(continued from front flap)

simple misperceptions to heightened tension, great political decisions and intractable attitudes. Against a backdrop of incidents preceding World Wars I and II, Mr. White suggests how the United States and other n~~~~ the conflict th~~~~ war in Vietnam

Both hawks ~ side Congress, h tivity of his appr~~~~ to the overheate~ ~~~roversy about Vietnam is a singular ability to see neither side in simple black or white.

Ralph K. White is Professor of Social Psychology at George Washington University; he has taught at Cornell and Stanford. He is well-known among psychologists for studies of autocratic and democratic attitudes in children, and has also followed particular professional interests in examining propaganda methods and Soviet-American relations, about which he has written for *Foreign Affairs* and other periodicals. Much of this book reflects his observations during the summer of 1967, which Mr. White spent in Vietnam.

Nobody
Wanted War

NOBODY WANTED WAR

•

Misperception in Vietnam and other Wars

RALPH K. WHITE

Garden City, New York
DOUBLEDAY & COMPANY, INC.
1968

Library of Congress Catalog Card Number 68–10553
Copyright © 1968 by Ralph K. White
All Rights Reserved
Printed in the United States of America
First Edition

PREFACE

Neither side wanted the Vietnam war. Nevertheless, step by step, it came. Most of this book is a study of how, in Vietnam, a thing so much feared and hated by both sides could nevertheless occur, and of the psychological reasons why it has been difficult or impossible for either side to extricate itself.

The essential subject of the book, however, is broader than Vietnam. Its purpose is to explore the psychological forces and rigidities that make any war possible, even at a time in history when nuclear weapons and chemical and biological techniques have made warfare perilous to a degree our ancestors never imagined. To prevent a World War III, we must understand the causes of war itself, including those that are exemplified by the comparatively tiny war in Vietnam. History has given the human race an object lesson in Vietnam, and time to study it before the holocaust comes. If we study it well we may be able to prevent that holocaust.

Accordingly, the examination of the Vietnam war in this book is preceded by brief case studies of World War I and World War II that try to identify the psychological factors common to all three wars. There is also, at the end, a psychological analysis that attempts to dig deeper for the general psychological roots of war, relating the historical evidence on all three wars to the relevant data and insights of psychology and psychiatry. There is now a body of knowledge in these disciplines that is more substantial and more relevant to the task of preventing war than most non-psychologists realize. The last three chapters of the book attempt to connect that body of knowledge to the other kinds of knowledge possessed by the historian, the student of present-day international politics, and the ordinary citizen concerned with preventing war.

The greatest hazard in such an analysis is, quite clearly, the writer's emotional involvement and the distortion of perception that emotional involvement usually brings with it. The ideal analyst would be a visitor from Mars, who could contemplate with detachment and perhaps with amusement the passions and delusions of that strange, self-destroying species, Man. But this writer is not from Mars, and, like the emotions of many others on all sides of the conflict (there are not just two sides), his are greatly involved. It will be wholesome for him to acknowledge the nature of that involvement. Psychologists are at last learning that a partial reduction of one's own perceptual distortion is achieved better by candidly admitting the nature of one's own feelings, and then consciously guarding against the effect of those feelings upon perception, than by pretending that the feelings do not exist. It may be that feelings always distort perception, but they distort it more when they are hidden than when they are in the open and under a greater degree of conscious control.

I have therefore stated my feelings, as plainly as I can, in Appendix A and Appendix B. Readers who want my "prescription" for getting out of the Vietnamese morass, and getting out honorably, with due regard for the evils of Communist dictatorship as well as for the evils of war, will find it there. But this book's essential purpose is diagnosis rather than prescription. In the body of the book I have done my best to keep my feelings about possible remedies from interfering with the main task of detached, dispassionate analysis. Policy implications (with one or two minor exceptions) have been relegated to the Appendixes, not because they are unimportant, but because this seemed the best way to emphasize their separation from the main body of the book. That separation was intended to remind me, and also the reader, that the proper time to consider policy implications is after, not during, a concentrated effort to see the facts.

The book is an expansion of a 167-page article entitled "Misperception and the Vietnam War," published in 1966 in the journal of the Society for the Psychological Study of Social Issues.[1] I want to express here my gratitude to SPSSI, and to four particularly qualified psychologists—Morton Deutsch, Jerome Frank, Herbert Kelman, and Charles Osgood—who served as consultants in the preparation of that article. The book in its present form differs from that article chiefly in three respects: Three new chapters of systematic psychological analysis have been added, two policy-oriented Appendixes, and a revision of Chapter 2, "The Conflict as Seen by the Vietnamese People," on the basis of two months spent in Vietnam in the summer of 1967.

[1] *Journal of Social Issues, 22,* No. 3, 1966.

Special thanks are due to the Vietnamese who helped me to understand their country, and most particularly to Nguyen-khoa Phon-anh (Director of the Center for Vietnamese Studies), Luong The Sieu, and Duang Thu Cuc.

Footnote references include only the writer's last name, the date of publication quoted, and, where possible, the page or pages referred to. Complete references can be found in the Bibliography.

R.K.W.

George Washington University

Contents

PART ONE

•

Other Wars

Chapter 1

MISPERCEPTION AS A CAUSE OF
TWO WORLD WARS

The fact of continuing war, in a world that desperately wants to avoid it, is a paradox too enormous to be evaded. It is the central problem of the human race in the second half of the twentieth century. Few reflective persons anywhere in the world have not thought that, in our nuclear age, only a madman could start a war. Yet wars continue.

Naturally, psychologists and psychiatrists have been especially inclined to see the problem in psychological terms. They know something about "madmen," since madness in all its forms and degrees, including the madness of ordinary people like ourselves, is in their bailiwick. Many of them have felt especially that *misperception* or cognitive distortion—a variegated psychological process that is accentuated in the psychotic but that pervades normal living as well—is a clue that may help to resolve the paradox. Misperception might explain how normally sane human beings can unwittingly, without intending the consequences, involve themselves step by step in actions that lead to war.

The following pages consist largely of an exploration of this idea. Psychological research and psychiatric experience are brought in where they seem relevant, but, since history can be described as "psychology teaching by examples," the main emphasis is on recent and contemporary history, psychologically interpreted. There is first a brief examination of the background of World Wars I and II, with an effort to discover the role of misperception in the crucial actions that brought about those wars. There is then a detailed examination of the background of the present conflict in Vietnam, again primarily focused on the possibility of misperception on both sides. There is no assumption that the amount of misperception is the same, or even similar, on the two sides. But a central hypothesis which the evidence seems to justify in all three wars is that each side is highly unrealistic in perceiving—empathizing with—what is in the minds of those on the other side. In the psychologist Hadley Cantril's phrase, they live in different "reality worlds." On each side, men assume that what seems real to them seems real to the enemy also.

To psychologists this emphasis on cognitive processes is very familiar. Lippmann, speaking as a psychologist, talked about "stereotypes" and "pictures in our heads"; Lewin, about "the psychological environment" and "the life space"; Tolman, about "cognitive maps." Freud took some form of distortion in perception for granted and proceeded to explore the mechanisms (such as projection) that lead to distortion in men's private worlds. Many now stress "empathy," defined as an effort to imagine realistically how the world looks to another person or group. The essential proposition running through all these is that different individuals, and their groups, perceive the world differently. We can scarcely begin to understand their behavior until we have begun to understand how reality as they see it differs from the reality we see.[1]

An enterprise such as this cannot invoke the safeguards and sanctions of a formal methodology. The value of the discussion depends, to a disconcerting extent, on the writer's efforts to recognize and transcend his own biases. That is too bad, because it goes without saying that every writer has biases (see Appendixes). Though the author has tried to avoid distortion, some undoubtedly remains. The reader should therefore be alert to discover—chiefly by comparing this discussion with everything else he knows about the subject—the nature and extent of the distortion.

Austria vs. Serbia

On the day when Austria-Hungary broke relations with Serbia, setting in motion the escalation that transformed a local dispute into a world war, the perception of the situation in Austrian minds was

[1] The word "perception" is used here in its broadest sense, including even the individual's most basic assumptions about the nature of the world and of man. The word "misconception" is more familiar than "misperception," and would be preferable in that respect, but it ordinarily refers to the end product of a psychological process rather than to the process itself. The word "misperception" lends itself to use in both senses. This study considers both the process of misperception (i.e., how a person's beliefs come to differ from the evidence available to him) and the products of that process, commonly called "misconceptions."

radically different from the perception of it in the minds of Austria's enemies—a perception that sustained those enemies (ultimately including the United States) through more than four years of one of the bloodiest wars in history. Austria's enemies saw her declaration of war on Serbia as cold-blooded, calculating aggression. In their minds, the militarists who ruled Imperial Germany and controlled Austria had decided to use the minor Serbian dispute as a pretext to launch a war that they believed would give them mastery, first of Europe and then of the world.

Historical scholarship in the 1920s established a view of these events that includes a more understandable conception of what was in Austrian minds at the time. Historians are now in fair agreement that Austria, not Germany, was the prime mover.[2] Germany clearly tried to prevent a major European war. From the Austrian point of view Serbia was carrying on an intolerable agitation against Austria-Hungary, not even stopping at assassination, that had to be punished. Unless Serbia was punished, nationalist agitation throughout the Austro-Hungarian Empire would get worse, threatening its very existence.

To be sure, there were other thoughts in the minds of Austrians. One was the terrifying possibility of a larger war.[3] Russia, with her enormous army, might come in. But surely (the Austrians thought) the Czar of Russia, who lived in fear of assassination himself, must realize that the Hapsburg emperor could not tolerate the sort of agitation that had prompted the assassination of the Archduke. He must see that Austria-Hungary's very existence as a bastion of civilization and order in Central Europe depended on her standing firm in this new crisis and teaching the conspirators in Belgrade an unforgettable lesson. Since the German Kaiser had seen the justice of Austria's position and was standing firmly by her, the Czar would hardly be so rash as to intervene; he must know that the consequences of a world war would be incalculable. In any case, the risk must be run; if the Serbian nationalist agitation among the Serbs and Croats still under Austrian rule were allowed to continue, it could quickly spread to the other nationalities within the Austro-Hungarian family of nations, and Austria-Hungary herself would disappear as a Great Power—which was, of course, unthinkable.

[2] Gooch, 1938, p. 445; North, 1967, pp. 105–16; Fay, 1928.
[3] Gooch, 1938, p. 446.

If this is a fair picture of what was happening in Austrian minds, it suggests that their reality world was distorted by six forms of misperception:

1. A diabolical enemy-image
2. A virile self-image
3. A moral self-image
4. Selective inattention
5. Absence of empathy
6. Military overconfidence

1. *The Diabolical Enemy-Image:* In the central focus of Austrian minds was the "criminal" character of the "assassins" who had violated all standards of human decency and were endangering the very survival of the beneficent Austro-Hungarian empire. In this black-and-white picture the black was more fully in focus than the white. To Austrians it seemed that such men, and the conspiracy in Belgrade that was responsible for their actions (though this point remained controversial to detached observers) were so flagrantly evil that all right-minded people, even Russians, must see the need to "punish" them.

The Germans too saw devils. Although before July 30 they only gave "loyal" support to Austria (and, on July 29, tried unsuccessfully to restrain her), on July 30 the news of Russian mobilization threw the Germans into panic. To the Kaiser it appeared that the Russians, French, and British were seizing upon the Serbian dispute as a pretext to attack both Germany and Austria. In an extraordinary instance of displacement of hostility, at precisely the moment when the British were trying desperately to stave off a major war, the Kaiser saw them as the head and center of a plot against him. On the margin of a diplomatic note he wrote: "The net has been suddenly thrown over our head, and England sneeringly reaps the most brilliant success of her persistently prosecuted, purely *anti-German world policy,* against which we have proved ourselves helpless, while she twists the noose of our political and economic destruction out of our fidelity to Austria, as we squirm *isolated* in the net (italics in the original)."[4] Though the Kaiser could scarcely be called psychotic, this passage has the ring of pure paranoia. To him, the British plot

4 North, 1967, p. 115.

was real. With Germany's very existence at stake, he felt that Russia should be given no more time to get its enormous but cumbersome military machine under way. He decided on a strike-first policy, and once that decision was made, the Great War had begun.

2. *The Virile Self-Image:* In 1914, the Austrians were not alone in their preoccupation with prestige and their feeling that humiliation would be intolerable. Each of the Great Powers feared "losing our position as a Great Power" and sinking to the status of a second-class power. In each case, after a firm stand had been taken, governments were acutely conscious of the danger of backing down, or seeming to back down. They were less vividly aware of the pain and death of tens of millions of human beings that might result if there were no compromise. This was true until the general Russian mobilization, when fear took over as the ruling emotion in Germany, if not in Austria-Hungary, and led directly to a strike-first policy. Before that time, the ruling emotion had been not fear of attack but fear of humiliation. The chief dimension in which national decision-makers judged themselves, and expected to be judged by others, was not good *vs.* bad, or right *vs.* wrong, but strong *vs.* weak. The essential goal apparently was to be, and to seem, strong and courageous. The essential thing was to take a firm stand, a strong stand, and to do it with such firmness and such obvious lack of fear, on one's own part and on the part of one's allies, that the potential enemy would surely back down.[5]

3. *The Moral Self-Image:* In the crisis of 1914 the Austrians had a black-and-white picture in which only evil was attributed to the Serbian enemy and only good to the Austro-Hungarian self. While their own moral nobility was perhaps less salient in the Austrians' minds than the diabolical character of the enemy or their own need to take a firm stand in the interest of self-preservation, the Austrian self that they thought worth preserving was also noble: peace-loving (they never for a moment sought a bigger war, and always feared it), civilized (they were a bastion of civilization in a Central Europe threatened by the barbarian tide of Pan-Slavism), economically rational (their empire was prospering in unity and would suffer economically if broken up), orderly (the Serbian assassins were violating elementary standards of law and order), and democratic (theirs was

[5] Schelling, 1960.

a limited monarchy, and the subject peoples were advancing toward full autonomy as rapidly as possible).

It is not necessary to deny some truth in each of these propositions; it is necessary only to notice that the Austrians' picture was expurgated at one crucial point. It did not include even a candid consideration of the possibility that this noble nation might now be committing aggression. The Austrian ultimatum to Serbia included what the Serbs regarded as a virtual demand for submission to Austrian authority, and when this was not clearly accepted by Serbia, Austria broke relations and began to mobilize for war. In the eyes of most of the world, this was aggression. It was aggression also by almost any clear definition of the term; for example, if aggression is defined as the use of force or threat of force on another nation's territory and against the wishes of the majority of the politically conscious people of that nation, Austria's action was aggression, however much it may have been provoked. But the Austrians did not call it that, or seriously think about what to call it. To them it was not aggression at all, but a firm stand, or bringing the criminals to justice. Here again there was selective inattention. The charge of aggression was not answered in their minds; it was ignored.

There was also in their minds a curious sort of automatism—a feeling that they could not do otherwise. The initial steps on the road to war were taken with a feeling of necessity; to do otherwise would be suicide. Once the initial steps were taken, Austrian minds were gripped by what Anatol Rapoport has called "the blindness of involvement."[6] As the Emperor Francis Joseph put it, "We cannot go back now."[7] All moral guilt was thus shifted from the Austrians themselves to an impersonal Fate or Necessity. This was shown most strikingly at two key points: Austria's refusal to reconsider her course of action on July 25, when the conciliatory Serbian reply to the Austrian ultimatum was seen even by the German Kaiser as "doing away with every reason for war,"[8] and her refusal to draw back even when Germany, on July 29, exerted very strong pressure on her to do so. On that day the German Chancellor, Bethmann-Hollweg, wired the Austrians: "we cannot allow Vienna to draw us lightly, and without regard to our advice, into a worldwide conflagra-

6 Rapoport, 1960, pp. 259–72.
7 Gooch, 1938, p. 437.
8 Montgelas, 1925, p. 137.

tion."[9] Berchtold, the Austrian Foreign Minister, had the bit in his teeth, and had put on his blinders; with a "courageous" unwillingness to consider any alternative course of action, he stepped over the brink of the precipice.

The strong German pressure on Austria to draw back also points up how mistaken our own diabolical image of Germany was, throughout the First World War. Americans generally assumed that Austria, much weaker than Germany, must have been playing a subordinate role in the Kaiser's plans for war and world conquest. Actually Austria, encouraged by the "blank check" which Germany had heedlessly given her on July 5, went a good deal further than Germany wanted her to. The "puppet" got out of hand. Like much of history, this series of events was largely a matter of sheer thoughtlessness and failure to communicate. Germany can be blamed not so much for malice or for dreams of world conquest as for ordinary carelessness. She should have tried sooner and harder to stop Austria. But one thing is now fairly well agreed upon by scholars: Germany did not try to precipitate a European war. She tried to prevent it.

4. *Selective Inattention:* Of all the psychological mechanisms involved in the misperceptions we have been considering, perhaps most pervasive is one that in some contexts may be called "resistance" or "repression" (though the Freudians give a more restricted meaning to each of these terms). Harry Stack Sullivan has referred to it more broadly as "selective inattention." It is involved on both sides of a black-and-white picture, when white or gray elements on the enemy side are glossed over and attention focuses only on the black, and vice versa.

In nations stumbling toward war there are usually at least three other definable types or aspects of selective inattention: narrow time-perspective, narrow space-perspective, and absence of empathy. The Austrians in 1914 were vividly aware of only one aspect of the future as they perceived it: the catastrophic disintegration that they thought likely (with much reason) if they could not cope firmly with Serbian nationalism. But the parts of this anxiety-filled image were not cognitively well defined. It did not distinguish clearly, for example, between what would happen if they merely dealt firmly with Serbian and other agitators within their own borders and what would happen if, in the process of punishing Serbia, they sent troops across

[9] *Ibid.,* p. 148.

their borders into a neighboring state. To the rest of the world this distinction seemed the distinction between legitimate maintenance of internal stability and illegitimate aggression that could precipitate world war. But in anxious Austrian minds it was all of a piece: a need to punish Serbia, as vigorously as possible, in order to prevent destruction and to vindicate the image of Austria-Hungary as a virile nation.

In addition, the Austrians failed to pay attention to other future possibilities, including Russian intervention, and the kind of breakup of the Austrian empire that later occurred as a result of the war that Austria herself precipitated.

A restriction in the Austrians' space-perspective was represented by their failure to pay much attention to countries other than the two that were the main focus of their attention (themselves and Serbia), and the two that were somewhat in the periphery (Russia, whose intervention they feared, and Germany, whose strong stand by Austria was counted on to deter Russian intervention). Two countries that were soon to become involved, France and England, were present in Austrian minds but apparently not seriously considered. America, which was to join the Allies nearly three years later—partly because of the American impression at the outset that Germany and Austria had committed aggression—was apparently not considered at all.

5. *Absence of Empathy:* Even in the case of Serbia, the enemy that was in the bright central focus of Austrian attention, the Austrians seemed to fail almost completely to realize how the situation looked from another point of view. They did not see that to a Serbian patriot the Austrian demands appeared to be naked aggression, calling for a struggle to the last drop of patriotic Serbian blood. They did not see how Russian pride, smarting after a number of setbacks including the high-handed Austrian annexation of Bosnia six years earlier, would respond to a new arbitrary extension of German-Austrian power in an area where the Russians felt that their honor and their interest were involved. They failed to see that, while the Russian Czar himself was peacefully inclined and would try to avoid a major war, his close advisers were not necessarily so pacific, and that Russia might become entangled in a situation in which its pride and prestige were so deeply involved that war might seem the only alternative to intolerable humiliation. Like the Germans, the Austrians resisted negotiations, which would have compelled them to see

clearly and to cope with other viewpoints.[10] They failed to anticipate the swing of the pendulum of the Kaiser's mood from careless
overconfidence to panic once the Russian general mobilization had
started and the British entry into the war seemed likely.[11]

The Austrians failed to see how the British and French would fear
a collapse of the balance of power if they left Russia to fight alone
against a smaller but far more efficient German army, or how British
public opinion would react if the panicky Germans, anxious to capi-
talize on their one great asset, the superior efficiency and speed of
their forces, were to invade France through Belgium. They did not
realize that America would regard their attack on Serbia as a big
country bullying a small one, and would similarly regard Germany's
march through Belgium—that America's sympathies would be immediately engaged on the side of the Allies, and the way would thus be
prepared for America ultimately to enter the war. In short, the Austrians were so wrapped up in their own anxiety and their own righteous indignation that they had little attention left for considering
what was real to anyone else.

6. *Military Overconfidence:* It is paradoxical but true that exaggerated fear can be combined with exaggerated military confidence.
The Austrians, for example, had what now seems an exaggerated
fear of the spreading disaffection of nationalities within their empire
that would result if they failed to take a firm stand against Serbia.
At the same time, until the Russian mobilization, they were excessively confident that they could teach Serbia a lesson and, with strong
German support, keep Russia from intervening. Like the Germans,
they pinned their hopes on the possibility of localizing the issue, enjoying mastery and venting righteous indignation within a small
sphere while remaining safe from the mastery impulse and the righteous indignation of others in a larger sphere. They were wrong. They
misperceived. Reality differed from their perception of it chiefly in
that they were inattentive to the possibility that strong allies of Serbia
(Russia, France, Britain, America) might scorn to be intimidated by
the Kaiser's appearance at Austria's side "in shining armor." They
did not see that their potential enemies, like themselves, might be
living up to an indomitable self-image, fearful of showing fear, and
therefore irrationally ready to fight.

[10] The Kaiser's comment was: "In vital questions and those of honor, one
does not consult with others." (North, 1967, p. 112)
[11] Taylor, 1963, pp. 214, 219, 228.

UNDERLYING CAUSES

The causes of any war are usually discussed under two heads: immediate, "precipitating" causes—assumed to be relatively superficial—and long-term, underlying causes. Up to this point our analysis of World War I has been only in terms of its immediate or precipitating causes. Is this superficial? Were there deeper causes that have not been touched?

Certainly there were other forces at work. Four factors often cited as underlying causes are nationalism, militarism, economic imperialism, and the system of competitive alliances into which Europe was divided in 1914. Each of these had deep historical roots, and the mere mention of them is enough to suggest how much has been omitted in the above historical sketch. But even in this brief discussion it is appropriate to ask two questions:

Were the immediate, precipitating causes perhaps less superficial than is commonly supposed?

After all, these are the causes that were most directly, demonstrably related to the fateful decisions that directly produced the war. Austria's breaking of relations with Serbia and her mobilization for war, Russia's general mobilization, the panicky German response to Russian mobilization—these actions, and the motives, assumptions, and misperceptions that produced them, were direct and unequivocal causes of the war's outbreak. Abstractions such as militarism and economic imperialism are both more indirectly and more equivocally related to what occurred.

Take, for instance, militarism. This high-level abstraction, insofar as it means anything beyond our dislike of war and of the arms associated with it, has two concrete meanings: an arms race, with its concomitant of heightened fear and suspicion, and a disproportionate influence of military men in the decisions that lead to war.

An arms race certainly existed in the years before 1914, especially in the competition between the German and French armies and between the German and British navies. But it would be hard to show that either race contributed even indirectly to the decisions of the Austrians, the Russians, and the Germans that directly precipitated war.

As for undue influence of military men upon diplomatic decisions, it probably existed in Russia but not, to any high degree, in either

Austria or Germany. In Austria the decisions were apparently made primarily by the civilian Foreign Minister, Berchtold, backed by the Emperor, Francis Joseph, and in Germany by the civilian Chancellor, Bethmann-Hollweg, backed by the Kaiser. In neither case is it clear that militarism had any essential part in what occurred.

Economic imperialism as a cause of war has been the favored explanation of Marxists and others who have pictured the First World War as the inevitable outcome of capitalist rivalry for markets, raw materials, and investment opportunities. Innumerable writers have discovered in economic imperialism a profound and "scientific" explanation for the mystery of the occurrence of war in a world in which the common people, at least, hate war. But this explanation is hard to reconcile with the stubborn, inconvenient fact that the prime movers in starting the First World War were not the advanced capitalist nations, Great Britain, France, and Germany. The prime movers were Serbia, Austria-Hungary, and Russia, which were engaged not in a scramble for overseas markets and raw materials but in an old-fashioned struggle for territory, power, prestige, national independence, and (at least in Austrian minds) national survival.

Competitive alliances also call for consideration as one of the forces behind the war. It is true that the alliance of Germany with Austria-Hungary, the alliance of France with Russia and the looser entente that included Great Britain as well as France and Russia were crucial factors in the immediate, dramatic spread of the war. Once Austria and Russia were embroiled, the war spread and became a conflagration that included Germany, France, and Great Britain. A local conflict was transformed, senselessly, into a general one. A distinction should be made, however, between factors that caused the war and factors that caused it to spread. The initial conflict was essentially between Austria and Serbia, with Russia's support of Serbia serving to bring two major countries, Austria and Russia, into collision. That presumably would have occurred whether either country had allies or not. Germany at first gave Austria a blank check, but later tried to restrain her. If that attempt had succeeded, the war probably would not have occurred, and the alliance system would have had to be credited with stopping a war instead of producing one.

Nationalism, however, was clearly a basic cause. The crisis of 1914 was shot through with nationalism from beginning to end. To take just one country: Austria's diabolical image of Serbia was an image of a national enemy, endangering Austria's national survival. Her virile and moral self-image was an image of a national self. Her selective inattention shielded her from disturbances of a national black-and-white picture and from reconsidering a course of action that she regarded, however mistakenly, as essential to national survival. (Sinking to the status of a second-class power seemed to the Austrians almost equivalent to national extinction.) The empathy that Austria's decision-makers did not have was empathy with national enemies, and Berchtold's jaunty, feckless overconfidence was overconfidence in a national self, backed by a national ally.

Every step in our analysis could be described also as a study of one or another aspect of nationalism, defined provisionally as identification (of individuals and governments alike) with a national self-image and a consequent mobilization of powerful motives—such as the desire for power and prestige—on behalf of that image. Negatively, nationalism can be described as an absence of any concept of a self larger than the nation. With the possible exception of the Catholic Church, and of course their alliance with Germany, the Austrians in 1914 had virtually no supranational self-images (such as Europe, or the United Nations, or the human race), with which they could identify. The same can be said of all other actors in the drama.

Earlier national history and underlying causes—including psychological ones—may be important, then, in helping to account for the growth and shaping of the nationalism that now seems to have been of decisive importance during the war crisis itself. And that leads to a second question:

Were psychological factors, including misperception, important also in the growth of nationalism, and should they therefore be recognized among the underlying as well as the precipitating causes of the war?

For full understanding of the nationalism that pervaded Europe in 1914, the history of the preceding two or three centuries must be studied. For example, Austria's glorious victories over the Turks and Metternich's special dynastic version of nationalism help one to understand the atmosphere and rhetoric of Vienna in 1914.

The historical record alone, however, is hardly enough to explain it. It is also important to ask whether Austrian and other nationalists derived unconscious satisfactions, throughout these centuries, from picturing their own nations as virile and moral, whether (more mysteriously) they also drew unconscious satisfaction from picturing their enemies as diabolical, and if so, why. One must ask whether there is a deep psychological need to identify with symbols of *something* larger and better than the individual self, and try to analyze the social factors that link this need to some symbols (religious, ideological, or national) rather than others. Here are psychological problems in plenty (some of which will be considered in Chapters 8, 9, and 10 of this book).

Hitler vs. Poland

The essential facts of Hitler's attack on Poland are familiar, and the historians' view of the origins of World War II has not yet been subject to the general and radical revision their view of World War I encountered. We can proceed immediately, therefore, to note in this context the six forms of perceptual distortion that emerged from our review of Austrian thinking in 1914. All six were present, in the extreme degree that might be expected from the fact that Hitler, though probably not psychotic, was one of the least rational, least evidence-oriented of men, with unmistakably paranoid tendencies.

1. *The Diabolical Enemy-Image:* It is now fairly well established that in Hitler's mind the diabolical character of the enemy, especially the Jewish enemy, was absolute. Postwar studies have confirmed the proposition that his anti-Jewish delusions of persecution were no mere propaganda technique; he seems to have actually believed them. The central role played by these delusions of persecution in justifying his more outrageous aggressive acts needs further elaboration.

Hitler faced the enormous task of reconciling these actions with the posture of peacefulness he had maintained consistently since 1930. He had abandoned his earlier, franker war propaganda, represented by certain passages in *Mein Kampf,* and adopted a peace line that was far more acceptable to the German people. It was urgently necessary, therefore, in order to keep their full and willing support, to present his bloodless conquest of the Czech part of Czechoslovakia, his bloody attack on Poland, and his still more bloody attack on Russia in ways that would at least half-convince the German people that he was no war-mad conqueror but a man of peace, forced to act by the provocation of diabolical opponents. Hitler's skill in doing so suggests that he was at least half-convinced of it himself. Also, his apparent strength of conviction seems to have at least half-convinced most of the German people.

Three quotations will suggest how he attempted to justify these aggressions. According to him, the march into Prague was legitimate and necessary for several reasons, including the need to remove a threat to German security. The role that had been assigned to Czechoslovakia by its Jewish and democratic masters was "none other than to prevent consolidation of Central Europe, to provide a bridge to Europe for Bolshevik aggression, and, above all, to act as the mercenary of European democracies against Germany. . . . What was expected from this State is shown most clearly by the observation of the French Air Minister, M. Pierre Cot, who calmly stated that the duty of this State in case of any conflict was to be an airdrome for the landing and taking off of bombers from which it would be possible to destroy the most important German industrial centers in a few hours." (Speech to the Reichstag, April 28, 1939)[12] Note Hitler's use of the time-honored device of treating arms in the hands of an enemy as proof of aggressive intentions.

The attack on Poland was justified, he claimed, not only by the Poles' "increased terror and pressure against our German compatriots" but also by "the sudden Polish general mobilization, followed by more atrocities. . . . I have therefore resolved to speak to Poland in the same language that Poland for months has used toward us." (Speech to the Reichstag, September 1, 1939)[13]

The attack on Russia was an attempt to break through a ring of encircling enemies. There was "a new policy of encirclement against Germany, born as it was of hatred. . . . Internally and externally there resulted that plot familiar to us all between Jews and democrats, Bolshevists, and reactionaries, with the sole aim of inhibiting the establishment of the new German People's State, and of plunging the Reich anew into impotence and misery. (Proclamation, June 22, 1941)[14]

2. *The Virile Self-Image:* Readers of *Mein Kampf* are familiar with Hitler's glorious image of himself and his country, which emphasizes strength and courage more than softer qualities such as

[12] Hitler, 1941, p. 638.
[13] *Ibid.*, pp. 685–87.
[14] *Ibid.*, pp. 977–78.

peacefulness and good will. Although after coming to power he greatly stressed peacefulness, his emphasis on the hard qualities, strength and courage, continued. As a study in how aggressive actions can come to appear acceptable to their perpetrators, his great emphasis on the courage theme during the crises of 1938 and 1939 holds special interest. When a hard action has to be given some label, the label "courage" is far more acceptable than the label "aggression."

In a speech on September 1, 1939—the day Hitler precipitated World War II—he avoided even the word "war." He was not attacking Poland, committing aggression, or starting a war. He was "speaking to Poland in the language that Poland for months has used toward us," he was recognizing that "no Great Power can with honor long stand by passively and watch such events," he was showing that his patience and love of peace must not be "mistaken for weakness or even cowardice," he was "meeting bombs with bombs," he was showing a "stout heart," he was "seeing to it that a change is made in the relationship between Germany and Poland that shall insure a peaceful coexistence." The final sentence of the peroration was: "If our will is so strong that no hardship and suffering can subdue it, then our will and our German might shall prevail."[15] One can almost feel the lump in the throats of German listeners as they contemplated their own indomitable selves.

3. *The Moral Self-Image:* A basically mistaken conception of Hitler's propaganda technique is still current in American minds: the assumption that he openly and cynically glorified war, announced his program of world conquest, advocated the "Great Lie" technique, justified oppression of weaker races, etc. This conception can be supported only by selecting extremely atypical quotations and removing them from context. Actually, as one might expect of such a thoroughly authoritarian personality, Hitler's propaganda after he came to power in 1933 was characterized by an extreme adherence to conventional standards of morality: peacefulness, respect for the rights of neighbors, truthfulness, etc.[16] In his words, and perhaps in some sense in his thoughts also, Der Führer and Germany were morally spotless. Three quotations give the flavor:

"I wish to point out first, that I have not conducted any war;

[15] Hitler, 1941, pp. 686–90.
[16] White, 1949, pp. 160–64.

second, that for years past I have expressed my abhorrence of war and, it is true, also my abhorrence of warmongers, and third, that I am not aware for what purpose I should wage a war at all." (Speech, April 28, 1939)[17]

"We have given guarantees for the States in the West, and to all those States bordering on our frontiers, we have given assurances of the inviolability of their territory as far as Germany is concerned. These are no mere words. That is our sacred determination." (Speech, September 26, 1938, at the height of the Munich crisis)[18]

"I will not war against women and children. I have ordered my air force to restrict itself to attacks on military objectives." (Speech, September 1, 1939, declaring war on Poland)[19] This is actually the only point in the speech in which Hitler permits himself to use the word "war," and here it is used only negatively, thoroughly embedded in a moral, humane context.

4. *Selective Inattention:* When he made his fateful decision to attack Poland, what was in the focus of Hitler's conscious mind? What was pushed out of the focus but still important in determining his decision? And what was not present? We can only speculate, using whatever clues his words and his actions give us, but that speculation may be fruitful.

Adolph Hitler had an exceptional capacity for doublethink—though doublethink may be more widespread in the human race than we usually realize. According to Konrad Heiden, "On this day (October 26, 1930) Hitler began his peace propaganda, which continued uninterrupted for almost ten years. Inexplicable and incredible, it moved men by this very fact, but also by an undeniable breath of passion. With the same passion Hitler had said the exact opposite."[20] He apparently had a knack of working up a noble passion that he could, in a sense, sincerely feel at the time of making a speech, though it would not necessarily remain salient at a moment of decision.

Probably when Hitler decided to attack Poland he took more elements of hard reality into account, and was more conscious of long-range plans of conquest than he proclaimed in his prepared

[17] Hitler, 1941, p. 661.
[18] *Ibid.,* p. 520.
[19] *Ibid.,* p. 688.
[20] Heiden, 1944, p. 414.

speech to the German people and to the world. His behavior suggests that in his conscious mind there were at least these emotions and ideas: elation at the immediate prospect of triumphantly crushing Poland and extending the boundaries of the Reich; elation at the thought (clung to somewhat anxiously) that, by the great coup of the Nazi-Soviet Pact, he and Ribbentrop had successfully divided his enemies, making it probable that the British and French either would not dare to fight—they had not fought when he marched into Prague—or would succumb quickly to his mighty military machine; real anger at the long-standing injustice of Danzig and the Polish Corridor, now about to be eliminated; consciously inflated anger at Polish "atrocities" and unwillingness to negotiate about the Corridor; pride in Germany's moral grandeur as contrasted with her vindictive, encircling, Jewish-controlled enemies; pride in his personal courage to face dangers which in lucid moments he recognized as real, though he evidently underestimated their probability; clear plans already forming in his mind for capitalizing on this triumph to extend German hegemony throughout Central Europe and the Balkans, while preserving the appearance of national autonomy in countries such as Hungary and Rumania; vague and wonderful private fantasies, which he probably recognized as fantasies that Fate might or might not permit him to fulfill, of total destruction of the Jewish world-octopus and the extension of beneficent German hegemony throughout the world. (When he was preparing or delivering a speech and presenting his peaceful, moral, Dr. Jekyll self, Hitler must have at least partly succeeded in pushing these morally dubious thoughts out of his mind, but at times of decision-making they were presumably more powerful.

Hitler's behavior suggests that he tended to overlook other facts and probabilities, or took them lightly: the tough nationalism of the Poles, the Yugoslavs, the Russians, the British, and others who stood in his path; the cumulative fear and anger of those who might be so mean-spirited and so influenced by the Jewish press that they would describe his courageous act as aggression; the enormous potential military strength of the United States; his own recent promise and "sacred determination" that the territory of all of Germany's neighbors would be inviolable, and the probable psychological effect of breaking that promise; the word *aggression* as possibly applicable to what he was doing, the word *imperialism* as possibly applicable to the beneficent control of Central Europe that he was immediately contemplating, the word *dictatorship* as applicable to his totalitarian form of government, and the word *paranoia* as applicable to his delusions about a Jewish-plutocratic-Bolshevist plot against Germany.

Among these blind spots indicated by Hitler's words and actions may be discerned the three overlapping categories that emerged from our discussion of Austrian thinking in 1914: he tended to ignore major future contingencies, actors such as America that were geographically far from his immediate focus of attention, and the reactions of enemies and neutrals. With certain exceptions Hitler's time-perspective and space-perspective appear to have been drastically limited, and he was almost totally devoid of empathy.

5. *Absence of Empathy:* Several of the blindspots mentioned above exemplify failure of empathy: Hitler failed to give due weight to the tough, defensive nationalism of peoples who stood immediately in his path, such as the Poles, the Yugoslavs, and the Russians. He failed to realize that onlookers such as the French, the British, and the Americans would certainly regard his action as naked aggression and as another violation of his pledged word, with the probable result that they would eventually overcome their extreme distaste for war and that, as his threat drew nearer, their defensive nationalism too would be fully mobilized. He was almost totally unable to comprehend the minds of Jews (instead of seeing their helpless terror he continued to attribute to them a plot to rule the world that must have been, essentially, a projection of his own world-conquering fantasies). He could not see that others, from their vantage points, might honestly attribute to him such things as war-making, aggression, imperialism, dictatorship, and paranoia.

Hitler also grossly underestimated, if he perceived at all, the great change in British public and governmental opinion after March 1939, when German troops moved into Prague and took over the purely Czech part of Czechoslovakia. For the British this was the last straw —a final demonstration to all doubters that Hitler was not merely trying to unify Germany (a plausible interpretation of the occupation of the Rhineland, the *Anschluss* with Austria, his taking of the Sudetenland, and even the claim to the Polish Corridor), but that he had embarked upon the conquest of non-German lands, in a career of conquest that might include Britain herself.

Hitler apparently could see none of this. He had a stereotype of the British: partly proud Nordics like the Germans, and therefore capable of sharing German scorn for the Russians and the inferior peoples of Central Europe; partly calculating imperialists capable of jealousy at Germany's new success, but apparently unwilling to risk war in order to block Germany's ambitions in Central and Eastern Europe—they had not stopped him even when he marched into Prague; partly co-conspirators with the Jews; partly muddleheads or cowards, such as Chamberlain had proven to be at Munich and after Prague.

There may have been some truth in this picture, but to a greater extent it was a projection of his own arrogance and craving for power. Except perhaps for the elements of fear and weakness which Hitler's own basic weakness enabled him to see in others, his picture of the British was external. He did not even try to imagine how the world might appear to them, on the assumption that they were ordinary peaceable but proud human beings. He apparently never really tried to assess his own behavior from their point of view. As a result, his stereotyped picture was also rigid and static. He could hardly have predicted the great mobilization of pride and of militance that his own behavior evoked in Churchill's Britain, any more than the Japanese militarists could predict the great mobilization of pride and militance that their attack on Pearl Harbor would evoke in the United States. (In Hitler's speech on September 1, his only reference to Britain, France, or the United States was: "When statesmen in the West declare that this affects their interests, I can only regret such a declaration. It cannot for a moment make me hesitate to fulfill my duty.")

6. *Military Overconfidence:* Two extreme examples illustrate Hitler's overconfidence: his assumption that, after the Nazi-Soviet Pact, Britain and France would not dare to fight; and his suicidal attack on Russia. Although he was presumably not psychotic, he showed to an extreme degree, within the normal range, not only the typical paranoid delusions of persecution (in the form of diabolical enemy images) but also the typical paranoid delusions of grandeur (in the form of military overconfidence).

It should not be assumed, however, that military overconfidence is a rare thing, associated mainly with unusual personalities such as Hitler. In recent history it has appeared again and again. Both the Russians and the Austrians were militarily overconfident in 1914. The Allied generals continually prophesied an early victory throughout the First World War. During the period from 1917 to 1924, the

Communists grossly overestimated their chances of an early world-wide victory. Stalin apparently thought he could defeat Finland easily and quickly. The Japanese militarists who attacked Pearl Harbor had little conception of the anger and the ultimate military strength that their action mobilized in the United States. The French doggedly underestimated the difficulty of holding both Indochina and Algeria. In the Suez conflict, the British, French, and Israelis were too confident that they could win quickly before worldwide opposition could be mobilized. Nasser and other Arabs in 1967 apparently thought that they could defeat Israel. To be sure, there are in recent history some contrary instances of too little military confidence. The rule, however, seems to be overconfidence, while too little confidence and strict realism appear to be the exceptions. This is not surprising, since overconfidence is a form of the wishful thinking that is the rule, not the exception, in human affairs.

Three characteristic forms of military overconfidence can be described. One is common to Austria in 1914 and Hitler in 1939: a failure to take seriously enough the possibility that other countries may intervene in support of one's enemy. Austria belittled the chance that Russia, France, Britain, or America would intervene in support of Serbia, or be later drawn into the war; Hitler belittled the likelihood that France, Britain, or America would intervene or be later drawn into the war. Similarly, the British, French, and Israelis were apparently surprised by the speed and strength of opposition to their 1956 Suez adventure, especially on the part of the USSR and the United States.

As we have seen, this is related to lack of empathy. It is difficult to realize that one's own behavior, the justification of which seems so obvious to oneself, can appear in the eyes of a neutral or hostile observer as actual aggression. There is also often a failure to realize that, in such a situation, the ally of one's enemy, even if relatively weak, may be too proud to be easily intimidated by one's own or one's allies' threats of intervention. Russia was too proud to be intimidated by the Kaiser's appearing at the side of Austria; Britain and France were too proud to be intimidated by Hitler's tirades or by the great coup of the Nazi-Soviet Pact, even though they felt militarily inferior. This is especially true when the enemy's ally feels bound to him by ties of mutual loyalty or by formal or informal commitments. Russia in 1914 felt honor bound to protect her Slavic protégé, Serbia; France felt bound by her firm alliance with Russia; Britain felt somewhat committed by her new entente with France. Similarly, though Britain and France had not come to the aid of Czechoslovakia, they became more deeply committed to Poland, and in September, 1939, they felt that if they did not honor their commitments to Poland, Hitler would hardly respect other commitments elsewhere. To a proud, self-respecting nation, there is something particularly repellent in the thought of letting down an ally and violating a commitment because of intimidation, even when such prudence seems militarily rational. Yet the enemy often fails to give enough weight to this factor of obligation compounded by pride, assuming that rational calculations of military advantage and fear of war will be enough to keep outsiders from intervening.

Another form of overconfidence was present to a conspicuous degree only in Hitler's case: underestimation of the difficulty of coping with an aroused people fighting on its own soil against what it regards as foreign invasion. Hitler encountered this on a vast scale in Russia, as Napoleon had done before him. Others who have encountered it have been Napoleon in Spain, the Allied forces in Russia in 1918 to 1920, the Italians in Greece, the Germans in Yugoslavia, the Japanese in China, the French in Indochina, the French in Algeria, the Russians in Poland and Hungary, and the Chinese in Tibet.

Here, too, a main reason appears to be lack of empathy. The occupying or invading power usually argues plausibly. Characteristically it focuses on the violence, often including atrocities, committed by activists in the local population, and on its own good intentions. But such black-and-white thinking leads to selective inattention to the human, non-diabolical characteristics of the local patriots, including their conviction that they are defending their homeland against foreign invasion; and this in turn leads to an underestimate of how difficult handling the activists may be, helped as they often are by many of the non-activist population.

A third form of overconfidence is the tendency to see another nation or group as disunited, with only its evil rulers hostile, while the mass of people is believed to be neutral or friendly to one's own side. This has been called the "black-top" enemy-image.[21] It is a typical form of the black-and-white picture; as a rule only

[21] White, in Kelman, ed., 1965, pp. 249, 259, 269–74.

the leaders at the top of the enemy group are seen as wholly black. The mass of the Serbs and Croats under Austrian rule were not seen by the Austrians as particularly hostile; to them the real enemies were the assassins, the agitators, the nest of conspirators supported by the Serbian government in Belgrade. Similarly, Hitler did not regard the common people of the countries around Germany as his enemies; it was their Jewish-plutocratic-Bolshevik leaders who were plotting Germany's downfall.

The conspiracy theory of history—the idea that history is largely a story of groups of conscious villains plotting with each other and operating behind the scenes—has fallen into disfavor among historians. Since it resembles what is called here the "black-top image of the enemy," it follows that seasoned historians would be likely to look askance at the black-top image. Yet it survives in full force in simplistic popular notions of what is at issue in any particular conflict.

There are many familiar examples of the conspiracy theory: the American public's focus on the Kaiser and the German militarists as the villains of World War I, the complacent employer's conviction that his employees are loyal and content but misled by union agitators, the Southerner's belief that Negroes in the South would be content were it not for "nigger-loving agitators" from the North. It is a wonderfully consoling conception. It simultaneously eliminates the guilt of feeling hostile to a large number of people; creates a positive image of oneself as saving the underdog masses from their conniving, oppressive leaders; provides a personal, visible devil on whom to center all hostility; and sustains hope that, once the opposing leaders have been defeated, the battle will be over.

UNDERLYING CAUSES

World War II differed greatly from World War I in that Hitler was a much more calculating aggressor than the Austrians had been in 1914. The Austrians at least believed, with some reason, that they were acting in self-defense to stave off Serbian aggression by means of internal subversion. Hitler had no reason to entertain such a thought. As for his enemies, in the light of history they seem more open to the charge of appeasement (up to September, 1939) than to that of belligerence. War guilt was therefore far more clearly one-sided than it had been in 1914.

Nevertheless, our brief sketch of the deeper causes of World War I has some parallels in the background of World War II. Militarism as an explanation does not seem to have much validity in either case. The years before 1939 saw no arms race comparable to that before 1914, and Hitler in 1939 was by no means a tool of his generals.

Capitalism and economic imperialism were even more clearly not crucial in 1939 than they had been in 1914. It is true that Hitler talked about *Lebensraum* and that his economic exploitation of conquered or occupied countries after 1939 suggests a certain economic imperialism as one motive for the conquests themselves. But his was by no means the typical capitalist form of competition for markets, raw materials, or investment opportunities, and his capitalist opponents in Britain, France, and America were, if anything, too slow to enter the lists against him rather than too belligerent. Hitler's one-party totalitarian state—in several ways resembling Communism more than Western capitalist democracy—was much more aggressive than capitalist democracy. Also this was a period in which capitalist imperialism was retreating in the Middle East, in India, and elsewhere. The Marxist theory of capitalism as a major cause of war could hardly have been more decisively refuted.

The idea of competitive alliances as a major cause of war again seems somewhat irrelevant. Hitler's alliance with Japan had little bearing on the events of 1939 and Italy did not enter the war for some time. The disunity of his opponents, rather than their solidarity, emboldened Hitler in 1939 and made his initial conquests easier than they would otherwise have been.

Nationalism again emerged as decisively important. Hitler's virulent, almost paranoid form of nationalism directly motivated German aggression. All six forms of misperception typical of Hitler in 1939 had been present also in Austrian minds, and influenced the formative stages of Nazism. As in the weeks preceding World War I, they were present in 1939 among the immediate or precipitating causes of war, but they were also important in the long term.

* * * *

These historical examples of typical, recurrent forms of misperception may alert us to possibilities in our study of perception in relation to the present conflict in Vietnam. Since history seldom approaches an exact repetition of itself, all historical analogies should be taken with a large grain of salt and with equal sensitivity to differences between a past situation and a present one. It is always legitimate, however, to formulate the analogies as questions to be asked about the present, such as: Is there now a great absence of empathy on both sides, as there was in Austrian minds in 1914 and in Hitler's mind in 1939? If so, what thoughts and feelings in the minds of those on one side of the Vietnamese war are typically ignored by the other side?

A word is in order also with regard to our own frame of mind as we approach these emotionally explosive questions of fact. The most appropriate frame of mind can perhaps be described as *tough-minded empathy*.

As the examples just cited indicate, the effort to empathize is particularly necessary in the case of one's own worst enemy. For the sake of realism in dealing with him, if for no other reason, it is important to try to see the enemy's world as he sees it—from the inside, recognizing that even his worst accusations against oneself may be sincere. At the same time it is advisable to combine empathy with several aspects of tough-mindedness. One can realize that the enemy's leaders are capable of lying, both to oneself and to their own people, for propaganda purposes, and that therefore no single public statement can be taken as necessarily sincere—though all are worth listening to. One can be alert to self-deception on the part of the enemy, even when one sees his belief as probably sincere. One can have a similarly tough-minded skepticism about the beliefs of one's own group. With no illusions about the possibility of fully achieving such a synthesis, we can aim at empathy combined with toughness—that is, empathy without gullibility, without shirking our responsibility to make an independent appraisal of facts, and without weakness in acting, even when action must be based on much less than a perfect case.

PART TWO

•

The Case of Vietnam

Chapter 2

THE CONFLICT AS SEEN BY
THE SOUTH VIETNAMESE

Who Wants Us There?

A question has been disturbing a good many Americans for several years: Do most of the people of South Vietnam want us to be there?

The evidence on this question is complex and much of it is ambiguous. There is no simple or certain answer. Nevertheless, the question is fundamental. If we mean it when we say we want the people to determine their own destiny, we are obliged to look at whatever evidence is available, and to try to arrive at an answer that is at least an evidence-oriented guess.

Partly because of the importance of the question, and partly because no one else seems to have attempted a systematic, detailed analysis of all the available evidence on both sides of the question, this chapter attempts such an analysis. Readers who do not want to go so fully into the question may prefer to read only this first section of the chapter and the summary at the end.

Two answers are commonly given, one optimistic and the other semi-optimistic.

The optimistic answer is very simple: "the people" of South Vietnam are on our side. As the State Department put it in February, 1965: "The people of South Vietnam have chosen to resist this threat. At their request, the United States has taken its place beside them in their defensive struggle."[1]

The semi-optimistic answer is more complex, more widely accepted by informed Americans, and much more in accord with the available evidence (though it omits one essential element of the picture). This answer is that there are actually three important groups in South Vietnam: (1) The Viet Cong itself—an active group of dedicated, ruthless men, with a core consisting of Communists who accept direction from Hanoi, extremely well-organized, disciplined,

[1] State Department White Paper. In Raskin and Fall, eds., 1965, p. 155.

and effective in intimidating other villagers, but numerically only a fraction of the population; (2) the active, militant anti-Communists, who are also only a fraction of the total; (3) a much larger mass of people, caught between the two extremes, who are largely passive and indifferent. Their main goal is survival under any sort of government. They obey whichever side has effective power in their locality at the moment. They have suffered at the hands of both sides; they know little or nothing of Communist ideology and now they are much less concerned about which side wins than they are about whether they and their families can survive and whether peace comes soon. What they want most is to be left alone.

As far as it goes, this answer is supported in its essentials by the available evidence, including my own observations in Vietnam in the summer of 1967. However, it says nothing about one politically central question: Which is the larger of the two active minorities—the Viet Cong, together with the segment of the peasantry that willingly and actively supports it, or the militant anti-Communists? In fact, by failing to raise this question, the semi-optimistic answer gives the impression that the balance of political forces within Vietnam is nearly even. The evidence suggests that this is far from true. There is a formidable amount of evidence that the active, *highly-motivated* pro-Viet Cong people in South Vietnam outnumber, by a considerable margin, those whose motives are strongly anti-Communist.

This more pessimistic interpretation focuses upon the sizable number of peasants who have been actively helping the Viet Cong by feeding them, helping them find concealment, giving them intelligence about American and government troop movements, and denying such intelligence to the government side. It is generally acknowledged that, without such help by a large proportion of the peasants, the Viet Cong cadres could never have survived and held their own—as they have, at least until early 1968—against the enormous weight of weaponry that has been mobilized against them. It is generally acknowledged that one factor promoting active cooperation has been intimidation by the Viet Cong. The essential question is: Has intimidation been the primary reason for cooperation? According to the pessimistic interpretation, most of the active minority have been motivated not only by fear but also by strong, genuine pro-Viet Cong conviction. The basic grievances of the ordinary peasants against the landowners and the Saigon government have been deep, and Viet Cong propaganda and organizational methods in playing upon them have been skillful enough to bring this about.

Evidence presented later in this chapter suggests that the size of the pro-Viet Cong group may be of the order of fifteen to twenty-five percent of the adult population of South Vietnam. This figure is based partly on the following estimates: the Viet Cong itself, three or four percent of the population; other strongly pro-Viet Cong peasants who are now or have been in hamlets fully exposed to the extraordinarily effective propaganda and organizational activities of the Viet Cong, perhaps ten to fifteen percent of the population; a very small minority of the rest of the population, including city dwellers and peasants not exposed to the full Viet Cong treatment, perhaps two to six percent. These figures do not include the large additional number of peasants who actively help the Viet Cong but who (even according to this interpretation) do so reluctantly, largely because of intimidation or social pressure.

Such a modest minority would not be of great importance if it were balanced by an equally large, equally well-organized and highly motivated minority on the other side. According to the pessimistic interpretation, however, it is not. While the great majority of the people in the cities and government-controlled hamlets pay lip service to anti-Communism, and while most are probably consciously sincere in doing so, their actual behavior on the anti-Communist question is, as a rule, perfunctory. This is as true of the ARVN (the South Vietnamese Army) as of civilian officials. There are many exceptions, but the rule is half-heartedness, with individual self-interest ready to overwhelm public spirit. From my observation, well-informed anti-Communist Vietnamese are usually quite ready to grant this half-heartedness, and call urgently for the kind of leadership which, they believe, would transform it.

Chiefly on the basis of the prevalence of perfunctory behavior, my own very tentative estimate of the number of Vietnamese who are strongly motivated on the anti-Viet Cong side is that they constitute some five to fifteen percent of the population. (This has been confirmed by a number of well-informed anti-Communist Vietnamese; their most frequent estimate has been ten percent.) This estimate includes a minority (including many Catholics from the North) of the middle-class and upper-class city dwellers (who are themselves a small minority of the total population), some peasants in Hoa Hao and Catholic villages, some refugees, a few relatively well-to-do peasants who are not yet refugees, and a few others whose close relatives have been physically mistreated by the Viet Cong. The estimate does not include the fairly large number of middle-class and upper-class people whose long-run class interest makes them quite genuinely anti-Communist, but in whom immediate personal interest outweighs loyalty to their class or to their country.

According to this interpretation, the remaining sixty percent to eighty percent of the population are outwardly passive and obedient to whatever authority controls their locality. Inwardly, they are indifferent or ambivalent, perhaps leaning toward one side or the other, but not so strongly that the claims of personal and family interest are outweighed. This group may include as many as half the peasants in Viet Cong-controlled hamlets (where much disillusionment has occurred in recent years), more than half the peasants in disputed hamlets, the great majority of the peasants in government-controlled hamlets, nearly all the urban poor, and a fair proportion of the middle and upper class. It probably includes also nearly all of the Chinese, Cambodian, and *montagnard* minorities.

Because of this group's numerical importance, and because the anti-Communist effort to "win the hearts and minds of the people" is directed primarily toward the passive majority, we will first analyze it more carefully. However, this group seems politically and militarily less important than the two dedicated, active groups at the two extremes. We will therefore return to them, more carefully considering the evidence for and against the pessimistic hypothesis that the pro-Viet Cong minority is much the larger.

The Passive Majority

It is necessary first to look at the cultural and social background of the Vietnamese peasants and to consider how the formation of political opinion in their society may differ from the same process in ours. We must at least try to struggle free of the habitual American frame of reference, in which the making of political choices is taken for granted, and try to grasp a way of life in which such choices have been largely meaningless. Most of the peasants in Vietnam, as in other developing countries, are not used to thinking they have any role to play or any choice in political affairs. Therefore, in the absence of any special stimulus, they do not presume to choose. "How can I know what is right?"

Susan Sheehan has described graphically an unusually clear instance of this non-choosing frame of mind.[2] The elderly peasant woman whom she describes "has never heard of the Geneva agreements. She does not know that her country has been partitioned. The words 'North Vietnam' and 'South Vietnam' mean nothing to her; she only knows that she lives in Vietnam." Though her son was killed by a Viet Cong mine, she bears the Viet Cong no animosity because of it. "I can't afford to resent the Viets because my son's injury is beyond my control. It's useless to be angry. It's a waste of emotion. I have to bear the consequences of the war. I don't understand the war but I can't do anything about it. I might as well save my words and my feelings. . . . How can I know anything? Living here is like living in a jug."

This is not to say that the minds of all Vietnamese peasants are as unfurnished as this old woman's. Among the younger men there are probably many whose feelings are more complex. Those feelings may include a good deal of sullen resentment of the oppression and exploitation they have suffered at the hands of absentee landlords and corrupt local officials. Such resentment presumably pulls them toward the Viet Cong, but it must be diminished, at least consciously, by an ingrained habit of fatalistic resignation to such injustice as part of the natural order—"that's what officials are like"— and also a partial acceptance of the officially approved viewpoint. Nearly all the poor people in the cities and perhaps half or two-thirds of the peasants—roughly speaking, those whose hamlets have never been fully exposed to the Viet Cong—have been one-sidedly exposed to the official view.

In addition, they probably have the usual human need to look to persons in authority for the kind of firm benevolence they received from their parents in childhood, the usual human tendency to think wishfully, and the usual human need to rationalize and legitimize the activities they find themselves engaged in—such as serving in the Vietnamese Army and saying the things that will please those in power. There would be painful dissonance in their minds if they let themselves become clearly conscious rebels or heretics.

Their impulse to obey is probably stronger than ours. In the Viet-

[2] Sheehan, 1967, pp. 3–24.

namese culture, children are usually kindly, permissively treated. More regularly than in the United States, apparently, they grow up as "good" children, respecting and loving their parents, and rejecting all conscious feelings of non-love or of disrespect.[3] The Confucian way of life, with its stress on filial virtue and the respect due to one's elders and to those in authority, is firmly built into their value system.[4] The good-child role then tends to persist. Obedience and a certain respect for authority tend to be accepted by adults also as necessary characteristics of a decent, acceptable person. It is probably easier for such a person to shift loyalties completely, deciding that the Mandate of Heaven no longer rests upon Saigon and that his true political father is Ho Chi Minh, than to become a conscious rebel against all authority.

The nearest parallel to this state of mind in the West is, perhaps, a Negro sharecropper whose main concern is to stay out of trouble, who thinks of himself as a completely loyal American citizen, and who feels no conscious resentment when he is drafted to fight in Vietnam. Or a Russian peasant who grumbles bitterly at the sins of the bureaucrats in Moscow but does not dream of opposing the authorities or the system, and who thinks of himself as a loyal Soviet citizen. Or an American boy in Iowa City who responds with apathy, not rebellion, to autocratic group leadership.[5]

Perhaps the search for such parallels in Western societies is presumptuous, since we cannot know how accurate they may be. The members of the passive Vietnamese majority themselves cannot be expected to know all the elements in their conscious and unconscious motivation, or to judge with any accuracy the relative importance of the elements that are conscious. In appraising them we have—perhaps—the advantage of detachment, but far less intimate knowledge. It is understandable, therefore, that on this point responsible American students of present-day Vietnam disagree most fundamentally. Where we see through a glass darkly, perceptions of what exists behind it necessarily differ.

For example, most of those who now think the passive majority is inwardly turning against the Viet Cong focus on, and emphasize, the resignation and habitual obedience described above. They focus also

[3] This generalization is based primarily on depth interviews conducted by the psychoanalyst Walter Slote (private communication).

[4] Hickey, 1964, pp. 276–77.

[5] White and Lippitt, 1960, pp. 138–59.

on what is said by Vietnamese in government-controlled territory, especially their frequent complaints about Viet Cong violence and Viet Cong taxation (although this involves a major problem of frankness). They note the strong tendency of peasants to migrate from Viet Cong-controlled territory into government-controlled territory, apparently "voting with their feet" against the Viet Cong (though this may be also an escape from the physical danger and privation imposed on Viet Cong areas by our side). They often quote the frequent statements by Vietnamese on our side that "things are better now" than in 1963 or 1965, though things were so bad then that a change for the better does not necessarily mean arrival at the good.

Among the reasons for thinking that the passive majority may inwardly feel more hostile to the Viet Cong than to the government, perhaps the most persuasive is the apparently widespread tendency to associate the Viet Cong with physical violence. On the verbal level, at least, that is the most frequent accusation against them. Peasants continually complain to government officials about the lack of "security," meaning that Viet Cong violence continues. This was also the most frequent complaint against the Viet Cong registered in the CBS-ORC (Opinion Research Corporation) survey (see below, pp. 40–46). In reply to the question "In your opinion what do people around here dislike about the Viet Cong?" the most frequent response was "terrorism and sabotage" (fifty-eight percent); it was far ahead of the second most frequent complaint, "exploitation of the people; heavy taxes" (thirty-six percent).[6]

Since most of the Viet Cong violence is pinpointed—confined to outsiders or government-appointed officials rather than directed against the ordinary peasants—there is some question about the emotional intensity of this complaint when voiced by a rank-and-file peasant. It is a "good thing to say" when talking with a government official, since it indicates that the speaker is on the right side (from the government standpoint). It can also be said with some degree of sincerity by anyone, since everyone has heard of some such violent incidents. But, in view of the elemental character of physical fear, it seems likely that such fear is, in emotions as well as in words, the

---

[6] CBS, 1967, p. 35. A balancing question was asked: "On the other hand, what do people like about the Viet Cong?" The most frequent response, "skillful propaganda," was given by only ten percent. But one must question the frankness of the respondents.

primary element on the negative side of the passive majority's ambivalence about the Viet Cong.

On the other hand, students of the present situation who guess that the passive majority is inwardly more anti-government than anti-Viet Cong focus on, and emphasize, the many sins of Saigon governments past and present—absentee landlordism, exorbitant rents, and chronic corruption. They also observe that nationalistic feelings mobilized during the long war of independence against France are now associated more closely with Ho Chi Minh than with the Saigon government (though there is some doubt about the intensity of nationalism in the passive majority). They see that peasants tended to "vote with their feet" against Ngo Dinh Nhu's strategic-hamlet program, which allegedly gave them security against Viet Cong violence (though Nhu's mismanagement of the program may have been the major reason it collapsed).

Those who think the majority of peasants oppose the government also focus on the extraordinary military success of the Viet Cong against great odds, inferring that it must have enjoyed widespread popular support (though intimidation is clearly one reason for that success). In fact, all the reasons for thinking that the pro-Viet Cong minority is larger than the anti-Viet Cong minority, which are discussed in detail below, may also be reasons for thinking that the same feelings exist in diluted form among the passive majority.

In view of the number of different psychological factors involved here, their intangible nature, the different levels of consciousness on which they exist, and the difficulty of getting direct evidence about them, the wisest course might be to suspend judgment and to admit that we simply do not know, yet, whether the minds of the passive majority tend in one direction or the other.

In any case, most of these people are probably ambivalent, hostile to both sides, often with no conscious conviction that one side is worse. In such a frame of mind they have probably found survival in rendering unto Caesar the things that are Caesar's—perhaps a Viet Cong Caesar at night and a government Caesar in the daytime, with a shoulder-shrugging acceptance of the duplicity that this involves. Such alternation seems to have become for millions of peasants a way of life, with fatalistic acceptance of the need to do and to say what the Viet Cong wants when its cadres are present, and to do and to say what the government wants when its officials are present.

In relation to each side, they are then playing, somewhat hypocritically, the good-child role. The literal demoralization (that is, the breakdown of morals) that this involves can be readily imagined. With a basic ambivalence toward both sides, the outwardly passive, conforming individual naturally puts first what is important to him individually—the survival and welfare of himself and his family.[7]

A final point should be made, underlining our lack of good direct evidence. The great, generally acknowledged gap between urban and rural life in South Vietnam means that very few city people even claim to know the peasants intimately on the basis of frank face-to-face conversation. This was one of the few aspects of Vietnam today for which I was not prepared by previous reading. I kept asking, "Who knows the peasants intimately? Who can tell me what their real feelings are?" The answers were few and unsatisfying. Few Americans and, what is more surprising, few urban Vietnamese, seem to have a relationship with the peasants sufficiently intimate to enable them to give up-to-date testimony on the attitudes of peasants, free from serious question regarding its frankness. I did not meet any such persons. No formal survey or social-science project that I know of, not even the otherwise excellent CBS-ORC survey of early 1967, can yet claim to have bridged this gap. The size of the gap itself indicates that a pessimistic interpretation may be justified. The peasants seem to feel deeply alienated from the city and from the city people's government, estranged from them if not rejected by them.[8] There is no equally convincing evidence of a deep feeling of alienation from the Viet Cong, which has always drawn its main (in fact almost its only) strength from the peasantry. It should never be forgotten that most of the Vietnamese people are peasants.

Evidence That the Pro-Viet Cong Minority Is the Larger

The politically central question still remains: Which of the two active minorities is larger?

The pessimistic hypothesis that the pro-Viet Cong minority is larger is supported by six major arguments:

(1) *Vietnamese nationalism is now and has been for some twenty*

[7] Hickey, 1964, pp. 279, 282, 285.
[8] Donnell, 1966, pp. 49–53.

years mobilized more in favor of Ho Chi Minh than in favor of the French-backed or American-backed government.

About the central importance of nationalism there is apparently no serious controversy. For example, in the Washington teach-in of 1965, Professors Kahin and Scalapino, who were on opposite sides, completely agreed on the importance of Asian nationalism.[9] Pike speaks of "profound resentment against foreign control";[10] Fall speaks of the "deep love" of the Vietnamese people for their "war-torn homeland";[11] both Buttinger's histories stress the struggle of the Vietnamese for independence over two thousand years.[12] Scholarly emphasis on nationalism has become a commonplace. It has often been remarked that the greatest single political force in our times is not Communism but nationalism, and that Communism itself is unlikely to succeed except where it is fused and identified with national aspirations.[13]

Regarding the mobilizing of nationalism primarily on the Viet Cong side, the evidence is less clear-cut, since it is fairly clear that most of the Vietnamese, North and South, want to avoid being dominated by outside forces, Communist or non-Communist. Most of them see in Communist China, as well as the United States, a threat to their independence. However, there is much reason to think that in Vietnam, perhaps more than anywhere else in the developing countries, the Communists have succeeded in fusing Communism and nationalism and identifying themselves with the cause of national unity.[14] The long and finally victorious struggle against the French was conducted, essentially, under Communist leadership by peasants who regarded their leaders more as patriots than as Communists.[15] As President Eisenhower put it, "I have never talked or corresponded with a person knowledgeable in Indochinese affairs who did not agree that had elections been held as of the time of the fighting, possibly eighty percent of the populace would have voted for the Communist Ho Chi Minh as their leader rather than Chief of

[9] Kahin, in Raskin and Fall, eds., 1965, pp. 289, 294; Scalapino, *ibid.*, p. 305.
[10] Pike, 1966b, p. 1.
[11] Fall, 1964b, p. vii.
[12] Buttinger, 1958, 1967a.
[13] Katz, in Kelman, ed., 1965; Doob, 1964.
[14] Toynbee, 1965.
[15] Buttinger, 1967a, pp. 301–3, 667–68, 701; Fall, 1964b, pp. 104–29; Lacouture, 1966, pp. 5, 8, 32; Pike, 1966b, pp. 33–41.

State Bao Dai."[16] Others corroborate this; for instance, Leo Cherne, one of Diem's leading advocates, in 1955 said, "If elections were held today, the overwhelming majority of Vietnamese would vote Communist."[17]

Since President Eisenhower's statement has often been misinterpreted, it should be noted that he did not say that Ho Chi Minh would probably have won by eighty percent the elections that Diem refused to hold in 1956. He said "possibly"; he carefully said "had elections been held as of the time of the fighting"—that is, in 1954 or earlier, not in 1956; and he specified as Ho's hypothetical opponent not Diem but Bao Dai, who was generally regarded as a French stooge. Although Diem was installed partly by the Americans, he was regarded even by many of his enemies as an honest man and a staunch anti-French patriot. The dates are also important. Diem's performance was impressive enough during his first two years in office,[18] and Ho's performance was bad enough during the same two-year period—those were the culminating, terrible years of the so-called "land reform" in North Vietnam[19]—to make it fairly certain that in a fair election in 1956 Diem would have gained more than twenty percent of the votes[20] both in the South and in the country as a whole. He might even have won.

Nevertheless, President Eisenhower's figure might not be too high an estimate of how Ho Chi Minh would fare today if he personally ran for office in a fair election, and if his opponent were a representative of the military government. The general personal regard for Ho is much higher than the regard for his regime, or for the word *Communism*. Also, things have changed since 1956. In the North, Ho corrected his worst errors,[21] and peasant uprisings, such as those that occurred in Nghé-An in 1956, apparently have not been repeated. Meanwhile in the South, along with certain kinds of economic progress, things became worse.[22] Diem refused to hold the plebiscite that had been expected to unify the country; he failed to reform a corrupt, oppressive, and inefficient bureaucracy that had

[16] Eisenhower, 1963, p. 372.
[17] Cherne, 1955.
[18] Fishel, 1959, in Gettleman, ed., 1965, pp. 195–204.
[19] Hoang Van Chi, 1964, pp. 90–239; Carver, 1966, pp. 353–55.
[20] Lansdale, 1964, p. 81.
[21] Fall, 1964b, p. 157.
[22] Carver, 1966, pp. 358–59.

never achieved psychological contact with the peasants;[23] he conducted a witch hunt, executing many whose only crime had been to fight against the French under Viet Minh leaders;[24] he permitted the use of torture on a large scale; he listened to his brother and his brother's wife. And, though he had been regarded as a staunch anti-French patriot, he became more and more identified in the xenophobic Vietnamese mind with another group of foreigners, the Americans.[25]

The governments that have come after Diem have apparently been more popular than his was (there are many who say "things are better now"), but they have been perhaps even more closely associated in the public mind with the Americans because of the very great increase in American troops. There is a chasm of incomprehension between the American troops and most of the Vietnamese people.[26]

As the Vietnamese probably see it, big-nosed tall white men are now increasingly prominent on the government side of the war, and obviously in positions of great influence if not of control. In contrast, the brown skins and small stature of the Viet Cong are familiar and authentically Vietnamese even though now a significant fraction of them have come down from the North. This contrast must create an impression—false or partly false as it may be—that alien rule is being imposed as it was by the French. The psychological concept of perceptual assimilation is relevant here. Perception of the Americans must have been partly assimilated, in many Vietnamese minds, to their previous perception of hated French overlords. The Americans, like the French, have white skins, big noses, a strange tongue, terrible weapons—and a nominally independent Vietnamese government that consists largely, to the ordinary Vietnamese mind, of officers who fought for the French and rode roughshod over the interests of their countrymen.

This is not to say that the typical Vietnamese sees no differences between the French and the Americans. Most of them appear to have positive as well as negative feelings toward the Americans, and often give them credit at least for blundering good intentions. In the

[23] Malcolm Browne, 1965, pp. 214–16.

[24] Devillers, in Gettleman, ed., 1965, pp. 221–25; Lacouture, 1966, pp. 28–31; Chaffard, 1965, p. 4.

[25] Fall, 1964b, p. 399; Robert Browne, 1965, p. 14.

[26] Carthew, 1966, p. 20; Clos, in Gettleman, ed., 1965, pp. 432–34.

countryside, more than in the cities, the friendliness of the G.I. has evoked a warm response. The Americans are apparently not often seen, in accordance with Communist propaganda, as imperialists in the sense in which the French were seen as imperialists. George Carver makes the strong statement that "persistent propaganda efforts to portray the Americans as successor imperialists to the French have simply never taken hold."[27] But there are many indications of anti-American feeling, puzzlement about America's ultimate motives,[28] and some outright hatred. There is, for instance, the letter left by Pham Tri Mai, who burned herself in protest: "Most of us Vietnamese hate, from the bottom of our hearts, the Americans who have brought the sufferings of this war."[29]

It is sometimes asserted that the Vietnamese peasants are politically too unsophisticated to be activated by nationalism. Were this true, it would be difficult to see how they could have won their war, in the face of great odds, against the French. Certainly Vietnamese nationalism has a different quality than ours; its core is perhaps a feeling about their village, and against outsiders who violate its values. Perhaps at bottom there is a feeling of simple identification: "this is my village," "this is my country," "these are my people," "we Vietnamese." But such an identification could be quite enough to produce an attitude more inclined toward the Viet Cong than toward the remote city people's government.

With an effort of empathy we may reconstruct some of the peasant's village-centered world. As the villager might see it, the guerrillas are "our boys," born and brought up in our village or in villages similar to ours. Their aims are good since they are fighting for us against our natural enemies, the rich city folk, the landlords who take our rice although they have done no work to grow it, the government officials who cheat us, the soldiers who torture us when they want information about our relatives, and now the strange-talking Americans with their bombs and napalm. (Literally speaking, the government troops are also "our boys," since most of them are peasants, but they are probably regarded as having been pressed into the service of the peasants' natural enemies. At least until recently, this

[27] Carver, 1966, p. 371.
[28] Langguth, 1965; Neil Sheehan, 1966, E3; Robert Browne, 1965, p. 14; Malcolm Browne, 1965, pp. 246, 259, 267–68; Marr, 1966, pp. 256–58.
[29] *New York Times,* May 17, 1967.

contrasted with the more voluntary process of recruitment by the Viet Cong.)

It is true, a peasant might think, that "our boys" are now acting very tough. They are impressing even their early teen-age brothers into military service, and it is almost impossible to pay the taxes they are now demanding. They are cutting down our freedom in many ways. When they hide in our village bombers are more likely to come. But they are still our boys. Although naturally I want to save my own life too, and my wife and children, I certainly hope they win. I will therefore help them, when the risk of doing so is not too great. And of course it is unthinkable that I would betray them to the enemy when the soldiers ask me questions. I am not a coward. I am a Vietnamese.

For this kind of thinking and feeling, no political sophistication is necessary.

(2) *There is an acute need for economic reform, especially land reform, and the Viet Cong have initiated reforms more broadly than has the Government.*

It may well be that another motive—hunger—is even more basic than village-centered nationalism in the mind of a typical illiterate Vietnamese peasant. He wants to safeguard the bowl of rice that represents his next meal, and the rice field that represents next year's meals for himself, his wife, and his children. From the peasant's standpoint, his rice and his rice field have been under attack, not only by the crop-destroying chemicals that have been dropped in some areas by government planes, but also by the absentee landlords who have in many instances demanded between thirty and fifty percent of his crop. This fact of absentee landlordism in the South is too little known in the United States. South Vietnam is one of the places in the world where drastic land reform is most badly needed. It has been estimated that, in 1955, in South Vietnam proper (Cochin China), only two percent of the people owned forty-five percent of the land.[30] According to Fishel, in the Mekong Delta eighty percent of the land was tilled by tenant farmers.[31] Land reform since then has not drastically changed the situation.[32]

[30] Fall, 1964b, pp. 308–11; Pike, 1966b, pp. 62–63, 167–68, 267; Buttinger, 1967, p. 932.

[31] Fishel, 1964, p. 32.

[32] Buttinger, 1967a, pp. 930–35, 1135.

In many newly developing countries a somewhat similar situation exists but is not psychologically explosive because the landless peasants have never known anything better; they are caught in the rut of a traditional society with its traditional mood of apathy and fatalism,[33] a mood that resembles the apathetic response to autocracy in experimental settings.[34] But no such psychological palliatives exist in South Vietnam. During the period before 1954, when large areas in the South were controlled by the Viet Minh, it put into effect a drastic land reform that really took the land away from the landlords and gave it to the peasants who tilled it. One of the greater grievances of the peasants against the city people and the city people's government is that when Diem replaced the Viet Minh in 1954, about eighty-five percent of the land that had been given to the landless peasants was forcibly taken back and given again to the landlords.[35] Some of the peasants were able to buy it back under the conditions of the new land reform, but that was a slow process, contrasting sadly with what the Viet Minh had done and with what the Viet Cong was still doing.[36] As of June, 1967, the Viet Cong claimed to have seized nearly 2.3 million acres from prosperous landlords and to have turned them over to the peasants.[37]

Many Americans have a vague impression that, since the death of Diem, reform by the Saigon government has been progressing as fast as it could under the circumstances, and that progress toward democracy, as represented, for instance, by the elections of 1966 and 1967, has been accompanied by revolutionary development on a considerable scale, including land reform. The facts hardly bear this out. With neutralists excluded from the elections, with some 4000 Buddhist activists in jail,[38] with the semiliterate masses handicapped in running for office, and with about three-quarters of the peasant hamlets not participating in the elections because they were either

[33] Lerner, 1958.

[34] White and Lippitt, 1960, pp. 138–59, 246–53.

[35] Shaplen, 1965, p. 143; Carver, 1966, p. 359; Buttinger, 1967a, p. 990.

[36] Gittinger, 1960; Ladejinsky, 1961; Montgomery, 1962.

[37] A recently reported study by the RAND Corporation gives evidence that there is some tendency for government control to be *less* where land reform has occurred. This paradoxical fact suggests that the local and immediate effect of land reform may be bad for our side. However, it does not prove that the long-term, countrywide effect of drastic land reform would not be good.

[38] Buttinger, 1967b, p. 80.

in Viet Cong hands or in dispute, the Constituent Assembly was by no means a peasant-oriented body. Not one peasant was elected to it. It was packed with men who profited directly or indirectly from the oppressive landlord system. A proposal to declare publicly that the land belonged to those who tilled it was defeated, 114 to 3.[39]

The façade of reform that has been erected since the early days of Diem has remained very largely a façade. For example, there has been little or no public discussion of the proposal, which Buttinger regards as entirely feasible, that the payment of rent on land (at least to absentee landlords) should be abolished immediately.[40] Only a drastic step such as this, one might think, would convince the peasants, after decades of broken promises,[41] that the Government is at last ready to act on their behalf. If the United States were to bail out the landlords and pay them all the rents that they formerly collected, these would amount to only about 1/120 of the present annual cost of the war.

The gap between words and deeds has been particularly glaring. Nguyen Cao Ky has continually talked reform, and has often sounded sincere. In a conversation with Robert Shaplen, for instance, he said, "We realize that during eighty years of French control and ten years of Diem, a small minority profited, but never the common people of Vietnam. But to get ourselves accepted by the people takes time."[42] In the 1967 election campaign he described his government as "the Government of the poor." A "revolution" has often been proclaimed, even under Diem. But Thieu, Ky, and their group, even if they fully realized how great is the need for drastic action, would still be in a bind. Their supporters are chiefly the landlords and the landlord-oriented upper and middle classes, and beneath their liberal façade these groups apparently want no real reform.[43]

(3) *There has been much physical suffering that has probably led to greater anger at the Government.*

Although few Americans realize it, there is much reason to believe that, for reasons essentially unrelated to the moral character of either side, the sheer amount of violence inflicted on the peasants by

[39] *New Republic,* March 18, 1967.
[40] Buttinger, 1967b, p. 11. Cf. Pool, 1967, pp. 563–66.
[41] Buttinger, 1967a, pp. 920, 947, 951, 1137.
[42] Shaplen, 1966, p. 62.
[43] Montgomery, 1962, p. 124; Buttinger, 1967a, p. 1136.

the Government and its American allies has been much greater than the amount inflicted on them by the Viet Cong.[44]

On this point there have been misperceptions of two quite different kinds. On the one hand there is the misperception of those Americans who, shocked by occasional television pictures of weeping mothers, roughly handled prisoners, and deliberately burned villages, have failed to realize that the atrocities of the Viet Cong, less accessible to Western photographers and less vividly depicted, are just as real. On the other hand, however, there is the misperception of those Americans who, focusing primarily on the widely publicized Viet Cong murders of teachers, health workers, and so on, have remained ignorant of the fact that, because of the nature of guerrilla war, much more suffering has been inflicted by the anti-guerrilla side than by the guerrillas.

There are two reasons for this. The more familiar one is that, even though there has been a real effort to minimize civilian casualties, the present process of using American firepower and mobility to break the back of the guerrilla force has meant a large amount of killing and maiming of villagers in the villages where the Viet Cong are known, or believed, to be hiding,[45] and in rough country napalm has been used. Chemical (though apparently not biological) warfare has been conducted in many forms.[46] American awareness of such action is limited: Few, for example, have permitted themselves to realize fully what napalm does. (A British observer has said that the special horror of napalm lies in the fact that it tends to leave its victims still alive.)

The less familiar reason for it is that, in the conduct of counter-guerrilla operations, it is urgently necessary to obtain intelligence about the hiding places and identity of the guerrillas.[47] This has been interpreted by the South Vietnamese soldiers as justifying torture to obtain information from captured Viet Cong prisoners and also from wives and relatives of men suspected of being Viet Cong. The water torture, the electric-current torture, and the wire-cage torture are all widely used. There are also other kinds even less well

[44] Fall, 1965b, p. 19; 1966b, p. 8.

[45] Lansdale, 1964, p. 81; Pouget et al., cited by Fall, 1965a, p. 14.

[46] Brightman, Carol, "The Weed Killers," *Viet Report*, June–July, 1966, pp. 10–14, 33–45.

[47] Mok, 1966.

known in the United States (perhaps chiefly because of unofficial censorship in Saigon) which have been well documented by observers such as Bernard Fall, Malcolm Browne, Denis Warner, and Susan Sheehan.[48]

Fall spoke in 1965 about "the universally callous attitude taken by almost everybody toward the crass and constant violations of the rules of war that have been taking place. . . . As personal questions to both American and Vietnamese unit commanders have shown (and I made a point of touching on the subject with most of them), there is only the vaguest idea among them as to what exactly *is* covered by the 1949 Convention (on the treatment of prisoners of war; ratified by the United States in 1955). . . . If total disregard of signed treaties is allowed to continue, then the Vietnam war will degenerate to an ignominious level of savagery far below that experienced in other guerrilla wars since World War II. . . . To me, the moral problem which arises in Vietnam is that of torture and needless brutality to combatants and civilians alike. The issue has been side-stepped in the United States; or worse, simply ignored as not being an 'American' problem. . . ."[49]

Malcolm Browne is more specific. "There is a small American field generator used extensively in Vietnam for powering pack radios. . . . The generator produces a high enough voltage to produce a severe but not fatal shock. The 'ding-a-ling' method of interrogation involves connection of electrodes from the generator to the temple of the subject, or other parts of the body. In the case of women prisoners, the electrodes often are attached to the nipples. The results are terrifying and painful, but subjects are not perma-

---

[48] Fall, 1965d, pp. 18–21; Malcolm Browne, 1965, pp. 114–18; Warner, 1962; Sheehan, 1967, pp. 94, 97. See also Robin Moore, 1965, pp. 46–50; Buttinger, 1967a, pp. 942, 962, 976, 987, 1165; Devillers, 1962, p. 13; Eden, 1966, pp. 233–34; Pike, 1966b, pp. 437–39; Schell, 1967, pp. 49–52; Duncan, 1967. On the canister bombs dropped in North Vietnam, see Lockwood, 1967, p. 44D. They "spray hundreds of pea-sized steel pellets at high velocity over a wide area. The pellets are coated with napalm and stick when they hit."

On the question of which side has caused the greater amount of physical suffering, Bernard Fall's testimony is relevant. The Viet Cong's "ability to do harm is immeasurably smaller than that of the other [our] side, and there is no doubt in anyone's mind, and that includes the Intelligence specialists in Saigon, that the Viet Cong are deliberately keeping terrorism at a low level because of its psychologically adverse effects." (*The New Republic*, October 9, 1965)

[49] Fall, 1965b, pp. 19–20.

nently damaged. . . . Some of the forms of torture employed are more sinister, in that they maim or disfigure. . . . Many a news correspondent or U. S. Army military adviser has seen the hands whacked off prisoners with machetes."[50]

These facts have not been presented at this length as an accusation against the United States. Some of the Viet Cong atrocities are at least as bad. The direct participants in torture have as a rule been South Vietnamese, not American, and (partly as a result of the article by Bernard Fall quoted above) the American authorities have since seen to it that American soldiers are provided with clear instructions about the 1949 Convention and also about the counterproductive character of torturing prisoners. Recent interviews with prisoners suggest that there may have been marked improvement in Vietnamese behavior—perhaps because of American influence in this respect. The facts are presented rather as a case study in certain psychological processes to be discussed in later chapters (especially selective inattention, which the American public has exhibited on a large scale, and the clogging of channels of communication). The facts are relevant to our immediate problem of making an educated guess as to how the more politically conscious peasants probably feel about the two sides. If the amount of suffering inflicted on the peasants by the Government, as compared with that inflicted by the Viet Cong, has been as one-sided as it now appears, the emotional response of the peasants can be readily imagined.

A closely related fact that can hardly be overemphasized is the war-weariness that now exists.[51] Those who picture the peasants as neutral speak of a numbness in which practically the only desire remaining is a desire for peace. The September, 1967, elections brought out clearly this craving for peace. Up to now there have been no clear indications whether it takes the form of resentment against one side or the other, but if the peasants and the war-weary urban population thought that the military government was prolonging the war, in opposition to an elected body or a faction that publicly favored a compromise peace, it seems likely that this war-weariness could quickly become a politically potent force against the military government. The survey reported by Mohr is said to "indicate that the people harbor—or at least show—less open resentment

[50] Malcolm Browne, 1965, pp. 114–16.
[51] Robert Browne, 1966, p. 12; Chaffard, 1965, p. 4; Clos, 1965, p. 435; CBS Survey, 1967; Mohr, 1965.

of military force that endangers them than a Westerner might think likely." This suggests again how risky it is to take much stock in any of our Western inferences about how we would feel if we were in the position of the Vietnamese peasants. Perhaps their culture and experiences during the past twenty years have hardened them to degrees of physical violence that we would find intolerable.[52] Yet the wording of the statement suggests that this inference, too, may be wrong; they may feel more resentment than they show openly. The hypothesis of callousness to violence cuts both ways; according to Mohr, "it has been found that there is less resentment of Viet Cong terrorism than is often supposed."[53]

(4) *The Viet Cong has a record of remarkable military success against enormous obstacles, and it seems unlikely that such a success could have been achieved without widespread popular support.*

To see the Viet Cong's achievement in its proper context, a number of unfavorable factors operating against it should be given proper weight. One basic factor, for example, is the inherent power advantage possessed by any police state, such as that of Diem, within its own borders. George Orwell's *1984* gives some notion of what propaganda, control of information, police surveillance, fragmentation of opposition and state-sanctioned torture of prisoners can accomplish when there is no stubborn population in opposition, and the success of the Nazi, Soviet Communist, and Chinese Communist regimes, using similar techniques, shows that Orwell's picture is by no means wholly fictional. Diem had all of those factors on his side (though at a much lower level of efficiency). Another factor is the amount of material help, including military equipment, that has been given to the government side by the United States during the past fifteen years—an amount far greater than the help the rebels got from the North. Another of the key facts that are too little known in the United States is that the rebellion did not begin in the part of South Vietnam near Laos and the Ho Chi Minh Trail, where an appreciable amount of help from the North might have been possible; it began primarily in the far South, in the Mekong Delta, where it was necessary to use mainly homemade or captured weapons,[54] and where it was necessary therefore to make up in organization, dedication, and extent of popular support for the gov-

[52] Reston, 1965a, p. 117.
[53] Mohr, 1965.
[54] Stone, in Raskin and Fall, eds., 1965, p. 157.

ernment's great advantages in material equipment.[55] As recently as early 1964 only about ten percent of the guerrillas' weapons came from the North,[56] though the proportion now is much higher.

Also, in contrast with the impression given by the State Department's White Papers,[57] it is important to notice that the rebellion began to a significant extent in 1957,[58] at least three years *before* its surprising success and the urging of Communists in the South led the Communist authorities in the North to give it their official blessing and begin to give it a significant amount of material help.[59] It is true that the infiltration of "regroupees" from the North (i.e., Viet Cong cadres "regrouped" in the North after 1954) began in 1956 or 1957 and that they were very efficient in organizing, but they brought few weapons, and the main psychological motive force behind the movement came rather clearly from local sources. (Diem's persecution of anyone he suspected of opposing him made it easier for the organizers to function.) Often the only choice a man had was whether to join the regroupees in the woods or go to jail. Naturally, they chose the former.

There is much controversy on the related question of whether the actual decision to start the movement was pushed by local Communists or by headquarters in Hanoi, and the issue is relevant to the question of outside aggression versus a civil war. If the impetus came initially from Hanoi, the case for the war itself being a result of North Vietnamese aggression is somewhat strengthened. If the local Communists pushed it, with Hanoi reluctantly agreeing, the case for calling the war essentially civil is strengthened.

The issue is not as crucial as some suppose it to be, since the general subordination of local Communists to Hanoi seems well established.[60] If Hanoi did not take the initiative, it must have at least permitted the local Communists to go ahead. The case against calling this aggression rests on other grounds (see below, Chapter 6). The answer to the question, in any case, seems to be that we simply do not know. The inner workings of the Vietnamese Communist or-

[55] Fall, 1964b, p. 317; Shaplen, 1965, p. 57; Lacouture, 1966, p. 213.

[56] Lacouture, 1965, p. 20.

[57] State Department White Papers, 1961, 1965.

[58] Carver, 1965, p. 406; Fall, 1965, p. 317.

[59] Devillers, in Gettleman, 1965, pp. 224–30; Clubb, 1962; Buttinger, 1967a, p. 983; Pike, 1966b, pp. 75–80.

[60] Pike, 1966b.

ganization are not yet enough known to the public for us to arrive at a clear answer; if we are wise and tolerant of ambiguity, we will admit our ignorance. Devillers' well-known 1962 article in the *China Quarterly,* which argues that the main impetus was local, is persuasive but not wholly convincing.[61] The North could have given the movement impetus under the table while trying to make it appear otherwise.

This question should be separated, however, from the clear fact of the success of the Viet Cong during the years 1957 to 1960 with very little *material* help from the North.[62] The implication also seems clear that there must have been a great amount of local discontent which the Viet Cong articulated and led. This is one of the many instances in which it would be a mistake to attribute too much independent power to propagandists and organizers. Their role is indispensable, but it is a role of catalyzing, articulating, and organizing discontent, not creating it. They could do little if there were no strong popular feeling to work with.[63]

It is true that one major compensating advantage possessed by the Viet Cong has been the tactical advantage of concealment and of surprise attack that guerrilla forces usually have. It is this advantage of concealment and surprise that has led to the conventional estimate that counterguerrilla forces must have a ten-to-one numerical superiority over guerrilla forces in order to defeat them. General Taylor in February, 1966, put it at "ten to one or twelve to one." But what is sometimes forgotten is that the tactical advantage exists to this high degree only when guerrillas have the active support of the people (which they could hardly get by intimidation alone—see below, pp. 57–60) in helping them to conceal themselves, in helping to supply them with the intelligence they need in order to have the full advantage of surprise, and in denying to the counterguerrilla forces the same kind of intelligence.[64]

There is also direct testimony to the partisanship of a large seg-

[61] Pike, 1966b, pp. 75–80.

[62] *Ibid.,* pp. 75–80, 320–25.

[63] The role of the organizer may have been a good deal more potent in this case than in most cases in which organizers have capitalized on popular discontent; cf. Pike, 1966b, pp. 373–77.

[64] Pustay, 1965. The Israeli General Moshe Dayan, after first-hand observation, calls Vietnam "an ideal country for guerrilla warfare . . . with an abundance of natural places of concealment." (Dayan, 1966, p. 33)

ment of the peasantry, as indicated by their unwillingness (at least in the Mekong Delta) to supply intelligence to the government. Jerry Rose, who reported for *Time* and *The Saturday Evening Post,* said in 1963,

It only takes one government-oriented peasant to inform on the movements of the Viet Cong, one peasant actively supporting the government. . . . Incredible though it is, that one active individual is lacking in most areas of the Mekong Delta, the economic heart of South Viet Nam. . . . Today the grass-roots strength of the Viet Cong appears so strong, particularly in the Delta, that it seems unlikely any leader could shake it.[65]

This would now be an exaggeration. The collection of intelligence from paid informers by our side is increasingly efficient, and the Viet Cong have built elaborate mechanisms to keep the peasants from informing on their movements. But the broad picture is still one of remarkably little informing,[66] even in the face of torture.[67] This was one of the most significant elements in the coordinated Viet Cong operations in the cities in February, 1968. There must have been thousands, even in the cities, who knew about the operations in advance and did not inform on them.

Convincing direct evidence on the feelings of the peasants toward the American soldiers is hard to come by, but it is clear that they are not often welcomed as liberators. Michael Mok quotes a Marine: "Sometimes I feel like one of the bad guys. I mean, in World War II it was more clearcut. You know, the Nazis on one side and us on the other. But when we go into these *villes* and the people look at you in that sad kind of way they have, it's pretty hard for me to imagine I'm wearing a white hat and riding a white horse."[68] General Dayan, quoting the American Major General Depuy, says, "There is a race between two horses, the American war horse and the horse of resentment over the American presence. It is up to the Americans to insure that the war horse gains victory over the Viet Cong before it is overtaken by the horse of resentment."[69]

Another tangible factor is recruitment. Viet Cong casualties have

[65] Rose, 1963.
[66] Mok, 1965.
[67] Moore, 1965, pp. 47–48.
[68] Mok, 1965.
[69] Dayan, 1966, p. E3.

been variously estimated to be between fifteen and fifty percent per year.[70] Since this is probably much greater than the rate of reinforcement from the North, at least up to 1965, recruitment must have been active and successful in spite of the deterrent provided by the heavy casualty rate itself. Until recently, too, recruitment by the Viet Cong—in contrast with Government recruitment[71]—does not seem to have been primarily through conscription, but rather through the special blend of persuasion and strong social pressure, well described by Malcolm Browne,[72] which presupposes a generally friendly and receptive attitude in the village community. Viet Cong troopers are paid only from 30¢ to 50¢ per month, while a Government recruit's pay is $27 per month.[73] Yet the Viet Cong often become fired with a type of motivation rare on the Government side. ARVN leadership is said to be poor. "How else do you explain the fact," asked one regimental adviser, "that the Viet Cong can take the same unwilling recruit and turn him into a tiger in six months, while after six months ARVN recruits are still unwilling recruits?"[74]

Such evidence suggests the familiar analogy of the iceberg. The fighting Viet Cong appear to resemble the portion of the iceberg that shows above water, while the much larger number of peasants playing supporting roles are like the submerged, invisible ice.

(5) *There is some reason to think that, if democracy is defined as government for the people and in communication with the people, most of the peasants feel they have been shown more democracy by the Viet Cong than by the officials of Diem or by the military government.*

The evidence on this point is more mixed and ambiguous than on any of the four previous points, and should probably be given much less weight than any of those four. Nevertheless, it calls for rather careful discussion, if only to divest ourselves of our ingrained American habit of assuming that Communism means dictatorship, and that anything other than Communism must necessarily be more democratic.

It is necessary first to push aside those meanings of democracy

[70] Fall, 1965b, p. 258; 1966a.
[71] Malcolm Browne, 1965, pp. 146, 240; Fall, 1966a, p. 67.
[72] Malcolm Browne, 1965, pp. 121–36.
[73] *Time*, August 25, 1967, p. 21.
[74] Jonathan Randal, *New York Times*, June 11, 1967, p. 4E.

that are familiar to us but foreign to the Vietnamese peasant: free speech, a free press, political parties, voting in national elections, having and expressing opinions on a number of national issues. Relatively speaking, he neither knows nor cares about such things, and certainly has not been given much chance to practice them by either side. It is necessary to focus more on such concrete village concerns as building a frame for a new roof panel[75] or forcing a local landlord to allow farmers to take a shortcut through his property to the village well.[76] In such matters, the evidence suggests that the Viet Cong has been much closer to the people than the Government officials have been. The impression of many Americans that the relationship of the Viet Cong to the *ordinary* peasant has been primarily one of intimidation is quite wide of the mark. While there has been plenty of intimidation, the violence (at least until rather recently) has been carefully directed against outsiders, and relatively prosperous peasants who were collaborating with the Government, rather than against the rank-and-file. As far as the rank-and-file are concerned, the effort has been in strict accordance with the Maoist philosophy of keeping in the closest possible touch with the common people and their needs. An example is the "Three Withs" program: "a good cadre lives with, eats with, works with the population."[77]

To understand what is in the back of the peasants' minds today, it is necessary to go back to the period when the predecessor of the Viet Cong, the Viet Minh, was in control of large areas in South Vietnam. (The two organizations should not be confused. Although the Viet Minh also was Communist-controlled, it attracted many on nationalist grounds, and contained many non-Communist individuals, some of whom have served in post-Diem governments.) The Viet Minh was "for the people" in that it identified itself with and led their anti-French struggle and in that it actually gave land to the peasants rather than, like Diem, merely permitting them gradually to buy it; and in local matters it was apparently also "by the people" to some extent. Testimony on this is provided by Joseph Alsop, who was one of the few Westerners to get first-hand contact with Viet Minh-controlled areas. In a *New Yorker* article, he reported on a 1954 visit:

[75] Malcolm Browne, 1965, p. 123.
[76] Mecklin, 1965.
[77] Fall, in Raskin and Fall, eds., 1965, p. 256; Malcolm Browne, 1965, pp. 109, 123.

I would like to be able to report—I had hoped to be able to report—that on that long, slow canal trip to Vinh Binh (Mekong Delta) I saw all the signs of misery and oppression that have made my visits to Germany like nightmare journeys to 1984. But that was not so.

At first it was difficult for me, as it is for any Westerner, to conceive of a Communist government's genuinely "serving the people." I could hardly imagine a Communist government that was also a popular government and almost a democratic government. But this is just the sort of government the palm-hut state actually was while the struggle with the French continued. The Viet Minh could not possibly have carried on the resistance for one year, let alone nine years, without the people's strong, united support.[78]

The fact that Alsop now takes a militantly anti-Viet Cong position should not lead one to accept this earlier testimony at full face value. In 1954 he apparently did not see certain elements of anti-Viet Cong feeling in the South that are described by Pike, who goes so far as to say:

From the start the Viet Minh alienated the South Vietnamese. Old Communist Tran Van Giau and his successor, Nguyen Binh, dealt too harshly with the easy-going Southerner. The scorched-earth policy, copied from the Chinese revolution, appalled the South and proved unworkable. The Cochin Chinese regarded the Resistance as Northern-oriented. . . . The Communist organization was simply unable to consolidate its position late in the war. Its chief failure in this respect was its inability to achieve a Viet Minh alliance with the Southern nationalists, particularly the sects, for the Resistance and the attendant dislocations had enabled them to grow strong and to develop their own military forces and administrative units."[79]

It seems likely that the truth lies somewhere between Alsop's picture and Pike's.

To a considerable extent the for-the-people aspect of this movement has been continued by the Viet Cong,[80] if only as a military necessity, since it was vital to have the people's help in gaining intelligence, in denying intelligence to the enemy, and in keeping a flow of new recruits. An entry in a Viet Cong soldier's diary is worth mentioning here: "I answered the call of the Party when I was very young, and what did I do for the people of my village? I devoted myself to

[78] Alsop, 1955.
[79] Pike, 1966b, p. 48.
[80] Malcolm Browne, 1965, pp. 121–28.

the people. . . ."[81] There is a certain kind of controlled but dynamic political participation by the rank-and-file villagers that is much more characteristic of Viet Cong villages than of Government-controlled ones.[82]

In recent years there has been an important other side to the story. Viet Cong cadres have often been authoritative or even dictatorial, and there has been a good deal of resentment of their highhanded ways. Massive American participation in the war since early 1965 has forced the Viet Cong to scrape closer to the bottom of the barrel in money and manpower, and they have used strong-arm methods in conscripting early teen-age boys and levying heavy taxes. One of the frequent complaints of refugees is that the traditional village structure has been broken down and replaced by a centralized mechanism that is experienced by many as very oppressive. The peasant cannot go to market without special permission, contact with the outside world is often forbidden; sometimes villages are even broken into zones and a villager cannot go from one zone to another without advance approval. People are often afraid to talk freely even with relatives or friends. Refugees frequently express wonderment at the amount of freedom of speech that is allowed in Government-controlled areas. This sometimes comes in the form of criticizing the Government for allowing too much latitude.

All in all, it seems clear that if democracy is defined as individual freedom, the Viet Cong (like the government of North Vietnam) permits even less of it than the post-Diem military governments in the South have permitted, and in that sense is less democratic. On the other hand, as their criticism of "too much free speech" suggests, this is not the aspect of democracy that matters most to the ordinary peasants. What they want most is a village official who will not cheat and exploit them, who actually does what he can for their welfare. It looks as if the Viet Cong officials have done this much more than the Government-appointed officials have (although there is much variation among the latter; there are popular province chiefs and district chiefs, and in their areas, the peasants might spontaneously vote for them, or for their side). Most of the peasants may give the Viet Cong credit for good intentions, and for being basically "on their side," even when their methods are highhanded. Remembering

[81] Viet Cong soldier's diary, in Raskin and Fall, eds., 1965, p. 227.
[82] Pike, 1966b, pp. 111, 114, 124–26, 129, 148–49.

the better performance of the Viet Minh and the Viet Cong in the past, when they were not faced with the terrible difficulties and dangers that face them today, many peasants probably take that into account and give the Viet Cong the benefit of the doubt.

They are probably much less likely to do the same with the similarly highhanded methods of Government-appointed officials and government troops. There is apparently no disagreement among responsible observers about the amount of deliberate cheating of the people by government officials,[83] and, as we have seen, the brutality of the troops in handling Viet Cong or Viet Cong suspects is proverbial. It should be remembered also that the initial breaking down of the traditional village structure—the fine old semi-democratic system of election of village councils and mayors that survived even during the period of French rule—was accomplished by Diem in 1956.[84] In the village-centered minds of the peasants, this was probably more shocking than his refusal to hold the national elections required by the Geneva Agreements (which he had not signed).

It seems possible that an anthropologically enlightened American-sponsored or UN-sponsored program that genuinely respected and attempted to restore all that was good in the old Vietnamese village culture might be more democratic than the Viet Cong regime in the villages, and much more democratic than the rule of Saigon. The pacification and reform program has appeared to be a real effort in that direction. To be effective, however, such a program would have to cut cleanly through the tradition of arrogance toward the peasantry and socially accepted cheating of them that evidently exists in the city-based, upper-class-based officialdom of the Saigon government. Perhaps it would have to set up a wholly new bureaucracy with a wholly new tradition and value system. Failing that, the peasants will still confront their present hard choice, which is between two essentially dictatorial governments, one of which (Saigon) now permits somewhat more individual freedom, while the other (the Viet Cong) must seem to most peasants to be basically more *for* them and in touch with their needs.

(6) *There is a fair degree of consensus among the well-informed that the active pro-Viet Cong minority is larger.*

[83] Mok, 1966, p. 71; Buttinger, 1967a, pp. 949–54; Malcolm Browne, 1965, pp. 214–16.

[84] Fall, 1964b, p. 274; Shaplen, 1965, pp. 133, 140; Hickey, 1964, pp. 282–83; Buttinger, 1967a, pp. 944–46.

In Vietnam I found a surprising degree of agreement with this proposition, not only among the better-informed Americans but also among knowledgeable anti-Communist Vietnamese. In both cases wishful thinking might be expected to lead to the opposite conclusion, but in spite of whatever tendency to wishful thinking they may have had, nearly all agreed that the strongly motivated pro-Viet Cong minority seems much larger than the comparable group at our end of the political spectrum. Although they greatly deplored the half-heartedness of most of those on the anti-Viet Cong side, they accepted it as a fact. There is consensus also on the great skill of the propaganda and organizational methods of the Viet Cong.

There is no such consensus about the inner feelings of the "passive majority." As we have seen (above, pp. 34–35), some well-informed Americans believe that the inner feelings of most of this group, as well as their outward behavior, incline against the Viet Cong. If they are correct, this would mean that more than half the adult population leans at least mildly toward our side. But even these individuals tend to agree that the *strongly motivated* minority on our side is smaller than its pro-Viet Cong equivalent.

Evidence That the Pro-Viet Cong Minority Is Not the Larger

We must now consider the evidence on the other side: psychological factors that might incline the people to take the pro-Government or anti-Viet Cong side, and evidence that considerable numbers of them do so.

Objections can be raised to most of the arguments that are usually presented on this side. Each, however, seems to contain at least a kernel of truth that should be given due weight. Six major arguments will be examined:

(1) *There is widespread physical fear of Viet Cong violence, and anger at the Viet Cong's use of physical intimidation.*

The evidence that a great many people in Government-controlled territory see the Viet Cong as dangerous and lawless has already been considered in our discussion of the passive majority. Unlike fear of Communism, which to many of the peasants must seem a far-off and abstract concept, fear of the hand grenade, the sniper's bullet, or the assassin's knife is a primitive, elemental emotion. In its emotional quality, it is comparable to the fear of American bombs, shells, and napalm that is often cited as a reason to believe that the people are hostile to our side. At the very least it probably operates in the minds of a great many non-political persons to balance and neutralize their impression of violence on the Government side. It must be easy for such persons to adopt a plague-on-both-your-houses attitude. As an argument against the Communists' propaganda proposition that the people of South Vietnam are on their side, it carries more weight than most opponents of our involvement realize.

It also adds some weight to the argument that a sizable fraction of the South Vietnamese people are active, dedicated anti-Communists. There is a great deal of violence on both sides; knowledge of it is therefore unlikely to produce dedication to either side except in one special type of person—those whose close relatives have been injured, tortured, or killed by one side or the other. In a family-centered culture such as that of Vietnam, in which family loyalty probably matters more and national loyalty less than in the United States, abiding hatred for those who have injured a relative is a potent source of commitment. Probably it swells the ranks of extremists on both sides, and perhaps especially on the pro-Viet Cong side, for reasons we have considered (pp. 41–47), but at least it strengthens the case for thinking that as many as five to fifteen percent are emotionally and actively opposed to the Viet Cong. It is also a reason not to rate very high the proportion of active, dedicated pro-Viet Cong people even in the hamlets fully controlled by the Viet Cong.

There is no doubt about the fact of intimidation. For years (very effectively as early as 1957), the Viet Cong has been liquidating not only tax gatherers and other natural objects of peasant hostility but also Government-appointed officials—teachers, health workers, and others—whose only crime has been competence plus a desire to help the peasants in ways that did not increase the power of the Viet Cong.[85] Recently the strong-arm methods have increased,[86] though actual assassination has apparently decreased.[87] Sometimes the killings have been in public, with embellishments such as the disembowelment of the man himself, his wife, and his children.[88] Beheading has also been frequent, and it "is a terrible thing to do to a man in Vietnam. Most people believe that the loss of the head damns the

[85] Lansdale, 1964, p. 81; Moser, 1965.
[86] Reston, 1965, p. 43.
[87] Fall, 1965b, p. 19; Pike, 1966b, pp. 102, 248.
[88] Malcolm Browne, 1965, pp. 103, 128–29.

spirit to an eternity of restless wandering. It is the worst way to die."[89] In recent years recruitment, which in the past had been voluntary, has often been at the point of a gun.

The problem lies rather in determining what inferences can be appropriately drawn from the fact of intimidation. Can we legitimately infer what many Americans have inferred: that intimidation is the only or the main reason for overt peasant cooperation with the Viet Cong, and that such strong-arm methods must create a great deal of resentment that is not openly expressed?

There are four reasons to question such inferences: First, the emphasis of the Viet Cong has not been primarily on violence but rather on political "struggle." Until 1964 and 1965, when increasing control by cadres from the North and the increasing involvement of the United States led them to shift the emphasis from the political side to the military, the emphasis was always on agitation, demonstrations, etc. There was even a myth of non-violence, remotely resembling the philosophy of Gandhi and Martin Luther King in that it included a great deal of open defiance of officials and protest against injustice by unarmed, defenseless persons, especially women.[90]

Second, the peasants are Vietnamese, and there is much in the behavior of Vietnamese, on both sides of the conflict, to suggest that their standards of acceptable behavior, especially to an enemy, differ considerably from what we like to think our own standards are.

Third, the violence of the Viet Cong, in contrast with that of the government, has been combined with a strong desire to win the good will of the peasants. As we have seen, it has in general been directed against persons who appeared as enemies or at least as outsiders.[91] The Viet Cong have gone all out (at least until recently) to help rather than to hurt the majority of the villagers, so as to consolidate their image of the Viet Cong as representing them and fighting on their side.[92]

Fourth, there is reason to doubt that the general human response to violence, if it is perceived as being on "our side," is as negative as we sheltered Americans tend to assume. The truth seems to be that, even in Western cultures, if there is a strong group consensus, and a

[89] Malcolm Browne, 1965, p. 100.

[90] Pike, 1966b, pp. 54, 87, 90, 99, 155, 264; Burchett, 1965, pp. 62–71; Malcolm Browne, p. 129.

[91] Dudman, 1965; Clos, 1965, p. 436.

[92] Malcolm Browne, 1965, pp. 121–27; Chaffard, 1965, p. 4.

part of the group enforces by violence what the large majority of the group agree with, resentment against that violence by the conforming majority is often minimal. This does not prove, of course, that such a consensus exists in the villages of South Vietnam, but it does suggest that the fact of intimidation is not in itself a strong basis for inferring where the natural sympathies of the peasants lie,[93] and it suggests that in the Viet Cong-controlled hamlets those who are strongly repelled by the violence probably do not often go to the opposite extreme (unless the victim of the violence is a close relative), but merely become ambivalent and join the passive majority.

(2) *In recent years the taxes imposed by the Viet Cong have become increasingly burdensome.*

With the Viet Cong's shift in 1964 to a military rather than a political emphasis, and with the massive intervention of the United States in and after 1965, the economic exactions of the Viet Cong have greatly increased. Especially when compared with the promises of victory made by the Viet Cong in 1964 and early 1965, this has understandably led to much disillusionment. It will be remembered that in the CBS-ORC survey, conducted in late 1966 and early 1967, the second most frequent complaint against the Viet Cong, second only to "terrorism and sabotage," was "exploitation of the people, heavy taxes" (thirty-six percent).[94] Since a person's pocketbook is as tangible as his skin, it seems likely that this too is a more acute grievance than intangible ones such as the threat of Communism or the increasing control of the Viet Cong by cadres from the North. Money means food and other necessities for oneself and one's family. Money payments to the Viet Cong are therefore probably a more important source of antagonism than most opponents of U.S. involvement realize.

It has been argued that this factor is more a liability to the Viet Cong than its land policy has been an asset. Counted in piasters, this may well be true. It may be questioned, however, whether the two "transfers" are psychologically equivalent. Since the recent exactions by the Viet Cong have obviously been imposed out of dire necessity, while the exorbitant rents previously demanded by the landlords were not, it is possible that the Viet Cong levies are often seen in this context and regarded as more reasonable and forgivable. Also,

[93] Tanham, 1961; Hilsman, 1965.
[94] CBS, 1967, p. 35.

though the current activities of the Viet Cong have largely eliminated rental payments to absentee landlords, the Government has not yet promised drastic land reform even when peace returns. The peasants have reason to fear that, if the Government and the Americans win the war, they will again have to pay exorbitant rents; if the Viet Cong wins, however, the present heavy taxes may be greatly reduced.

(3) *The prevailing picture of the Communist North appears to be unfavorable, and the Viet Cong is now generally seen as Communist-controlled.*

The proposition that there is an unfavorable picture of the Communist North is supported by the virtually unanimous anti-Communist statements of other leaders and groups, including the Buddhists. It is supported also by the testimony of some on-the-spot observers who are least open to the charge of pro-Government bias. Max Clos, a French journalist who is intensely opposed to the military government, nevertheless says that the Vietnamese "know perfectly well what they have to fear from the installation in South Vietnam of a government comparable with the one imposed by the Viet Minh on North Vietnam. They don't want a government of that kind at any price."[95] This apparent fear of the North is the more remarkable because it conflicts with the undoubted personal regard of most of the people for Ho Chi Minh as the hero of the victorious struggle against the French. He personally is seen as the George Washington of his country, yet his type of government is widely dreaded.

The unfavorable picture of the North does not seem to be primarily economic in origin. Economic comparisons between North and South raise complex and controversial issues, with much to be said on both sides.[96] Rather, it seems to be based mainly on the first-hand reports of life in the North that must have been brought down by the more than 800,000 refugees who fled the North in and after 1954. They had much to report. Harsh treatment was being meted out to Catholics and others who had sided with the French in the long and bitter war that had just been victoriously concluded, and during the period of the so-called "land reform" of 1953 to 1956 there was much torturing and killing of the more prosperous peasants. In brutality this period can be compared only with Stalin's treat-

[95] Clos, in Gettleman, ed., 1965, p. 437.
[96] Fall, 1964b, pp. 242, 302, 312, 389; Scalapino, 1965, pp. 302–3.

ment of the kulaks, and the negative reaction to it by most of the peasants themselves was indicated by the Nghé-An uprising in 1956, which is another item that critics of our involvement have too often ignored. An extremely negative picture of the whole situation in the North must have been brought to the South by the hundreds of thousands of escapees, and they must have had this picture confirmed by rumors or reports of what was happening to their relatives in the North during the next two years. Exaggerated and selective as these reports by the escapees may have been,[97] they came with the authority of first-hand observation, and the subsequent official depiction of Communist oppression and slavery, by Diem and his successors, has therefore probably had a firm basis of credibility in the minds of many people. (However, since the great majority of those who came South were Catholics, and the Catholics settled mainly in the cities or in new Catholic villages in the countryside, this strongly negative picture of the North may exist much more in the cities and in the relatively few Catholic villages than in the non-Catholic villages, which contain most of South Vietnam's population. Also, the non-Catholics tended to regard the newcomers from the North with some suspicion, and did not necessarily give much weight to what they said.)

The next question is the extent to which the Vietnamese in the South regard the Viet Cong as Communist-controlled, the spearhead of an attempt by the North Vietnamese Communists to impose their rule on the South. To the extent that they make this identification, the negativity of their conception of Communism in the North should carry over to their conception of the Viet Cong.

Until after the fall of Diem, the Viet Cong made a continual effort to avoid the word Communism and to picture themselves as a grass-roots movement representing all patriotic elements among the people of South Vietnam. The fact that they did so lends further support to the proposition that most of the South Vietnamese want to avoid rule by the Communist North; the Viet Cong were apparently realistic in regarding the word Communist as primarily negative to most of the people, and association with it as a stigma to be avoided. After the fall of Diem, however, in the process of exerting increased discipline within their somewhat heterogeneous front organization, the Communists have been much more frank about their

[97] Mus, quoted by Scheer, 1965, p. 28.

alignment with Hanoi. They have "regularized" their position.[98] At the same time, the flow of supplies and men from the North has made the association impossible to hide. It seems likely, therefore, that today there are few if any politically conscious persons in the South who do not regard the nucleus of the Viet Cong as Communist and as closely associated with the North.

Putting these two facts together—the generally negative picture of the Communist North and the recently obvious association of the Viet Cong with the Communist North—we can probably infer that the Communist stigma has hurt the Viet Cong in the eyes of most of the city people, though probably not, to any considerable extent, in the eyes of most of the non-Catholic peasants. As we have seen, most of the villagers probably do not see the rank-and-file Viet Cong guerrillas as inherently evil at all, but as "villagers like us," with "our" welfare at heart. If now they begin to believe that the leaders of the Viet Cong are Communists, this may evoke in their minds only vague and partly disbelieved images of Communist oppression in the North.

In fact, the stigma of association with the Communist North probably has emotional significance only to intellectuals who know what Communism means as a threat to intellectual freedom, to some devout people who oppose it on religious grounds, to some men of property who oppose it on grounds of class self-interest, and to refugees who vividly recall their escape from the North. Many of these can be counted among those who are actively, militantly anti-Viet Cong. But it is doubtful that anti-Communism is an emotional, important factor even in the ambivalent feelings of the passive majority. To many of them, Communism must often have seemed a mere scarecrow used by landlords and rich city people to fend off and discredit those who were trying to help the poor, just as the word socialism seems to many liberal Americans to be a scare word used by conservatives to discredit sound progressive measures.

The negative potency of anti-Communism is probably weaker than the positive potency of the term *liberation forces,* which the peasants habitually use when talking of the Viet Cong, or the negative potency of the term *nationalist,* which they habitually apply to the Government forces. These two terms have been carried over directly from the war of resistance against the French, when the Viet Minh

[98] Malcolm Browne, 1965, p. 244; Chaffard, 1965, p. 6.

forces were generally called liberation forces, and the pro-French, Bao Dai troops were called nationalist. In semantic terms, the present government has two strikes against it in the minds of the peasants, since all the pride and patriotism of the successful war for independence are bound up in the word liberation, while the stigma of aiding the hated French and the stigma of ignominious defeat are attached to the word nationalist. It is almost as if nationalist has come to mean unpatriotic.

(4) *Many Americans who have been in Vietnam, including some who have conducted systematic interviews, have the impression that most of the people are definitely against the Viet Cong.*

It is necessary to note that all such impressions are questionable on two grounds: selectivity of contacts, and lack of frankness in what is said to Government officials, city-bred interviewers, and other persons associated with the Saigon government, as Americans inevitably are in the minds of many peasants.

In Vietnam the selectivity of contacts means, for instance, that an American is most likely to meet precisely those groups that are most anti-Viet Cong; army officers, officials, educated people, city people, Catholics, foreign-oriented people who can speak either English or French.[99] Although he often has some awareness of this selectivity, he may fail to give it more than a fraction of the emphasis it deserves. It presumably applies even within a refugee camp, since the peasants who have escaped from the villages to the cities or to refugee camps are presumably, in general, those who have the most to fear from the Viet Cong and the least to fear from the military government.

The other vitiating factor is the worldwide human tendency to say what it seems expedient to say, or what the listener wants to hear. It does not seem likely that a pro-Viet Cong peasant or lower-class city dweller would be frank about his position when talking to an American or to an official of the military government. Why should he be so foolish? Why not pretend that he is anti-Viet Cong—or, more plausibly, that he is simply not interested in politics, or that he hates both sides equally? The widespread use of torture by the South Vietnam troops to gain information about the location of Viet Cong suspects is not well calculated to promote frankness about leanings in that direction. There is also evidence that anti-American feeling

[99] Malcolm Browne, 1965, p. 202; Fall, 1964a, p. 175.

is much stronger under the surface than on it,[100] and that the same is true of anti-Government feeling.[101]

What about more systematic opinion studies, resembling opinion polls in the United States and other advanced countries, but adapted to the circumstances of interviewing in South Vietnam, with a special effort to circumvent the obstacles of unrepresentative sampling and of non-frankness? Isn't it possible to get useful results by, for instance, relying more on descriptions of what has happened than on opinions, asking about the opinions of "others in your village" rather than about the respondent's own opinions, and including questions yielding answers that can be factually checked?

Unfortunately, such studies do not seem to have been done by any investigator who is in a position to report his findings freely. If it were done, the qualitative findings would certainly be useful, but it is doubtful whether the particular hypothesis we are considering here—that most of the people are definitely anti-Communist—could be convincingly supported by such a study. The pro-Viet Cong people of Vietnam have had many years of practice in concealing not only their own real attitudes but also the real attitudes of others like themselves, and it is hard to see how any known technique could fully circumvent this well-practiced façade of conformity. The burden of proof, at least, is on the investigator who thinks he has succeeded.

A case in point is a "study of Vietnamese village attitudes" described briefly by Douglas Pike.[102] He says the study indicates that "ten percent of the villagers are true believers [in the Viet Cong], twenty percent waver between the Viet Cong and the Saigon government, while the attitudes of seventy percent range from a sort of determined neutralism to outright hostility toward the Viet Cong." Since it presumably was not his own study, Pike was under no obligation to report it at greater length, but the reader would feel more reassured if he had at least shown some awareness of the possible biases by making some statement indicating that the investigators were aware of the dangers of unrepresentative sampling and of non-frankness, and used various methods to avoid them. Until we are so reassured we must leave open the possibility that, for example, the sample may not have included a proper proportion of peasants from the southern part of the Mekong Delta (who are probably the most

[100] Robert Browne, 1965, p. 14.
[101] Halberstam, in Gettleman, ed., 1965, p. 262.
[102] Pike, 1966a, p. 24.

pro-Viet Cong and by the same token the least accessible), and that the respondents' statements may have been simply taken at face value. The reader wonders also what the attitudes of these same peasants toward their own government were. Perhaps they were even less favorable than attitudes toward the Viet Cong. How many, for instance, were true believers in Premier Ky? As many as ten percent?

Two other surveys have been publicly though only partially reported in the United States: a "confidential report by American representatives in Vietnam's forty-three provinces" sketchily reported by Jack Foisie,[103] and "a recent survey by a group of American civilian officials here" reported from Saigon by Charles Mohr.[104] Neither of them modifies substantially the picture as presented in this chapter. The first asserts that "the rural people have taken heart and are willing to provide more assistance to allied troops" (without describing the previous situation implied by the word *more*), and presents a discouraging picture of the pace of rural reconstruction. The second reports "increasing anxiety among South Vietnamese over the growing intensity of the warfare and its effects on civilians" but says "the study could find no evidence that the population had begun to go over to the political control of the Viet Cong."

An extensive survey, already cited, was conducted in late 1966 and early 1967 by the Opinion Research Corporation (ORC) for CBS; like the others, it does not seem to have discovered any method that circumvents the two great biases (see below, p. 82). There may be confidential surveys the results of which have not been given any public circulation. If so, one wonders why their findings on this crucial point have not been communicated (with proper safeguards) to the American public. If the findings permit a more optimistic interpretation than the ambiguous one that results from putting together the publicly available information, one would expect the American government to publicize them. As long as it does not do so a non-government observer will necessarily wonder whether the unpublicized information is even less reassuring than what is publicly available.

(5) *Very few non-Communist leaders and organized groups in the South have clearly allied themselves with the Viet Cong.*

[103] Foisie, *Washington Post*, September 29, 1965.
[104] Mohr, *New York Times*, November 27, 1965.

This is true, for instance, of the anti-Diem intellectuals in Saigon, the Buddhist leaders such as Thich Tri Quang and Thich Tam Chau, the Catholic hierarchy, and the indigenous religious sects, the Cao Dai and the Hoa Hao.[105] The Cao Dai, which had opposed Diem, switched sides after his death.[106] Government employees, understandably, appear to be quite generally loyal to the Government;[107] the Overseas Chinese in Cholon, who have great economic power, have shown almost no pro-Viet Cong sentiment;[108] even the Buddhists do not seem to have been much infiltrated or converted.[109]

Such facts certainly justify renewed emphasis on the proposition that the dedicated, organized group at the Viet Cong end of the continuum is a minority. Those who have gone so far as to join the fighting Viet Cong organization are probably no more than 200,000 or 300,000 at most[110] in a country of 17,000,000—less than one in forty. As in most other countries, even in times of great inner stress and polarizing of attitudes, the number of able-bodied adults who are so highly motivated and so undeterred by urgent family responsibilities that they can give themselves wholly to a guerrilla unit is far less than the total population.

The fact that leaders of other Vietnamese groups have not flocked to the Viet Cong may also serve as a salutary reminder of Ho's free use of assassination as a means of getting rid of non-Communist nationalist leaders who threw in their lot with him in 1945 and 1946. This characteristic crime of a single-mindedly power-seeking authoritarian apparatus is also a source of weakness at times such as the present, when it frightens off important potential allies.

On the other hand, it should be remembered that many other factors of self-interest may induce these leaders, living in the cities and other Government-controlled areas, to play a waiting game. Whatever the extent of their distrust of the military government or their resentment of American intrusion, or their degree of agreement with the Viet Cong, they now have much reason not to display these attitudes fully. Those who advocated a neutralist solution have some-

---

[105] Scalapino, 1966, p. 136; Carver, 1966, p. 365; Chaffard, 1965, p. 7; Pike, 1966b, p. 268.

[106] Pike, 1966b, pp. 68, 201, 369; on the Hoa Hao, see p. 69.

[107] *Ibid.*, p. 258.

[108] *Ibid.*, p. 204.

[109] *Ibid.*, pp. 203–4, 353.

[110] Carver, 1966, p. 369; Pike, 1966b, p. 115.

times been repressed, notably the Buddhist leader Thich Quang Lien.[111] And in any case, the leaders' personal fear of a too-close embrace by the Communists does not necessarily apply to the rank-and-file.

Observers agree that the Viet Cong exhibit intense motivation, which is a major factor in their extraordinary organization and fighting efficiency. Georges Chaffard, a French journalist who was able to observe the Viet Cong directly and who appears to be a relatively objective witness, describes them as "incredibly serious and equalitarian."[112] The events of early 1968 bear this out. The picture on the government side is quite different; most of the reports agree that there is much corruption, individual self-interest, factionalism, and—with many honorable exceptions—a perfunctory attitude toward the prosecution of the war.[113] Few, for instance, have much stomach for the dangerous business of staying in disputed villages throughout the night. Conscription is very difficult.[114] According to R. W. Apple, Jr., of the *New York Times,* desertion in 1966 "threatened to demoralize the entire army," though strenuous efforts to combat it have reduced the rate from about twenty-four percent to about twelve percent annually.[115] On the other hand, few have defected to the Viet Cong.[116]

(6) *After the Geneva settlement of 1954, a great many more Vietnamese moved from the North to the South—"voting with their feet" against Communism—than moved from the South to the North.*

While it is estimated that nearly 900,000 left the North, a much smaller number, estimated variously between the figures of 80,000 and 150,000, moved North when Diem took over in the South.[117] This is a ratio of at least six to one, and perhaps ten to one in favor of the non-Communist alternative.

The disproportionate numbers recall the outcome of similar foot-voting in Korea and in Germany. All three examples suggest that, when people can choose freely between a Communist and a non-

111 Robert Browne, 1965, p. 13.

112 Chaffard, 1965, p. 4; Clos, in Gettleman, ed., 1965, p. 431.

113 Shaplen, 1965, pp. 229–31; Malcolm Browne, 1965, p. 240; Clos, in Gettleman, ed., 1965, p. 431.

114 Fall, 1966a.

115 Apple, *New York Times,* May 5, 1967, p. 2.

116 Fishel, 1966.

117 Shaplen, 1965, p. 114.

Communist way of life, they are likely to reject Communism. This is much more impressive than any mere words or ballot-box voting, since it normally involves a pulling up of roots and personal sacrifice in both social and economic terms. Those who do it must mean it.

On the other hand, to be properly evaluated this particular instance of foot-voting should be seen in its context. The great majority of those who came South were Catholic,[118] which meant that a relatively large minority of them were educated, mobile, and well-to-do, although numerically peasants probably predominated. Whether they were well-to-do or poor, however, being Catholic meant that they were in some degree identified with the French, both in their own minds and in the minds of most of the South Vietnamese, who tended to regard them as semi-alien and as the natural stooges of alien white intruders.[119] Since about ninety percent of the South Vietnamese remain non-Catholic, even after the influx from the North, the immigrants can scarcely be regarded as a representative sample of the population as a whole.

This brings up the question: How do the Catholics stand now? Optimistic Americans often start their calculations as to South Vietnamese attitudes with the assumption that the roughly ten percent who are Catholics are unequivocally anti-Communist and therefore "on our side." Some others (e.g., Drew Pearson), while assuming that the Catholics are on our side, assume by the same token that the remaining ninety percent are probably against us. Both generalizations seem too simple. As we have seen, many non-Catholics *are* intensely or moderately anti-Communist, and at the same time many Catholics are intensely critical of the way in which the military government and the United States have conducted the war.[120] The survey described by Charles Mohr "indicated that . . . Roman Catholic leaders were among the most vocal critics of the use of too much military force." Many priests have been critical of the bombing of villages. In fact, Norman Morrison's self-immolation in the United States was directly influenced by an article reprinted from a Paris newspaper giving a priest's account of the napalm bombing of a Vietnam village. "I have seen my faithful burned up in napalm," the priest was quoted as saying. "I have seen all my villages razed. By

[118] Fall, 1964b, pp. 154, 170.
[119] Carver, 1965, pp. 387–408.
[120] Robert Browne, 1965, p. 14.

God, it's not possible. . . . They must settle their accounts with God."[121] The proportion of Catholics who are intensely anti-Communist is clearly much higher than it is among non-Catholics, but this is not at all equivalent to saying that most of the Catholic rank-and-file, or even most of the Catholic hierarchy, are "on our side."[122]

Returning to the question of the relative numbers moving South and North, we must consider why so few went North. Several things should be remembered. In 1954, as in later years, the economic level was decidedly higher in the South, and many probably believed that there was a prospect of massive American help in the South. (They were right.) Also, most of those with a strong Viet Minh involvement were villagers, and villagers are proverbially difficult to uproot. Normally, they stay rooted in their village unless there is an extremely strong incentive to move, as the failure of the strategic-hamlet program demonstrated.[123] And a third inhibiting factor, probably, was that the Geneva Agreements gave the Viet Minh a prospect of an election victory in 1956 if they stayed and used their influence in the villages to ensure that victory—or, if necessary, to resume the armed struggle. The Communists probably directed most of their own men to stay put. The small number moving North, therefore, cannot be regarded as a valid indication of the feeling of the peasants in general.

It should also be noted that hundreds of thousands of peasants are now "voting with their feet," escaping from Viet Cong-controlled villages to the safety of Government-controlled cities or refugee camps.[124]

The obvious question here, however, is: Are they escaping mainly from Viet Cong domination or mainly from the shells, bombs, napalm and crop-destroying chemicals that the Government and the American armed forces are dropping on them? As yet there appears to be no convincing evidence that hostility to the Viet Cong plays a large part in the process.[125] Statements to that effect by the refugees themselves can hardly be taken at face value, since their self-interest is on the side of dissembling.

[121] *Washington Post*, November 4, 1965, p. A1.
[122] Hickey, 1964, p. 282.
[123] Fall, 1964b, p. 179.
[124] Carver, 1966, p. 370.
[125] Hilsman, 1965.

How Large Is the Middle Group?

Six arguments have been examined on each side of the proposition that the strongly pro-Viet Cong group is larger. In order to see the entire picture in perspective, a further question must be considered: How large is the relatively indifferent group in the middle? Is our initial estimate of sixty to eighty percent realistic? Four factors that apparently contribute to neutrality will be considered first, then four factors that could make for an active taking of sides. Reasons for inferring widespread indifference on the part of the Vietnamese:

(a) There is evidence (p. 47) of tremendous war-weariness; it seems likely that a considerable majority of the people care more about ending the war quickly than they do about victory for either side. This majority probably includes many who,[126] if they take sides, tend to align with the side they think most likely to win, chiefly out of self-interest but also to press for a speedy end to the war.

(b) A matter-of-fact acceptance of the winning side may be more common among Chinese and Vietnamese than among Europeans and Americans. Lucien Pye, partly on the basis of interviews with defectors from the Chinese guerrillas in Malaya, has argued that the structure of the Chinese conscience or superego differs from the typical Western pattern; it more matter-of-factly accepts changing sides when one's self-interest seems to be to do so.[127] A number of social scientists (Pye, Pool, Davison) think the same is true of the Vietnamese, whose cultural traditions and mores are similar to those of the Chinese.

(c) The hypothesis that a large majority are indifferent also fits the mass of evidence that the majority are ignorant and indifferent on most political issues, even in advanced countries such as the United States, and usually all the more in the less developed countries with less widespread education and democratic political experience. It seems natural enough to extend this generalization to Vietnam and to assume that there also the majority, being composed

[126] CBS, 1967.
[127] Pye, 1956.

of "illiterate oriental peasants," is likely to be similarly indifferent to politics.

(d) A fourth reason to infer indifference is the impression of many Western observers in Vietnam that the typical peasant is simply numb and confused by the battering he has taken from both sides, with no strong conscious desire except to end the war. In the survey described by Mohr, "the attitude of the population was summarized as being mainly passive, fatalistic, and somewhat confused."[128]

Reasons for inferring a widespread taking of sides:

(a) A simple logical point should be noted: The desire for peace could be paramount in the ordinary peasant's mind, yet he could still prefer one side to the other. To say that peace is what he wants most is not equivalent to saying that it is the only thing he wants. He might also want an end to a viciously oppressive system of land rent, and he could regard as the lesser evil the side that offers it to him. He also could naturally identify more with one side than with the other, hating the thought that "we," the common people of Vietnam, might be defeated by a coalition of alien Americans, semi-alien landlords and corrupt officials, while being willing to accept even this coalition if the alternative might be prolonged war.

(b) Most of the reports that the peasants are neutral are open to a serious methodological question: Perhaps those who lean toward the Viet Cong find that an apathetic and apolitical pose is the best way to conceal their real feelings when talking with an American or an interviewer whom they suspect of being associated with the Government.

(c) While the Vietnamese superego may differ from that of the West insofar as personal and family concerns more often take precedence over larger causes such as nationalism, by the same token *family* (as opposed to individual) loyalty may matter more there than here.[129] How often does family loyalty lead to feelings and actions on the Viet Cong side, and how often does it lead to feelings and actions on the Government side? The point has already been made that those whose wives, brothers, or children have suffered intensely at the hands of either side are likely to hate that side, and

[128] Mohr, *New York Times*, November 27, 1965.
[129] Hickey, 1964, pp. 279, 282.

may dedicate their lives to its defeat. As we have seen, there is reason to think that many more have suffered physically (torture, shelling of villages) at the hands of the Government. In a family-centered culture this could be the chief means by which fanatics are made.

(d) Finally, there are historical as well as psychological reasons to think that numbness and confusion are not necessarily the most probable response to the experiences the Vietnamese have been through. The emotional impact of civil war is usually to promote an intense partisanship, not apathy. We too have known civil war, and Civil War history shows no indifferent majority. A process of polarization occurred that tended to range nearly everyone, with varying degrees of intensity, on one side or the other of the great issue. In the American Civil War polarization occurred even in the border states, and violent cleavages within families were not uncommon.

This factor of polarization under stress counts most strongly against the easy assumption frequently expressed in the United States that because the Vietnamese people are largely "illiterate oriental peasants," less "politically sophisticated" than ourselves, they probably "couldn't care less" which side wins. There is a danger here of a kind of snobbery on our part. Perhaps we overestimate our own kind of "political sophistication," based as it often is on second-hand or third-hand knowledge, and underestimate the kind of simple, direct knowledge that a Vietnamese can have, based on living in the situation throughout his own life. We may leap too readily to the conclusion that the Vietnamese peasants are like the politically apathetic majority of Americans, only more so. What we often forget is that Vietnam differs from the United States and from most other developing countries because for over twenty years it has been deeply plowed by civil war. War is the expected, not the exceptional; thus numbness is created in many Vietnamese; in many others, fierce hatred and dedication to the destruction of one side or the other are born.

On balance, the initial estimate of sixty to eighty percent "relatively indifferent" seems reasonable. The word "relatively" is important here, however, since a great many in the middle group probably are ambivalent, with real feelings on both sides and with some preponderance of one set of feelings over the other. Probably only a minority within this majority are as resolutely uncommitted as Susan Sheehan's old woman. There is room for the speculation that most of the middle group are inclined mildly toward the Viet Cong (including those who dislike both sides but dislike the Saigon government more), or that most of them are inclined mildly against it (including those who dislike both sides but dislike the Viet Cong more). All of this is consistent with the proposition that sixty to eighty percent are "relatively" indifferent. It is probably inaccurate and complacently snobbish to draw the sweeping conclusion that "most of them couldn't care less" about which side wins, but it is probably still fair to say that in this large middle group inner preferences are not strong enough to override considerations of personal and family self-interest. Consequently, in Vietnam as in a great many other countries, the crucial question continues to be the balance of side-taking among those who, unequivocally and with a feeling of commitment, take one side or the other.

Changes Since Diem

The evidence covered so far consists largely of the experiences and behavior of the Vietnamese before November, 1963, when Diem was deposed and assassinated. There are many observers who believe that the psychological atmosphere has improved since then, and some who think it has improved considerably.

Indications of significant improvement include first the evidence of how bad the situation actually was in Diem's last days. It was catastrophic. Buttinger, Fall, Pike, Halberstam, Mecklin, Malcolm Browne, Scigliano, and others have documented the catastrophe in detail,[130] and so convincingly that Washington's slow realization of the actual situation emerges as a striking and puzzling phenomenon,[131] deserving psychological study (see Chapter 9). Diem, his half-mad brother Nhu and his brother's wife had alienated one by one every important group in the country, including most of the realistic anti-Communists who saw how the Ngo family was debasing and weakening the anti-Communist struggle, and at last including the upper echelons of the armed forces, on which every

[130] Buttinger, 1967a, pp. 925–1010; Fall, 1964b, pp. 389–99; Pike, 1966b, pp. 57–73; Mecklin, 1965; Malcolm Browne, 1965, pp. 169–99, 214–17; Scigliano, 1963, pp. 88, 91.

[131] Pike, 1966, pp. 69, 72–73.

unpopular dictator must rely for survival.[132] According to Malcolm Browne, there was a "sweeping hatred" of the regime throughout the country.[133] If the Ngo family had remained in charge there is little doubt that Vietnam would be entirely Communist today.

There has grown up a legend in the United States, held still by some militant anti-Communists whose information on this point is secondhand and selective, that America withdrew support from Diem *because* he was anti-Communist and that this betrayal destroyed the one strong, authentically Vietnamese anti-Communist who knew how to rule and who could have saved the situation.[134] The legend rests on a single kernel of truth: The military situation did deteriorate rapidly in the months immediately after Diem's death. The Communists themselves apparently believed for a year or two, somewhat wishfully, that the end of the Diem regime helped them by accelerating the disintegration of anti-Communist forces that were already crumbling.[135] If the central element in a large organizational structure is removed and there is nothing ready to take its place, a temporary deterioration is probably inevitable.

Although the short-run effects, from an anti-Communist standpoint, were bad, there is little doubt that the long-run effects were good. While Khan, Ky, Thieu, and the others who succeeded Diem have scarcely been popular, there has been no sweeping hatred of them comparable to the hatred of the Ngo family that existed in 1963. The special, peculiar elements injected into the situation by Diem's fatuous rigidity (with its curious religious coloration), Nhu's arrogant hypocrisy, and Madame Nhu's poisonous dynamism were removed. The Cao Dai, which had opposed Diem, switched sides. The Buddhist *bonzes* stopped self-immolation. The military was stabilized; the generals, once they gained control, were no longer a danger to the Government. Many of the people say (at least when talking with Americans or with officials of the Saigon government) that things are better now.

Other indications of improvement include the massive American military effort, which has largely removed the militant anti-Communists' fear of a Communist takeover, the decrease of

[132] Buttinger, 1967, pp. 925–30, 935–39; Schlesinger, 1967, pp. 41–43.
[133] Malcolm Browne, 1965, p. 215.
[134] Labin, 1964, pp. 27–40, 61–79.
[135] Burchett, 1965, pp. 216–18.

unemployment with improvement (albeit inflationary and unnatural) in the economic situation,[136] real efforts to help the peasants with American money, some progress toward democracy and civilian representation in the Government, an easing of the formerly acute conflict between Buddhists and Catholics, resentment against the Viet Cong's strong-arm recruitment and high taxes.

On the other hand, there are a number of reasons to think that the improvement has not been as great as some believe, and that the over-all psychological situation remains not very different from what has been described earlier in this chapter:

(1) There has been no real land reform (see above, pp. 42–44). An immediate abolition of land rent, which might have convinced most of the peasants that Saigon's claims of "revolutionary development" were genuine, has not occurred. Most of the peasants had stopped paying rent by 1964 and 1965, but for this they can thank the Viet Cong, not Saigon.

(2) The extreme corruption of local officials appears to continue. It would be difficult to exaggerate the extent of this evil. Malcolm Browne says, "Personally, I feel the biggest factor in the disenchantment of the Vietnamese people with the Diem regime was his failure to do anything to change the French colonial system of administration. And this fatal flaw appears to be no less true of Diem's successors."[137] It is not realistic to brush this off with the thought that "there is corruption even in the United States." The difference in degree between Saigon and Chicago or between Saigon and the Viet Cong is very great.

(3) The program of "revolutionary development" designed to "win the hearts and minds" of the peasants has not yet fulfilled the hopes invested in it. It has gone the way of its predecessor programs, and for the same reasons, especially the halfhearted fashion in which it was administered, by Vietnamese appointed by local bureaucrats whose power in turn depended on the indulgence of the landed oligarchy and its political allies.[138]

---

[136] Shaplen (1967, p. 80), however, stresses the privation caused by continuing inflation. "The average person's purchasing power . . . continues to decline."

[137] Malcolm Browne, 1965, p. 216; see also pp. 214–15; cf. *New York Times*, April 16, 1967.

[138] Shaplen, 1966, pp. 58, 108; Apple, *New York Times*, March 26, 1967; Buttinger, 1967b, p. 5.

(4) The terrible insecurity and demoralization of the peasants who live in disputed villages, often Government-controlled by day and Viet Cong-controlled by night, continues without much change. As of mid-1967 perhaps one eighth of the hamlets were securely held by the government,[139] and claims of significant change since then are controversial.[140]

Unless there is capitulation by the Viet Cong leaders, the shortage

[139] Shaplen, 1966, p. 107; Richard Harwood, *Washington Post*, August 13, 1967, p. B2.

[140] Official figures publicized by William Bundy and Ambassador Bunker in November, 1967, described two-thirds of the population as under a "reasonable" degree of Government control, one-sixth under Viet Cong control, and one-sixth living in disputed hamlets. There is a major discrepancy between these and the "official" figures cited by Harwood, who said that only 168 of the roughly 12,500 hamlets were under "total" Government control, and some 2000 under "partial" Government control, with nearly 4000 under Viet Cong control and the remainder, some 6300, in dispute.

Even allowing for the fact that Viet Cong-controlled hamlets are likely to be smaller in population, this is a big discrepancy. In view of the long history of overoptimistic official interpretation of such facts, and in view of the Administration's special need to show evidence of "winning" the Vietnam war, it seems likely that what happened was a new interpretation of old figures. The initial classification is in terms of Viet Cong-controlled hamlets and five degrees of Saigon control: A, B, C, D, and E. The discrepancy would be accounted for if Harwood, or the officials who informed him, counted only the A hamlets as under total Government control, and only the B hamlets as under "partial" Government control, with C, D, and E counted as in dispute, while the more recent figures give the Government the benefit of the doubt and classify also the C hamlets as under "reasonable" Government control. (My own observations in the Delta tend to support the earlier interpretation presented by Harwood.)

The official claim in early December, 1967, was that the proportion of the South Vietnamese population under a "reasonable" degree of Government control increased from sixty-one percent to sixty-eight percent during the period since January, 1967. Presumably this comparison, unlike the other one, involved a constant definition of what constitutes a "reasonable" degree of control. The amount of increase, seven percentage points, is substantial. It should be remembered, however, that during this period many villagers were literally forced to become refugees (which would automatically transfer them into the category of "Government-controlled") while many others became refugees because of the bombing and shelling of their villages (which would have the same effect on the statistics). Increase of physical control over hamlets is not equivalent to "winning hearts and minds."

The degree of Viet Cong strength exhibited in early 1968 strongly supports this skeptical interpretation of the official figures.

of competent Vietnamese personnel apparently means that security and reform can only inch forward slowly. Shaplen, Pike, and others have brought out the great difficulties resulting from spreading available personnel too thin.[141] The job could well take ten years at its present pace, assuming that other military and political events do not overtake it.[142]

(5) Anti-American feeling is clearly increasing.

(6) Progress toward democracy, though real, has hardly been substantial.[143]

(7) The events of early 1968 showed that the cities, including Saigon, are much more vulnerable than most Americans realized. Though past Viet Cong efforts had been concentrated upon the peasants, there has been increased infiltration of the cities since 1965, and further major trouble there for the Saigon government cannot be ruled out.[144]

(8) Although at least one competent opinion survey has been conducted, its more encouraging findings are open to serious question.

Several references have been made in this chapter to the only large-scale, systematic published study of how the people of South Vietnam feel about the war. It was done for the Columbia Broadcasting System by the Opinion Research Corporation (ORC) in the last two months of 1966 and the first two months of 1967. Since the survey has been well publicized in the United States and is regarded by many as the best available information on the whole complex of Vietnamese attitudes, it warrants full and careful analysis.

The conclusions (which must be viewed in the light of conditions under which the interviews were conducted) provide grist for the mills of both militant and non-militant Americans. For example, militant Americans may be gratified to learn that, out of the 1545 persons interviewed, only one[145] said he preferred a government "led by Communists":

141 Pike, 1966b, pp. 57–58.

142 Shaplen, 1966, p. 108.

143 New York Times, April 16, 1967; Just, 1967.

144 Shaplen, 1968, pp. 104–7.

145 One person did express this preference, but since 1/1545 is less than half of one percent, it was rounded to zero percent in the table that is reproduced here. (CBS, 1967)

"Thinking of the time when the war is over, which of the following sentences do you think is closest to your opinion?" (Alternatives read to respondents.)

Life would be better for you and your family if the government is led by the Communists.	0%
Life would be better for you and your family if the government is led by the Nationalists.	83
You don't care who would lead the government; it would be the same to you.	10
No opinion; not reported	7
	100%

Apparently a considerable majority would not want the Viet Cong even included in a postwar government:

"In your opinion, when the war is over, will people around here like to see the National Liberation Front of South Vietnam take part in the government?"

Yes, they would want the NLF to take part	6%
No, they would not	73
No opinion; not reported	21
	100%

On the other hand, non-militant Americans may find their feeling supported by the frequently expressed desire for negotiation:

"Would you like the Americans to devote more attention to finding a way to negotiate with North Vietnam, or do you want them to concentrate on their military efforts against the North?"

More negotiation	63%
Concentrate on military efforts	15
No opinion; not reported	22
	100%

To be sure, the disproportion between sixty-three percent and fifteen percent is not as great as it seems, as a fair proportion of the sixty-three percent added qualifications such as "intensify the war and then negotiate," while hardly any of the fifteen percent of respondents who wanted concentration on military effort made any such qualification. Nevertheless the figures tend to confirm the strength of the peace sentiment that showed itself unmistakably in the elections of September, 1967.

A similar peace sentiment seems to influence attitudes on withdrawal of American troops:

"What do you think the American forces should do in the South? Should they go on fighting, should they stop fighting but remain here as advisers to the GVN forces, or should they stop fighting and go back to their country?"

Americans should go on fighting	39%
Should stop fighting, stay as advisers	21
Stop fighting, go back to their country	10
No opinion; not reported	30
	100%

Although the most frequent single response is "go on fighting," less than a majority of the respondents expressed it; the two "stop fighting" responses total thirty-one percent, and a relatively large number (thirty percent) express no opinion.

How much confidence can be placed in these findings? Are the different findings equally worthy of confidence?

In several ways the survey was a competent, professional job. The sample (1545) was adequate in size. It was a probability sample, carefully drawn to represent the adult population of South Vietnam living in "secure" areas. Only about one fifth of the total adult population was excluded because it lived in "insecure" hamlets under firm Viet Cong control. The interviewers were not Americans but Vietnamese (employees of the respected Center for Vietnamese Studies, directed by Nguyen-khoa Phon-anh), and they were trained and experienced.

On the other hand, some of the ORC's findings are undermined by three limitations inherent in the circumstances of the interviews:

(1) It seems likely that most of the strongly motivated pro-Viet Cong peasants live in the hamlets that are most strongly Viet Cong-controlled, and that were therefore necessarily excluded from the

population sample. If, for instance, twenty percent of the adult population are in this category, as many as fifteen of the twenty could easily have been excluded from the survey.

(2) Since it focused on words rather than actions, the survey would have had difficulty in making a valid distinction among degrees of motivation. In fact, it made no attempt to do so; the relatively indifferent "passive majority" was not differentiated from the strongly motivated anti-Viet Cong minority. The survey therefore cannot test the hypotheses that the passive majority is as large as sixty to eighty percent, and that the strongly motivated anti-Viet Cong minority is as small as five to fifteen percent. It would be easy for the outwardly passive majority to conceal whatever pro-Viet Cong sentiment existed in their ambivalent attitudes, presenting to the interviewer a proper, officially acceptable amount of anti-Viet Cong feeling. Through words alone it would thus be nearly impossible to distinguish them from those whose anti-Viet Cong convictions were genuine.

(3) On certain questions (notably those involving attitudes toward the Viet Cong) there may have been a very great lack of frankness.

ORC was reassured of the respondents' frankness by the considerable number who willingly expressed criticism of their own government—moderate, not basic criticism—and criticism of the Americans. The majority did not consistently follow the officially approved "nationalist" line of uncompromising prosecution of the war. As we have seen, as many as sixty-three percent favored negotiation more than escalation, and those who said they wanted the American forces to stop fighting (thirty-one percent) were only eight percentage points fewer than those who said they wanted the Americans to continue fighting (thirty-nine percent).

It is doubtful, though, whether we can infer from this that respondents were equally frank about their feeling toward the Viet Cong. It is possible to be frank on a relatively uncharged question, such as the superficial faults of the Saigon government or of the Americans, and to be quite opaque on the extremely sensitive subject of sympathy with the Viet Cong. In the eyes of the military government, such sympathy is treason, punishable by imprisonment, sometimes torture, even death.

In the hamlets that are Government-controlled by day and Viet Cong-controlled by night (and many such hamlets must have been included in the survey, which could only be conducted during daylight) the peasants presumably have a strong tendency to say, during the daytime, what Government officials want to hear. The ORC interviewers were nearly all middle-class, urban Vietnamese, probably (from the peasant's point of view) connected with the Saigon government, and therefore people with whom it must have seemed wise to be wary. Under these circumstances it is hardly surprising that only one of the 1545 respondents was willing to brand himself a traitor by admitting to a strange interviewer that he favored the Viet Cong. Nor is it surprising that only six percent were willing to say openly that they would like to see the National Liberation Front included in a coalition government.

A methodological principle is involved here that is familiar to those who work with inherently biased data, such as interviews with escapees from Communist countries:[146] It is necessary to discount all findings that are in the direction of the inherent bias, and to give special weight to findings that are in the opposite direction—findings that must be *in spite of,* not because of, the bias.

In the ORC survey this means, for instance, that special weight should be given to the thirty-one percent who say they want the American forces to stop fighting. This sentiment is opposed to the militantly anti-Viet Cong policy of the military government, which welcomes American support. Some courage is needed to express it. It is impossible to say how many respondents who felt this way were not prepared to say so. Many of them, perhaps, resorted to the "no opinion" response, which on this question was unusually large (thirty percent). By the same token, the figure of thirty-nine percent, representing those who overtly favored continued fighting by the Americans, requires substantial discount. The true balance of opinion on this question, therefore, may have been the reverse of what it appeared.

ORC did not attempt to interpret its findings according to this principle. It apparently took at face value the largeness of the thirty-nine percent, for example, and the smallness of the thirty-one percent. Perhaps this happened because ORC is an American survey organization, accustomed to the survey techniques that are standard in the United States, where the problem of frankness is not nearly so acute as it is in Vietnam. Readers of the ORC report, however,

[146] USIA/IRS, 1963.

should take into account the probable effect of reticence and concealment on its findings, giving much more weight to the pro-peace than to the anti-Viet Cong findings. If this is done, there is no reason to regard the result as inconsistent with the estimates of Vietnamese attitudes that have been suggested here.

Summary

Every reader will have his own impression of the relative weight of the arguments and evidence presented here. Mine is that only the first two on the side of optimism about Vietnamese attitudes carry much weight: anger at the physical violence of the Viet Cong (especially when one's own relatives are victims), and the burdensome scale of recent Viet Cong taxation. On the other hand each of these substantial reasons for optimism is matched by an argument on the other side that seems equally valid and important. Anger at the violence of the Viet Cong is probably matched by anger at the violence of the Government and the Americans; anger at taxes imposed by the Viet Cong is probably matched by the peasants' recognition of the benefits of land reform. Three additional substantial arguments then tip the balance toward a pessimistic estimate: that nationalism is associated mainly with Ho Chi Minh and the war of liberation from France, that the military success of the Viet Cong against odds is impressive, and that the consensus of informed observers seems pessimistic on this point.

Concerning the inner attitudes of the outwardly passive majority there is much disagreement among informed observers. Some firmly believe that most of the passive majority lean (though not fervently) to the Government side. My own impression is that we just do not know, nor have we means of ascertaining, whether this is true; the middle group is as likely to have a net leaning in one direction as in the other. Our uncertainty is unfortunate because, though perhaps politically unimportant, this middle group is very large, as the fourth section above reports; changes since Diem have not drastically modified this picture.

The estimates suggested at the beginning of this chapter seem, on the whole, to be supported: strongly pro-Viet Cong probably fifteen to twenty-five percent; strongly anti-Viet Cong probably five to fifteen percent; relatively indifferent probably sixty to eighty percent.

Those who find six figures hard to remember may make it easier by taking the midpoint of each of the pairs of figures suggested above. The estimate would then be: twenty percent strongly pro-Viet Cong, ten percent strongly anti-Viet Cong, and seventy percent relatively indifferent. If the uncertainty of the estimates is kept in mind there is no harm in using the simpler figures. The trouble is that when single figures are used there is a tendency to quote them without qualification, forgetting the fallible processes of inference on which they are based. Therefore I prefer to keep all estimates in the form of a pair or range of figures, with the word "probably" always attached, as a double reminder that this is educated guesswork, not science.

Chapter 3

THE CONFLICT AS SEEN BY
THE COMMUNISTS

The NLFSV and the South Vietnamese people warn the U.S. imperialists and their lackeys: If you take risks by expanding your war of banditry throughout all of Vietnam and if you intend to blow the flames of war to spread them to all of Indochina, the invincible strength of the thirty million Vietnamese people and the mountain-displacing and ocean-filling strength of hundreds of millions of people in Indochina and Asia will overflow and bury you alive. (NLF broadcast, March 23, 1965)

The most important methodological problem involved in interpreting this and other Communist statements can be summed up in six words: Do they mean what they say?

Or rather, since it is usually a question of degree: To what extent do they mean what they say? After all, this is a propaganda statement, an attempt to persuade—like nearly all public political statements and a great many private ones. The NLF clandestine radio that broadcast it had a purpose in mind, and what it said was instrumental in relation to that purpose, not a detached attempt to describe reality. So it is necessary to ask: To what extent are the Communist propagandists aware of exaggerations and omissions in what they say, or of outright lies? For instance, how literally do they believe that "the" South Vietnamese people are on their side, and that "thirty million" would rise in anger if the United States extended the war? If pinned down and speaking frankly, would they admit any awareness of the peasants who are apathetic, and of the millions who are hostile to them as well as to the Americans and the military government? How fully do they believe that American "imperialism" caused the war? Do they have any awareness of Communist expansionism and terrorism as causes of American involvement? And when they say that if we extend the war in the North they will "bury us alive," rather than going under cover or perhaps settling for a compromise peace, do they fully mean it? Or is there in the back of their minds the doctrine of both Lenin and Mao that it is sometimes wise to resort to a strategic retreat, a temporary going under cover, when at a given moment the enemy seems too strong to be met in open combat?

Such questions are impossible to answer with confidence or with any approach to precision; yet we all answer them after a fashion, and we must do so because our action or our non-action depends on the guesses we make. It behooves us, therefore, to make our guesses as educated as possible, and to consider first what makes a guess "educated." Three guidelines can be suggested:

(1) An awareness that the Communist leaders, probably even more than our own, have an instrumental attitude toward what they say in public. The cause is what matters most, and words are weapons. The entire history of Communist propaganda has shown a readiness to exaggerate, to omit, and on occasion to lie.

(2) At the same time, an awareness that the Communists are also human, and that most human beings, most of the time, believe most of what they say. There are psychological factors that simultaneously pull thoughts into line with what is publicly said,[1] and, partly for reasons of long-run credibility, keep what is said from diverging very much from genuine thought. As Gunnar Myrdal put it, those who make policy "fall victim more or less completely to the stupefying effects of their own propaganda. It is difficult for normally honest persons to distort the truth without coming to believe their distortions."[2] While presumably the Communists are less "normally honest" than some others, the same tendency probably exists in them too.[3]

(3) A continual search for other evidence that will confirm or deny the sincerity of a given verbal statement or propaganda theme, with no prejudgment of the degree of sincerity in any particular statement. It is often possible to check words by comparing them with actions. For example, North Vietnamese statements of intransigence in response to U.S. bombing of the North have been to some extent verified by the actual continuing refusal of the North Vietnamese to come to the conference table.

Also, a knowledge of the facts that the speaker has been exposed to, combined with recognition of normal human mechanisms of wishful thinking and cognitive distortion, may permit some inferences

[1] Kelman, 1953; Janis and King, 1954; Scott, 1957, 1959.

[2] Myrdal, 1965, p. 26.

[3] Honey, 1965.

about sincerity. For instance, there is little doubt that the Vietnamese Communists have been exposed to most of the evidence considered in Chapter 2 on the negative side of the proposition that most of the Vietnamese people want American help. They may not have been exposed to most of the evidence on the positive side, and it is virtually certain that their human tendency to buttress their own black-and-white picture (not to mention their extra measure of Communist dogmatism) has led them to exaggerate evidence on the negative side and minimize evidence on the positive side. Given the fairly large amount of evidence that is actually on the negative side, their wishful thinking would almost certainly make them see it as still larger. If, for instance, the actual fact is that sixty or seventy percent of the South Vietnamese people are less hostile to the Communists than to the Government and the Americans, their perception could easily be that eighty or ninety percent are, and they could interpret "less hostile to us than to the Government" in all-or-none terms as "on our side."

It is legitimate, then, to study the Communist viewpoint on Vietnam through the Communists' own words, if we do so with proper skepticism.

The Diabolical Enemy-Image

We Americans know how basic in our own thinking the idea of Communist aggression is. Most of us feel that appeasement—failing to stop Communist aggression—is not the way to preserve either peace or freedom; that if Communist aggression is not stopped, by force if necessary, we will only have to fight a bigger war under worse conditions in another place.

There is a parallel to this in the words of the Communists and perhaps in their thoughts also. To the extent that they mean what they say, aggression on our part seems as obvious to them as their aggression seems to us:

It is crystal clear that the United States is the aggressor who is trampling under foot the Vietnamese soil.[4]

Vietnam is one, the Vietnamese people are one. As sons and daughters

[4] Ho Chi Minh, 1966, p. A12.

of the same fatherland, our people in the north are bound to extend whole-hearted support to the patriotic struggle waged by the people of the south against U.S. aggression.[5]

Under the cruel policy of the U.S. aggressors and their henchmen, this beautiful and prosperous territory of South Vietnam has become ragged and desolate.[6]

The United States is rapidly escalating the war in an attempt to subdue the Vietnamese people by armed force.[7]

Normalization of our relations (with the U.S.) is incompatible with the armed aggression of American imperialism against a fraternal Social-ist country—Vietnam.[8]

In our minds aggression is evil in two ways: the evil of war and the evil of one country imposing its rule on another. Communist ag-gression brings thoughts not only of bloodshed but also of countries such as Hungary, Poland, Lithuania, Tibet, subjected to alien Com-munist rule. This imperialism theme also finds a parallel on the Com-munist side:

Faced with their imminent complete defeat, the U.S. imperialists dropped their neocolonialist mask and appeared as the most cruel soldier of old colonialism, which actually they are.[9]

(I am) leaving temporarily the beloved North to return to my native South to liberate my compatriots from the yoke of misery imposed by My-Diem (U.S.-Diem). This has been my ideal for a long time.[10]

We are familiar with the thought that the Viet Cong uses terror and assassination to enforce its rule in the villages, and picks for as-sassination especially competent persons such as village officials, teachers, health workers. President Johnson has called it "a war of unparalleled brutality. Simple farmers are the targets of assassina-tion and kidnapping. Women and children are strangled in the night because their men are loyal to their government."[11] The theme of

[5] Ho Chi Minh, 1965, p. A10.

[6] NLF broadcast, March 23, 1965, in Raskin and Fall, eds., 1965, p. 238.

[7] Chou En-Lai, 1966, p. 4.

[8] Brezhnev, 1965, p. A16.

[9] NLF broadcast, March 23, 1965, in Raskin and Fall, eds., 1965.

[10] "Viet Cong Soldier's Diary," 1961, in Raskin and Fall, eds., 1965, p. 266.

[11] Johnson, in Raskin and Fall, eds., 1965, p. 344.

the enemy's brutality and inhumanity is also frequent on the Communist side:

Over the past eleven years, they (the U.S. imperialists and their lackeys) have conducted more than 160,000 large- and small-scale mopping-up operations, killed about 170,000 people, wounded and crippled through torture about 800,000 people, detained more than 400,000 people in more than 20,000 prisons, raped more than 40,000 women, including old women, children, and religious people; cut open the bellies of and buried alive more than 5000 people; destroyed innumerable villages and hamlets; herded more than 5 million people into 8000 concentration camps disguised as agrovilles, land-development centers, and strategic hamlets; and sprayed chemicals over many areas to destroy tens of thousands of hectares of crops and fruit trees and poisoned thousands of people.[12]

As this quotation suggests, the official Communist picture of the United States is at least as intensely and consistently evil as the official American picture of the Communists. To get some rough check on this and other points a modest-scale value-analysis[13] was conducted with the four Vietnamese Communist statements contained in *The Vietnam Reader,* edited by Raskin and Fall,[14] and the two outstanding American statements in the same volume, by President Johnson and Secretary McNamara. One of the findings was that, out of the 337 Communist characterizations of their enemy in evaluative terms, 337—literally 100 percent—were in terms of evil rather than good. The corresponding figure for the Americans was 127 out of 130, or 97.7 percent. The three exceptions on the American side were somewhat ambiguous: Johnson at one point said that nations "in dispute with us" may "honestly fear our intentions"; McNamara once spoke of "loyalty" within the Viet Cong, and once acknowledged that the Viet Cong had "large indigenous support." But nothing even ambiguously positive appeared within the Communists' image of "U.S. imperialism and its lackeys." This suggests a generalization for which we will find further evidence: The Communists are, if anything, even more susceptible to absolute black-and-white thinking, and therefore presumably more authoritarian, more dog-

[12] NLF broadcast, March 23, 1965.
[13] For the nature of value-analysis, see White, 1951.
[14] Raskin and Fall, eds., 1965.

matic, and less evidence-oriented, than their American opposite numbers.

To what extent do the North Vietnamese and the Viet Cong mean what they say? To what extent is this diabolical enemy-image real to them?

In all probability there is a sizable element of conscious, deliberate exaggeration in many of their propaganda statements. The figures given on numbers of women raped, etc., may well be greatly and consciously inflated. But the fact that their accusations seem fantastic, from the standpoint of our own black-and-white picture, should not lead us to minimize the truth they may contain (which our own wishful thinking might lead us to ignore or to minimize), or the Communist capacity to misperceive in line with their own black-and-white picture. A moderate element of truth inflated by Communist misperception (which is not the same as conscious exaggeration) could look very large indeed.

It goes without saying that whatever kernels of truth may exist in their beliefs about America, including the belief that we are "aggressors" in Vietnam, there has been much to be said on the other side, and that the Communists would have to ignore the other side in order to perceive our actions as diabolical. In particular, there has been a persuasive rationale for even our "worst" actions in Vietnam in the thought that, in a developing country such as Vietnam, true democracy has been impossible in any case, and that a temporary non-Communist dictatorship was preferable to a permanent Communist one which would augment the threat of Communist dictatorship on a worldwide scale. But it would be unrealistic to expect this rationale to seem plausible to the Communists. When we have supported a government that they regarded as unpopular, in Vietnam or elsewhere, they have perceived it within their frame of reference, not ours, and in their frame of reference—if we acknowledge that they think their side is "democratic" in any sense of that word—our quite sincere belief that Communist dictatorship is the ultimate disaster is not likely to seem sincere. It is likely to appear as a transparent rationalization of our own desire to rule.

But aren't the Communist leaders quite aware of their own aggressive desires, and don't they know, basically, that what we are doing is simply to block their path to world domination? Isn't this probably the case in the minds of the Soviet, Chinese, and North Vietnamese leaders, even if not in the minds of the general public in any of these countries, nor in the minds of the rank-and-file Viet Cong guerrilla fighters, who may indeed think that they are fighting in defense of their homeland?

With regard to the Viet Cong and North Vietnamese the judgment of competent observers seems to be that they do mean most of what they say, especially about the diabolical character of their enemies.[15]

As for the broader question of the diabolical enemy-image in the minds of Communists generally, the writer has discussed this question in some detail elsewhere.[16] A brief answer, however, would be this: It is true that conscious expansionism has been a major element in Marxism-Leninism from the beginning. In this respect the situation is not symmetrical; the "mirror image" does not exist at this point, since there is no comparable expansionism on the Western side—at least not on the conscious level. In the minds of the Communist leaders there is also probably an absence of what they sometimes call "petit bourgeois" scruples against using force for the sake of expansion whenever they think it is reasonably safe to do so. In this sense, in my judgment, they are aggressors, and their talk about peaceful coexistence is a sham. This probably applies as fully to the North Vietnamese Communist leaders—whose behavior in Laos and at the Geneva Conference suggests that they would be trying to extend their power in Southeast Asia whether they had Chinese support or not—as to the Soviet leaders or the Chinese.

On the other hand, the existence of this aggressive motive is not in the least inconsistent with the existence of another and perhaps much stronger motive: the desire to defend what they have against what they probably perceive as Western aggression. The fear of being overwhelmed by encircling capitalist enemies has been in the Leninist tradition from the beginning,[17] and was revitalized when the West achieved nuclear superiority. Some of America's actions since 1950—as misperceived by the Communists—have contributed to it, notably America's missile bases around the USSR, the U-2 incident, the Bay of Pigs, the "alliance with Germany," the policy in Vietnam, and—of great emotional importance to the Chinese—America's support of Chiang Kai-shek in Taiwan.

In the case of the Chinese Communists especially there is a great deal of evidence that they interpreted America's earlier military sup-

[15] Pike, 1966b, pp. 53, 378–79, 437–39; Chaffard, 1965.
[16] White, 1965, pp. 250–52, 268–74.
[17] Leites, 1954, pp. 27–30, 38–39, 379–416.

port of Chiang as aggression against "the Chinese people," that they actually do regard our support of Chiang in Taiwan as a violation of China's territorial integrity,[18] and that their fear of a nuclear attack by the United States is now entirely genuine.[19] That the Chinese feel a need for buffer territory between their own border and a hostile America was illustrated by their intervention in Korea when MacArthur crossed the 38th Parallel and pushed on to the Manchurian border,[20] and could be illustrated again if a similar danger appeared in North Vietnam.[21] Such actions support the hypothesis that the Chinese truly fear Western attack, as do statements such as that of Hanson Baldwin: "The intellectual and physical isolationism of their Government and their paranoiac suspicions tend to make them victims of their own propaganda. They view the world through prismatic glasses of their own making and tend to believe what they say about the United States."[22]

This hypothesis, that genuine suspicion and paranoid fear can coexist with genuine aggressive impulses, seems well supported by historical evidence (for example, the Austrians in 1914). It is also consistent with a great deal of psychological evidence, especially what we know about the authoritarian personality and about the mechanism of projection.[23]

The Virile Self-Image

We have seen how both the Austrians in 1914 and Hitler in 1939 emphasized power and prestige more than moral goodness. The most accurate single term to describe the national self-image, at a time of impending war such as 1914 or 1939, is apparently not "noble" but "virile," or some near-synonym such as "courageous," "firm," or "indomitable."

We Americans know how prominent such thoughts are in our own minds. We know how most Americans scorn those who would

[18] Fairbank, 1962, pp. 275–77, 307; Barnett, 1961, pp. 78, 406–9; Snow, 1965, p. 16.

[19] Gayn, 1965, pp. 180–82; Snow, 1965, p. 78.

[20] Barnett, 1961, pp. 78–79.

[21] Ibid., p. 78.

[22] Baldwin, 1966, p. 81.

[23] Below, Chapter 10, C, F.

"tuck tail" or "scuttle and run" simply because the job to be done is a hard and bloody one, especially when we feel that we have committed ourselves and would be disloyal as well as weak and cowardly if we violated that commitment.

There is a close parallel to this, at least on the verbal level, on the Communist side:

For the liberation of our compatriots in the South, a situation of boiling oil and burning fire is necessary. . . . But in my heart I keep loyal to the Party and to the people. I am proud and happy.[24]

Our people are determined to persevere in the fight and to undergo sacrifices for ten or twenty years or a longer time, until final victory, because there is nothing more sacred than independence and freedom. We are determined not to flinch. . . .[25]

The South Vietnamese people are fond of peace, but the South Vietnamese people cannot stand idle and let the U.S. aggressors and their lackeys freely trample on the country and dominate the nation. They prefer death to bondage.[26]

Rivers can dry up, mountains can erode, but the South Vietnamese people and their armed forces will never drop their weapons as long as the South Vietnamese people's fundamental objectives—independence, democracy, peace, and neutrality—have not been achieved.[27]

Along with this courage theme, we Americans sometimes permit ourselves the luxury of action-images, such as "clobbering" the North, or "breaking the back" of the Viet Cong, that we might never think of using except in a context of defense or retaliation. More often we avoid such words, along with the word war itself, preferring to speak of opposing, resisting, defending, saving, backing, coping with. In this respect the Vietnamese Communists are as a rule more frankly belligerent; a psychologist might infer that their aggressive impulses are stronger—or, perhaps, less disguised. They not infrequently use terms such as strike, hit, crush, deal the heaviest blow, kick out, chase away, annihilate, exterminate. The terms fight and struggle are very common, and terms such as anger and even hatred are not rare:

[24] Viet Cong Soldier's Diary, 1961, in Raskin and Fall, eds., p. 228.
[25] Ho Chi Minh, 1965, p. A10.
[26] NLF broadcast, March 23, 1965, in Raskin and Fall, eds., 1965, p. 239.
[27] NLF broadcast, March 23, 1965, in Raskin and Fall, eds., p. 242.

Naturally the criminal actions of the U.S. imperialists and their lackeys aroused hatred throughout Vietnam and gave rise to a wave of boiling anger throughout the world.[28]

The conscious, explicit cultivation of hatred under that name appears characteristic of the Viet Cong and not of the United States. Pike, for instance, quotes a Viet Cong document, *Needs of the Revolution:* "The demonstration [or struggle meeting] must strongly promote hatred, and this requires an assembly of several hundred people. The person who delivers the main speech must be well prepared and must [so arrange it] that at the end of his speech the masses will shout slogans expressing their determination to struggle. . . ."[29] There is a chilling echo here of the "two-minutes' hate" in Orwell's *1984*.

Another related theme in Vietnamese Communist propaganda that hardly appears at all on our side is scorn for compatriots who are so lacking in pride that they play the game of the alien ruler. As the quotations above indicate, the word lackey, especially in the recurrent stereotyped expression "the U.S. imperialists and their lackeys," is by far the most frequent for expressing this scorn.

To what extent is this virile self-image genuine, and potent in determining their actions as well as their words?

The amazing tenacity of the Vietnamese Communists through twenty years of recurrent warfare suggests that it is quite genuine. So does the history of Vietnam's two-thousand-year struggle against Chinese domination, the more recent thousand years of which were largely successful.[30] So does their typical resistance to giving useful information even when tortured.[31]

Their pride in their own courage is also relevant to predictions about their response to punishment inflicted on them in the North. In this respect, they are probably not unique or even exceptional; the results of the Strategic Bombing Survey in Germany after World War II indicated that the practical effect of Allied bombing of Germany, which the Allies had hoped might break German civilian morale, had the opposite effect.[32] In any case it seems to be true of the

28 NLF broadcast, March 23, 1965, in Raskin and Fall, eds., 1965, p. 235.
29 Pike, 1966b, p. 94; cf. Sacks, 1959; Trager, 1959; Tanham, 1961.
30 Buttinger, 1958.
31 Malcolm Browne, 1965, p. 115.
32 Strategic Bombing Survey, 1945.

North Vietnamese. After talking with neutrals as well as belligerents in Hanoi, Gottlieb reported that "on this there was unanimity among the North Vietnamese, the NLF, and the neutral observers: no proud people would go to the bargaining table as the result of punishment through air power."[33] James Cameron, of the London *Evening Standard,* has reported from North Vietnam that our bombings so far "have worked miracles in creating unity and strengthening morale throughout the countryside and in the city."[34] The fact of a hardened official position tends to bear this out.[35]

Another aspect of the virile self-image that was important in 1914 was a general preoccupation with national prestige; even frightening risks of war were considered worth taking if the alternative was "sinking to the status of a second-rate power." This is a factor to be considered in predictions of possible intervention by the Chinese and, if China should appear in danger of defeat, by the Russians. On this there is, of course, much to be said on the optimistic side. For example, China, knowing her own vulnerability to American airpower and the logistic difficulties of fighting in South Vietnam, has the strongest of reasons not to intervene. But circumstances might develop in which Chinese "face" could become more deeply involved, and, judging by history, rational prudence might then be outweighed by considerations of prestige-plus-commitment.

The same could occur in the USSR. According to Morgenthau, the chief reason why Soviet intervention is "likely" is fear of humiliation. "The critical observer is struck by the motivating force which considerations of prestige exert both in Washington and Moscow. That this is so in Washington hardly needs extensive elaboration. . . . Similarly, the Soviet Union operates on assumptions of prestige, both for itself and for North Vietnam. It cannot allow Hanoi to go to the negotiating table under a hail of American bombs; for to do so would be tantamount to admitting that the United States can impose its will upon a small Communist nation by force of arms. It cannot afford to remain indefinitely passive while American bombs destroy North Vietnam; for to do so would be tantamount to admitting that the Soviet Union cannot protect a small Communist nation against

[33] Gottlieb, 1965, p. 2; cf. Snow, 1965, p. 19; Susan Sheehan, 1966, p. 80.
[34] Paraphrased by Rovere, 1965, p. 198; cf. Cameron, *New York Times,* December 10, 1965.
[35] Fall, 1965a, p. 14; Zagoria, 1965, E3.

America's military power. When I mentioned to a Soviet official American considerations of prestige and pointed to the need for a face-saving device and for Soviet cooperation in providing it, he replied: 'Other nations must take care of their prestige too.' "[36]

As Morgenthau interprets it, this is not necessarily a matter of prestige for its own sake, in either Washington or Moscow. In Washington the solidarity of the world anti-Communist front is seen as dependent on American prestige, defined as reputation for strength plus willingness to back up anti-Communist commitments, and this is thought of in defensive terms as something vitally needed to prevent further Communist encroachments. But according to Morgenthau the same blend of prestige-for-its-own-sake and prestige-for-the-security-of-allies exists in Soviet minds too. A psychologist can question whether, in both cases, the virile self-image and the goal of prestige-for-its-own-sake may be much more important emotionally than either American or Soviet decision-makers realize.

The Moral Self-Image

To most Americans there are several reasons for being in Vietnam: to resist aggression, thereby protecting both peace and the freedom of the Free World; to teach all Communists that the Chinese emphasis on "wars of liberation" simply does not pay off; to preserve the independence of the South Vietnamese, and at least a future possibility of democracy and self-determination for them; to fulfill a commitment to anti-Communists in Vietnam, thereby saving their lives and keeping our honor clean. War to us is abhorrent; domination of any other country by us is abhorrent. On the conscious level, at least, our conception of our own motives is that they are wholly good.

To judge by their words, the same is true of the Communists. Not only that, but, to judge by their words, they regard themselves as wholly good in terms of much the same value-system by which we and most of the rest of the world judge ourselves: peacefulness, respect for the independence of other nations, patriotism, loyalty to

[36] Morgenthau, 1965b, p. 13.

THE CASE OF VIETNAM

allies, social justice, truthfulness, humanity, and even "democracy" (with a meaning somewhat different from the meaning it has for us):

Humanity:

"American prisoners (at least those released) received reasonably humane treatment. The author [Pike] talked with four, and all said that although life as prisoners was harsh it was not much worse than what the guerrillas themselves endured. . . . A leaflet said: 'Prisoners of war are not maltreated or insulted.' "[37]

Democracy:

"People's War, People's Army" [the title of a book by Giap[38]]

I answered the call of the Party when I was very young, and what did I do for the people of my village? I devoted myself to the people. I took part in propaganda and aroused the people to carry out the policy of the Party and the Government and helped organize village defense and fighting forces.[39]

Especially in the case of a term so ambiguous as the word democracy the question comes up: To what extent does the other side mean what we mean by it? The statement is sometimes made that the Communist definition of such terms as peace and democracy is completely different from ours. This is a complex question that can only be touched on here. The writer has done a fair amount of research on it, the upshot of which is that these semantic differences are not as great as they are often supposed to be. The most ambiguous term is democracy and the chief difference in its usage is that to us it necessarily includes freedom of expression, while to the Communists it does not. This is, of course, a major difference. But the meaning the Communists attempt to convey when they use the term democracy—which implies nothing as to their actual practice—does clearly include government *by* the people (through "the Party of the people") as well as for the people. (See Chapter 2, pp. 55–56)

The extent to which the Vietnamese Communists believe their own words is, as always, a question on which it would be dangerous to speak with confidence. It should be noted, however, that the white part of the Vietnamese Communists' official black-and-white picture

[37] Pike, 1966b, pp. 266–67.
[38] Vo Nguyen Giap, 1962.
[39] Viet Cong Soldier's Diary, 1961, in Raskin and Fall, eds., 1965, p. 227.

is no whiter than the genuine national self-image of many Americans and of many others in the world. It should be noted, too, that all they need to do in order to purge their self-image of all conscious evil is to deny, ignore, or interpret in terms of their own frame of reference each of the crimes we habitually attribute to them.

There is no suggestion in any of their official words, for instance, that they have ever for a moment taken seriously the idea that their aid to the Viet Cong might be genuinely regarded by anyone as "aggression." Felix Greene in a 1965 interview with Ho Chi Minh raised this question, citing the 325th Division and other Northern units fighting in the South, and Ho did not deny the fact but immediately reinterpreted it within his own frame of reference as aid to the South Vietnamese people in resisting American aggression: "The truth is that the United States and its satellites have brought in foreign troops to wage aggression in South Vietnam in contravention of the 1954 Geneva Agreements. . . . As sons and daughters of the same fatherland, our people in the north are bound to extend wholehearted support to the patriotic struggle waged by the people of the South against U.S. aggression."[40]

Similarly, there is no apparent thought given by Hanoi or the Viet Cong to any of the following: (1) Ho's free use of assassination to rid himself of nationalist anti-Communists who joined with him against the French. (2) The cruelties and injustices of the so-called land reform that culminated in the Nghé-An uprising of 1956. (3) The use of terror and assassination against village officials and their families. (4) The many instances of Communist aggression since 1939 as seen by the West: Finland, Poland, the Baltic States, Eastern Europe, the Berlin blockade, Korea, the crushing of the Hungarian uprising, threats to Berlin, Tibet, etc. (5) Chinese Communist thought control and brainwashing techniques, and the probable spread of such totalitarian methods if Chinese control expands to other Asian countries. These things are not defended or discussed. They appear to be simply pushed out of the consciousness of the Vietnamese Communists.

It can be argued too that their moral self-image is even more absolute than ours. In the value-analysis described above (p. 89) the figures for the white side of the picture are very similar to those for the black side. Among the 287 evaluative references to the self by

[40] Ho Chi Minh, 1965, p. A10.

Communists, 287—again 100 percent—were positive. Among the 220 evaluative self-references by Johnson and McNamara, 217—98.6 percent—were positive. Again there were three somewhat ambiguous exceptions: President Johnson acknowledged that "some of the people" of South Vietnam are not on our side; McNamara acknowledged that in 1963 "President Diem lost the confidence and loyalty of his people" and that "there were accusations of maladministration and injustice." No similar admissions were made by the Communists.

More important as an indication of their higher degree of dogmatism is, of course, the fact that the amount of unofficial challenge and discussion of the government's policies is far greater here than in North Vietnam or Communist China. (In North Vietnam as in China, there was a "Hundred Flowers" period, but it lasted only a few months during the fall and winter of 1956–57.)

Selective Inattention

The tendency to ignore what does not fit the Communist black-and-white picture has appeared many times in the previous pages. The Vietnamese Communists tend to ignore every bad aspect of themselves, and every good aspect of the United States—its democracy, intellectual freedom, prosperity, aid to other countries, progress toward social justice, etc. They do not see how most Americans perceive the situation in Vietnam, including the prevailing American assumption that Communist dictatorship is the ultimate evil, beside which every other evil, including even a non-Communist dictatorship, is relatively unimportant. This absence of empathy is probably of central importance in explaining the Vietnamese Communists' hostility to the United States.

Absence of Empathy

There is little to be said about the Communists' capacity for empathy except that, as far as our evidence goes, it seems almost totally absent. They do not seem to have the faintest inkling of the defensive motivation of American actions, or of the fact that the great majority of the American people are *not* on their side (as they have often claimed). Nor do they recognize the fact that probably a considerable majority of the South Vietnamese people are not on their side (according to our best guess) even though the same people may be even more hostile to the Government and to the Americans. In the all-or-none, black-and-white Communist pattern of thought, "the people" must always be unequivocally on their side and their enemies must always be devoid of any human characteristics such as a defensive motive or a mistaken assumption. It is difficult to conceive of anyone in any Communist country being permitted to undertake any such sustained effort to "empathize with the enemy" as this study.

One psychological observation should be added: The Vietnamese Communists' absence of empathy is not merely passive. It is buttressed by an official and probably also by an intrapersonal severing of contacts with the outside world. Much more than the Soviet Union today, North Vietnam has been a xenophobic country, distrustful of all Westerners and fearful of contact with them. There has been much of what Newcomb calls "autistic hostility"—a vicious circle of perpetuating hostility by cutting off the human contacts that might tend to end it. This has occurred partly by cultivating an image of the enemy as a lying, deceitful propagandist:

At the very moment when President Johnson talks a lot about peace discussions, the U.S. imperialists are expanding further the war of aggression. . . .[41]

U. S. President Lyndon Johnson has spread the smoke screen of independence, freedom, peace, and negotiation in an attempt to whitewash the towering crimes and aggressive and war-seeking policy of the U.S. imperialists in Vietnam.[42]

According to them, the promises of the West are made only to be broken:

To sabotage the unity of Vietnam, the U.S. imperialists have completely violated the Geneva agreements.[43]

And orders to cadres are explicit:

[41] Ho Chi Minh, 1965, p. A10.
[42] Hoang Quoc Viet, 1965, p. 419.
[43] Ibid., p. 420.

Rule 5. Do not take the liberty of listening to enemy broadcasts or of reading their newspapers or documents. Do not spread false rumors. Rule 6. Do not have any relations with . . . evil segments of the population which are harmful to the revolution.[44]

This too, of course, has its parallel on our side. Few Americans have listened with an open mind to a Communist broadcast or have read with an open mind more than fragmentary quotations representing the Communist point of view. Most Americans justify their inattention by picturing the Communists as nothing but lying, deceitful propagandists whose Party line is wholly boring and predictable. Unfortunately, there is much truth in this stereotype of the official black-and-white picture, and of all who accept it uncritically, including the typical official propagandists, on *both* sides. But there are many other sources of information besides official propaganda: personal contacts, books and magazines written in countries not directly involved, etc. The real tragedy is that so many on both sides, but especially those on the Communist side, because they are much more hemmed in by official barriers and pressures, fail to avail themselves of sources of knowledge that would be interesting and varied and might also promote empathy.

Military Overconfidence

Many Americans have been baffled and exasperated by the Communists' scornful rejection of our effort to achieve "unconditional discussions." They have rejected them even though we indicated some willingness to have the Viet Cong included as part of the Communist delegation, and even though our war effort had been stepped up to such an extent that, rationally, one would think the Communists would be ready to discuss a compromise peace. American public opinion was consolidated to some extent behind President Johnson's position by this Communist intransigence, and world public opinion in the UN and elsewhere was made more receptive to the American position and more hostile to that of the Communists.

Inside Vietnam, too, it is a good guess that the Communists are losing by their present unwillingness to consider a compromise peace.

[44] Rules copied in diary of Viet Cong soldier, 1961, in Raskin and Fall, eds., 1965, p. 229.

The enormous buildup of American troops and weaponry makes it seem more and more that the Americans are not going to be defeated. Whether the Americans and their Vietnamese allies can "win" or not is quite a different question. Americans, too, may be deluding themselves when they hope for and expect a victory rather than stalemate; that is a different question, to be discussed in Chapter 7. Our present question is whether the Vietnamese Communists and their Chinese allies are responding to external evidence or to internal psychological needs when they cling to the hope of victory, rather than accepting the probability of a stalemate and trying to get as soon as possible a peace that approximately reflects the present balance of military strength.

If they were to seek such a peace, they might gain politically as well as militarily. War-weariness is clearly very strong and growing among the civilian population; one would think, therefore, that the Communists could gain politically and psychologically by capitalizing on this war-weariness, proclaiming their own willingness to settle for a compromise peace with a broadly based neutralist government, and putting on the United States the entire blame for continuing the war. They have not yet done any such thing. They have refused even to discuss peace, holding out for the rather clearly undemocratic and probably unpopular position that the NLF must be recognized as the "sole" representative of the South Vietnamese people. (At least that position seems undemocratic and probably unpopular if our guess is correct that most of the peasants are not pro-Viet Cong, but intensely anti-government, intensely pro-peace, and much more ready for a broadly-based neutralist government than for total Viet Cong control.)

Why? Why are they clinging so stubbornly to a course of action that seems self-defeating?

One hypothesis would be that they do have a good chance of complete victory in the fairly near future, and that Americans are the ones deluding themselves—including those who do not expect victory and are thinking of stalemate as the most probable outcome. Another hypothesis would be that they already see the probability of stalemate and are simply putting up a bold, belligerent front in order that, when the time for compromise comes, it will be made on terms as favorable to them as possible. In fact, it seems likely that this bold-front hypothesis represents a part of the truth. But a larger part of the truth probably lies in the hypothesis that they are genuinely overconfident—misperceiving and overestimating by a large margin (if our expectation of probable stalemate is correct) their chance of total victory.

One indication of this, though it is a minor one, consists of their public statements, such as "We are absolutely convinced that we will certainly be victorious."[45] Such evidence is ambiguous, however, since it could have the instrumental purpose of "whistling in the dark" to keep up their courage. More important is the evidence of three specific types of overconfidence which it is plausible, under the circumstances, to believe that they have.

(a) An overestimation of the importance of "people"—that is, primarily their own organization, skill, and courage—as compared with the military technology in which the United States excels.

To be sure, the United States may tend to be overconfident in the opposite way, by focusing attention too much on the power of modern weaponry and underestimating the importance of "people" (events in early 1968 suggest that this is all too true), but the fact that Americans may distort reality in one direction is no indication that the Viet Cong and the North Vietnamese do not distort it in the other.

In the first half of 1965, it looked as if they might well be right. They were winning, and since their enemies were clearly better armed, the Viet Cong appeared to be superior in "people" (including the ability to obtain civilian support in the villages, partly through voluntary partisanship and partly through intimidation). Since that time, however, the superiority of their enemies in materiél has become so enormous that (together with the quality of the American troops) it now appears to be—or did appear to be, up to February 1968—at least as great a factor as the Viet Cong's continuing net superiority in "people."

Bernard Fall, who knew from first-hand experience in the French *maquis* what is needed to preserve the morale of guerrilla fighters, changed his once very pessimistic view of the possibility of an American military victory and was, nearer the time of his death, inclined to rate much more highly the chance of victory in a purely military sense (though he was aghast at the human cost, and not at all optimistic about the possibility of winning the people after fighting the war with such methods as we have been using). But when the facts

[45] NLF broadcast, March 23, 1965, in Raskin and Fall, eds., 1965, p. 248.

changed, and Fall's relatively detached appraisal of them changed, it could well be that the Communists' appraisal did not change, or did not change enough. This would be an instance of perceptual lag— that is, the rate of change in perception not keeping up with the rate of change in objective reality. This lag could be considerably greater in Hanoi and Peking than in the jungles and rice paddies of the South, where the new and overpowering strength of American weapons is most vividly and directly perceived.

The hypothesis that the Communists greatly stress the decisive importance of "people" is consistent with all that we know about the previous course of the fighting in Vietnam (against the French and during the period 1959 to 1965) and also about the civil war in China. In both cases the side able to command the support of the peasantry, by whatever methods, was able after great struggle and sacrifice to win against enormously better-armed opponents. As Mao put it:

China's liberation forces had grown in numbers and strength by recruiting to their side the troops trained and armed by the Americans for Chiang Kai-shek. The movement was called "changing hats." When Nationalist soldiers changed hats in large numbers because they knew the peasants would kill them for wearing the wrong hat, the end was near.[46]

The virile self-image seems clearly important here. The image of empty-handed men wresting weapons from well-armed opponents and proceeding to outfight them is an extraordinarily satisfying one:

With empty hands the South Vietnamese people have fulfilled a great task and achieved many glorious victories. . . . Previously, with empty hands the southern people dealt heavy blows on the U.S. imperialists and their lackeys and fulfilled a great and glorious revolutionary task.[47]

In addition to being emotionally satisfying, the Communists' emphasis on the military importance of "people" must seem to them to have been borne out by history. The Chinese Communists after many years of struggle finally won out over the Nationalists; the Vietnamese Communists eventually won after a nine-year struggle against

[46] Mao Tse-tung, 1965, p. 215; interview with Edgar Snow.
[47] NLF broadcast, March 23, 1965, in Raskin and Fall, eds., 1965, p. 241.

the better-armed French, and were winning (to 1965) against the better-armed Government troops and Americans.

A behavioristic psychologist might say that their rewards in the form of victory and political power have constituted "positive reinforcement" of the most potent sort. A non-behaviorist might say that tenacity in adversity has become an integral part of the Communists' self-image.

Both of these descriptions sound appropriate. But, while the Communists are clinging to these glorious memories of the recent past, it is only human for them to pay attention too exclusively to such memories and to push out of their minds certain ways in which the present differs from the past. America, for instance, is not France.

Moreover, the Communists have been hardened by some bitter setbacks in the past which, in view of their courage and tenacity, turned out to be only temporary. The Long March was only one of them. The Vietnamese Communists have had serious setbacks several times—in 1931, 1941, 1945, 1950, 1956. Success after such setbacks has been in effect a reward for patience and tenacity, and must be especially conducive not only to a hardening of the virile self-image, but also to the view that History reserves its rewards for those who can hold out long enough. (Compared with such first-hand experiences, the merely verbal potency of Marxist-Leninist ideology, which pictures History itself as being on the side of the "socialist" cause, may be of secondary importance; but whatever weight it may have is, of course, on the same side.)

It may be that once again Communist tenacity will triumph. Americans would be in danger of military overconfidence if they assumed otherwise. The point is only that *if* the Communists are now overconfident (as their apparently self-defeating behavior seems to indicate), there is much in psychology as well as in Marxist-Leninist ideology that could account for it.

(b) An overestimation of the extent to which "the people" of South Vietnam are now on their side and will continue to be so.

Here, too, American misperception may be in the opposite direction, but this is no reason to rule out a similar distortion in Communist minds in the direction of their own black-and-white picture. As we have suggested, if the actual facts are that sixty or seventy percent of the people are in a sense leaning in their direction, (that is, less against them than against the military government) they might easily perceive this as eighty or ninety percent unequivocally on their side. When they talk about "the fourteen million South Vietnamese people" being on their side, then, it is not necessarily a very great conscious exaggeration of their perception of the facts. They could easily fail to perceive adequately the falling away of their rapport with the peasants as a result of their recent strong-arm tactics of taxation and conscription (just as we could wishfully exaggerate the extent of this falling-off). They could have at all times failed to realize the extent to which their control of the peasants was a result of intimidation rather than spontaneous mutual trust (just as we could have wishfully exaggerated the extent to which it has been a result of intimidation). This feeling of being at one with perhaps eighty or ninety percent of the people must give them not only a strongly reinforced sense of moral rightness but also a very great—and partly spurious—feeling of strength. And it might also, quite specifically, lead them to underestimate the extent to which they are alienating the peasants by prolonging the war until the NLF is recognized by its enemies as the "sole" representative of the South Vietnamese people. This demand, which to us seems outrageous, may seem to them quite natural and right.

(c) An overestimation of the extent to which American opinion and world opinion will force the "U.S. imperialists" to give up completely.

As Ho Chi Minh put it:

The American people are essentially well intentioned. That is why the great majority of the American people cannot support President Johnson's policy of aggression. . . . U.S. imperialism is the common enemy of our two peoples. With our united struggles, it will certainly be defeated.[48]

This "black-top image of the enemy" is reassuring, it should be noted, not only with regard to the justice of one's own cause but also with regard to the chances of ultimate victory. It seems likely, therefore, that Ho partly believes it, even though he also wants to use it for all it may be worth as a propaganda theme. And similarly, the Communists may overestimate the extent of support for their cause among "the peace-loving peoples" of the world (just as we may tend to underestimate it):

[48] Ho Chi Minh, interview with Felix Greene, 1965, p. A10.

The criminal actions of the U.S. imperialists . . . gave rise to a wave of boiling anger throughout the world. . . . Now, with their own strength, with the wholehearted support of powerful North Vietnam and the rich and powerful Socialist countries, and with the sympathy, support, and encouragement of the Asian, African, and Latin American countries and all peace-and-justice-loving peoples the world over, the South Vietnamese people will surely and gloriously triumph over the U.S. aggressors and their lackeys . . .[49]

It is possible to argue that such statements have only a propaganda purpose and that the real decision-makers in the Communist world are too realistic to take them seriously. According to Marquis Childs, "seasoned diplomats both here and in Europe doubt that either Peking or Hanoi has illusions about the significance of the small minority that continues to protest against the war."[50] But other observers take what the Communists say on this point more seriously. James Cameron, on the spot in Hanoi, reported that "Hanoi is making long-range calculations based on the belief that American opinion is now turning against the war and will in time force the government to call its troops home" (paraphrased by Rovere).[51] According to Seymour Topping, "In trying to dissuade the Vietnamese Communists from negotiations, Peking has put great stress on its contention that public opinion, especially that in the United States, would be decisive in compelling Washington to halt the bombings of North Vietnam and eventually to withdraw from the South."[52] It is always possible, too, for the Communists to recall the failure of the French people to support a long-continued fight to hold Algeria, though militarily they clearly had the upper hand. No matter how great the present American military effort in Vietnam may be, then, and no matter how heavy the support of the President's policy may be in opinion polls, the Communists can always think, "They'll get tired," citing history in support. As Mao put it, "the United States troops would find it boring and might go home or somewhere else."[53]

These last two sources of overconfidence—overestimation of support for the Communist cause among the South Vietnamese people and overestimation of the support in other countries, including

[49] NLF broadcast, March 23, 1965, p. 241.
[50] Childs, 1965a, p. A24.
[51] Rovere, 1965, p. 198.
[52] Topping, 1965, p. E3.
[53] Mao Tse-tung (paraphrased by Snow), 1965, p. 215.

America—differ in form but not in essence from two discussed in connection with Hitler: the historically frequent tendency to underestimate the chance that other countries will enter a war on the enemy's side, and the frequent tendency to underestimate the resistance of a people fighting on its own soil against what it regards as foreign invasion or occupation. The common element in all four is a tendency to regard the attitudes of others as more favorable to oneself than they actually are—as less hostile, in the case of an enemy's potential allies or a people fighting on its own soil, and as more favorable in the case of the Communists' estimate of Vietnamese and of American opinion. In each of these four cases, the attitudes of others toward one's own group seem to be shifted toward the favorable end of the continuum. A generalization begins to emerge: While the leaders of an enemy group may be seen as more aggressively hostile to oneself than they actually are (the black-top image), the common people in an enemy group and also the enemy's potential allies are likely to be seen as less hostile than they actually are.

This offers a problem for the psychologist. Is it perhaps simple wishful thinking based on a desire to be liked? That would be plausible, since human beings normally do like to be liked and dislike being hated. Is it often wishful thinking about the chances of victory, or of victory without having to fight too big a war? That would be plausible too. Is it often an assumption that one's own moral case is so obviously strong that all decent, right-thinking people in the world must recognize it as valid—that is, a naïve universalizing of one's own "reality world"? That too seems plausible.

It seems, then, that all six of the forms of misperception detected in 1914 and in 1939 exist on the Communist side of the war in Vietnam. The phenomena of misperception in situations of acute group conflict do show some order and predictability.

Underlying Causes: Communist Ideology as a Refracting Lens

One underlying cause of the war clearly calls for further discussion: the Communist ideology, and Communism considered as a worldwide expansionist movement. No informed person doubts that Ho Chi Minh, Le Duan, Vo Nguyen Giap, and the other top decision-makers in North Vietnam are tough, disciplined Communists. While their nationalism is perhaps as genuine as their Communism, it has undoubtedly been cast in a Communist mold and has become something decidedly different from, for instance, the nationalism of Nehru, or that of Austria in 1914, or that of Hitler in 1939. How, precisely, has it been modified?

There are many in the United States who see the modification as a total or almost total substitution of Communist imperialism for ordinary nationalism. As they see it, nationalism has become little more than a disguise, serving the purpose of the aggressive, world-wide Communist conspiracy, doubly headquartered in Moscow and Peking. That purpose is world conquest. Nationalism is a device to attract the masses of people throughout the world, hostile to "capitalist imperialism," who can be drawn by slogans of national independence if not by those of social justice and socialism. It is a mask to be cast aside when the nation in question has been taken over by one of the two varieties of Communist imperialism. The short shrift that true patriots will then receive is illustrated by Ho's assassination of nationalist colleagues in 1945–46, and by the fate of nationalists in the Baltic area, Eastern Europe, Central Asia, and Tibet.

While there is surely a large measure of truth in this interpretation, another one can be set beside it: that the Communist ideology primarily provides a lens through which a nationalist perceives the situation and the needs of his own country. To him, nationalism does not necessarily conflict with Communism, any more than the book a person reads conflicts with the spectacles through which he reads it. In the discussion that follows, this will be called the "refracting-lens hypothesis."

In South Vietnam, for instance, even a non-Communist might fully agree that there are two great and genuine evils: a cruelly oppressive system of absentee land ownership and of official corruption, and an undemocratic government sustained by foreign money and foreign arms. It is possible to see both of these as great evils without seeing Communism as the only way of eliminating them. Americans, too, are opposed to cruel oppression, oligarchic land ownership, official corruption, undemocratic government, and excessive foreign influence. Whether most Americans tend to shut their eyes to the actual extent of these evils in South Vietnam is not now the point at issue. The present point is that, no matter how genuine the evils may be, they do not necessarily point toward a Communist accession to power as the only way out; as seen through the Communist refracting lens, they do.

Looking through his own lens, the nationalist-Communist tends to see the oppressive land-ownership system as an inherent, inseparable part of "capitalism" or perhaps, if he is a relatively sophisticated Marxist, as part of an outmoded "feudal" system that is now being sustained by an unholy alliance between "feudal" landowners in South Vietnam and the capitalist ruling circles in the United States. (Actually, although liberals feel that American efforts to promote land reform have been exasperatingly halfhearted and have far too often been outweighed by immediate considerations of military advantage or political necessity, these efforts have been quite genuine. Even conservative Americans are likely to favor land reform, feeling that it is required for a consistent free-enterprise philosophy.)

Similarly, when he looks through his lens at the United States, the nationalist-Communist tends to see it as the last citadel of an evil, moribund system called capitalism. In the light of this assumption, he strongly tends to perceive our role in Vietnam as aggressive, imperialistic, anti-democratic, anti-national, and in every other respect evil. Once these premises are fully accepted, a number of consequences follow. Seeing America in these terms he can hardly fail to see the Vietnamese who collaborate with America as, quite literally, traitors. Believing that only Communists see clearly the long-run needs of the country and have the discipline and courage required to satisfy those needs, he is able to give himself single-mindedly to establishing and maintaining the Communist Party in positions of power. Seeing his nation's role as only one part of a global struggle to achieve power and welfare for "the people" (or for the Party that is assumed to represent them), he can feel that he is also serving humanity itself. He can believe that his own nationalism is purged of the narrow chauvinism that all intelligent, historically educated citizens of the twentieth century instinctively mistrust, and he can draw great courage and confidence from the thought that History itself, embodied in the mighty forces of the whole socialist camp, and in the latent power of the common people in every other part of the world, is on his side.

Believing this, the nationalist-Communist in Vietnam or elsewhere could easily take a further significant step: He could really believe that his side is the side of peace, not only in the long run (by hastening the advent of a peaceable socialist world) but also in the short run. He could take at face value the protestations of Chinese as well as Soviet Communists that their role at this stage of history is militarily purely defensive (though offensive in the ideological sphere), that they oppose the export of revolution as well as the export of counterrevolution, and that if war occurs it must be due to the aggression of their capitalist enemies. As we have seen, a genuine belief in capitalist aggression is not at all inconsistent with a basically expansionist Communist philosophy. Even a thorough-going, aggressive Communist could think, "We have no desire to commit aggression—at least not now, before we are ready for an all-out offensive. If war occurs now, therefore, it must be due to capital-ist aggression."

This is the point at which the perceptual or refracting-lens theory most clearly conflicts with the simple diabolism of the theory of a Communist conspiracy. Adherents of the conspiracy theory are often quite willing to grant that Communists want peace, but only in the very special sense that they believe the ultimate establishment of Communism on a world scale would usher in an era of peace, through eliminating the causes of capitalist wars. The Communists are seen either as cold-blooded gangsters who pretend to believe this or as blind fanatics who really do believe it and are willing to engage in aggressive small wars, which means running the risk of plunging the world into a large war, partly because a warless Utopia is their vi-sion and ultimate goal.

The refracting-lens hypothesis does not deny that Communists may derive part of their sense of idealism from this long-range hope of eliminating the root causes of war, but it takes much more seri-ously the idea that Communists may also really believe that they are peaceful (at least in the *present* phase of history), and really believe that a war such as that in Vietnam is wholly caused by capitalist aggression. They can easily feel they are good Communists (focus-ing mainly on the orthodox Communist doctrines of peaceful coexist-ence and no export of revolution) and at the same time satisfy their own war-hating consciences, reconciling these things—inconsistent to us—chiefly through the belief that capitalists are diabolical warmon-gers and that any war now going on must be due to capitalist war-making. The sense of outraged virtue which this world-view might sustain, especially in the minds of North Vietnamese leaders, could be very strong.

The refracting lens is of course just another way of describing what is called cognitive distortion elsewhere. It produces all the characteristic forms of distortion—the diabolical enemy image, the virile self-image, etc.—that this book describes and interprets. The capitalist world, or its ruling circles, is the Devil. (In a paranoid extreme of diabolism worthy of Hitler himself, the Maoists in China have even spoken of their domestic Communist opponents as "monsters and demons."*) The socialist camp is seen as virile, suffering manfully the hardships and perils of the present phase of history. It is seen as moral, dedicated to a better world and also to peace (with some possible exceptions). There is selective inattention to many things, such as the social justice achieved by democratic welfare societies in the West, and the worldwide, largely voluntary retreat of Western "imperialism," coinciding with the expansion of Communist imperialism. The Communists almost totally lack empathy with the capitalist point of view, and are sublimely confident that, with History and the peoples of the world on their side, ultimate triumph is assured.

Reactions to the Bombing of the North

To a great many Americans one proposition seems to be obvious common sense: If the enemy will not listen to reason, then the only language he will understand is the language of force, and it must be employed to whatever extent is necessary. The enemy must be made to hurt until he does listen to reason. To most of our military men in Vietnam, from the lowest echelon to the highest, this assumption apparently seems axiomatic, as it does also to a great many civilians in the United States. Those who even question it are often regarded as verging on soft-headed pacifism.

Nevertheless, like any other axiom, this one calls for testing on the basis of the evidence available to us.

A major piece of evidence is the Strategic Bombing Survey conducted for the American government immediately after World War II to determine what had been the physical and psychological effects of the heavy strategic bombing of Germany.[54] One purpose of

* Much of this diabolism was already present in Marx, as Tucker makes clear (1961). And capitalism in the West is now clearly much less evil than it was in Marx's day.

[54] U. S. Strategic Bombing Survey, 1945; cf. Rumpf, 1962—a German who arrived at similar conclusions seventeen years later after surveying a much larger amount of evidence.

that bombing had been to reduce the physical ability of the Germans to make war, and another had been to impair their fighting spirit and induce them to come to terms more quickly. The findings were negative on both counts. The ability of the Germans to repair the physical destruction of their industrial facilities proved to have been far greater than was expected; the industrial underpinnings of their military effort actually increased, in spite of the bombing, until near the end of the war. As for the psychological effect, it was clearly a hardening and embittering of their fighting spirit rather than a breaking of it. Their emotional response to the bombing of cities resembled that of Churchill and the British when British cities had been bombed earlier in the war: a mobilization of pride and patriotism to defy an enemy who was going beyond ordinary methods of warfare and was attacking defenseless women and children. Similar findings were obtained in a similar study in Japan.

Relevant experience has also been gained from the Korean war. As in Vietnam now, the United States had command of the air and an opportunity to concentrate its air power in an effort to interdict supply routes, etc., in North Korea. Again the effect was surprisingly small, as General Ridgway and others have testified.[55] Effective supplying of the North Korean and Chinese troops continued, and there was no breaking of the North Korean fighting spirit. Although a threat of possible use of nuclear weapons finally ended the deadlock at Pan Mun Jom, heavy non-nuclear bombing did not produce "meaningful negotiation."

As for direct evidence on reactions to our bombing of military targets in North Vietnam (which apparently result in many unintended civilian casualties), we now have such evidence from a number of Western observers, including Cameron,[56] Gottlieb,[57] Lockwood,[58] Salisbury,[59] Gerassi,[60] and Ronning,[61] not to mention the Quakers of the *Phoenix*. All of these have reported what they believe to be a genuine reaction of intense anger and defiance, with

[55] Ridgway, quoted by *U. S. News & World Report,* August 22, 1966.

[56] Cameron, 1966; cf. Barrymaine, 1966.

[57] Gottlieb, *New York Times,* March 17, 1967.

[58] Lockwood, "Recollections of Four Weeks with the Enemy," *Life,* April 7, 1967.

[59] Salisbury, *New York Times,* January 15, 1967, p. E2.

[60] Gerassi, "Report from North Vietnam," *New Republic,* March 4, 1967, p. 16.

[61] Ronning, quoted by Schlesinger, *The Bitter Heritage,* 1967, pp. 108–9.

no indication of readiness to "listen to reason." It is true that they may have been given an exaggerated picture of North Vietnamese determination. The Communist leaders, pinning their hopes of victory on a revulsion of feeling against the war in the United States and in the West as a whole, would want to give an impression of indomitable determination to visitors from outside. But the observers have consistently returned with the impression that the Communist leaders meant what they said.

Their actions have been in line with their words. The North Vietnamese and the Viet Cong have steadily refused to come to the conference table during the period of the bombing from early 1965 to 1968, and there has been an actual hardening of their position during that time, though their hopes of victory must have been greatly diminished by the simultaneous build-up of massive American strength in the South. It seems likely, therefore, that they do mean what they say, and that their emotional reaction to heavy bombing is like that of the British, the Germans, and the Japanese.

It will be noticed that none of these examples counts against the clearly valid generalization that when force is overwhelming it is usually effective in ending a war. Many wars have ended with the final capitulation of one side in the face of overwhelming force mobilized by the other. The Confederate army finally surrendered at Appomattox; the Nazi armies gave up after their country had been completely overrun; the Japanese submitted after defeat in the Pacific was followed by the wholly new terror of the atomic bomb, against which they had no defense. There is at least this much truth in the common-sense assumption that increased use of force is the way to end a war.

On the other hand, there is now an impressive accumulation of evidence that a proud people, wound up in the emotions and assumptions that war brings, is likely to absorb an amazing amount of punishment without admitting defeat, and is likely to stop fighting only when the force against it becomes physically overwhelming. The assumption implicit in much current American thinking seems to be that the North Vietnamese are calculating aggressors who are rational enough to reconsider their aggression when we have demonstrated to them that it is not paying off. It seems to be assumed that this point is likely to be reached long before North Vietnam is confronted with total destruction or hopeless defeat. The evidence reviewed here calls that assumption into question.

If we ask why this reaction of anger and defiance should prevail, two reasons suggest themselves. First, the punished people are not likely to see their new sufferings as punishment for aggression, even when their government has been, from its opponents' standpoint, as unequivocally aggressive as the Nazi and Japanese governments. They ordinarily see their new suffering in the context of an over-all definition of the war in which they are the innocent victims of the enemy's wrongdoing. By a process of cumulative collective rationalization, with mutual reinforcement of each others' individual rationalizations, they have come to assume that their enemy is essentially aggressive. In such a context, adding the bombing of the population to the enemy's catalogue of crime seems but another, particularly flagrant, particularly naked example of aggression. The enemy is now taking off his mask and showing himself in his true colors. The leaders as well as the general population of the bombed nation are likely to feel that their case has now become unequivocally clear in the eyes of honest men everywhere.

It is very difficult in time of war for an ordinary person on either side to realize how innocent the enemy feels, and therefore how unprovoked and outrageous, from the enemy's point of view, an intensified war by one's own side is likely to appear. The usual picture of the enemy is that "he" (we tend to use the singular when speaking of the enemy, thinking of one devil rather than several million devils) is not only diabolical but also calculatingly, cold-bloodedly, rationally diabolical. Although we assume that he is capable of fear—"the only language he can understand is the language of force"—we seldom attribute to him other emotions resembling our own, such as patriotism, an endangered virile self-image, and (from his own point of view) righteous anger. It is therefore all too easy to assume optimistically that if the enemy is made to hurt enough he will rationally decide that his calculations have been mistaken and that he had better leave his neighbors alone. At that point he may actually be nerving himself to die rather than submit to what he sees as naked aggression.

If the Germans and the Japanese reacted this way, it seems extremely likely that the North Vietnamese Communists do. Since 1945 they have been fighting on what they apparently regard as their own soil, in defense of their homeland, and their rationale for regarding their opponents as aggressors is a good deal more persuasive than the rationale of the Germans or the Japanese was.

When the citizens of a great power speak of punishing a small one, they may also be carrying over—perhaps without clearly realizing that they are doing so—the analogy of a firm and righteous parent punishing a bad child. He must be brought to see the error of his ways. Actually, if we are to turn to child psychology for examples, a better analogy might be the infliction of punishment on a child who feels (rightly or wrongly) that he is being unfairly punished for something he never did.

A second reason for the reaction of anger and defiance may be the mutual reinforcement of hope and rejection of "defeatism" that is typical of a fighting group. This may result in maintaining a kind of spurious hope long after the point at which, objectively considered, it would be wise to seek a compromise. Every slim basis for hope is seized upon and overemphasized; every indication of defeat is ignored or explained away. No one wants to be the first to admit stalemate or defeat; each is on his mettle to stand as firmly as the next man and to deny the doubts that may be slowly gathering beneath the surface of his mind. As a rule, only when defeat is so overwhelming that no one can lose face by admitting it (as it was for the Confederate States in 1865, or for the Germans or the Japanese in 1945) does the group's hope and fighting spirit finally and suddenly break. Because of mutual reinforcement, such a delay in recognizing distasteful reality is much more likely in a group than in an individual.

In the case of North Vietnam this mutual reinforcement of exaggerated confidence seems likely to have full scope in view of a number of relatively realistic grounds for hope on which the North Vietnamese can focus their attention. The terrain is favorable for guerrilla warfare in both North and South Vietnam. The Communists have had long experience in guerrilla fighting in the favorable terrain of the Delta region in the South (where food is plentiful) and also in the mountainous jungle regions of North and Central Vietnam. They know how well they can fight there; in their minds that kind of fighting is an obvious alternative to ignominious surrender. It seems likely that they would choose to fight on as guerrillas rather than to surrender or to disband the Viet Cong in the South even if we invaded the North, and even if we used nuclear weapons. Also, North Vietnam is economically a relatively undeveloped country, much less dependent on fixed industry and transportation than Germany and Japan were, and thus less immediately vulnerable to aerial bombardment.

Evidence from a number of sources supports the tentative generalization that, while extreme degrees of bombing may bring an enemy to terms, intermediate degrees are likely to have the opposite effect. If one country is able to pulverize another and chooses to do so, accepting whatever consequences may follow, its bombing can have the intended psychological effect. Up to that point, increased bombing seems likely to stiffen resistance.

Chapter 4

THE CONFLICT AS SEEN BY
ONLOOKERS

How Important Are the Onlookers?

Why should we care what others think about our policy in Vietnam? We Americans care too much about whether we are loved by all the world —including our faint-hearted allies who in their hearts must be thanking God that we are protecting them from Communist aggression, but who don't have the guts to stand by our side when the going gets rough. What we should care about is respect, not love—and what we are doing now must at least command their respect. If we do what *we* know is right and necessary, that is enough.

This is a familiar line of thinking, and a very attractive one to many Americans. It is in line with an individualistic tradition, an ideal of inner-directedness, and a distaste for Madison Avenue's preoccupation with selling an image. It is also in line with a virile self-image. We Americans like to think of ourselves as having the courage to do what is right and necessary regardless of the price we may pay in popularity. Surely there is much that is psychologically healthy as well as emotionally satisfying in such an attitude.

Yet this attitude could lead us very far astray if it led us to pay too little attention to certain aspects of the world's response that could catastrophically affect our own future, and the world's, in ways more tangible than mere popularity. There is a striking similarity between our own tendency to narrow our horizon almost deliberately, focusing strongly on a small patch of land on the eastern rim of Southeast Asia, and the Austrians' tendency in 1914 to narrow their horizon almost deliberately, focusing strongly on a small patch of land on the western rim of the Balkan peninsula. In both cases the rest of the world, which in the case of Austria was to become vitally involved within a matter of days, has been pushed to the fringes of conscious thought. In both cases there has been a sense of courage and of virility in doing what has to be done, regardless of consequences.

The same mood finds a disturbing echo in Hitler's brush-off of world reactions on September 1, 1939: "When statesmen in the West declare that this affects their interests, I can only regret such a declaration. It cannot for a moment make me hesitate to fulfil my duty." Satisfying and simplifying as it may be to shut the thoughts and feelings of others out of our minds, we live on a planet that has grown too small for autism on a national scale. Nuclear weapons have made empathy a necessity for survival.

One curious thing about many Americans who show little or no interest in criticism of our Vietnam policy in other countries is that in some ways they themselves base their support of the war on what they expect will be the reactions to the conflict outside of Vietnam. The "domino theory" itself, which in one form or another is perhaps the most important single reason for America's involvement, essentially consists of the proposition that appeasement or retreat in Vietnam would have serious psychological effects elsewhere, encouraging Communists, discouraging anti-Communists, and seeming to confirm the Chinese Communist philosophy of war by assassination. This domino theory cannot by any means be dismissed by calling it too simple or too mechanical. General Taylor stated persuasively a more sophisticated version of the domino theory when he said, "I personally do not believe in such a theory if it means belief in a law of nature which requires the collapse of each neighboring state in an inevitable sequence, following a Communist victory in Vietnam. However I am deeply impressed with the probable effects worldwide, not necessarily in areas contiguous to South Vietnam, if the 'war of liberation' scores a significant victory there."[1] These "probable effects worldwide" are psychological in nature, and deserve empirical study along with whatever other psychological effects the conflict may have. Similarly, many Americans feel that the credibility of America's promises, in the minds of people all over the world, is at stake, and many are concerned that we may lose our "position of leadership" if we retreat or compromise in Vietnam. Credibility is a psychological fact too, subject to empirical study, and so is the followership that makes leadership possible.

Even if these were our only goals, then, certain empirical questions about the attitudes of onlookers would still need to be answered in order to make well-educated guesses about what to do in

[1] Taylor, 1966, p. A18.

Vietnam. What if extending or (from others' point of view) need-lessly prolonging the war in Vietnam should provide a propaganda bonanza to the Communists that would help them more than they would be helped by our settling for a compromise peace? What if the spectacle of an America claiming to be peaceful and anti-imperialistic, and at the same time fighting a war that hundreds of millions regarded as imperialistic, should greatly increase the tend-ency to regard Americans as hypocritical? What if this, together with a widespread feeling that America had violated her non-intervention commitments contained in the charter of the United Nations,[2] should undermine the credibility of America's words more than it would be strengthened by proof that we were fulfilling our commitments to anti-Communists in Vietnam? What if our rapport both with the neutrals and with our allies should be impaired to such an extent that our "position of leadership" would be weakened by this, more than it would be strengthened by proving our fighting spirit? Suppose evidence should indicate that a policy of all-out, long-continued war in the South (as compared, say, with settling quickly for some kind of strongly enforced compromise peace) would probably mean a net loss in all three of these dimensions: anti-Communism, America's credibility, and America's leadership in the world. What then? Would not those for whom these are the crucial goals necessarily have to modify their position on the Vietnam conflict?

These are all in principle empirical questions, capable of being answered (to the extent that they can be answered at all) only by an empirical study of the minds of people in countries that are not yet actively involved in the war. Even those who favor the most militant policies in Vietnam are usually making certain assumptions about the psychology of other countries, and can build their case on a sound foundation only if they examine those assumptions in the light of whatever evidence is available. They cannot shrug off the whole task by merely asking the self-flattering question: "Why should we care what others think?"

There are at least six other tangible ways in which world reactions may affect American interests adversely:

(1) Onlookers may become participants against us. Just as the Austrians in 1914 and Hitler in 1939 underestimated the chance

2 Wright, in Raskin and Fall, eds., 1965, pp. 7–12; Larson and Larson, in Raskin and Fall, eds., 1965, pp. 99–108.

that certain other countries would sooner or later enter the battle against them, so we may make a similar miscalculation. In the case of Communist China such involvement would not be because of any selective inattention on our part; the possible involvement of Communist China is a matter of continual anxious attention in American minds. We may underestimate its likelihood, but we do not ignore it. On the other hand, the possible involvement of the USSR is a thing that a great many Americans have tended to push out of their minds, with the comforting thought that the Sino-Soviet split is so deep that we do not need to worry about it. If this is a miscalculation, it could be a miscalculation of catastrophic proportions. In addition, there are other possibilities, less catastrophic but deserving more attention than they have usually received. Russia or China could open a second front elsewhere. Small countries such as Cambodia could give increased help to the Communist side, even if it fell short of all-out war. A movement to condemn and restrain the United States could gather strength in the United Nations. The British, French, and Israelis were startled by the strength of the opposition to their Suez policy that was quickly mobilized in the UN, and we could be startled in the same way.

(2) We can fail to get help from others and be left to carry the burden alone. The other major countries that, from our point of view, are most endangered by Communist China are India and Japan. Many Americans have hoped that they would become directly and vitally involved on our side. They have not yet become so involved.

(3) Our long-term relations with the Soviet Union could suffer, with a serious effect on the long-term chances of peace. This is the aspect of the whole matter that Kennan, for example, regards as most serious and as most dangerously ignored by Americans.[3]

(4) The unity of the Western alliance could be seriously impaired. Both De Gaulle and Gaston Defferre, a leading anti-Gaullist in France, have been disturbed by our policy. Defferre recently said: "Many French disapprove, as I personally do, of the policies of the United States in Santo Domingo and in Vietnam, but they do not think that blustering communiqués will influence American policy. On the contrary, they are convinced that it is by creating Europe, and speaking in the name of Europe, that European statesmen will

[3] Kennan, 1966, p. 25.

exert a real influence on the American Government and lead it to change its foreign policy in the direction of what they consider progress and peace.[4] We may draw too much comfort from the official support that our position has had, on the whole, from the leaders of Great Britain and West Germany, and underestimate the strain in our alliances that already exists and that could grow if our allies felt we were extending the war or needlessly prolonging it. According to Richard Rovere, the President "today is being told by his allies that he is fighting a fundamentally unjust war."[5]

(5) Our relations with the less developed two-thirds of the world may suffer, while the Communists' may improve. To be sure, rapport with the less-developed countries may not be as vital for our survival as is sometimes assumed. Perhaps they could all "go Communist" or tilt toward the Communist side, and with firm allies in Europe and tolerable relations with the USSR we might still survive. But those who regard a significant domino tendency in the less-developed countries as a major loss to the United States should be much concerned with the possibility that the nationalism and anti-imperialism of these countries might be mobilized against us, on the basis of an impression that in Vietnam we are trampling the peace and independence of a small country like their own. Whatever the degree of truth of this belief, we can scarcely afford to ignore it. The reality of the danger is illustrated by the position of Norodom Sihanouk, who is himself clearly fearful of a Communist takeover: "This 'anti-Communist' war, by reason of the imperialist character that it forcibly assumes in the eyes of the masses, on the contrary, *favors Communism*."[6] It is illustrated by the statement of a correspondent in Vietnam published in *La Croix,* the daily of the Catholic Archepiscopate in Paris: "Have they [the militantly anti-Communist Catholic refugees in Vietnam] reflected that such a war, which accumulates dead and wounded, material and moral destruction, will finally become the best ally of Communism? . . . We know the slogan: Asia for the Asians, and its corollary: Africa for the Africans. Who would dare to say that such slogans do not impress the masses!"[7] Thich Tri Quang has said, "The more the war goes on,

4 Defferre, 1966, p. 440.
5 Rovere, 1966, p. 199.
6 Sihanouk, in Raskin and Fall, eds., 1965, p. 359.
7 *La Croix,* in Raskin and Fall, eds., 1965, pp. 277–78.

the stronger Communism becomes, the more Americans become colonialists, and our people are destroyed."[8]

(6) All of this could weaken the UN and our position in it. For those who believe that there can be no solid and lasting peace until the world is organized along federal lines, preserving national independence in non-military matters but with a world government strong enough to enforce world law, any weakening of the United Nations is a setback in a movement that in the long run seems as important for freedom as for peace. Others who would not go so far may nevertheless regret disunity in the UN. Although there has not yet been an overt, active movement against us in the UN, the strains beneath the surface are now too strong to be ignored. According to Rovere, "given a fair chance, the United Nations would almost certainly find against us."[9] U Thant, a moderate and tactful man who has done a masterly job of keeping rapport with the diverse viewpoints represented in the UN, would clearly be enormously relieved if there could be a compromise peace that would not involve precipitate American withdrawal: "Of course I have never advocated the immediate withdrawal of United States troops from the Republic of Vietnam . . . but . . . I am sure that the great American people, if only they know the true facts and the background to the developments in South Vietnam, will agree with me that further bloodshed is unnecessary. . . . As you know, in times of war and of hostilities, the first casualty is truth."[10] During the Arab-Israel crisis of June, 1967, many Americans wished that the UN had been stronger and America's position in it firmer; many felt that the Vietnam war had detracted from both.

Finally, there is the possibility that by listening to the best-informed of those who are not directly involved in the conflict we may be able to come closer to the truth, especially the truth about ourselves, than if we enclose ourselves in a psychological cocoon of our own making. Any group that is emotionally involved on one side of a conflict suffers handicaps in balanced perception of the situation as a whole and of itself. Onlookers have the immense advantage of relatively need-free perception.

[8] Tri Quang, *New York Times,* April 9, 1967.
[9] Rovere, 1966, p. 199.
[10] U Thant, in Raskin and Fall, eds., 1965, pp. 264, 266.

To be sure, those directly involved are likely to perceive some facts, such as the evil acts committed by their opponents, more fully than onlookers do. There is some truth, no doubt, even in the insistence of Southern white-supremacists that meddlers from the North do not understand the situation as they, who are on the spot and dealing with the situation all the time, understand it. Doubtless there were facts about Suez that the British, French, and Israelis understood better than their critics, and facts about Indochina and Algeria that were understood better by the French than by anyone else. Yet this advantage seems quite overbalanced by the highly selective inattention and consequent distortion of the overall picture that is typical of the combatants themselves.

There are substantial advantages, then, in continuing the American tradition of "a decent respect to the opinions of mankind."

The Validity of the Domino Theory

In the sophisticated form in which General Maxwell D. Taylor has stated it, the domino theory seems to have a good deal of validity. It seems entirely consistent with psychological evidence to suppose: (1) that complete withdrawal by the United States would encourage the Communists to attempt seizures of power in various developing countries, including some where they would not have the degree of popular support they have had in Vietnam; (2) that the degree of cruelty and ruthlessness on both sides is now such that complete withdrawal by us would leave our anti-Communist friends exposed to some very rough treatment, which would tend to discourage anti-Communists in other countries who might otherwise have the courage to resist terror and threats of assassination; and (3) that complete withdrawal would in Communist eyes confirm the Chinese Communist philosophy of village-centered warfare against the structure of government in newly developing non-Communist societies.

The gain for the Chinese philosophy is an argument that the opponents of our involvement find particularly hard to answer. General Giap of the North Vietnamese army has said, "If the special warfare that the U.S. imperialists are testing in South Vietnam is overcome, then it can be defeated everywhere in the world."[11] Robert Scalapino, one of the best-informed of the more militant Americans, observed that "withdrawal would prove that Peking was right and make it virtually impossible for moderation to prevail inside the world Communist movement."[12]

Each of these processes could operate especially in countries near the borders of South Vietnam (Laos, Cambodia, Thailand, Malaysia) where the salience of events in Vietnam is greatest and guerrilla warfare can be supported by direct infiltration of men and weapons across a border or a limited stretch of open water. Each could presumably operate also in any country in the world where conditions are ripe for violence and men have images of the physical and psychological strength of Communism and anti-Communism. If Communists gained a decisive victory in Vietnam, Communists elsewhere would tend to be confirmed in their belief that Communism is the wave of the future. Anti-Communists would tend to be disheartened, and many Communists, presumably, would decide that Mao's strategy for dissolving the power of anti-Communist governments is a strategy that pays off in the long run.

Doubts about this more complex and sophisticated version of the domino theory do not center around the probable fact of such a tendency; they center around its probable importance in the over-all scheme of things. There are many informed persons who doubt that the domino tendency is likely to be very strong, and who doubt especially that it would be very strong *if* America does not withdraw completely but settles for some kind of compromise peace and remains in the country indefinitely with enough troops to enforce it. We have seen in the previous chapter how thoroughly the Communists have apparently set their hearts on total victory and how confident they have been that in the end they would achieve it. Politically conscious persons in other countries have also tended to see a probable Communist victory.[13] If they were denied such a victory, and were compelled, with or without negotiations, to settle for approximately the parts of South Vietnam that they now control, they would probably be acutely frustrated. They probably would continue to denounce American "aggression" on Vietnamese soil, and the rest of the world

[11] U Thant, in Raskin and Fall, eds., 1965, p. 11.
[12] *Ibid.*, p. 12.
[13] Myrdal, 1965, p. 21.

would have not an enhanced image of Communist strength but about the same image it has had for the past three or four years. Many would see us as still "holding the line."

Even the effects of a complete Communist victory, if such a victory should occur, are regarded by a number of informed persons as not likely to be catastrophic. Kennan, for instance, told the Fulbright committee: "It is difficult to believe that any decisive developments of the world situation would be determined in normal circumstances by what happens [in Vietnam]."[14] Richard Lowenthal says, "The success of guerrilla war depends primarily on the internal condition of the country under attack—as the contrast between developments in Vietnam and those in the Philippines and Malaya has shown."[15] And Morgenthau strongly doubts the theory on historical grounds: "The so-called 'domino theory' assumes that as South Vietnam goes so will Thailand, and as Thailand goes so will India, and so forth, until the whole world will have gone Communist. This theory is a slogan born of fear and of a misconception of history and politics. It is unsupported by any historic evidence. The Soviet Union went Communist in 1917 and China in 1949, but no other nation followed suit. In 1945, Poland and Hungary went Communist, but Finland did not, and all the Balkan states went Communist, but Greece did not. In 1948 Czechoslovakia went Communist but no other nation did. In 1954 North Vietnam went Communist all by herself, and in 1960 or so Cuba went Communist without being followed by any other Latin American nation. Social and, more particularly, revolutionary change is not the mechanical result of imitation and prestige but of objective conditions peculiar to individual nations."[16] Psychologists can confirm Morgenthau's generalization at least to this extent: Imitation is not an automatic or inevitable process; a great deal depends on the other psychological factors—especially motivation and recognition of opportunity—that exist at the same time. (However, to supplement Morgenthau's version of recent history it should be noted that foreign support given to anti-Communist governments in Greece, Korea, South Vietnam, West Germany, and other countries on the borders of the expanding Communist empire

14 Kennan, 1966, p. 20.
15 Lowenthal, 1965, p. 70.
16 Morgenthau, 1965c, p. 13.

has had a gool deal to do with their not succumbing, as Czechoslovakia did, to the Communist juggernaut.)

Perhaps the most telling critique of the domino theory comes from a Southeast Asian specialist, George Kahin: "Non-Communist governments of Southeast Asia will not automatically collapse if the Communists should come to control all of Vietnam. So long as Southeast Asian governments are in harmony with their nations' nationalism, so long as they are wise enough to meet the most pressing economic and social demands of their people, they are not likely to succumb to Communism."[17] This too is not, it may be noted, a reason to think that the domino tendency is negligible. It is, however, a reason to grant it less importance than certain other factors, such as whether a government is "in harmony with its nation's nationalism" and the extent to which it "meets the most pressing economic and social demands of the people." It therefore offers hope that America can be effective in diminishing the spread of Communism to other developing countries if it consistently allies itself with rather than pitting itself against the burgeoning nationalism of these countries, and helps them to fulfill their hopes of economic and social progress.

It should not be forgotten, also, that there is a "reverse domino theory" held by Tri Quang, Sihanouk, and others. This theory maintains that America's conduct of the war actually helps Communism and promotes its spread to other countries. This is "reversed" in that it pictures Communism spreading not because of American weakness but because of American belligerence. The truth may lie somewhere between the domino theory and the reverse domino theory. Onlookers may object most not to America's willingness to stand firm in Vietnam, but to America's other sins (as they perceive them) of omission and commission: escalation, napalm, unfulfilled promises of land reform, apparent unwillingness to settle for a compromise peace. Perhaps these are the things that most fuel Communist propaganda and most promote the spread of Communism elsewhere. If so, then a holding strategy, a policy of simply standing firm against further Communist encroachment, without these attendant evils, might be most effective in preventing the spread of Communism.

A word should be added, too, about non-rational factors that

[17] Kahin, in Raskin and Fall, eds., 1965, p. 294.

could make us unduly ready to accept a picture of spreading catastrophe within the non-Communist world. The data on the authoritarian personality[18] and the analysis of the Bolshevik mentality by Leites[19] both suggest that there can be such a non-rational factor, resembling certain paranoid delusions, in obsessive fear of infection or fear that "all would be lost" if one's outer defenses are breached. Metaphors such as the row of dominoes, or fire, or an epidemic, or the flooding in of the sea through a broken dike, all suggest a non-rational inflation of anxiety and a great lack of empathy with the human beings whose human responses are represented by these dehumanized images. Such metaphors recall also the Austrians' fear that their empire would quickly disintegrate if Serbia were not severely punished. In that case there was clearly truth in the fear of disintegration; its irrationality lay largely in exaggerating the seriousness of the danger and in an all-or-none feeling about what Austria had to do. There was a blurring of the distinction between legitimate firmness within the borders of the Empire and the illegitimate and extremely dangerous firmness (more accurately described as aggression) that consisted of a use of force against Serbia herself. Perhaps that is the most important way in which anxiety-ridden perception tends to be unrealistic. It often blurs essential distinctions. In our own case, the danger of unrealism lies in a similarly exaggerated anxiety about the catastrophe that would follow if the outer defenses of the "Free World" were breached, leading to a similar lack of discrimination in the methods we choose to combat the danger.

It goes without saying that neither clinical analogies nor historical analogies can substitute for direct study of the evidence on the present situation. The most relevant evidence for us lies in a case-by-case study of countries such as Thailand that are now most directly threatened, and a case-by-case study of other countries similarly threatened in the recent past, especially those in which an indigenous insurgent movement has been partly or wholly captured by the Communists. But if this most relevant type of evidence gives only moderate support to the domino theory (as, judging by the testimony of such men as Kahin, it does), then it is legitimate to look at clinical and historical analogies to explain why so many Americans perceive this probably moderate factor as catastrophic and decisive.

[18] Adomo, Frenkel-Brunswik, Levinson and Sanford, 1950, pp. 442–48.
[19] Leites, 1953.

The Positive Image of American Policy

It would be a great mistake to conceive of the world's response as wholly negative. Statements by political leaders, editorial comment in the press, and public opinion surveys have all shown a large amount of approval of America's actions so far, as well as a large amount of disapproval. The evidence of approval includes these facts:

The governments of Great Britain, West Germany, and a number of other countries have on the whole supported us.

Most of the urban and politically conscious people in the small countries that are directly in the path of possible Chinese Communist conquest (Laos, Thailand, Malaysia, Singapore, the Philippines, Taiwan, South Korea) are fearful of such conquest and reassured by the knowledge that America is standing against it. For instance, Tunku Abdul Rahman, as reported by Richard Nixon, said, "If one small country is unsafe from Communist domination, all are. The United States stands for the safety of all free nations in Asia by defending South Vietnam."

Most of the people of Australia and New Zealand appear to be similarly anxious, and eager for our help in fending off possible Communist conquest, as their tangible contributions have demonstrated.[20]

Opinion-survey evidence indicates that, throughout most of the non-Communist world, the image of Communist China is strongly negative. Negative reactions to American involvement in Vietnam tend to be matched by negative reactions to Chinese Communist

[20] William Bundy (1967, p. 135) quotes Drew Middleton of the *New York Times*: "Despite some misgivings, non-Communist leaders from Tokyo to Teheran largely support United States policy in South and Southeast Asia." It seems clear that most of those political leaders—though not necessarily most of their people—want us to stay in Vietnam and hold the line against further Communist advance. What is unclear is whether they would define "holding the line" as an insistence on victory rather than a compromise peace. These leaders apparently conceive the issue rather simply, in terms of two alternatives: fight or get out. Between these two they clearly choose fighting (that is, that America should fight). But they still might prefer a strong holding policy (see Appendix A) if the alternative were prolonging or spreading the war. We do not know.

involvement (which is often assumed to be greater than, up to now, it has actually been). The Indian statesman C. Rajagopalachari has written, "There is not the slightest doubt that if America withdraws and leaves Southeast Asia to itself, Communist China will seize the continent. There is no hope for freedom of thought in Asia if the hegemony, if not the empire, of China is established."

Surveys in many countries have shown that the *basic* image of America has been on the whole (at least until recently) much more favorable than unfavorable. There is ambivalence everywhere, but the positive image of our wealth, productivity, willingness to help others, democracy, and commitment to peace has strongly tended to predominate. In the great majority of the countries in which surveys have been conducted, the United States has been more favorably regarded than the USSR, and much more favorably regarded than Communist China. (To be sure, the Western type of survey has not been conducted in certain especially anti-American spots such as Egypt and Indonesia.) Other things being equal, people probably have tended to give America the benefit of the doubt in their judgments about the Vietnam war.

Some of those who do not publicly support the American action are willing to say privately that they are glad America has taken up the bloody and thankless task of balancing Communist power and (as many see it) resisting Communist aggression. As Senator Russell has suggested there is a genuine and understandable "let-George-do-it" reaction.

There was a warm response throughout most of the world to our bombing pause at the end of 1965, and the failure of the Communists to respond to it set them back in their effort to enlist world support on their side.

The Negative Image of American Policy

Even after all of this has been said, however, the fact remains that the world's response has been mainly negative.[21] The reasons are worth exploring. There are at least six negative reactions that seem clearly more frequent in other non-Communist countries than in the United States:

[21] Markel, 1965, p. 69.

1. *That the United States is "making war," and that this sets back the great hopes for peace in the world that were created during the Kennedy administration.*

To most Americans of course we are not "making war" but accepting war with utmost reluctance in order to resist aggression. It is understandable that to others who are only vaguely aware of this rationale or consciously skeptical of it we should appear to be "making war," especially since our bombing of the North made it seem that we were unequivocally crossing the line separating the Communist from the non-Communist world, and using force on the Communist side of it.

There is also another factor in their perception that is so distasteful to Americans that it seems to be rather seldom thought of even by those who oppose our involvement: To many onlookers our claim to be fighting a defensive war is made to seem ridiculous by the fact that we are the world's strongest military power and North Vietnam is one of the weakest. In plain terms, it looks to them like a case of a big country bullying a small one.

We ought to know how it feels to identify with a small country being bullied by a large one. We felt that way when Austria-Hungary seemed to be bullying Serbia, when Germany seemed to be bullying Belgium, when Hitler was bullying Austria, Czechoslovakia, and the Jews, when Russia attacked sturdy little Finland, when Russian tanks crushed the uprising in Hungary. Americans pride themselves on their tradition of fair play, and the code of "pick on somebody your own size" is in fact strong among American boys even if it is often violated.[22] America has entered at least three wars, including the Spanish-American war, partly because of its feeling for the underdog. There is a paradox, then, in the fact that we have been so insensitive to this possible definition of what we have been doing in Vietnam. Few of us have even allowed it to occur to us that others might see our behavior in this way.

Once the question is raised, a partial answer to it is obvious: In our own eyes we are not picking on a weak country but defending one, South Vietnam, against attack by a stronger neighbor which in turn is backed by the enormously greater power of Communist China. We are standing in the path of Communist China's ambition

[22] White & Lippitt, *Autocracy and Democracy: An Experimental Inquiry,* 1960, pp. 166–67.

to dominate, one by one, the many weaker countries on its periphery. We are for the underdog, not against him. But few of those who favor our involvement have taken the next step in thought, which is to note that, from an onlooker's point of view, American intervention has been up to now on a much larger scale than that of Communist China. It could look as if we, with our terrifying nuclear power, are insisting that the situation remain what it is now—a very powerful country fighting a very weak one—and are threatening to attack China herself (that is, to "spread the war" further and make it dangerously close to a world war) if China dares to intervene in defense of her small protégé. As they could see it, the big bully is continuing to beat up the very small boy, and is telling the small boy's older brother (who is also smaller than the bully) that if he helps the little one he will be beaten up too.

It is true that onlookers seldom express their disapproval in precisely these terms. They are more likely to say simply that America is "making war" or perhaps that it is fighting "a colonial war." Alex Campbell, for instance, describes the typical Asian reaction as follows: "To most Asians the war in South Vietnam is not a 'small war,' as Defense Secretary McNamara recently pigeonholed it; nor is it a war in defense of civilization against the onslaught of Communism in Southeast Asia. . . . In the eyes of the Asians it's much more like a colonial war, or at least a war that is now being fought and directed by whites in pursuit of white Western rather than indigenous Asian interests."[23] But against the background of a century of white Western domination of the economically less developed countries, including China, and willingness to fight "colonial wars" to maintain that domination, the charge of fighting a "colonial war," or a war in pursuit of white Western interests, must be psychologically more or less equivalent to a charge of bullying the weak.

2. *That the United States is opposing what most of the people of South Vietnam want.*

As we have seen, this more basic assumption, or its opposite, is likely to determine perceptions as to who is "the aggressor." Those who assume that most of the people in South Vietnam are opposed to American intervention are likely to define that intervention as "aggression," while those who assume that most of the people are opposed to intervention by the North are likely to define it as "the

[23] Campbell, ed., 1966b, p. 13; cf. Ahmad, in Gettleman, 1965, p. 362.

aggressor." As we have also seen, the available evidence on this point is complex and somewhat ambiguous. Most of the South Vietnamese people seem to resent intervention *both* by the United States and by the North Vietnamese Communists, but probably resent American intervention more intensely because it is on the side of an intensely unpopular government.

If this is the case, and if most of the American people are capable of the oversimplification and distortion involved in thinking that "the Vietnamese people" have asked for our help in repelling aggression from the North, it is not surprising that many onlookers have an oversimplified perception of the opposite nature, regarding "the people" of South Vietnam as resenting and resisting our intervention as they resented and resisted French rule. If this is their basic picture then they must perceive the North Vietnamese intervention not as aggression but as helping "the South Vietnamese people" to resist aggression (or imperialism) and they must see our military actions in both North and South as a strong power bullying a weak one.

Since people tend to assume that their own perception as to what the Vietnamese people want is an obvious fact, evident to both sides, they do not often put it into words. Those who oppose America's action are likely to call it "aggression" or "war-making" or "a colonial war" without realizing that to most Americans it seems evident that most of the Vietnamese people do want our help (or are, at worst, neutral). But Americans traveling abroad are likely to recognize and make explicit the implicit assumptions on which our critics base their judgments. For example, C. L. Sulzberger reported from Paris: "The French admit their primordial difference with Washington is the U.S. belief that there actually is a Government in Saigon and that this is being opposed by Communist and foreign intervention. France insists the U.S.A. is in fact fighting against the population of South Vietnam which is aided by others including North Vietnam. They claim this is an evident truth which some day must be acknowledged by Washington and that until then there can be no negotiations."[24]

This should not be taken as necessarily typical of West European opinion; the French, who burned their fingers badly in Vietnam and think they have learned a lesson, are apparently much more anti-

[24] Sulzberger, 1966, p. E12.

American on this issue than most other European countries.[25] But if this assumption about the Vietnamese people is as widespread in France as Mr. Sulzberger says, it is probably fairly widespread in other countries, too, especially in the developing countries, whose predisposition to see us as fighting a colonial or a white man's war is much stronger than that of West Europeans.

There are also more direct indications that in other West European countries, as well as in France, the Vietnamese people are as a rule believed to be anti-American. Marquis Childs gives his impression of "the privately held view of many European chancelleries" as including the following: "You can stay in Vietnam indefinitely if you have the will to stay, since you have the resources. But you can never win over the people after subjecting them to months, if not years, of area bombing with napalm and your deadly canister bombs. So, eight thousand miles from your shores, you will be like the British in Ireland—being shot at from behind the hedgerows for as long as you choose to stay."[26]

Such a perception would not necessarily mean that they basically lean more toward the Communist side than toward the American. There is abundant evidence in opinion surveys that the majority of West Europeans, though ambivalent, are much more pro-American than anti-American, and basically much more antagonistic to the Communist countries, especially Communist China, than to the U.S.[27] Their present perception of our behavior in Vietnam is, for a great many, a reluctant perception; it exists in spite of their basic pro-Western leaning, not because of a pro-Eastern leaning, as some Americans, impatient of European criticism, have tended to assume. In their minds there is puzzlement and dismay that "those good guys, the Americans, are now doing a thing like this."

To a much lesser extent, the same can be said about the developing countries. They are not, on the whole, leaning toward Communism. To be sure, in many of them there is a strong latent stereotype, all too ready to surface, of Western imperialism and of America as a Western capitalist power that engages in economic imperialism and might easily become politically imperialistic, too.[28] Opinion surveys and other evidence shows that their basic picture of the

25 Markel, 1965, p. 69.
26 Childs, 1965b.
27 White, 1966.
28 Chanakya Sen, 1965.

world is usually a neutralist one, with America and the Communist countries both appearing as potentially dangerous to the independence of small, newly developing nations. But most of them are at least as ready to believe evidence of aggressive Communist Chinese intervention as to believe evidence of aggressive American intervention. They are jaundiced and hypersensitive in their perception of both. And they usually have a strong positive image of America alongside the negative one.

It is a mistake, therefore, when impatient Americans assume that most of these onlookers "would have been against us anyway, whatever we did." If the facts were actually as much on our side as most Americans believe—if it were actually a clear case of Communist aggression against a gallant small nation fighting to maintain its independence, as it was when Russia attacked Finland or put down the Hungarian uprising—we could expect at least a leaning toward our side on the part of most of the people in the developing countries, and certainly in Western Europe. Instead, the evidence shows that their leaning is against us.

3. *That the United States—the strongest nation in the world—is irrational and obsessive in its fear of Communism.*

It is not that these people are themselves pro-Communist. As we have seen, most are anti-Communist, even in the developing countries. But it is precisely because they feel fairly sure of the anti-Communism of their own country and of other countries like it that they are skeptical of the typical American assumption that if the outer defenses of the Free World are breached, Communism would spread like a fire or an epidemic. Anti-Communism is not for them the essence of foreign policy, as it is for most Americans (along with the quest for peace).[29] The possibility of several other developing countries "going Communist" is not for most of them an unthinkable eventuality, justifying almost any sort of preventive action, as it is for many Americans.[30] As U Thant has put it, "When American policy did concern itself with what was happening in the rest of the world, it did so out of fear and suspicion—fear of Communism and suspicion of Communist motives. Fear and suspicion are very undesirable states of mind. They breed hatred, and hatred in turn breeds cruelty and intolerance. Fear of Soviet Communism has led the

[29] Pool, in Kelman, ed., 1965, p. 118.
[30] Markel, 1965.

United States, and those who follow her lead, to take a distorted view of the world situation and of the forces that are at work in modern society."[31] And again, "You know, I was once a paranoid anti-Communist myself, in Burma, in the years after the war. But a great deal has changed in these years, and the increasing liberalization within the Soviet Union and other Communist countries has made generalizations about Communism no longer valid."[32]

One way in which this basic difference in amount of anxiety about Communism shows itself is less alarm at the danger of expansion by Communist China. China is in general viewed negatively but there are many in India and Japan, for instance, who are not greatly disturbed by the danger of Chinese expansion. They point out that Chinese actions are often less belligerent than Chinese words: that the recent bristling manifesto by Lin Piao, for example, has not coincided with a clear attack on any neighbor. On the Sino-Indian border conflict there are well-informed persons who think China had the stronger legal case. There is a great deal of reason to think that the present mood of the Chinese is mainly defensive; they are acutely afraid of an attack by the United States.

Another indication of a lesser degree of anxiety than is typical in the U.S. is the apparently greater readiness of European and other onlookers to regard Ho as a potential Tito—to believe there is a good prospect that Vietnam may remain largely independent of Communist China if the war is not too prolonged and North Vietnam does not in desperation appeal for Chinese intervention. Marquis Childs, reporting again the privately held view of European chancelleries, describes it as including the view that "six months more of bombing, both in the north and in the south, and North Vietnam will be a Chinese dependency."[33]

4. *That atrocities are at least as frequent on the anti-Communist side as on the Communist side.*

For reasons related to the nature of anti-guerrilla warfare rather than to the moral character of either side, this impression may be essentially correct. "Atrocities" by the South Vietnamese troops (not the Americans) may in fact be more frequent than those the Viet Cong commit. Perhaps those in America who do not recognize the correctness of this impression may have been defending their

---

[31] Stated in 1958; quoted by Mannes, 1966, p. 11.

[32] Mannes, 1966, p. 11. For similar American comments, see Nevin, 1966.

[33] Childs, 1965b.

national self-image against a peculiarly disturbing form of dissonance. In America, the emotional, dramatic character of pictures
and news stories about torture practiced by our South Vietnamese
allies has been counteracted in some degree by our intense dislike of
having to associate such things with anyone on our side of the conflict. But in other countries there has been no such counteraction;
the dramatic quality of stories of torture and other atrocities on our
side has ensured maximum distribution. As Marquis Childs put it
during a visit to Stockholm: "Hardly a day passes without a battlefield photo of Viet Cong prisoners subjected to abuse or torture."[34]
Among the onlookers there are not many (as there are in the U.S.)
who are ready to point out that the Viet Cong commits atrocities,
too, and that it takes the greatest pains not to let Western newsmen
or cameramen see them.

5. *That a major motive in American policy is fear of losing
prestige.*

In the eyes of many Americans the only reasons for a militant
policy in Vietnam are praiseworthy, morally unexceptionable reasons: to preserve the freedom of the Free World; to promote peace,
which would be endangered by appeasement; to preserve the right
of the South Vietnamese to determine their own destiny; to fulfill
commitments to our friends. A goal much less talked about is prestige for its own sake—though prestige in the form of keeping our
commitments credible is mentioned unhesitatingly. Occasionally
there is talk about preserving our "position of leadership in the
world" or "our status as a great power," and in such phrases the
goal of prestige for its own sake becomes almost explicit. To many
Americans, however, it seems morally a little unworthy to admit that
we are actuated in any degree by fear of losing prestige, fear of
losing face, or fear of having to admit past mistakes.

People in other countries whose own self-image is not involved
are less inhibited. Perhaps they are enabled by their detachment to
see motives in us that we cannot see; perhaps they tend to exaggerate, cynically, the less worthy motives of a country that is more powerful than their own. In any case, they have a notable tendency to
see in us not only a desire for prestige but also a desire for power.

The British historian Arnold Toynbee, after conjecturing that "the
probable outcome of free play of the local forces" in Vietnam would

[34] Childs, 1966b; cf. Fall, 1965a, p. 15.

be a reunification of the country under a Communist regime, says that "the U.S. government and people would be inclined to take this as a defeat for the U.S.—a local defeat which, they fear, would deal a blow to the prestige of the U.S. all over the world." But, Toynbee insists, "the risk of the appalling slaughter and devastation of an atomic war is a far graver one than the risk of a diminution of national prestige."[35]

Similarly, Gunnar Myrdal, the Swedish economist and social scientist, speaking broadly about governments in general, but in a context that makes his remarks clearly applicable to the U.S., says that "in the case of foreign affairs governments invariably attach the greatest importance to convincing themselves, their people, and the world for as long as possible that their policies remain *unchanged*. Too often, no lessons are drawn other than the pretended one that experience proves these policies to be right, and to have been right from the beginning. There is an altogether irrational stress on sticking to a line. This may be due in part to the fear that a change in policy would mean 'losing face,' which is supposed to be dangerous. . . ."[36]

General de Gaulle is more caustic: "The United States, in fact, considered itself as being invested throughout the world with the burden of defense against Communism. . . . It can be added, without any intention of being derogatory, that the conviction of the United States of fulfilling a sort of vocation, the aversion which they had to any colonial work which had not been theirs, and finally the natural desire in such a powerful people to ensure themselves of new positions determined the Americans to take our place in Indochina."[37]

6. *That there is a pattern in three recent events: the murder of Kennedy, the Dominican Republic intervention, and the Vietnam war.*

Impressed as most Americans have been by the Warren Commission Report and by the apparent lack of evidence to support the belief that Oswald was put up to his crime by some anti-Kennedy group, it is hard for most of us to understand how differently the assassination is perceived by the rest of the world. Recent challenges

35 Toynbee, 1965.
36 Myrdal, 1965, pp. 21–23.
37 De Gaulle, 1964, p. 269.

by various writers have not greatly changed our prevailing interpretation. Knowing the sheer inefficiency of many local police forces, we can accept the proposition that Oswald's murder in the police station was a matter of inadequate vigilance rather than an expression of the active desire of powerful political interests to do away with Oswald before he could tell the story of how he came to kill the President. It is hard for us to realize how impossible it is for most onlookers abroad to accept this unmelodramatic verdict, and how naïve they tend to think we are for accepting it.

We also tend to forget how greatly Kennedy stirred the imagination of the world, not merely because of the youth, vigor, and rationality attributed to him but also because he had become a symbol of the world's longing for peace. He seemed to combine legitimate firmness, in his Berlin and Cuban missile crisis policies, with a statesmanlike vision of a long future of gradually improving East-West relations, illustrated in his inaugural address, the test-ban treaty, the wheat deal with Russia, and the speech at American University.

Perhaps our first-hand knowledge of the complexity of American politics and our daily observation of the legitimate motives of those who disagree with us keep us from fully realizing the tendency of foreigners to see the American political scene in highly colored, simplified, good-guys and bad-guys terms. We therefore tend to underestimate the strength of their fear, when Kennedy was killed, that the bad guys were about to take over.

In the light of all this it is not surprising that a great many onlookers tend to put a melodramatic interpretation upon the two more recent American actions that have most engaged their attention: intervention in the Dominican Republic and increasingly active participation in the war in Vietnam. (The fact that Kennedy himself took an active part in the earlier build-up in Vietnam is, typically, forgotten.) Each of these two events was tailormade to fit into their preconceived pattern: the bad guys in America—the war-makers, the economic imperialists, the Pentagon, the CIA, Wall Street, the racists, the reactionaries, the McCarthyites, or whatever other group fills out the picture of "bad guys" in a particular onlooker's perception of America—must have taken over and are now ruling from behind the scenes. From their standpoint the picture hangs together too well. "It couldn't be just coincidence."

For some this takes the form of an actual suspicion that the collusion of people in high places was involved in Kennedy's murder.

For others there is merely a conviction that some evil group in America engineered the murder. As they see it, the balance of forces in America has tilted from good to bad. As a result, America is no longer leading the world toward peace; she is instead, wittingly or unwittingly, leading it toward nuclear war.

Chapter 5

THE CONFLICT AS SEEN BY
NON-MILITANT AMERICANS

Four Viewpoints, Not Two

One of the major obstacles to realistically differentiated thinking about Vietnam is the tendency to conceive the issue in either-or terms: hawks or doves, war or peace, stand up and be counted or scuttle and run. Actually there are at least four major choices: to escalate in the North, to try to reclaim the entire South for a non-Communist government without escalation in the North, to hold essentially our present power position and try to get a compromise peace, or to withdraw. Within each of these choices there are a number of variations. To speak of only four choices is therefore an oversimplification, but perhaps it is tolerable. To speak of only two oversimplifies too much.

It distorts our thinking in at least two ways.[1] In the first place, it immediately emotionalizes thought. Dichotomies tend to become black-and-white pictures, separating good guys from bad guys and setting the stage for struggle rather than thought, discussion, or investigation. An either-or tends to become a good-or-bad. Once the issue has been defined as war versus peace or aggression versus non-aggression, for example, the mind leaps to the only possible conclusion: peace. And once the issue has been defined as courage versus cowardice, it has been virtually settled: We are men, not cowards.

In the second place, a dichotomy denies the existence of even one middle position. When there are at least two middle positions, this is inaccurate and unfair. For the sake of compactness, we will speak here of four groups: the escalators, the reclaimers, the holders, and the withdrawers. If confronted with these four choices, a great many of the American people would describe themselves as either reclaimers or holders, rejecting both further escalation and with-

[1] Cf. McGeorge Bundy on "The End of Either/Or," 1967.

drawal.* But unless confronted with four choices, both the holders
and the reclaimers would probably tend to think in terms of three,
with themselves in the happy-medium, middle-of-the-road position,
between undue risk of a major war at one extreme and weak cowardice at the other. The reclaimers, those who want to fight and win
in the South but oppose any serious further escalation in the form
of bombing the North or extending the ground war to the North,
naturally resent being regarded as war-makers, aggressors or hawks
by those whom they perceive as deviants in the direction of cowardice. Equally naturally, those who want neither to attack nor to retreat, but to hold fast to our present military position and
consolidate it, see this as a sensible middle position between the
risks of prolonging or intensifying the war, on the one hand, and
retreat or surrender on the other. To them the word dove applied
to themselves, with its devastating connotations of softness and
naïve pacifism, is an insult. They do not feel like doves, and resent
being labeled as such by those whom they perceive as deviants in
the direction of war and aggression.

What is happening here psychologically, it may be suggested, is
a shift in the whole frame of reference. The reclaimers and the holders reduce four choices to three in somewhat different ways. The
reclaimers tend to collapse the third and fourth choices, holding and
withdrawing, into a single choice of soft, cowardly compromise-or-
retreat, and see themselves as in the middle between it and escalation. The holders collapse the first and second categories, escalating
and reclaiming, into a single category of aggressive, war-making action, and see themselves as in the middle between it and withdrawal.
By a very moderate foreshortening of perspective and shifting of the
frame of reference, a person who takes either of the non-extreme
positions can in this way see himself as precisely in the middle,
endowed with all the dignity and sanity associated in his mind with
middleness. He may combine the two and call himself a "dawk" or a
"hove." In any case, he quite properly resents the dichotomy of
hawks versus doves, which is highly ambiguous and, in addition,

* During the period 1965–67 both extremes seem to have gained at the ex-
pense of the middle positions. In the summer and fall of 1967, many Americans
were in a frustrated, impatient mood that included an impulse to win and get
it over with. As in many other conflict situations, there was a tendency for
attitudes to become polarized, that is, to pull away from the normally preferred
middle position.

fails to recognize the middle position that he regards as the only sane and sensible one.[2]

To be sure, there are times when it seems useful to dichotomize and when, with both categories clearly defined, it also seems legitimate to do so. At such times, in the remainder of this study, we will use the term "militants" to include both the escalators and the reclaimers, and the term "non-militants" to include both the holders and the withdrawers. Psychologically, this distinction has some significance, since the motives and assumptions that are characteristic of the militants (for example, the motive of preserving the virile self-image and the assumption that the Communists have clearly committed aggression) do tend to differ from the motives and assumptions characteristic of the non-militants. This choice of terms also has advantages from the standpoint of reducing to a minimum the question-begging emotional connotations that attach to such terms as hawk, dove, war, aggression, appeasement, and retreat. "Militant" has positive connotations of vigor and courage (Martin Luther King advocates "militance without violence") as well as negative connotations of war and militarism, without a clear preponderance of either, and "non-militant" has a similar balance of positive and negative.

The chief aspect of the picture that this approach still leaves out of account is the difference between two questions: What should the United States do now, in its effort to get the Communists to the conference table, and what terms should the United States be willing to settle for, if and when the Communists do sit down and talk? It is quite possible to be militant on the first question and non-militant on the second. It is quite possible to say, Let's clobber them in the North—since there seems to be no other way—in order to get them to sit down and talk, but at the same time, If they talk, let's be very reasonable about terms of peace; that will be our chance to pull out without seeming to retreat or surrender. It is possible to have a very great abhorrence of the war, with a very strong impulse to pull out, and still say, Let's clobber them in order to end the war and get out.

In fact, the two broadest generalizations that emerge from all the opinion-polling in the United States correspond rather closely to this combination of superficially inconsistent attitudes. The ordinary

[2] For a psychological discussion of frames of reference in general, see Krech, Crutchfield, and Ballachey, 1962, pp. 19, 30–34.

American wants two things: to get out of the mess, and to do so on terms more honorable than retreat or surrender. The differences among Americans lie mainly in the fact that some define "honorable" in one way and others in another.

A thoughtful analysis of the opinion-poll evidence by S. M. Lipset[3] brings out this double picture clearly. On the militant side there is, for instance, general approval of bombing the North. A Harris poll reported in February, 1968, that only twenty-nine percent of the respondents wanted to stop the bombing; fifty-three percent wanted to continue it.[4] The holding strategy, defined as holding "defensive positions around the cities," was rejected about two to one in March, 1966.[5] An NBC-National Analysts poll asked at that time whether we should "pursue a more offensive ground war in Vietnam than we are presently doing, or establish defensive positions around the cities we now control." Over half (fifty-five percent) chose "a more offensive ground war" and only twenty-eight percent favored holding defensive positions around the cities. There is little comfort here for Communists who think the American people are on their side.[6]

On the other hand, the evidence of non-militant attitudes includes strongly predominant approval (eighty-eight percent) of "American negotiations with the Viet Cong if they were willing to negotiate," and a majority of those with opinions (fifty-two percent as against thirty-six percent) willing to approve "forming a new government in which the Viet Cong took some part" in order to "end the fighting." (The wording of questions makes a big difference. When, as in this case, the wording touches the pro-peace feeling of the public more clearly than its anti-Communist feeling, pro-peace feeling tends to dominate the replies, and vice versa.) There is strong sentiment in favor of shifting the burden to the UN if possible; more people (forty-nine percent) said the U.S. should submit the Vietnam question to the UN and abide by the UN's decision *no matter what it is* than opposed the idea (thirty-seven percent). It seems clear

[3] Lipset, 1966, pp. 19–24.

[4] *Washington Post*, November 13, 1967, pp. A1, A3. A Gallup poll at about the same time reported an even more striking margin of approval of bombing: sixty-four to twenty-four percent (*Washington Post*, October 29, 1967, pp. F1, 5).

[5] National Opinion Research Center, reported by Lipset.

[6] Reported by Lipset.

that most Americans would give President Johnson wide latitude to settle for terms of peace that he regards as honorable.

This hawk-dove combination of attitudes on Vietnam reflects a more basic hawk-dove combination of attitudes on world affairs generally. The two keynotes are peace and unwillingness to permit the expansion of Communism. According to Lipset, "the great majority of the American people desire peace in Vietnam, do not want war with China, are prepared to accept some sort of compromise truce with the enemy, and, in fact, anticipate a negotiated peace rather than a victory which will see the defeat of the Viet Cong. On the other hand, a substantial majority is strongly hostile to Communism and all the Communist countries, including Soviet Russia, Cuba, and China. Almost nobody interviewed by NORC (five percent or less) believed that our foreign policy toward any one of these countries is 'too tough'; a large majority agree with statements that the U.S. is 'too soft' in dealing with China and Cuba; almost half think we are 'too soft' in our relations with the Russians. Most of those who do not think the policy is 'too soft' say it is right."[7]

Here too there is small comfort for Communists who think the American people are on their side, and no support at all for the Communists' black-top image of the United States, wherein the capitalist-imperialist-militarist ruling circles hate Communism and foment war while the people do not. But there is much comfort for those who hope for some compromise peace, if the Communists are willing to come halfway from their position.

Reality Worlds of the Holders and Withdrawers

First a brief sketch of how the conflict looks to the non-militants, the holders and withdrawers in this country. It is brief, because months and years of intense discussion (especially since early 1965, when we began to bomb the North) have probably made both positions familiar to nearly all readers.

For the purpose of this discussion a holder will not be defined as a person who wants to retreat to enclaves. A holder will be defined rather as one who wants to use a primarily defensive strategy to hold approximately the same power position that the Saigon government and the United States now have, probably including much of the

[7] Lipset, 1966, p. 20.

good agricultural land and more than half of the population of South Vietnam. He wants to use this power position as leverage to get a fair compromise peace through negotiation or—if the Communists continue to be unwilling to negotiate or unwilling to compromise—to hold that position indefinitely. It includes those who would settle for permanent partition of the South, preferably with Communist agreement to some new boundary line and with international policing of it; and it includes also those who would settle for a coalition government with Viet Cong participation, preferably with strong international backing of the non-Communist majority in South Vietnam to keep the organized and disciplined Communists from gaining control as they did in Czechoslovakia. It does not necessarily imply optimism about the possibility of fruitful negotiation. It includes those who are pessimistic on that score and who would be willing to forego negotiation if necessary, with a unilateral military policy decision to withdraw from overexposed positions where the Viet Cong are especially strong and the peasants are, relatively speaking, most opposed to the Saigon government, while consolidating genuine control, by night as well as by day, and vigorously prosecuting basic reforms, especially land reform, in the broad areas in which it is militarily most feasible to remain. Also, it does not necessarily imply reduction of the number of American troops in the country. There are some holders who think that the situation is so difficult that even this relatively modest program would require more troops than the United States now has there.

As we have seen, to the advocates of a holding strategy it usually appears as a happy medium between the needless, dangerous warmaking of the two more militant positions and the danger of appeasement in simply pulling out. As they typically see it, a holding strategy avoids the catastrophic possibilities inherent in escalation in the North; it avoids the immorality and futility of fighting to reclaim for a militantly anti-Communist government an entire country (South Vietnam) in which probably more than half the people hate that government. The strategy avoids helping Communism elsewhere by discrediting the United States, while fulfilling our genuine commitment. It avoids the danger to our friends that would occur if we simply withdrew, and it largely avoids the danger of encouraging militant Communism and increasing the likelihood of take-overs elsewhere.

While the advocates of complete withdrawal are at this writing still a minority,[8] this fact itself makes it worthwhile to discuss their viewpoint at some length. Even among the holders there may be some whose desire to occupy a relatively safe, socially acceptable middle-of-the-road position has kept them from doing justice to the case for the apparently extreme position of complete withdrawal. Among the escalators and reclaimers this is far more likely to be so.

The apparently extreme character of the withdrawal position may result partly from an unduly restricted frame of reference in those who find it extreme. Because we think about the situation in no more than four categories, of which withdrawal is the fourth, we tend to assume it is extreme—and to condemn it—when in a larger and perhaps more realistic frame of reference it might not seem extreme at all. Perhaps a more realistic perspective would extend all the way from militant, belligerent anti-Communism to militant, belligerent Communism. Within that frame, a withdrawal from Vietnam—doing nothing either for or against Communism—would seem the approximate middle. What most Americans have done is to focus on only half the larger frame of reference as *the* frame of reference, virtually ignoring the half stretching from neutrality to militant Communism. Many persons in other countries have a less restricted perspective. In countries where neutralism predominates, the modal position is neutrality and deviations from it occur in both directions with more or less equal frequency. In such countries, those Americans who want to pull out of Vietnam are probably perceived as plain, ordinary, sensible neutralists. This of course does not prove that the neutralists' frame of reference is right, but it does suggest that Americans should not accept their own habitual perspective without thinking critically about it, and should not regard those who favor withdrawal as obvious extremists.

Moreover, extremes are not necessarily undesirable. Persons who were regarded as extremists by those around them have sometimes been right. In the history of science there has sometimes been a final wholehearted acceptance of what was once regarded as radical heresy; the truth does not now seem to lie somewhere between the Ptolemaic and the Copernican pictures of the planetary system, or somewhere between the theory of special creation and the theory

[8] Gallup reports thirty-five percent and Harris forty-four percent (*Washington Post,* October 29 and November 13, 1967, respectively). This was a high point, just before confidence was partly restored by the public statements of Ambassador Bunker and General Westmoreland.

of evolution. (The point is relevant to our evaluation of escalation, too; the fact that escalation is extreme in all three frames of reference does not necessarily prove it to be wrong.)

With this preamble, a typical withdrawer's perception of the conflict can be sketched as follows: Withdrawal, like the holding strategy, would avoid the catastrophic possibilities in escalation; it would avoid the immorality and futility of fighting to reclaim, for a militantly anti-Communist government, all of a country where probably most of the people hate that government. It would avoid the probably unworkable proposal of a coalition government. To be sure, a problem of protecting our anti-Communist friends would arise, but perhaps emigration, financed by an affluent America, is the answer there. The charge that withdrawal would be appeasement is unfounded, since the Communists have not committed aggression in Vietnam. If any country has, it is the United States; our stooge, Diem, refused to hold elections there in 1956, and our moral position is therefore thoroughly unsound.

On the positive side, advocates of withdrawal feel that it has one tremendous advantage: It would end the war, cleanly and completely. In their view, we have no business in Vietnam and are in a sense aggressors as long as we are there; withdrawal would end the immorality and futility of our involvement in an essentially aggressive war against an essentially nationalist independence movement. It would end the prolonged torment of the Vietnamese people, with all the social and economic disorganization, moral disintegration, torture, and suffering that the war has produced. It would end the danger of catastrophic enlargement of the war, which exists as long as the war goes on. It would permit Ho Chi Minh to remain independent of Peking, end our disgrace in the eyes of most of the rest of the world, and permit us to begin the long, slow process of restoring our reputation as a country that wants peace and respects others' independence—as Britain restored hers after the Suez fiasco and as France restored hers after getting out of both Indochina and Algeria.

We could then take up again, in earnest, the far more important work of building a *modus vivendi* with the Soviet Union, establishing at least some effective communication with Communist China, restoring harmony within the Western alliances, and promoting sound non-Communist development in the other developing countries—thereby contributing, in the one way really open to us, to preventing future Vietnams. From this standpoint, a holding strategy would, of course, be better than escalating or trying to reclaim the whole South, but it would be temporizing with all the evils of continued war. Pulling out would cleanly end them.

Some Possible Misperceptions

What are the misperceptions in the two non-militant views of the conflict? A list of twelve possible misperceptions is presented below. Not all of them are necessarily misperceptions (in my judgment the first two are not), and not all are shared by all non-militants. But they are at least food for thought; to search for weaknesses in one's own position is as wholesome an exercise for non-militants as for anyone.

1. *Exaggerating the proportion of the South Vietnamese people who hate the military government more than they hate the Viet Cong.*

Chapter 2 examines with some care the publicly available evidence on both sides of this question and reaches the tentative conclusion that probably much more than half of those with strong feelings among the South Vietnamese hate the Government more (while the majority of people are indifferent). But this could be mistaken, and since it is crucial to the position of both holders and withdrawers, it calls for the most stringent examination and continual reconsideration in the light of new evidence.

2. *Exaggerating the catastrophic possibilities inherent in escalation.*

While psychological considerations and historical analogies strongly suggest that the Chinese or the Russians may escalate irrationally in response to further escalation by us, there are also persuasive arguments against this view (see especially the points made by Hanson Baldwin, below, p. 158).

3. *Ignoring or underemphasizing the danger that a Communist victory in Vietnam would, in many Communist eyes, confirm the Maoist strategy of "wars of national liberation."*

It has been persuasively argued that in this case the pro-Chinese faction and its philosophy would probably be strengthened within every Communist Party—in the USSR, in Peking, and throughout the underdeveloped two-thirds of the world.

Considering the vulnerability of a great many newly developing countries to this strategy, this is perhaps one of the two or three strongest arguments in favor of at least fighting the Communists to a standstill in Vietnam (that is, using whatever military force is necessary to establish a stalemate). But it has not often been discussed by non-militants. As a rule they do not answer it; they acknowledge it and give it some weight, or they ignore it.

4. *Not realizing how vulnerable a great many developing countries are to take-over by disciplined Communist groups even where the Communists are a small minority.*

Impressed by the evidence that in Vietnam the majority of those with strong feelings favor the Viet Cong or regard it as much the lesser evil, many opponents of our involvement fail to realize that in scores of other developing countries, where Communism has not had the good fortune to become fused with nationalism, the Communists are likely to remain a very small minority—which means that a take-over by them could not be democratic, as it might be, in one sense of the word "democratic," in Vietnam. If encouraged by a victory in Vietnam, the Communists in these other countries may nevertheless attempt to seize power, either by *coup d'état* in the cities or by the Chinese strategy of assassinating village leaders and destroying the infrastructure of a non-Communist society that might otherwise be viable. This danger stems only partly from the vindication of the Chinese philosophy which we have already considered. It stems also from simply encouraging Communists everywhere to do what Communists have often done or tried to do in the past—in Indonesia, Malaya, China, Czechoslovakia, Germany, and elsewhere—whenever they have thought they had a good opportunity.

5. *Assuming that, since "both sides have committed aggression," the historical record in this respect is therefore more or less equal.*

A person who is trying very hard to be fair-minded may assume that the truth lies exactly halfway between two extremes when a closer look at the evidence would indicate otherwise. For example, when Hitler attacked Czechoslovakia, the aggression was not equally divided between him and the Czechs. A question must therefore be raised: When some non-militants assume a general equality of aggressiveness on both sides of the East-West conflict, are they actually leaning over backward and distorting a body of historical evidence which—*even after* making all due allowance for our own ethnocentric and anti-Communist bias—indicates that aggression by the Communists has been much greater?

Let us look very briefly at the record. A hostile critic of the United States, putting on our actions the worst interpretation that would be at all consistent with the facts, might say that since 1939 the United States has been aggressive in China (by supporting Chiang against a majority of his own people, and later by using force to support him in Taiwan and Quemoy), in Guatemala, Cuba, the Dominican Republic, Laos, Vietnam, possibly in Indonesia and Lebanon, in our U-2 flights over Communist territory, and in our support of Israel in 1967.

A similarly hostile critic of the Communists, putting on their actions the worst possible interpretation, could easily prepare a much longer list. The clearest cases are probably Finland, the Baltic states, most of Eastern Europe in 1944–45 (Poland, Czechoslovakia, Hungary, Rumania, Bulgaria, Yugoslavia, Albania, and East Germany), the Berlin blockade, Korea, the crushing of the Hungarian uprising, Tibet, and (if one may define aggression as the effort of a clear minority to seize power) Indonesia. Somewhat less clear would be the partition of Poland (following the Nazi-Soviet Pact), threats to Berlin, the Berlin Wall, threats against Turkey, the temporary occupation of northwestern Iran, guerrilla warfare in Greece, the Philippines, Burma, Laos, and Vietnam, support of Mao in China, military aid to Arbenz in Guatemala, aid to Castro, the Cuban missile crisis, threats to Quemoy and Taiwan, rocket threats in connection with Suez, the Sino-Indian border, and support of the Arabs against Israel in 1967. About eleven items on our side and thirty-four on the Communist side, twenty-nine of which may be charged to the Soviet Union alone.*

If all these situations were carefully weighted according to their seriousness (for example, the numbers of people involved and the severity of political control over them) and according to their unambiguousness as instances of aggression (including the amount of provocation by the other side), which list would then be more weighty? The writer's interpretation, even after taking into account his own ethnocentric bias, is that the Communist list is much longer, and that it also includes a much greater number of relatively serious, unambiguous instances of aggression. The reader may disagree, but in doing so he should at least consider both lists on their merits.

* We can fairly compare the U.S. with the USSR alone, not with all Communist nations, unless other instances of Western "aggression," such as Suez, are included.

Those who simply ignore the long Communist list, or assume it to be no worse than our own, are indulging in selective inattention.[9]

6. *Forgetting the full horror of Chinese Communist methods of mass thought control.*

Even if one grants that physical torture and mysterious "brainwashing" techniques are not now the keynotes of Chinese thought control, as they are in the inflamed imagination of many Americans, the pervasiveness and skill of the Chinese techniques and their total disregard of the individual's right to critical, independent thinking are horrible enough.[10] So is the possibility that these techniques may spread to other countries.

7. *Not recognizing the ruthlessness of the Viet Cong and the helplessness of our militantly anti-Communist friends if the Communists win a complete victory.*

If anything has been demonstrated in the course of the long struggle, it is that cruelty and atrocities have occurred on a large scale on both sides. The Vietnamese value system, which is perhaps not very different from that of many other developing countries, and the special bitterness engendered by more than twenty years of civil war have caused great brutality on both sides. This is no reason to condone the preventable atrocities on our side, and it is one of the most powerful reasons for ending the war as soon as possible. At the same time, it is a valid reason to regard a coalition government as not feasible, and a strong argument for preserving at least some large areas in which our friends can be safe.

8. *Not recognizing that anti-war protests and demonstrations in this country are eagerly seized by the Communists to sustain hopes of victory that impede their acceptance of a compromise.*

There are good reasons why opponents of our involvement should speak out.[11] It can be argued that if dissenters do not speak freely, at such a time of danger as this, they would risk losing precisely what we are supposedly fighting for. Nevertheless, candor should compel non-militants to acknowledge that all public dissent tends to increase the unrealistic hopes of the Communists and probably in that respect tends to prolong the war.

9. *Not recognizing the genuine anti-Communism of many—probably most—of the people of South Vietnam.*

9 White, 1965, pp. 249–58.
10 Lifton, 1961, pp. 38–64.
11 Fulbright, 1966, pp. 29–103.

While the great majority of Americans probably misperceive in the opposite way, some opponents of our involvement are too ready to equate anti-government sentiment with pro-Communist or pro-Viet Cong sentiment. They probably underestimate the large proportion of South Vietnamese who prefer a broadly based, independent government to a Viet Cong-dominated one. Stories of tyranny in the North during the period 1953 to 1956, brought south by hundreds of thousands of refugees, may even have led to exaggerated ideas of how bad things are there.

10. *Assuming that Ho Chi Minh is another Tito.*

Though Ho is an extraordinary and in some ways very attractive figure,[12] there is little doubt that he is a thoroughgoing Communist as well as a nationalist. He has suppressed free thinking as thoroughly as the Chinese Communists,[13] and he has resorted to assassination (or betrayal to the French) of non-Communist nationalists who threw in their lot with him. He carried out the brutal "land reform" that drove the peasants of Nghé-An to rebellion in 1956, and he and his group aspire to control all they can of Southeast Asia whether Communist China backs them or not. Very probably Ho resembles Tito in wanting to remain independent of his powerful Communist neighbor, but this thought should not be as consoling as it often is in American minds. (The North Vietnamese ruling group that would hold power after his death appears to share these goals.)

11. *Not recognizing or not emphasizing the Viet Cong atrocities that more or less balance the cruelties on our side, which have been much more often photographed.*

Our cameramen have access to much that is done by our own troops or by the South Vietnamese; they have little access to what is done by the Viet Cong. Most Americans know about the teacher and the health worker murdered in their beds or stabbed in the back on a lonely path, and many Americans have a psychological need to dwell on the cruelties of the enemy rather than on our own. But some who oppose American involvement have the opposite psychological need, and the one-sidedness of our news stories and photos—the occasional vivid reminders of the village deliberately burned, the woman weeping over her wounded child, or the roughly handled Viet

[12] Fall, 1964b, pp. 81–103, especially p. 82.
[13] Honey, 1962.

Cong prisoner, and no corresponding pictures of the knife in the health worker's back—has made it easy for many Americans to react more strongly against the brutalities on our own side.

12. *Failing to give full credit to the Administration's desire for peace.*

In some Americans suspicion of the motives of the present Administration is very marked. We have seen that the suspicion is still greater among a great many onlookers abroad. Yet a fair-minded American or onlooker must grant that the country's leaders, like the great majority of Americans, became involved in Vietnam with extreme reluctance, hating the thought of another Korea and of getting bogged down in a land war in Asia. They genuinely wanted the people of Vietnam to choose their own form of government—though with the proviso that it must not be a Communist government—and stepped up American involvement only because they regarded the war as a clear case of aggression that we had to resist.

*   *   *   *

It would be easy to show the existence, in some American non-militants, of all six classical forms of conflict-perception described in earlier chapters. Many of them have a diabolical enemy-image including—perhaps on a par with the Communists—the military government in Saigon and American escalators such as Barry Goldwater and Ronald Reagan. Many have a virile self-image that takes the form of pride in their courage in going against the majority and daring to speak out for sanity in a country that, as they see it, has gone mad. Their moral self-image is often an image of themselves helping to save the world from nuclear war. They may indulge in selective inattention in any of the twelve ways we have just described. They often lack empathy with President Johnson. And if in the past they have failed to see that they have been outnumbered by the escalators, whose public pressure on President Johnson has been much greater than that brought by the non-militants, they have been indulging in a civilian analogue of military overconfidence.

Chapter 6

THE CONFLICT AS SEEN BY
MILITANT AMERICANS: COMMUNIST AGGRESSION

Reality Worlds of the Reclaimers and Escalators

Two central themes, common to both the reclaimers and the escalators, are that the North Vietnamese Communists have committed unequivocal aggression against their South Vietnamese neighbor, and that we must resist their aggression in order to avoid the tragic blunder of appeasement, and to deter further Communist aggression.

Probably these two themes, Communist aggression and anti-appeasement (which assumes Communist aggression) are more prominent than any others in the public statements of our leaders of both parties. President Johnson has said: "The first reality is that North Vietnam has attacked the independent nation of South Vietnam. Its object is total conquest. . . . Let no one think for a moment that retreat from Vietnam would bring an end to the conflict. The battle would be renewed in one country and then another. The central lesson of our time is that the appetite of aggression is never satisfied."[1] Secretary McNamara has said: "The prime aggressor is North Vietnam."[2] Secretary Rusk has said: "What we are seeking to achieve in South Vietnam is part of a process that has continued for a long time—a process of preventing the expansion and extension of Communist domination by the use of force against the weaker nations on the perimeter of Communist power."[3] Richard Nixon emphasizes the analogy of Hitler and Munich: "To negotiate with the enemy before we have driven him out of the South would be like negotiating with Hitler before the German armies had been driven

---

[1] Johnson, in Raskin and Fall, eds., 1965, pp. 344–45.
[2] McNamara, in Raskin and Fall, eds., 1964, p. 196.
[3] Rusk, 1966, p. A10.

from France. . . . The Communists claim it is a civil war. Actually it is naked aggression on the part of North Vietnam."[4]

Often the militant American feels he has a ready, convincing answer to every argument raised against either of these two central themes. He may ask: Can you deny that North Vietnam has sent troops and weapons to the South? Can you deny that the Viet Cong is essentially an arm of the North Vietnamese government? Can you deny that war by assassination in the villages is aggression, in principle, as much as is war by invasion? And can you deny that rewarding aggression is likely to encourage further aggression, as experience after Munich proved? When he finds that his opponent does not try to deny any of these statements, the militant is likely to feel he has established his case.

In his eyes, appeasement would endanger our two most important objectives: preserving peace and preserving freedom in the Free World where it still exists. We are confronted with a brutal fact: Communist aggression. As he sees it, we must determine our response to that brutal fact in the light of an unquestionable lesson of history: that allowing aggression to be rewarded by success only whets the appetite of the aggressor and makes it necessary to fight a bigger war on less favorable terms somewhere else. The domino process, in some form, begins to operate. This means we cannot allow the Communists to end the war with *any* territorial gain. The so-called holding strategy or enclave theory would leave perhaps half or more than half of South Vietnam in Communist hands; that would be appeasement.

To resist aggression and to push back the would-be conqueror to his starting point is not only right and wise from our own standpoint. From the militant's standpoint, it is also our commitment to the people of South Vietnam, whose opportunity to achieve some measure of self-determination in the near future and whose long-run possibility of developing genuine democracy and independence would be ruled out if the Communists took over. We have given them our promise. We cannot welch on it and preserve either self-respect, or the credibility of our promises to anti-Communists in other countries, or the credibility of present and future warnings to the Communists. Honor and interest therefore coincide. It is a matter of honor

[4] Nixon, 1965, pp. 50, 53.

to fulfill our commitment, and interest dictates that our future commitments should be completely credible.

It is at this point that the two militant reality worlds, that of the reclaimers and that of the escalators, begin to diverge. The reclaimers (that is, those who want to do whatever is necessary to reclaim all South Vietnam for an anti-Communist government, but without more escalation in the North) are likely to argue somewhat as follows:

"Important as it is to avoid appeasement, it is also important to avoid nuclear war. We must therefore exercise restraint. We do not want to risk much greater Communist Chinese or Russian involvement, nor do we want to cause avoidable suffering on the part of the innocent common people of North Vietnam. We should therefore refrain from any ground attack on the North, and should confine our bombing to military targets and to what is strictly necessary for our essential defensive enterprise of winning in the South. If we exercise restraint we will not only avoid the catastrophic possibilities of a larger war; we will also greatly reduce the negative impact of the war on other countries. We will not deeply alienate the Russians, nor drive them into the arms of the Chinese, nor deeply split the Western alliance, nor alienate most of the neutralists in the developing countries. This is the sane middle path, the only one that will simultaneously achieve three major goals of our foreign policy: to preserve the freedom of the Free World, to prevent a major war (both directly by avoiding escalation and indirectly by avoiding appeasement), and to preserve reasonably good relations with all the rest of the world."

The reality world of the escalators is much less familiar to non-militant Americans than that of the reclaimers, and in approaching it a conscious effort to listen and to empathize is therefore, for them, much more necessary.

Those who favor escalation are not "war-makers" in their own eyes. On the conscious level, at least, most of them feel that their desire for peace is as great as anyone's, but that they care more about freedom than some of the appeasers do, have more courage, and, above all, have a more realistic view of the brutal realities of the present situation. Even the "reclaimers," as seen by the escalators, are not fully realistic. Their own objective, as they see it, is exactly the same as that of the reclaimers: to win a decisive victory in the South. Neither has any desire to attack the North for the sake of attacking; both regard any operations in the North as strictly a means to an end, the end being the defensive one of decisively driving out the Communist aggressors in South Vietnam. As the escalators see it, the war in the South has bogged down and become an interminable, indecisive stalemate. A decisive victory in the South that would end the loss of American and Vietnamese lives, preserve South Vietnam's freedom and teach Communists all over the world to stay where they belong is simply not possible unless we have the courage and realism to strike at the heart of the beast, in Hanoi. That can be done—with some danger, but with no great danger—and it would quickly end the war. Let's get it over with. If we're going to fight, let's fight to win.

An impressive, clearly reasoned case along this line has been presented by the *New York Times* military specialist, Hanson Baldwin.[5] Like the great majority of his countrymen, but even more intensely, he rejects a pull-out. "Given the pledges of three Presidents, and the political, psychological, and military catastrophe that would result from such a surrender [pulling out], this course is unthinkable, even to most opponents of the war. Such a course would mean not only that the United States had decided to abdicate as a great power, not only that it was dropping the global struggle to contain Communism, not only that it reneged on its pledged word, but that it conceded complete defeat and was reconciled to withdrawal from Asia and the Western Pacific."[6] He then argues that we should both increase our forces considerably beyond their present level and "intensify the bombing and interdiction of North Vietnam and Laos (while at the same time holding open the prospect of an *acceptable* negotiated peace)." Any course of action short of this "would mean indefinite stalemate—deferred defeat, defeat on the instalment plan."

Baldwin acknowledges the possibility of Chinese Communist intervention but regards it as minimal for a number of reasons: the logistic difficulties of Chinese troops fighting in Vietnam, the reluctance of the North Vietnamese to permit it, the vulnerability of China to "devastating attack" by our air power. Similarly, he sees Russian intervention as only a remote possibility. "Would Russia risk her developed economy for the sake of Ho Chi Minh? And is

5 Baldwin, 1966.
6 Baldwin, 1966, p. 79.

Russia, at dagger's points with Peking, likely to invoke nuclear arms in a war, to her, remote in space and interest? The idea is preposterous. We scare ourselves with shadows."[7]

Controversial Implicit Assumptions

Like many other reality-worlds, that of the typical American militant contains some important assumptions that are taken so completely for granted that they are seldom put into words. To him they seem so obvious, so self-evident, that there is no need to discuss or even mention them. They are not "unconscious"; if challenged, they leap into the full light of consciousness and are vigorously defended. But as a rule they are unchallenged, and remain implicit.

A curious thing about these implicit assumptions, as a general human phenomenon, is that actually they are often controversial. Members of a conflicting group may actually regard the opposite assumptions as self-evident, and fail to argue for them on that account. It is quite possible, therefore, for two conflicting groups to "talk past each other," each defending itself and denouncing the other on the basis of assumptions that seem self-evident to it, while to the other side the same assumptions seem too fantastic to be taken seriously. In such a case, conflict-resolution is impossible until each side at least recognizes its own implicit assumptions, makes them explicit, and treats them as a legitimate subject of discussion. (For further discussion of implicit assumptions, see Kelman[8] and Brown.[9])

In Chapter 3 the "mirror-image" phenomenon has been described at some length. On the level of public, verbal discussion and propaganda, each side calls the other an aggressor, accuses it of various other crimes, asserts its own peacefulness, speaks of "the people" as being obviously with it, asserts its own manhood and courage, vows to drive out the aggressors no matter how long it takes or how much sacrifice it involves, etc. What now needs to be brought out is that the implicit assumptions on each side also tend to be mirror-images of those on the opposite side. Specifically:

[7] *Ibid.,* p. 82.
[8] Kelman, 1965, pp. 602–5.
[9] Brown, 1965, pp. 596–97, 724.

Communist	Militant American
The land that the enemy (American imperialism and its lackeys) have taken is obviously not theirs. It is ours (the Vietnamese people's).	The land that the enemy (the Communists) have taken is obviously not theirs. It belongs to our allies (the non-Communists in South Vietnam).
To be a Man obviously means to drive out completely those who invade one's own land, regardless of the cost.	To be a Man obviously means to drive out completely those who invade one's own land, regardless of the cost.
The idea that we (North Vietnamese Communists) are on *their* land is fantastic.	The idea that we (Americans) are on *their* land is fantastic.

No one of these assumptions appears in anything very close to this form in the quotations from Communists in Chapter 3 or in the quotations from militant Americans above. But it will be noted that a denial of all three would thoroughly undercut the case presented explicitly by either side. Suppose for instance that Americans were to grant that South Vietnam "belonged to" the Communists in the same sense in which North Vietnam does; suppose we felt that *even if* "invaders" were on South Vietnamese territory our manhood in no way required us to drive them out; and suppose we were to grant that we Americans were trespassers on Vietnamese soil in the first place, starting in 1950 or in 1954. Our case would not wholly disappear, perhaps, but a great deal of the psychological force that now supports it would dissolve.

The rest of this chapter will attempt to make some progress in separating the kernels of truth from the husks of misperception in these three implicit assumptions in the minds of militant Americans as well as in their explicit arguments.

Overlap and Conflict of Territorial Self-Images

Students of animal behavior have often remarked on how quickly an animal will spring to the defense of a piece of territory with which he has identified himself and which he perceives to be invaded by outsiders.[10] "Territoriality" is a major basis of animal fighting.

[10] McNeil, 1965, p. 17; Ardrey, 1963, pp. 33–58; Collias, 1944; Carpenter, 1934; Lorenz, 1952, 1966.

Similarly, history is full of examples of human warfare originating from the fact that more than one human group has identified itself with the same patch of land. Bosnia and other Yugoslav territory under Austrian rule, plus Serbia herself when Austria claimed a right to punish her, constituted the initial focus of World War I. The Polish Corridor, claimed by both Poland and Germany, and Danzig, an internationalized German city, were the initial focus of World War II. Both Germans and Czechs identified with the Sudetenland; Alsace-Lorraine long poisoned the relationship between France and Germany; Israelis and Arabs claim Israel; Pakistanis and Indians claim Kashmir; French and Algerians identified with Algeria (some striking quotations from French writers suggest that for them Algeria was almost a part of their own body); French and Indochinese claimed Indochina; Communist China and "the Free World" identify with Taiwan (both Communist and Nationalist Chinese treat it as self-evident that Taiwan is an integral part of China, though most of the Taiwanese feel differently). Areas along the Sino-Indian border have caused fighting and great bitterness on both sides, each side feeling that its own land had been infringed upon. Egypt claims the Strait of Tiran while others call it international. With the growth of nationalism during the past century, irredentism in scores of places has become a potent source of conflict.

It is somewhat surprising that psychologists have paid so little attention to the territorial self-images of human groups, when these bulk so large in both animal behavior and human history. Although there have been studies of the factors determining national identification,[11] they have not stressed this aspect of the problem. A study is needed of two distinct psychological processes: the process by which a human group comes to identify firmly with a given piece of land and to assume implicitly that it is "our" land, and the process by which strong emotions, some of which are probably unconscious, become mobilized when the territorial self-image is impinged upon by "outsiders."

The way in which feelings about manhood and virility become an integral part of the territorial self-image would be particularly interesting. Presumably, such feelings enter into both phases. In the first phase, the strength or potency of the national self-image is felt to be enhanced by expanding it into all territories actually subject to dis-

[11] Karl Deutsch, 1953; Katz, 1965; Doob, 1966.

pute and ambiguity. India, for instance, feels that its manhood would be diminished if it weakly gave up its claim to all Kashmir. There is pain at the thought of accepting a diminished image of one's own nation on the map, and map makers push their own nation's claims to the limit of what is plausible. In the second phase, once a given territorial image has become thoroughly identified with the national self, it is almost as if the territorial image becomes an image of the nation's physical body. Infringements upon it are reacted to as an individual might react to violations of his own body. The nation's territorial self-image becomes its body-image. The presence on one's "own" land of the "outsiders" who have conflicting claims to it is then perceived as obvious aggression, a challenge to one's manhood, requiring even the risks and costs of war in order to drive them out.

Although this emphasizes the importance of land, it should be noted that it is not an economic interpretation of war in the usual sense. According to this hypothesis, it is not the economic, or even the military, significance of the land, rationally considered, that matters. What matters is its symbolic importance as part of the national body-image. What counts emotionally in this context is not prosperity or even national power—there may be very little desire for power beyond the nation's own borders, as the nation itself conceives those borders—but national integrity and self-respect, symbolized by driving all invaders out of "our" territory.

The way this applies to the North Vietnamese is similar to the various examples above. They see South Vietnam as part of their national body, and our presence there as self-evidently a violation of it, and a challenge to their manhood. We have stepped over the boundary of their land with guns in our hands.

The way this applies to American militants is a variation on the usual pattern, since Americans do not regard South Vietnam as American land at all. We mean it when we say we have no territorial ambitions there. We see ourselves as defending the right of a small, weak nation to its own land and its own integrity. But it can be argued that we nevertheless have identified with the soil of South Vietnam. Since 1945, we have seen ourselves as the champion of the entire Free World in its attempt to defend itself against Communist aggression; in a sense, therefore, our national body-image has expanded until it has become co-extensive with our conception of the Free World itself, visualized as having a definite outer boundary that we feel we must defend at all costs, much as a nation feels it must defend its own boundary. In the eyes of American militants, that boundary in Vietnam is obviously the 17th Parallel.

Those who regard this boundary as part of the natural order of things may forget (or perhaps they have never learned) certain historical facts that are psychologically important enough to call for review at this point: The great majority of the Vietnamese were elated by what they thought was independence under Ho Chi Minh's leadership immediately after World War II. With much trickery and bloodshed, the French tried to reimpose Western, white rule upon Vietnam. Our own form of Western, white influence (which we have never regarded as "rule" but which a great many Vietnamese naturally assimilated to their perception of French trickery, French warmaking, and French rule) began to be exerted in 1950, when we began giving major financial help to the French, and became predominant after we contributed to setting up Diem's regime. During Diem's later years, while we still supported him, his regime became quite generally hated. The Catholics, of whom he was one and who were as a rule the most militant anti-Communists, were widely regarded by non-Catholics as semi-foreign and sometimes as the stooges of foreigners. Most of the present military leaders are tainted by association with the French during the period of the long war for independence from France, while Ho Chi Minh is the chief symbol of that struggle and of its final victory. The Communists' victory in 1954 gave them (and almost everyone else) the expectation that the whole country would in 1956 revert to the Communist government it had in 1945. The North Vietnamese made peace—giving up at the conference table what they could then have won rather easily on the battlefield—on the basis of what they took to be a general agreement, to be enforced by the French, that all-Vietnamese elections would be held in 1956;[12] chiefly because of actions by Diem and his American backers, this expectation was never fulfilled. This must have appeared to the Communists as a confession by Diem that the people would not support him.

All of this makes psychologically interesting the apparent assumption of a great many American militants that South Vietnam is self-evidently "our" (the Free World's) territory, that North Vietnamese Communists who cross the line as we have defined it are self-evidently invading "another country" rather than, as they claim, try-

[12] Devillers, 1962, pp. 211–12.

ing to "liberate" their countrymen from foreign rule, and that to regard our presence in Vietnam (from 1950 to the present) as an infringement on Vietnamese soil is fantastic.

Among the militants who care greatly about peace—and there are many such—an additional factor clearly has psychological importance: Many have hoped that peace between East and West might be preserved by an increasing tacit acceptance, on both sides, of the existing boundary line between the two worlds. Irrational as it may be at certain points (especially where it cuts a nation in two) it is the only clear line we have had. We respected it when the Hungarian uprising gave us a moral right to intervene on behalf of a people most of whom seemed to be greatly distressed and clearly hostile to Soviet rule. We cared more about peace, then, than about extending "our" territory (the Free World) or liberating a people who wanted to be liberated. In Korea we defended the line, and since then many of us have thought of "holding the line" as one of the two essential ingredients in keeping the equilibrium between East and West, the other essential ingredient being that our military power should at least equal that of the Communists. In 1954 we said to ourselves, in effect: Now the boundary line between the two worlds, as far as Vietnam is concerned, is the 17th Parallel; it has been divided as Korea was, and our job as keepers of the peace is to hold that line as we held the line in Korea.

In other words, we identified "ourselves" (the Free World) with South Vietnam, defined as a separate, non-Communist country. Very few of us were clearly aware, at that time, of the historical facts and of the psychological situation in Vietnam that made this a highly questionable identification. Partly because of the seeming analogy with Korea it became very firm in our minds before we were given any strong reason to challenge it. Many of us have used it ever since then as a fixed image and frame of reference for deciding who is "the aggressor," without challenging it at all.

At the same time, we have kept another standard for judging what is the legitimate government of a given country: the principle of national self-determination. That principle is still very much alive, as is shown by our present commitment to let the people of South Vietnam determine their own destiny. If this means that a country on our side of the East-West boundary line can freely "go Communist" if it wants to, then we have two criteria, one geographical and one psychological, that are capable of clashing. If and when they clash we may be forced to choose between them, instead of continuing to assume implicitly that it is always possible to retain both.

Four Meanings of "Aggression"

Since the assumption of Communist aggression is central in the reality-world of the typical American militant, while the assumption that there has been no clear, one-sided aggression is central in that of the typical non-militant, our most important question of "misperception" is: Which side is more nearly right? Has there been clear, one-sided Communist aggression or not? The answer depends partly on what we mean by "aggression."

Like many other intractable arguments in human affairs, this one has a semantic aspect that has to be grappled with before the relevant empirical questions can be asked in a clear, answerable way. About two central facts there is little disagreement: North Vietnamese troops and weapons have unquestionably been on South Vietnamese soil at least since 1960, and the general fact of control of the Viet Cong by the North Vietnamese Communists is also unquestioned (though there has been a good deal of doubt in the minds of Georges Chaffard, Bernard Fall, Sanford Gottlieb, and others as to the absoluteness of Hanoi's control). But as to the words to be used in describing these facts there is much disagreement depending on the definitions used, the criteria applied, and the interpretation given to certain other important facts.

We have just considered one definition that is probably implicit in much of the thinking of American militants: Aggression exists when either side uses force on the other side of the East-West boundary line that *we* regard as clear and well-established. In Vietnam, this is the 17th Parallel. Since there are North Vietnamese fighting south of that line, we assume that North Vietnam must have committed aggression. For convenience, let us call this the *boundary-line* definition of aggression. (Since the Communists think of the shoreline of South Vietnam as their boundary, they apply the boundary-line definition quite differently. Our landing troops on their shore may be to them an act of aggression.)

But at least three other definitions are possible, and perhaps all of them have been implicit in militant American thinking:

One is that aggression exists when any government uses force on a neighboring territory against the government of that territory. Since North Vietnam has quite clearly used force on the territory of South Vietnam against the present government of South Vietnam, by this definition it has clearly committed aggression. This can be called the *force-against-government* definition. (In their eyes, our bombing the North is aggression by the same definition.)

Another is that aggression exists when any government uses force on a neighbor's territory against the people of that territory (or the majority of the people, or the majority of those people who take sides). It can be called the *force-against-people* definition. Since the question of whether North Vietnam has done this is controversial and ambiguous (see Chapter 2), the question of whether North Vietnam has committed aggression by this definition is also controversial and ambiguous. One thing is clear, however: They do not think they have. They believe most of the people in the South are on their side. By this definition, also, they undoubtedly believe that America has committed aggression on a very large scale, since they believe America has been using force on the territory of South Vietnam against the people of South Vietnam since 1950.

Finally, one could say that if two governments are both using force on the territory of a third government, the one that first began to use force is the aggressor. This can be called the *first-use-of-force* definition.

According to a typical American militant's view of the facts, the first to intervene with force in South Vietnam was North Vietnam, because it either ordered or permitted the Viet Cong to start its campaign of assassination in 1957. North Vietnam officially declared war against the South Vietnamese government in 1960, and it has been intervening more and more openly, on a larger and larger scale, since then. Meanwhile, according to this view of the facts, America did not use actual force on any great scale until early 1965.

However, the Communists have a radically different picture of who used violence first. As they see it, violence was first used against the Vietnamese by white men from overseas in the late nineteenth century when France first conquered the country. It was used again when France tried to reconquer the country (with much American help after 1950) in the war of 1946–54. As they see it, force has been used by Americans ever since 1954 in the form of massive economic and military aid which Diem turned against "the people" in a brutal witch hunt that precipitated the militant reaction of the Viet

Cong in 1957. By the first-use-of-force definition, then, it would be fair to say that the question of who is the aggressor is at least controversial.

These differing interpretations illustrate the general type of irrationality that Osgood has called "psycho-logic" or "the Neanderthal mentality."[13] In this type of thinking, exactly the same behavior is interpreted as moral if *we* do it (whoever the *we* may be) but as immoral and aggressive if *they* do it (whoever the *they*—the enemy—may be).

Vietnam provides a prime example. The physical fact is that North Vietnamese and American troops are both fighting on South Vietnamese soil, but the interpretations put on that fact are radically different. The Communist interprets the presence of American troops as self-evidently aggressive and the presence of his own as moral, legitimate self-defense. The militant American interprets the presence of North Vietnamese troops as self-evidently aggressive and the presence of his own as moral, legitimate defense of the Free World.

The black-and-white picture produced by psycho-logic is, however, the end result of a rather complex psychological process. At the moment we are concerned only with the semantic aspect of it. That semantic aspect is important as a necessary preliminary to a discussion of the assumptions about reality that are relevant to the central problem of how perceptions of aggression can be so radically different. The definitions of aggression that are at least implicit in a given person's mind constitute necessary connecting links, psychologically as well as logically, between his beliefs about the facts and his judgment about who the aggressor is.

In addition, the semantic differences between the Communists and the militant Americans may supply a part (though probably only a minor part) of the answer to the question of why their reality-worlds are so different, each feeling so sure that the other is the aggressor. To some extent the choice of definition may itself reflect the black-and-white picture, and contribute to maintaining it. A militant American, for instance, can buttress his interpretation that the North Vietnamese Communists are the aggressors by focusing on that one definition of aggression according to which they are most clearly aggressors: the "force-against-government" defini-

[13] Osgood, 1962, pp. 18–36.

tion. Given the unchallenged fact that North Vietnamese troops are opposing the South Vietnamese government on land it claims as its own, the implicit adoption of this definition necessarily leads to the unconsciously desired conclusion—that the North Vietnamese are aggressors. On the other hand, since the North Vietnamese evidently think most of the people in the South are against America and its lackeys in Saigon, they can achieve the psychologically necessary black-and-white picture most easily by implicitly adopting the force-against-people definition.

The Assumption of Communist Aggression

We are now in a better position to tackle the central, decisive issue: *Are* the Vietnamese Communists aggressors, or not? Is this a misperception in the minds of American militants, or not?

One thing seems certain: The answer is not self-evident. Those who have treated it as such stand convicted of self-evident superficiality, ignorance of essential historical facts, and self-protective inattention. Any candid, open-minded approach, with even minimal attention to the most important historical facts, would immediately disclose that it is a complex issue, full of ambiguities and capable of being honestly interpreted in radically different ways. Those who see one answer as self-evident are exhibiting a rather extreme degree of intolerance of ambiguity, inability to suspend judgment, and selective inattention to the evidence that does not fit their preconceptions.

A statement by Richard Nixon provides an example of such intolerance of ambiguity: "This goes to the heart of what the Vietnam war is all about. The Communists claim it is a civil war. Actually it is naked aggression on the part of North Vietnam."[14] Mr. Nixon does not examine the rather elementary logical possibility that it might be both—both a civil war and naked aggression. He also refrains from discussing the definition of aggression according to which the intervention of North Vietnam (which is unquestioned) must be called naked aggression while that of the United States (which is also unquestioned, which began sooner and which has been on a larger scale) is regarded as a moral imperative. As a

[14] Nixon, 1965, p. 53.

matter of fact, the evidence covered in Chapter 2 would seem to make plain that it is a civil war, whatever else it may be in addition. If our definition of a civil war is a conflict in which the *primary* motivating forces come from within a specified area rather than from outside, then there can be little doubt that it is a civil war.[15]

Another thing seems certain or almost certain: As we have seen (Chapter 3), the Communists do not regard themselves as aggressors. Their picture of the situation is in this respect close to a mirror-image of that of the militant Americans, since all the evidence suggests that they feel as sure of their innocence as the militant American is of ours, and as sure of our aggression as the militant American is of theirs. For many practical purposes, such as predicting the response of the North Vietnamese to bombing or to a ground-force attack by us, this is what matters most.

Perhaps still another thing can be pinned down as definite: In the eyes of most of the rest of the world, the answer to the question of who is the aggressor is not self-evident (Chapter 4). The rest of the world recognizes ambiguity where many Americans do not. If anything, those who leap to the conclusion that we are now playing an imperialist role like that of the French, and that this war is an aggressive "colonial war" of white against non-white, probably outnumber considerably those who assume, as militant Americans do, that it is a clear case of Communist aggression. There are some, especially in small neighbors of Communist China (South Korea, Taiwan, Thailand, Malaya, the Philippines, Australia, New Zealand), whose overriding preoccupation is a fear of conquest by Communist China, and who see the war as militant Americans do, but they are the exceptions. The majority in most of the rest of the world either see the situation as ambiguous, with blame often attached equally to Communist China and to the United States, or as a clear case of "a colonial war" waged by America.

For many practical purposes this too is a thing we Americans need to know. For example, if we are wondering whether most of the world would regard us as "appeasers" in case we settled for a holding operation, the answer is clear: They would not. Not assuming as we do that the Communists are obvious aggressors, they would see a compromise peace not as a dishonorable temporizing

[15] For evidence of consensus of experts on this point, see Schlesinger, 1967, p. 50.

with aggression but as a statesmanlike ending, on more or less equal terms, of a war that has threatened to spread and engulf the whole world. There is little doubt that a compromise peace would be met by most of the politically conscious people in the world not with scorn for our weakness, but with respect for our reasonableness, and with an enormous sigh of relief.

This is relevant also to the way we should talk about the issue in discussing it with people in other countries. If in talking with them we take the line that militants habitually take in the United States, that the central issue is whether we have the courage to resist a clear case of Communist aggression, they are not likely to respect our courage; they are likely, rather, to question our candor or our intelligence. In their eyes, any reference to Communist aggression is merely begging the essential question: Which side is actually the aggressor? If we want to win their respect we will meet that issue head-on and discuss it candidly rather than seeming to ignore or evade it.

The insistent question remains: Apart from what various people think, which side is *really* the aggressor? After the ambiguities are clarified and the evidence weighed, what is the answer? Each reader will answer that question for himself—with, one may hope, a clear choice of some definition or definitions of the word "aggression," and with due attention to the most relevant historical facts.

There is a deeper semantic question that must finally be considered: Is there any real meaning or practical importance in the question of which side is "really" the aggressor, when obviously each side is utterly convinced that it is not and the other side is? Aren't both sides innocent, in that they are not guilty of conscious wrongdoing but only, at worst, of misperception? Aren't both sides guilty of gross misperception in failing to see that the other side, in its own eyes, is fighting a defensive war? The question itself, "Which side is the aggressor?," carries with it the controversial implicit assumption that one side must be "the aggressor," with all that that term implies of deliberate wrongdoing and of obligatory resistance to "aggression" in order to avoid appeasement and keep the peace of the world. If the North Vietnamese see themselves—however mistakenly—as carrying on a desperate struggle to defend their homeland against American aggression, are we obligated to "resist" them as we were obligated to resist Hitler? The term "the aggressor" carries with it a cloud of historical associations and moral imperatives, among which the Munich analogy and the feeling of obligation to "resist" aggression are central. If the situation is actually basically different from Munich, don't we beg the question when in our own thinking we seriously use the term "the aggressor" at all?

In the light of these considerations, how can we answer now the central question of this chapter: Is the major assumption of American militants—the assumption that the Communists have committed aggression—a misperception or not?

One answer would be: It is a misperception in so far as they assume Communist aggression to be self-evident when it is not. In glossing over—not resolving but simply glossing over—all the complexities and ambiguities, the typical American militant is indulging in an extreme form of selective inattention and is basically misperceiving the issue. It is a misperception also in so far as he fails to realize how completely the North Vietnamese Communists regard themselves as innocent and regard us as the aggressor. Finally, and most basically, it is a misperception in that it assumes the existence of an aggressor in the Munich sense of that word when, psychologically, the contrast with Munich is very great. In this ambiguous, in-betweenish war there is not necessarily a full-blown devil anywhere.

The Assumption of American Non-Aggression

To almost any American the most emotionally unacceptable thought about Vietnam is probably the thought that we ourselves might have in some way committed aggression. Yet, as every psychoanalyst knows, the most unthinkable thought may be precisely the one that most needs to be brought up into the sunlight and calmly, rationally examined if it and related problems are to be realistically understood and grappled with. An intensely unthinkable thought not only sinks below the level of clear consciousness itself; it tends to pull down with it into murky obscurity, in varying degrees, a whole network of related thoughts. There is partial, peripheral repression of, or selective inattention to, a number of ideas that are merely associated with a more deeply repressed idea.

In the case of Vietnam, if the most unthinkable thought is that we might have committed aggression, then we would be wise to try to react to the question not with moral indignation against those who ask it—which is a frequent indication of psychological vulnerability and one of the more immature responses to a psychological threat —but with a tough-minded willingness to consider the question factually, on its merits, letting the chips fall where they may.

At this key point in the analysis, it will be useful to bring together into a coherent pattern all of the evidence that seems most relevant, including a number of historical facts that have already been considered in other contexts. The most important facts stressed by those who think the United States has been aggressive (without implying that the United States has been thinking of its own behavior in those terms) can be summarized as follows:

(1) Our large-scale contribution of money and weapons to the French, starting in 1950, in a war against the Viet Minh, which was at that time rather clearly supported by a majority of the Vietnamese people.[16] To be sure, 1950–51 was a time of crisis. The Communists had just won in China and the Korean war was starting; it looked as if the Communists might be about to take over all of the Far East. But the acute crisis passed and our help to the French invaders—that word is not too harsh—continued.

(2) Our contributing role in installing Diem in 1954, and our decisive role in sustaining him from then on.[17] He was a promising choice at that time, but we alien, intruding Americans were playing a role that perhaps should have acutely embarrassed us. Some argue that we should have backed away from it as soon as possible.

(3) Our apparent approval of Diem's unwillingness to accept all-Vietnamese elections in 1956, or at any later time. To the Communists this must have seemed a frank abandonment of our traditional American commitment to national self-determination. To them it must have seemed that the U.S. and Diem had said to all Vietnamese: You cannot be allowed to unify your country and achieve full independence by peaceful, democratic means. If you want to do it, you'll have to do it by force.

The question here, it should be noted, is not whether we and Diem "violated the Geneva Agreements." Since neither he nor we signed those agreements there is, at least technically speaking, no question of violation. The question is rather whether we can without self-

---

[16] The French apparently managed to believe, at least for a few years, that they were not fighting against a majority. There are several parallels between their attitudes then and ours now.

[17] Buttinger, 1967a, pp. 845–93, 917–1010.

deception reconcile our apparent approval of his decision with our own basic commitment to national self-determination.

It is true that North Vietnam probably would not have permitted genuinely free elections within its own borders, but this does not explain the American failure to press publicly for internationally supervised elections, and to throw onto the Communists the onus of obstructing them.[18] Nor does it explain our lack of interest in internationally supervised elections in South Vietnam alone if North Vietnam refused to accept the necessary degree of supervision.

(4) Our failure to challenge publicly or to prevent effectively Diem's great witch hunt against all who opposed him. The amount of help and support we gave Diem presumably provided some leverage. Perhaps one lesson to be drawn from this whole experience (and from the American experience with Chiang Kai-shek) is that *if* the U.S. decides to play an interventionist role in a given country, it should frankly accept the implications of that role and insist, as a minimum, that our help is not used to support a tyrannical use of force against a majority of the politically conscious people.

(5) The role that many observers think we have played behind the scenes in determining the nature of post-Diem governments, especially in deposing Quat, who had been leaning toward neutralism.

(6) Our unwillingness, from 1954 until perhaps the spring of 1966, to press for immediate, scheduled steps toward a genuinely representative national government. Not until the Buddhist-led riots in the spring of 1966 did the wheels start turning toward a constitutional convention, and the approach to democracy was very limited even then. The exclusion of neutralist candidates for office from the 1967 election campaign implied also that many reform-minded candidates were shut out. The Constituent Assembly elected in 1966 still represented mainly the entrenched land-owning oligarchy, while some 4000 Buddhist activists, most of whom were not Communists, remained in jail.[19]

Whether any or all of these things should be called aggression depends partly on how we define aggression. No one of them could be called aggression by the force-against-government definition since we have not at any time clearly opposed by force a *de facto* government in South Vietnam. But in view of the clear, strong American

[18] Devillers, 1962, p. 219.
[19] Buttinger, 1967b.

tradition of support for democracy and national self-determination it is doubtful that many Americans would consciously adopt the force-against-government definition when it conflicts with any of the other definitions, and by each of the other definitions the hypothesis that America has committed aggression is at least arguable. By the force-against-people definition each of the actions listed above might be described as aggressive. By the first-use-of-force definition those that occurred before 1957 might be so described. And by the boundary-line definition it is arguable that the natural boundary, at least after 1945, was the boundary of Vietnam itself. If the boundary line is so defined, we stepped over the boundary of Vietnam with a gun, in effect, when in 1950 we began giving military aid to the French invaders.

As a case in point let us consider somewhat more carefully what is perhaps the strongest single argument of those who think America has been aggressive: our apparent approval of Diem's unwillingness to accept all-Vietnamese election in 1956. It is essential to see this as fully as possible in its historical context, including the artificiality and impermanence of the 17th-Parallel boundary as perceived by both sides at that time.[20] We often forget the key fact that the Communist-led majority of the Vietnamese really won their war for independence in 1954. The battle of Dienbienphu was decisive. The 17th Parallel therefore does not reflect a military stalemate, as does the 38th Parallel in Korea. With a few more months of fighting the Viet Minh, supported by a majority of the people, presumably could have had a total military victory.[21] They relinquished it, probably not with very much trust that the Geneva Agreements would be carried out, but with the formal assurance of the French (who were still the primary negotiating party on the opposite side, and who showed no intention then of pulling out completely) and of several other powers that the country would be unified in two years. At that time the Communists also had every reason to be confident that if free elections were held they would win. According to Philippe Devillers: "The demarcation line was to be purely provisional; the principle of Vietnamese unity was not questioned, and the idea of partition was officially rejected with

[20] Pike, 1966b, p. 51; Devillers, in Gettleman, ed., 1962, pp. 211–12; Buttinger, 1967a, p. 831.

[21] Pike, 1966b, p. 52; Buttinger, 1967a, pp. 829–30.

indignation by both sides. When military forces were regrouped and administrative divisions laid down, national unity would be restored by free general elections."[22]

Against this background it is understandable that the Communists and also a great many of the non-Communists who had fought with them against the French felt that somehow they had been tricked when in 1956 they were denied the opportunity to achieve peacefully the unity and independence for which they had fought through nine years of heartbreaking war. As they probably saw it, there must have been some sleight-of-hand, with the face of America appearing where the face of France had been, and with both Diem and John Foster Dulles blandly claiming that they were not bound by the decisions made at Geneva. The result was that a full half of the country the Viet Minh had fought to liberate and unify was snatched from it. It must have seemed to Ho Chi Minh and others to be quite out of line with the American claim to represent democracy.

On the opposite side there are a number of arguments: Vietnam was not ready for genuine democracy in any case. Diem's strongman rule was no more repressive than that of the Communists, it is argued; unlike Communist rule, Diem's offered a real possibility of evolution toward true democracy and individual freedom. In Diem we had found a strong, honest, patriotic, indigenous leader whom we could support with some enthusiasm. In his first two years he showed courage and decisiveness, creating order in a country where there had been a danger of almost total social breakdown. The Communists would surely not permit genuine elections in their half of the country anyway, so the possibility of genuine all-Vietnamese elections was a mirage. Over a million Catholics who were in the South would have been persecuted if elections had been held and the Communists won. A number of other countries would be safer from the Communist danger if we supported Diem in holding the line against the Communist North.

Whatever elements of truth there may be in this rather persuasive list of arguments, they have one common characteristic that should not be overlooked: Not one of them really comes to grips with the question of American aggression. Not one of them shows that we were right in regarding the decision as ours to make, or that we

[22] Devillers, in Gettleman, ed., 1962, p. 210.

were not using force against the people when we made the decision to back Diem in rejecting elections. Not one of them answers the arguments based on two of the other three definitions of aggression either. They do not refute the Communist claim that this was a continuation of our "first use of force" which began in 1950, nor the Communist claim that we stepped across the boundary of their country with a gun in 1950 and have been committing aggression by the very fact that we have been staying there, supplying our friends with guns "against the people," ever since. After due attention has been paid to definitions of terms and to relevant historical facts, these Communist claims now seem to constitute an intellectually defensible position. It can be argued legitimately that in 1954 the land of South Vietnam did not belong to us to do with as we liked. It belonged, in the sense of military power, to the ragged but victorious Viet Minh troops, and it belonged, in the sense of moral right as we ourselves have traditionally defined moral right, to the majority of the Vietnamese people. It can be argued that in effect we participated in tricking the troops and denying the majority the right to determine their own destiny; and it can be argued, by three of the four definitions of aggression outlined above, that this was—however unintentionally—aggression.

Since the arguments on both sides are essentially political and historical rather than psychological they can be left at this point for the reader himself to wrestle with. From a psychological standpoint, though, one fact is striking: the selective inattention that Americans have given to the whole question of whether our actions were aggressive. The points on this side of the argument have been rather thoroughly ignored and glossed over in the thinking of the great majority of the American people and probably, to a lesser extent, in the thinking of our decision-making leaders also. At any rate they have seldom if ever been publicly discussed by our leaders in these terms. Like the Austrians in 1914, we as a country have simply never candidly asked ourselves whether what we were doing could be legitimately called aggression. In this massive absence of thought there is strong support for the hypothesis that repression of an intolerable idea has been going on, on a very large scale.

A further psychological hypothesis is that when this most intolerable thought has been pushed down into unconsciousness (or, in our own terms, selectively inattended), it has dragged down with it a closely associated thought: that the Vietnamese Communists firmly *believe* we are aggressors, and firmly believe they are defending their homeland against our aggression. The lack of attention to this further thought, in the minds of most Americans, is perhaps even more remarkable in view of the fact that the evidence in favor of it is so very strong (above, Chapter 2). Whatever the actual rights and wrongs of this complex, ambiguous situation may be, it seems almost certain that the Communist leaders believe themselves to be right, in the very simple terms of foreign invasion and self-defense. But few militant Americans seem to have thought about this; most of them continually give evidence that they have not thought about it when they speak as if it were self-evident that the North Vietnamese are aggressors and have committed aggression by fighting in the South. (A person who believes he is defending his homeland may be tragically deluded, but he cannot be fairly called an aggressor without at least mentioning his delusions.)

Appeasement and the Learning of Aggression

Several aspects of learning theory and research on learning are relevant to the Vietnam conflict.

The well-established psychological principle of *learning by reward* powerfully supports a central proposition of the militants' case, which is that *there is a danger to peace whenever clear aggression is rewarded by success.*

If anything is well established experimentally and accepted now by all schools of learning theory, it is the principle of learning by reward (the law of effect, positive reinforcement, instrumental or operant conditioning). The effects of punishment are much more complex and problematic; the effects of reward are clear.

In fact, even those psychologists who prefer the general approach of Edward Tolman or Kurt Lewin[23] must grant that learning by reward is an extremely common and relatively predictable form of learning. They may interpret it not as reinforcement of a direct connection between situation and response, but as attentive perception leading to establishment of a cognitive connection between a particular path and a particular goal. Lewin might say, for instance, that it was unwise to allow Hitler to perceive intimidation of his neigh-

[23] White, 1943, for example.

bors as the "distinguished path" to further expansion of German power. But Tolman and Lewin, as well as Edward Thorndike, Clark Hull, and B. F. Skinner, would probably agree that if no firm barriers are placed in the path of aggression—if an aggressor can look back on a particular act of aggression as a clear and cheap success, well worth the price he paid for it—he is likely to be encouraged to do the same thing elsewhere, and the prospects of a stable peace are diminished.

There is also abundant evidence that fighting and aggression can be greatly influenced by various kinds of learning. McNeil has summarized much of this evidence.[24] For example: "The malleability of aggressive urges has been demonstrated in a series of experiments devoted to inhibiting or increasing fighting through training. In five days, for example, J. P. Scott[25] converted an inexperienced mouse into a successful fighter by 'fixing' its bouts so that it always emerged the uninjured victor. According to M. W. Kahn[26] this method of training makes mice so assaultive that, contrary to their usual habits, they may attack females and the young. Scott makes the interesting observation that methods quite similar to this are used by boxing managers who carefully match their fighters with opponents they can defeat to prevent them from undergoing a morale-killing beating." It will be noticed that in these examples no extraneous rewards are mentioned. Victory itself is apparently, in this situation, a sufficient reward. Unless counterbalanced by the pain and frustration of defeat, victory alone is enough to keep the fighting behavior going or even increase it. Successful fighting is in this sense self-reinforcing.

In recent history, as well as in the school and the psychological laboratory, the principle seems to be upheld. The leap from individual behavior to national behavior is great, but in this case a good deal of evidence supports the principle on both levels. Chamberlain at Munich thought he had won "peace in our time," but in about six months Hitler marched unopposed into Prague—probably his worst, most unequivocal act of aggression against a non-German people. This too was a cheap and well-rewarded act of aggression. It was therefore not surprising that in another six months he attacked Poland, precipitating World War II. Korea provides a sharp

24 McNeil, 1965, pp. 16–27.
25 Scott, 1958.
26 Kahn, 1951.

contrast. In 1950, North Korea attacked South Korea, as the climax of a period during which Communists seemed to be on the offensive in many parts of the world (Eastern Europe, Berlin, China, Burma, Malaya, Indonesia). The United States, wiser after seeing the results of the appeasement at Munich, used the force that was needed to see to it that aggression in Korea was not rewarded. The results were encouraging. World War III, which was widely feared at the time, did not occur. Though the Communists finished about where they started, they paid a high price in blood and material destruction and got nothing. On balance, they were unequivocally punished. Perhaps we, too, learned a wholesome lesson when we crossed the 38th Parallel and lived to regret it. In any case, the Korean war was followed not by world war but by some fifteen years of comparative peace and equilibrium of power. It is plausible to attribute this largely to the fact that in Korea both sides had fought and neither had been rewarded. In fact, both sides had burned their fingers badly when they crossed the line.

As we have seen, the answer of informed non-militants to the charge that they are appeasers is usually to question that the principle of non-appeasement applies to the case of Vietnam on the ground that the North Vietnamese have not committed aggression comparable to the aggression of Hitler against Czechoslovakia or that of North Korea against South Korea. Since a great deal hinges on the validity of this premise—the appropriateness of the analogy between Vietnam and Munich—it deserves some further thought. Which side is misperceiving, the militants who think there is a clear analogy between Munich and Vietnam, or the non-militants who think there is not?

Our whole discussion of aggression is relevant here. At Munich there was clearly an "aggressor." Hitler was on the rampage. Certainly when he marched into Prague he must have known in the back of his mind that he was aggressing by every definition of the term: He was crossing a boundary line, initiating the use of force, using force against the government of Czechoslovakia, and using force against the Czech people, who were clearly almost unanimously opposed to his take-over of their country. But, as we have seen, only one of these conditions exists in South Vietnam. The only definition of aggression according to which the North Vietnamese are clearly committing Hitler-like aggression is the force-against-government definition: They are clearly using force against the Saigon government on territory it claims as its own. But it is doubtful whether many Americans, if they were consciously making a choice, would choose this as their primary definition of aggression.

George Kennan, author of the term *containment,* has put it in this way: "I think that no episode, perhaps, in modern history has . . . been more misleading than that of the Munich conference. It has given to many people the idea that never must one attempt to make any sort of a political accommodation in any circumstances. This is, of course, a fatally unfortunate conclusion. . . . Hitler was a man who had made up his mind that he was going to conquer Europe by force of arms according to a certain timetable. I have never seen the evidence of anything comparable to that state of mind on the part of our Communist opponents."[27]

As Winston Churchill once said, "Appeasement in itself may be good or bad according to circumstances. . . . Appeasement from strength is magnanimous and noble and might be the surest and perhaps the only path to world peace."[28] In this case Churchill seems to have used the word appeasement in its broader, pre-Munich sense of negotiating and seeking legitimate compromise, rather than its narrower post-Munich sense of rewarding outright aggression by failing to resist it. Nevertheless, since Churchill has become for us a symbol of non-appeasement, his words can serve as a wholesome reminder that there are times when compromise with an enemy is an act of statesmanship rather than a dangerous rewarding of aggression, and that this is particularly likely to be true when one's own strength is greater than the enemy's.

Psychologists probably can agree that allowing clear aggression to be rewarded always tends to reinforce it and to make further aggression more likely. In the case of Vietnam, though, clear aggression has not occurred. We therefore cannot reward it. If unclear aggression has occurred, we ourselves may have committed it, at least as much as the enemy has. Is there a danger, then, that *our* aggression might be rewarded?

Before taking up this unpleasant subject let us look more closely at the conviction of American militants that "the Communists must be taught a lesson." There may be an element of validity in it that

---

[27] Kennan, 1966, p. 28; see Schlesinger, 1967, pp. 96–104.
[28] Quoted by Fulbright, 1966a, p. 103.

is not touched by the above discussion and rejection of the term aggression. Perhaps, if we at least held our own in Vietnam, the Communists *would* be learning that it is dangerous to tangle with the United States.

If we simply pulled out, there would surely be a feeling of victory over the United States in the minds of Communists all over the world. Might not that feeling of victory function psychologically as a reward—and as a basis for anticipation of future reward—that would embolden them to try to seize power elsewhere? Of course they would not say to themselves "our aggression triumphed in Vietnam." They would say rather "the people of Vietnam, under our leadership, threw out the imperialist aggressors." But the effect on their behavior might be somewhat the same. Since they have proved capable of misperceiving almost any situation, defining their own side as that of the people and defining their enemies as imperialist aggressors regardless of the facts, this means that they might be emboldened to attempt seizures of power even in countries where their claim to represent the people is much less valid than it is in Vietnam—in Indonesia, perhaps, Thailand, Malaya, the Philippines, Iraq, or even, someday, in India. In this line of thought the domino theory reappears with a new psychological twist. If the Communists have not committed what they regard as aggression in Vietnam, we cannot validly say, We must teach the Communists everywhere that aggression does not pay. But perhaps we can validly say, The Communists are likely to take fewer risks in the future if we teach them that the imperialist aggressors are utterly diabolical and willing to fight at the drop of a hat. If we fight an all-out war in South Vietnam and win a military victory with or without escalation in the North, Communists everywhere, seeing our action within their frame of reference and in the light of their assumptions, would regard it as a diabolical, flagrantly imperialistic and war-making act. However, they might at the same time acquire greater fear of our strength and of our easily aroused belligerence, and this fear might have a wholesome aspect in that it might deter them from attempting to seize power in other countries where, quite possibly, they would not have a majority on their side even among the politically active minority.

In this respect, then, the principle of learning by reward gives some support to the case for a militant policy of reclaiming or escalating, and a good deal of support to the case for at least a holding strategy that would deny the Communists the satisfaction of a clear-cut victory. (After their twenty years of suffering and sacrifice, it is doubtful that they would regard a military stalemate as a net reward at all.)

We must now return to the thoroughly unpleasant question touched on above: If the United States itself has committed unclear, ambiguous aggression, never recognized as aggression by Americans themselves, is there danger in allowing that kind of aggression to be rewarded by a feeling of clear-cut victory? *Might this reinforce our tendency to do in other countries what we have been doing in Vietnam since 1950?* This is the second major way in which the principle of learning-by-reward is relevant to Vietnam.

If we are honest enough to apply to ourselves the reasoning we have just applied to the Communists, we must regard this as a legitimate question. Learning experiments (Greenspoon, 1955; Verplanck, 1955) have shown that rewards tend to reinforce unclear, inadvertent behavior as well as clearly conscious, fully intentional behavior. If we should win militarily in South Vietnam (perhaps never fully facing up to the question of whether, in doing so, we had lost "the hearts and minds of the people") what learning would occur in American minds? Given the assumptions on which most American militants are operating, wouldn't their perception be that we had been firm and that firmness had paid off? Wouldn't they have a general feeling of success and satisfaction, probably marred by continuing difficulties in South Vietnam (which they could explain away as simply further examples of Communist deviltry), but with a triumphant sense of having taught the Communists a lesson, making both peace and freedom more secure throughout the rest of the world? Wouldn't this reinforce the American tendency to respond to similar troubles in other countries with the same mixture of self-deception and righteous indignation that has been shown in Vietnam?

Some non-militant psychologists, especially Charles Osgood, believe that this potentially disastrous learning process is already far advanced in American minds. As these skeptics see it, we have acted firmly in the past in many situations in which the rights and wrongs were actually ambiguous, as they have been in Vietnam. We have, as a rule, been intolerant of that ambiguity, imposing on the situation our own unilateral black-and-white interpretation and acting accordingly—and we have gotten away with it. We have tended to perceive in our own black-and-white terms not only situations that were actually fairly clear cases of Communist aggression and/or treachery (such as the take-over of Eastern Europe, the Berlin blockade, the Korean war, the intervention in Hungary, and the Cuban missile crisis) but also a number of relatively ambiguous situations such as China, Taiwan, Quemoy, Lebanon, Guatemala, Cuba, and the Dominican Republic. When we responded with unilateral military action or threat of such action our response has usually been rewarded by success. We have, therefore, been acquiring a continually deeper conviction that what we define as firmness is good. It works.

Like Austria after its annexation of Bosnia, we have become increasingly committed to firmness. According to Osgood, the core of what we have been learning is realistic and valid; his GRIT (Graduated and Reciprocated Initiatives in Tension-reduction) proposal—and this is a point some of his critics have overlooked—recognizes a danger in appeasement and insists that clear-cut aggression should be resisted, by force if necessary. But he would add that our learning has been overgeneralized. Like Austria, we have become capable of perceiving aggression by ourselves as firmness. What should have been rewarded is the rather clearly defined stimulus-response connection of seeing clear-cut aggression and responding with firm *resistance*—not counteraggression. But what has been rewarded, in addition to this, is a tendency to perceive trouble anywhere as Communist aggression, to classify it immediately as similar to Hitler's aggression against Czechoslovakia, and to feel that forcible resistance is the only right, realistic, and manly response—with no clear distinction between resistance and counteraggression, and consequently with a tendency to engage in counteraggression. Along with firmness in the situations in which it is appropriate, we have been learning (it can be argued) self-righteousness, self-deception, over-ready moral indignation, intolerance of ambiguity, an expanded territorial self-image, and a virile self-image unduly identified with a quick resort to violence. The adequate stimulus to a firm response has been too generalized, and the firm response itself has also been overgeneralized. The result is sometimes a form of military aggression that occurs with hair-trigger sensitivity even in situations that actually call not for immediate "firmness" (that is, unilateral military action) but for holding such firmness in reserve, while working with all interested nations toward a mutually acceptable compromise.

Learning theory suggests a third question that relates to Vietnam. What *other* learning would the Communists be doing if we fought a war in an ambiguous cause—a cause that they would naturally regard as diabolical if it seemed even ambiguous to many Americans —and if we won? What would they learn in addition to the wholesome lesson that they should not lightly risk another war with the United States by overturning governments in newly developing countries? *Wouldn't they be learning*—that is, getting more firmly ingrained in their minds—*the idea that America really is aggressive,* as Communist propaganda has always said it is, and that they must depend entirely on their own military power in order to be safe? Wouldn't this intensify the arms race and all the vicious circles of mutual suspicion, fear, and hostility?

In other words, the principle of learning-by-reward is a two-edged sword. It strengthens one argument, the danger of appeasement, on the militant side. At the same time, it strengthens two arguments—the danger of reinforcing America's inadvertent aggressiveness and the danger of reinforcing Communist suspicion and hostility—on the non-militant side.

Is there any way of resolving the conflict? Is there any course of action that would simultaneously teach the Communists not to aggress, teach Americans not to aggress (inadvertently), and reverse the vicious spiral that has been carrying both sides closer to nuclear war?

Perhaps there is. As we have seen, the Korean war suggests a clue. At the end of that war no one gained anything; everyone lost something. From the standpoint of learning theory, a more wholesome outcome would be difficult to contrive. The ensuing peace supports that interpretation. Perhaps a similar outcome of the Vietnam war is now at hand if we are wise enough to grasp it: the Lippmann-Kennan-Gavin proposal of a holding strategy. Since the Vietnamese Communists have set their hearts on "driving the imperialist aggressors into the sea," the firm establishment of sizable non-Communist areas would probably be for them an ambiguous, frustrating experience, which they could hardly regard, from the standpoint of rational self-interest, as justifying the enormous price in suffering and death that they have already paid. Since many American militants have set their hearts on a decisive victory, anything less would necessarily frustrate them too. A stalemate or holding operation, then, would probably be moderately punishing to both sides and rewarding to neither. As in the case of Korea, each side would have burned its fingers, and each side might be more careful from then on.

There is one great drawback here, however. This would be merely learning by punishment on both sides; as psychologists know, learning by punishment is a problematic thing, dependent on a number of not too well understood circumstances, while learning by reward is relatively clear and predictable. Is there any other course of action that would reward constructive, peace-maintaining behavior on both sides?

Osgood's GRIT proposal[29] is a systematic attack on this problem. No attempt will be made here to describe it or apply it to the case of Vietnam, as Osgood himself has done.[30] One point, however, can be made: If we Americans are clear about what we regard as good behavior by the enemy, if it actually is good in terms of his welfare and in terms of his reality-world as well as ours, if we communicate our conception to him clearly, and if we see to it that good behavior by him is rewarded as consistently as bad behavior is punished (or simply deprived of reward), we can contribute much to a reversal of the present psychological vicious circle of mutually stimulated suspicion, fear, and belligerence.

[29] Osgood, 1962, pp. 85–134.
[30] Osgood, 1966.

Chapter 7

THE CONFLICT AS SEEN BY
MILITANT AMERICANS: OTHER ASPECTS

The Diabolical Enemy-Image and the Moral Self-Image

The black-and-white picture (that is, the combined diabolical enemy-image and moral self-image) is one of the most inclusive psychological concepts that bears on the Vietnam war. In its most important form—the conviction that the enemy has committed self-evident aggression and that one's own country has done no such thing—it has occupied us throughout the previous chapter. Other elements of the diabolical enemy-image of American militants—imperialism, dictatorship, atrocities, deception—have been touched in Chapter 3. Some other points should now be added.

The typical American conception of the enemy follows the classical pattern of a black-top image. The ordinary Vietnamese peasants are not blamed; we do not feel we are fighting against them, but only against the Viet Cong fanatics who intimidate and oppress them. We feel only sympathy for the poor and the downtrodden in other lands who now for the first time are catching a glimpse of the good life they might be leading.

As President Johnson expresses it: "In Vietnam, Communism seeks to really impose its will by force of arms. But we would be deeply mistaken to think that this was their only weapon. Here, as in other places in the world, they speak to restless people—people rising to shatter the old ways which have imprisoned hope—people fiercely and justly reaching for the material fruits of the tree of modern knowledge. It is this desire, not simply lust for conquest, which moves many of the individual fighting men that we must now, sadly, call the enemy."[1] In the same speech he reiterates the official American thesis that "the South Vietnamese" (not some or most of them, but "the South Vietnamese") are on our side, which is another way of insisting that we are for, not against, the majority: "How incredible it is that there are a few who still say that the South Vietnamese do not want to continue the struggle. They are sacrificing and they

[1] Johnson, 1965b.

are dying by the thousands. Their patient valor in the heavy presence of personal physical danger should be a helpful lesson to those of us who, here in America, only have to read about it, or hear about it on the television or radio."

Similarly, former Undersecretary of State George Ball has described the Viet Cong as follows: "Only the leaders and the hard core have a strong ideological commitment. The rank and file are their puppets—those whom they have bought, coerced, or intimidated."[2]

Here, as in many other historical instances, the black-top image of the enemy serves a number of psychological purposes: It relieves us of the painful thought that we may be going against the majority of the Vietnamese, especially the poor and downtrodden; it replaces such thoughts with a glorious image of ourselves as actually helping them against those who have intimidated, duped, and oppressed them; it raises our own hopes that, once the evil leaders have been taught a lesson, the conflict will be over and stability can be established. Also, since we know we are virtuous and people in the enemy camp don't seem to recognize our virtue, it is natural to think that this must be because their leaders are preventing them from doing so.

While in the case of Vietnam the black-top image does seem to have some validity, the evidence presented above (Chapters 2 and 3) suggests that it is largely mistaken. The common people of North Vietnam and the Viet Cong-leaning peasants of South Vietnam probably share their Communist leaders' motives and assumptions to a much larger degree than most Americans realize, and the leaders are probably a good deal more human—more like their followers and more like us—than most Americans realize. The extent to which our militant American picture departs from this more realistic conception suggests that the forces of cognitive distortion acting in the direction of the black-top image of the enemy must be very strong.

There is a similarity to the thinking of the Austrians in 1914 in that in both cases there is a picture of the criminal actions of assassins on territory that does not belong to them, instigated by arch-conspirators elsewhere. The Austrians saw the Serbian nationalists who had assassinated the Archduke as only the tools of aggressors

[2] Ball, in Gettleman, ed., 1962, p. 62.

sitting safely in Belgrade; militant Americans see Vietnamese nationalists and Communists, the Viet Cong, as assassinating Vietnamese villagers who are loyal to their Government, and see them as only tools of aggressors sitting safely in Hanoi. And, just as militant Austrians felt that it was imperative to punish the real criminals in Belgrade, so militant Americans feel that it is imperative to "punish" the real criminals in Hanoi (and perhaps also in Peking), even though doing so may be regarded by most of the rest of the world as aggression.

There is a similarity to the thinking of the Austrians also in that in both cases there is a picture of rapid disintegration within one's own territory if its outer defenses are breached. The Austrians, with much reason, feared that their ramshackle empire might fall apart if they did not deal firmly with Serbia. American militants, perhaps with less reason, assume a domino theory that asserts the Free World will progressively fall apart if we do not deal firmly with North Vietnam. In both cases it is possible to ask whether a kernel of truth has been exaggerated by anxiety that is not wholly unrelated to paranoia. In both cases, too, there is reason to think that anxiety has led to excessive emphasis on the virile self-image and to a lack of discrimination between aggressive and non-aggressive forms of "firmness."

The Virile Self-Image

About the emotional importance of our own virile self-image there can be little doubt. The imagery of our leaders' public and private statements is full of it. On the positive side, a militant policy is described as determined, unflinching; we see ourselves as having the guts to stand up and be counted. On the negative side there is scorn for the softness of those who would bug out, turn tail, tuck tail (both President Johnson and Senator Russell have used this expression), scuttle and run. The word dove itself suggests weak, dim-witted pacifism. Student demonstrators are lumped with draft-card burners and both are pictured as effete bearded beatniks in contrast with the hard, clean-cut men who are fighting for their country in the jungles of Vietnam.

The mood is more grim than belligerent; there are few signs of enthusiasm for the war. As Secretary Rusk put it to Henry Graff,

"Dictatorship underestimates democracy's willingness to do what it has to do.[3] . . . The men around the President do not speak of conquest on the battlefield in Vietnam—as men from time immemorial have talked of victory—because they are honest men and know that there can be none. Nevertheless, they exude the resolution of people who do not mean to get licked, either. It may be said that beyond the specific advice they offer the President daily, they reinforce, without turning into sycophants, his own resolve to see this terrible episode through."[4]

Occasionally, though, the image of a tough, victorious fighter breaks through. We must clobber the North, or break the back of the Viet Cong. Refraining from more intensive bombing of the North is described by Representative Hale Boggs as expecting our men to "fight with one hand tied behind their back." There is a fierce pride in our strength; Joseph Alsop describes the launching and recovery of a mission from an aircraft carrier as a spectacle "to fill the mind with wonder and the heart with pride. The whole vast carrier was a single scene of elegantly, intricately efficient, and deadly purposeful activity with a single aim."[5] There is a strong tendency to equate compromise with surrender, and to insist on decisive victory, at least in the South. Richard Nixon declares: "The lesson of all history warns us that we should negotiate only when our military superiority is so convincing that we can achieve our objective at the conference table—and deny the aggressors theirs."[6]

Closely related to our image of ourselves as strong and determined is our feeling that others regard us as strong and determined, and our desire for the one involves a desire for the other. Our virile self-image and our desire for prestige are therefore intimately interrelated. It is not surprising, then, that fear of losing prestige is a potent motive today in America, as it was in many of Europe's chancelleries in 1914. As Lippmann puts it, "the critical question is whether and how Lyndon Johnson can bring himself to accept anything less than success in an enterprise where he has staked so much of his personal reputation and his country's prestige. In the perspective of history there is nothing unusual for the leader of a great power to settle for less than a victory, and to pull himself out of rather than to plunge

[3] Graff, 1965, p. 16.
[4] Ibid., p. 20.
[5] Alsop, 1965.
[6] Nixon, 1965, p. 51.

more deeply into a quagmire. This is difficult for a proud man like Lyndon Johnson."[7]

Some of the psychological roots of the virile self-image are obvious. Benjamin Spock, who knows something about children, has put it well: "A leader who may be quite mature in his ordinary dealings will, when feeling threatened in an international crisis, announce an inflexible determination to impose his will on the adversary. This is partly his fear of being considered timid, which is ingrained in every male beginning at the age of three and which automatically colors his actions the rest of his life. But for the leader, the compulsion to appear strong is enormously magnified: he must try to intimidate the officials of the other country, he must show his own people that he is up to the task of protecting them, he must prove to the political opposition at home that he cannot be accused of softness."[8] Other possible roots will occur to every psychoanalytically oriented psychologist: perhaps fear of sexual impotence, fear of castration, fear of homosexuality, fear of playing a "woman's" role or a role of weak dependence.

Virility is a good thing, and there are times when it is indispensable. But danger arises when enchantment with a virile self-image causes selective inattention to important aspects of reality and misperception of the situation as a whole.

There is reason to think that in America it has done just that, by leading militants to exaggerate the magnitude of the emergency and the degree of suffering and of risk that the war involves for America as compared with America's enemies. They often see it not only as "a terrible episode" (which of course it is) but also as a situation of imperative urgency, demanding all we have of courage and of manhood, a test of our moral fiber, a situation in which democracy must prove its "willingness to do what it has to do."

To the Communists and to a great many non-Communists in the rest of the world it seems like something very different: a bullying of one of the world's smallest and weakest countries by one of the strongest. That hardly seems a situation of imperative urgency, or one that requires much courage. In their eyes, the fact that America is risking intervention by the world's most populous country, Communist China, does not make our action seem much more courageous. Though more populous than America, China is clearly far weaker militarily. If she dared to intervene to protect her small protégé, it would seem to millions of non-Communists, in spite of their basic distrust of Communist China, to be not a step toward Communist conquest of the world but courageous protection of a small neighbor against destruction by an enormously better-armed opponent possessing airborne weapons that render the cities of North Vietnam and of China terribly vulnerable. The sufferings of American soldiers in Vietnam, real as they are, seem to these onlookers minor in comparison with the suffering, and the risk of torture and death, that the Viet Cong have faced without flinching for twenty years.

This raises a psychological question: Why are we so blind to the figure we cut in the eyes of much of the rest of the world, beating our breasts and proclaiming our courage in a situation that they perceive as a very strong nation beating up a very weak one?

A possible answer is that we may have an unconscious need to retain our picture of the situation as one requiring courage in order to retain—and continue to revel in—our own courageous self-image.

Military Overconfidence

The possibility of American overconfidence comes up in two main contexts: the question of whether the costs and risks of heavy bombing in the North outweigh its advantages, and the question of whether the costs and risks of all-out war in the South (as compared with a holding operation) outweigh its advantages. In both cases there are some who think we are in danger of blithely ignoring or underestimating the costs and the risks.

It may seem presumptuous for a non-military person to discuss this question at all. Perhaps it is. But with certain honorable exceptions (for example, General Ridgway) military men concerned with Vietnam, both French and American, have been so regularly, monotonously mistaken in their overoptimistic predictions that a non-military person can perhaps be pardoned for wondering why they have misperceived so badly, and almost always in the same direction.[9] The record of history (for example, the overoptimism of Allied generals in World War I, well described by Liddell Hart) does not

[9] Fall, 1966a, p. 59.

inspire a generally high regard for the realism of military men in predicting the over-all course of a war. Certainly on technical matters such as weaponry no amateur has the skill or information to argue with a professional, but there are political and psychological factors in warfare, as the best military specialists know only too well, and on these anyone who has done his best to cover the available evidence has a right to speak.

It is also legitimate for anyone to note the process of selective inattention when he sees evidence of it in the thinking of a general, or anyone else. In this discussion we will confine ourselves to an inventory of some legitimate grounds for confidence, and then some grounds for lack of confidence, a number of which seem to be usually ignored ("selectively inattended") or given too little weight by American militants.

The legitimate grounds for confidence are many; it is natural that a person who focuses mainly on them will come to an optimistic conclusion:

REASONS FOR OPTIMISM

America is enormously stronger—in population, science, industry, and military technology—than all of Vietnam together.

The government and some of the people of South Vietnam are still on our side.

Perhaps chiefly because of Secretary McNamara, America is better prepared for this war than it has been for others in its history. Partly because of the War College system, intelligence and imagination are respected in the present American defense establishment. There are few Colonel Blimps.

Our troops and airmen in Vietnam have performed well, especially when compared with the South Vietnamese troops. They are committed to doing the job.[10]

In contrast with Communist delusions about the American people being on their side, only a minority now want to pull out (unless, perhaps, the Vietnamese themselves ask us to). Our pride is now mobilized and rather thoroughly involved.

Counterguerrilla campaigns succeeded in Greece, Malaya, the Philippines, and—contrary to a widespread assumption—in Algeria.[11]

10 Raymond, 1965.
11 Pike, 1966b, p. 49; Ahmad, in Gettleman, ed., 1965, p. 354.

As Bernard Fall testified on the basis of his experience in the French *maquis,* great strain is put on guerrillas when they no longer have secure bases for supply and recuperation. We have attacked those bases more successfully than the French did. America's use of weapons is on a far more massive scale than was the French.

The logistic difficulties of Chinese or Russian intervention are great.

The Sino-Soviet split is deep. Russia would be reluctant to help China, and China would be reluctant to act alone.

China's cities, transportation centers, and incipient atomic industry are so vulnerable to our air power that she would be foolish to intervene.[12]

The Viet Cong are now alienating the peasants to a greater extent than before by strongarm methods of taxation and recruitment.

America is now verbally committed, more than before, to a reform program designed to "win the hearts and minds of the people."

As recently as January, 1968, non-Communists claimed control of two-thirds of the population, and claimed that the Viet Cong controlled only a sixth of it.

Death ratios and ratios of captured weapons now strongly favor the government side.

The Viet Cong tide has actually been stopped. In early 1965, the government seemed near collapse; while it is not yet clear that the tide has turned, there now seems to be general agreement that the Americans are not going to be defeated by military action. The setbacks in early 1968 do not disprove this proposition, since the price paid by the Viet Cong for their gains at that time may have been exorbitantly high.

The Communists have a long tradition, stemming from Lenin as well as Mao and Giap, of strategic retreat and acceptance of a temporary truce in the face of a strong and determined enemy. It can be argued from this that their response to bombing of the North should be rational rather than emotional. Even if they do not humble themselves by coming to the conference table, they could simply go under cover, let the fighting simmer down, and permit some kind of reconstruction in the South to occur.

Most of these are quite familiar and much stressed by optimists. Some of the points on the pessimistic side are also quite familiar,

[12] Gilpatric, 1965.

but a number of others are not, and it is doubtful that, taken all together, they have been given adequate attention and emphasis by most optimists.

REASONS FOR PESSIMISM

There are many indications that in South Vietnam there is no viable society to build on. The processes of social, economic, and perhaps even political disintegration are far advanced.

The political situation is still shaky. If it should again become worse, the military outlook is bleak, unless the war becomes thoroughly American.

"Revolutionary development," including land reform and reconstruction of village democracy, is generally regarded as essential in gaining popular support. Up to now little has occurred.

History is so full of examples of military overconfidence that Americans need to be on guard against being affected by it (Chapter 1, pp. 11, 21–23; Chapter 3, pp. 101–8).

One recurrent factor in these instances of overconfidence—the unexpected intervention of a more formidable power on behalf of one's enemy—is more than a possibility in the case of Vietnam. North Vietnam could fight in the South on a larger scale than it has yet; Cambodia could become more active; North Korea could make more trouble; Communist China could intervene and cause trouble elsewhere even if not in Vietnam itself; the USSR could intervene with catastrophic consequences.

Another recurrent factor in the historical instances of overconfidence—the unexpected effectiveness of a people fighting on its own soil against foreign troops—is already present in Vietnam if our appraisal of peasant attitudes toward the military government (Chapter 2) is at all close to the truth. The events of early 1968 underline the danger.

The strongest movement of our times, it has often been said, is nationalism. If the Vietnamese think of the war more and more as a defense of their homeland against alien invaders, then the force of nationalism, already probably mobilized much more on the Viet Cong side than on our side, would become mobilized on that side to an even greater extent.

If the war becomes more and more clearly a war of alien white men against Vietnamese, onlookers throughout the world who are still noncommittal might become aroused against American "aggression" and "imperialism," and it is debatable whether America could —or should—withstand that kind of world disapproval. There is a fair analogy with the French position in Algeria. According to Fall and others, from a military standpoint the French had more or less won the war, but pulled out because of a revulsion of feeling in world opinion and in metropolitan France.

Just as the Vietnamese Communists probably overstress the factor of "people" in modern warfare as compared with weapons, we may tend to overstress the factor of weapons as compared with "people." The Viet Cong have proved perhaps the most effective guerrilla fighters in all history.

This war differs from counterguerrilla operations in Greece, Malaya and the Philippines[13] in that the guerrillas have outside sources of weapons, reinforcements and hope.

Although American opinion up to now has been pressing the Administration more in the militant than in the non-militant direction, Americans could become convinced that "we're helping people who don't want to be helped," or get the idea that "They aren't willing to do their share so why should we keep on helping them?" If so, they might even swing to the opposite extreme and favor a pull-out rather than a holding strategy.

To be sure, none of this is necessarily reason to stop fighting. To brave men who feel sure that they are fighting for the survival of freedom in their own country and perhaps in all the rest of the world, difficulties are likely to appear only as a reason to put forth greater effort and make greater sacrifices. Given a certainty or even a high probability that the cause is worth fighting for, such a reaction would deserve more respect than a defeatist one. But to those who think our cause is basically dubious and who favor a holding strategy or withdrawal on moral grounds, the reasons for military pessimism appear as potent additional reasons for attempting no more than we can reasonably hope to accomplish. To sacrifice and risk much in a great cause is heroic; to sacrifice and risk much in a bad cause, or even a highly ambiguous cause—as Austria did in 1914 and as Hitler did in 1939—may be heroic but it is also blind and foolish.

[13] Ahmad, in Gettleman, ed., 1965, pp. 359–61.

Absence of Empathy

To avoid misunderstanding it should perhaps be repeated that the word empathy as used here does not mean sympathy. It does not mean a sneaking sympathy for the Communist cause, but a tough-minded effort to understand the viewpoints of both enemies and on-lookers, as a basis for realism in coping with enemies (without war if possible) and achieving cooperation with onlookers.

The nature of the empathy that most Americans need and do not have has been discussed especially in Chapters 2 to 4, so that little needs to be added here. One aspect, however, calls for further discussion: what Newcomb has called "autistic hostility"—the tendency to express hostility by cutting off communication (and with it, the possibility of achieving empathy), with the result that the hostility is perpetuated or even reinforced, and a vicious circle results. Autistic hostility is present to an extreme degree in the paranoid psychotic who believes himself persecuted and therefore cuts himself off from empathic communication with all or almost all of his fellow human beings. It can occur in any quarrel between individuals. It also tends to develop on both sides of any acute group conflict.

As we have seen (Chapter 3), xenophobia and autistic hostility are particularly marked today in North Vietnam and in Communist China. The obstacles to genuine communication are likely to come much more from their side than from ours. Their assumption appears to be the one that tends to occur in all group conflict: What the enemy says consists only of lies and propaganda; a loyal citizen, therefore, will simply not listen. Their underlying feeling seems to be similar to that which Leites describes as typical of Russian Bolsheviks: a fear of contamination, as if even the slightest contact with the evilness of the enemy will be poisonous, and perhaps spread an infection through one's own body politic.[14] It is a feeling that has given rise to Iron Curtains and buttressed dictatorships at many times and in many places.

It is more surprising to find the same feeling even in America, the strongest country in the world and one of the most democratic. Yet it does exist here. Few Americans except scholars have been ex-

[14] Leites, 1953.

posed to more than fragmentary glimpses of a Communist point of view. Few have wanted to be so exposed. Except for a few courses on the college or graduate-school level, our educational system contains little representation of the Communists' thinking in their own words, even as a basis for critical, analytical discussion. And our governmental policy has fostered autistic hostility in at least two ways: resistance to free communication with Communist China and resistance to direct communication with the Viet Cong.

The worst thing about autistic hostility is that it tends to become a vicious spiral when hostile words and actions on one side, untempered by empathy, evoke further suspicion and hostility on the other side, which in turn evokes further suspicion and hostility on the first side, and so on. There is then a self-fulfilling prophecy in that each group, expecting hostility from the other, does things that make the other more hostile. The system contains circular processes that may take on a runaway character.[15] This danger lends support to the view that in almost any human relationship, between individuals or between groups, a certain minimal amount of trust—or at least absence of acute distrust—is basic. Trust is a basis for communication and businesslike cooperation; and businesslike cooperation and communication are a basis for realistic mutual trust. The latter relationship has been shown experimentally by Morton Deutsch in laboratory situations[16]; and the theme has been elaborated in the context of international affairs by Osgood, Rock, and Pruitt.[17]

The characteristic absence of empathy between conflicting groups raises a psychological question: why? Like many other basic psychological questions, the answer to this one seems obvious on the common-sense level. One's first thought is: Of course conflicting groups don't empathize with each other; they are hostile by definition, and how can hostility be combined with empathy? There are nevertheless some genuine psychological problems here. For instance, is there active inhibition of a type of empathy that would naturally, spontaneously crop up if the hostility were not there? *Does* empathy naturally, spontaneously crop up between groups that are in any sort of contact, except when it is counteracted or inhibited by hostility? Or is empathy between groups always a product of other

[15] Richardson, 1960; Boulding, 1965, pp. 190–91; Pruitt, 1965, pp. 422–27.

[16] Morton Deutsch, 1958; cf. Deutsch and Krauss, 1962; Loomis, 1959; Sawyer and Guetzkow, 1965, pp. 473–79.

[17] Osgood, 1962, 1966; Rock, 1964; Pruitt, 1965.

factors, such as conscious striving for peace, or alliance against a common enemy, or working together toward superordinate goals?[18] To the extent that tough-minded empathy with a hostile group is psychologically possible, what factors promote or hinder it?

Selective Inattention and the Blindness of Involvement

Call it resistance, repression, ignoring, forgetting, non-learning, inhibition of curiosity, evading, card-stacking, perceptual defense, blind spots, or plain not paying attention. By whatever name, it is omnipresent. It has cropped up continually throughout this study. Absence of empathy—that is, not paying enough attention to the thoughts of others—is probably its most serious, most war-producing manifestation, but it has many others. Whatever is inconsistent with the black-and-white picture (that is, with the diabolical enemy-image and the moral self-image) and whatever is inconsistent with the virile self-image tends to drop out of consciousness. Space perspective, especially whatever has to do with distant onlookers (Western Europe, the USSR), tends to be restricted. Time perspective is restricted. Important distinctions (for example, between different meanings of aggression, between Munich and the present situation in Vietnam, between a holding operation and surrender) tend to be blurred or ignored. Individuals who raise issues that one does not want to think about are often not answered in terms of the issues; they are denounced as traitors, cowards, or naïve dupes of the diabolical enemy. Grounds for fear, including fear of atomic destruction, may be pushed out of the mind.[19] Elements of actual or potential strength in the adversary are often given less attention and less weight than they deserve. On each side of every acute conflict the tendency appears; we have seen it in the minds of the Austrians in 1914, in Hitler's mind in 1939, in the minds of Communists today, in the minds of non-militants in the United States, and in this chapter and the last one we have seen it, in many forms, in the minds of militants.

In fact, the forms it has taken in the minds of American militants are so numerous that at this point perhaps a sort of check list, pulling together all or nearly all of the examples noted on previous pages,

18 Sherif et al., 1961; Rock, 1964.
19 Janis and Feshbach, 1953.

would be useful. The reader can check each item as to whether he himself has heard it adequately discussed (and perhaps refuted) by American militants.

EXAMPLES OF SELECTIVE INATTENTION: A REVIEW

The large-scale help we gave the French in their war against a clear majority of the Vietnamese people.

Our role in maintaining Diem in office, and our failure to insist on genuine representative government at any time since 1954.

Diem's tragic blunder in taking away from the peasants the land that the Viet Minh had given them, and substituting a watered-down land reform.

Diem's abrogation of the traditional forms of village democracy in 1956. (His refusal to hold elections to unify the country in the same year is not included in the present list because it is now well-known and much discussed, though it was selectively inattended until perhaps three or four years ago.)

Diem's great witch hunt against all who opposed him, with a more than McCarthy-like lack of discrimination among liberals, patriots who had fought against the French, and Communists.

The amazing success of the Viet Cong against an enormously better-armed adversary, and the possible inference that they have had the spontaneous support of most of the peasants—that is, that peasant cooperation with them has not been solely or even primarily a result of intimidation.

The great headway made by the Viet Cong before 1960, when for the first time they received appreciable help from the North.

The fact that the area of greatest Viet Cong success was the Mekong Delta, so far south that they could not possibly have owed that success to help from the North.

The large-scale corruption shown by most of the provincial and district officials under Diem and his successors; their exploitation and cheating of the peasants.

The disintegration of South Vietnamese society, and its implications.

The continuing prohibition of neutralism, and the continuing imprisonment of some 4000 Buddhists.

The vote in the Constituent Assembly, 114 to 3, against paying more than lip service to land reform. The failure even to discuss remission of rents.

Other evidence—in addition to the above twelve items—indicating that, among those who really care which side wins, the majority are pro-Viet Cong.

The fact that omission and slanting in the channels of communication has resulted in a large amount of distortion that, with some exceptions, has been heavily on the side of the militants' black-and-white picture. (See below, Chapter 9.)

The defects (for example, selective contacts and the tendency to say what is expedient) that vitiate much of the evidence relied upon by most of those who think the majority of the Vietnamese people are more anti-Communist than anti-Government.

Historical examples of failure on the part of a formidable military force facing a seemingly less formidable population fighting on its own soil (Napoleon in Russia, Hitler in Russia, France in Indochina).

Historical examples of an enemy's ally entering a war unexpectedly (Russia in 1914, Britain and France in 1939, Communist China in Korea).

The Strategic Bombing Survey and its implication that bombing the North is likely to stiffen Communist morale.

The Korean experience and its implication that bombing the North is not likely to be very effective militarily.

The evidence of Cameron and others that bombing North Vietnam has actually stiffened its morale.

The failure of repeated American efforts to promote subversion in North Vietnam. (There is a prevalent myth that we have not made such efforts, but see Fall.[20])

The fact that North Vietnam's helping one side in the conflict is neatly paralleled by our helping the other—on a much larger scale, and starting as far back as 1950. The thought that we ourselves may therefore be committing aggression.

The thought that Ho Chi Minh's government in the North *may* be at least as popular as the government we have supported in the South. (There is extremely little evidence on this point, but it is a tenable hypothesis.)

Our nibbling attacks on China.

[20] Fall, 1964b, p. 402.

Our chemical warfare.[21]

Some specific forms of torture widely used by the South Vietnamese troops, for example, the electric-current torture.[22] Our willingness to turn over our prisoners to them.

Our commitment when we signed the UN Charter.

The problem of defining "aggression."

The fact that in the eyes of onlookers we may look like a bully beating up a much smaller boy, and the possible truth in this.

The harm done by Vietnam to our previously improving relations with the Soviet Union—and perhaps, therefore, to the long-run chances of peace.

The impression of many non-Communist onlookers that our anti-Communism is extreme and obsessive, and the possibility that there is some truth in their impression.

The ways in which the Vietnam situation differs from Munich and from Korea.

The ways in which a holding operation differs from pull-out or surrender—for example, fulfillment of our commitment to protect our friends, and perhaps a greatly lessened domino effect.

There are many arguments on the other side. Of course there is a great deal of selective inattention on the Communist side too (Chapter 3) and some, as we have seen, on the part of many American non-militants. But such *ad hominem* answers only reinforce our present psychological point, which is that in any acute conflict situation there is a strong tendency on each side to ignore rather than refute everything on the other side that it is psychologically possible to ignore, and to give too little attention to facts on the other side that are too obtrusive to be ignored completely. How many of the points in the above list, for example, have been given any attention—even in an effort to refute them—in the public speeches of President Johnson, Secretary McNamara, or Secretary Rusk? To some opponents of our involvement this seems almost a conspiracy of silence. More probably, it is not a conspiracy. It is human.

An element of conspiracy may exist though, in a very limited sense: a conscious agreement on the part of high government officials that certain points should be left undiscussed except when an

[21] Brightman, 1966.
[22] Malcolm Browne, 1965, pp. 114–18; Fall, 1965b, pp. 19–20.

opponent forces discussion, and perhaps a "gentlemen's agreement" between government officials and representatives of the mass media that "the national interest," "the war effort," and "support of our hard-pressed allies" require avoidance of certain topics. Free speech in America being what it is, such agreements would be impossible to enforce completely, but there are some indications that they exist —the initial handling of the Tonkin Bay incident by the American press,[23] for instance, and the extreme rarity of references to electric-current torture by the major mass media in the United States.

In spite of the American tradition of free speech, there is also reason to fear that selective inattention in the minds of the militant majority may continue or even increase. As De Tocqueville observed many years ago, America is not exempt from the pressures of conformity and "the tyranny of the majority," which tend to penalize and discourage dissent, including the efforts of dissident individuals to get the majority to notice what the majority does not want to notice. Asch, Crutchfield, and others have demonstrated the power of conformity to influence thinking as well as behavior in our American society,[24] and Milgram has shown how Americans, like Germans, can perform cruel acts if they are commanded to do so by established authority.[25] Such research suggests how, through circular processes in a society, selective inattention may become self-reinforcing and cumulative. Anatol Rapoport, in a brilliant phrase that perhaps sums up better than any other the state of mind in which nations do the things that lead to war, has spoken of "the blindness of involvement."[26] Woodworth has stressed the tendency for "an activity to become a motive," and Festinger and others have re-emphasized the common-sense observation that, once an activity is well launched, there is a tendency for thoughts in harmony with it to be retained while dissonant thoughts tend to drop out.

While there is much controversy about some of the experiments that Festinger's thinking has stimulated, the criticisms do not necessarily contradict the large amount of historical experience and everyday observation in support of this common-sense version of his theory. Historical experience bears out the idea that the psychology of a nation at war contains self-reinforcing elements. On both sides

23 Stone, in Raskin and Fall, eds., 1965.
24 Asch, 1951; Crutchfield, 1955; below, Chapter 9.
25 Milgram, 1965.
26 Rapoport, 1960, pp. 259–72.

in World War I there was enormous war-weariness by 1916; yet the war continued to the bitter end. Why? Probably one reason was "the blindness of involvement." Those who thought unthinkable thoughts about a compromise peace knew how little they could accomplish by voicing their thoughts; they would have been called pacifists, defeatists, unwitting dupes of the enemy, or, perhaps, traitors. They were caught in what Martin Buber has called "the speechlessness of slaughter."[27]

The blindness of involvement—a special case of selective inattention—has been well described by the psychologist and psychiatrist Jerome Frank: "As a conflict progresses, each side sacrifices more blood and treasure and endures more hurts and humiliations from the other. These pressures heighten each individual citizen's sense of identification with his nation, so that he feels threats to it as personal attacks. These include threats to any area the nation defines as its territory, however geographically remote, atrocities inflicted on fellow nationals, and efforts to make a nation abandon its moral commitments. Thus threats at the national level mobilize psychological forces in each individual, at all levels of consciousness, that operate to intensify the conflict. These include the desire to recoup one's losses, the determination to defend one's honor, moral indignation at the enemy's outrageous behavior and, at less conscious levels usually, the need to prove one's masculinity and courage, the urge for revenge, and primitive blood lust. The enemy becomes a monster that threatens life, property, and one's own self-image, and who must therefore be opposed to the absolute limit of one's strength. Furthermore, he must be made to suffer for the suffering he has caused.

"These forces promote escalation of the conflict, and each step up the ladder in turn intensifies them, until destruction of the enemy becomes the overriding goal, and compromise becomes impossible. As Homer put it some three thousand years ago, in describing 'Strife, the War-god's sister': 'Once she begins, she cannot stop. At first she seems a little thing, but before long, though her feet are still on the ground, she has struck high heaven with her head.' "[28]

Charles Osgood, commenting on a discussion of escalation by Herman Kahn, expresses a similar thought in very different words:

[27] Quoted by the American Friends Service Committee, 1966, p. 10.

[28] Personal communication. A similar statement by Frank appears in the *Congressional Record,* March 9, 1965, inserted by Senator Gruening.

"It may be true that, *physically*, escalators can run down as easily as up, but, *psychologically*, it is much easier to keep on going up than to stop and back down. Each step in escalation makes it more difficult to achieve the 'accurate communication' and 'shared understandings' Kahn himself considers necessary for de-escalation. Escalation produces the very conditions, both internally and externally, which make it harder and harder to stop moving up. Internally, particularly in a democracy, a sense of commitment is created which makes backing down come close to political suicide for leadership. Externally, escalation up to some indefinite point produces hardening, rather than softening, in the opponent's resolve—which is likely to carry the escalator far beyond the level originally intended. The analogy with sexual arousal may be disturbing, but it seems valid; as every practiced seducer knows, each threshold whose passage can be induced makes it easier to induce passage of the next."[29]

The concept of cumulative involvement has cropped up under several different names. Withey and Katz, for instance, speak of "progressive commitment,"[30] Lippmann speaks of a "vicious spiral,"[31] and Morton Deutsch, stressing the "unwitting" aspect of the phenomenon, has described several different "processes of unwitting involvement and commitment."[32]

Or, as Mephistopheles said to Faust, "At the first step you are free; at the second you are a slave."

[29] Osgood, 1966, p. 6.
[30] Withey and Katz, 1965.
[31] Lippmann, 1965b.
[32] Morton Deutsch, 1966. See also Osgood, 1962, Crow, 1963, and Guetzkow, Alger, Brody, Noel, and Snyder, 1963.

PART THREE

•

Black-and-White Thinking

Chapter 8

PSYCHOLOGICAL PROBLEMS
POSED BY HISTORY

"Power is not a means; it is an end. . . . We are the priests of power," he said. "God is power. But at present power is only a word so far as you are concerned. It is time for you to gather some idea of what power means. The first thing you must realize is that power is collective. The individual only has power insofar as he ceases to be an individual."

—George Orwell, *1984*, pp. 200–1.

"After much thought Snowball declared that the Seven Commandments could in effect be reduced to a single maxim, namely: 'Four legs good, two legs bad.' This, he said, contained the essential principle of Animalism. Whoever had thoroughly grasped it would be safe from human influences. . . . All the humbler animals set to work to learn the new maxim by heart. FOUR LEGS GOOD, TWO LEGS BAD was inscribed on the end wall of the barn, above the Seven Commandments and in bigger letters. When they had once got it by heart the sheep developed a great liking for this maxim, and often as they lay in the field they would all start bleating 'Four legs good, two legs bad! Four legs good, two legs bad!' and keep it up for hours on end, never growing tired of it."

—George Orwell, *Animal Farm*, pp. 40–41.

Orwell did not call himself a psychologist, but he was one of the first rank. He knew from history, as he had studied and lived it, that the inner evil mankind has to contend with contains two central elements: the craving for power and the black-and-white picture. The two chapters that follow will have something to say about both.

First, however, a pulling together of strings is needed. The main connections between history as presented here (including that of Vietnam) and psychology should be made clear.

The craving for power underlies both the virile self-image and military overconfidence. Absence of empathy also serves the purposes of the craving for power in a way that is not so immediately clear. It dulls awareness of the suffering caused by one's individual or collective craving for power.

It is probably true, as Orwell and the psychoanalysts insist, that there is an unacknowledged pleasure in having the power to hurt others and also in using it for that purpose. This is the essential evil in human nature that some optimistic liberals have fought hard not to see. In most men it is constantly combated and pushed down by more positive forces: good will, conscientiousness, enlightened self-interest. Yet in most men, to some degree, that force exists, submerged and struggling to assert itself. When it does so successfully, the fact of its doing so, and the resulting pleasure, cannot be acknowledged. It would be difficult for ordinary men to live with themselves if their pleasure in hurting others came too close to clear consciousness. The pleasure must therefore be dulled, limited, kept in its shadowy, half-conscious place, and absence of empathy is the major means of keeping it there. The enemy, if he is to be tortured or killed, must first be dehumanized. He must be viewed as a devil or the dupe of a devil, not as a full human being.

The black-and-white picture embraces most of what has been described in previous chapters. The diabolical enemy-image is the black part of it; the virile and moral self-images are the white part. Military overconfidence is a self-deluding manifestation of the virile self-image. Selective inattention is the chief means of sustaining both sides of the black-and-white picture, and absence of empathy is the most dangerous, war-producing form of selective inattention. If we want to survive, we would do well to study the nature and origins of black-and-white thinking as systematically as we can.

Accordingly, the word "psychology" in the next two chapters will be broadly interpreted. It will include, first, some of the substantial research done in social psychology, especially during the past twenty years. Ideas will be drawn from psychiatry, from daily observation and, as before, from history, including the war in Vietnam. Now, however, the main focus will be on psychological processes illustrated by history, rather than on the contexts and continuities of history itself. Many of the same historical examples will be mentioned, but this time in a different context, as raw material for psychological generalizations and deeper psychological understanding.

In trying to analyze the sources of the black-and-white picture, it is necessary to avoid at the outset one assumption: that a black-and-white picture of a particular conflict is always wrong. There are situations in which one side is clearly committing aggression against neighboring states. In these situations, is it "black-and-white think-ing" to recognize a danger and cope with it?

There is a special kind of sentimentality and wishful thinking that consists of not recognizing the genuineness and the extent of evil, even in an enemy. Optimistic liberals often exhibit it. Neville Cham-berlain showed it when Hitler was blustering and he could not quite believe his ears. At that point, the dark part of Chamberlain's black-and-white picture was not black enough. This sentimentality, too, can cause war, as the events immediately after Munich demon-strated.

History has contained quite a number of real devils, or at least semi-mad semi-devils who were dangerous enough to require for-cible restraint. Hitler, with his conquests and gas chambers, was not the only example. Stalin's purges come to mind, the persecution of the *kulaks,* the anarchy and cruelty of Mao's "cultural revolution," Ho's terrible "land reform," the pious corruption and brutality of Ngo Dinh Nhu, slavery in the American South. If decent men band together to oppose such evil, or simply to limit its spread, should their decency be impugned as "black-and-white thinking," with all the irrationality and all the war-producing belligerence implied in that term?

The answer, clearly, is No. But we can distinguish between the black-and-white *picture* and black-and-white *thinking*. The black-and-white *picture* (or something close enough to it to justify fighting) may in particular cases be arrived at by realistic, evidence-oriented thinking rather than by the biased thinking that is properly impugned by the term "black-and-white." We can define black-and-white thinking as a *straining toward* a black-and-white picture, con-sciously or unconsciously distorting evidence, slanting and selecting it. This is what is irrational, what creates unnecessary wars; there-fore, it is what we now must try to understand and explain.

Chapter 9

SOCIAL FACTORS IN
BLACK-AND-WHITE THINKING

Conformity

Seven college men are sitting in a half circle. A psychologist, Professor Asch, shows them two large cards, one containing a single heavy vertical line, the other containing three heavy vertical lines numbered 1, 2, and 3. Number 2 is the same length as the line on the first card; Number 1 is a little shorter, and Number 3 seems quite perceptibly shorter. Professor Asch asks, "Which of these three lines is the same length as the one on the first card?"[1]

Our particular friend in the group, John Jones, thinks he knows the answer; it is Number 2. But, as each man in turn is called on, each confidently answers, "Number 3." John is fairly sure this is not what he sees, though not absolutely sure, since the cards are far enough apart to keep him from being certain. He thinks, "Could anything be wrong with my eyes?" Five other men have answered, "Number 3," and he is being called on. He feels a strong impulse to say, "Three," like the others. But he knows that is not what *he* sees. He resists the temptation and says "Two." Many cards are then shown. On some of them he finds himself agreeing with the rest of the group, but on several occasions there is a baffling contradiction between what the others in the group unanimously say, and what John thinks he sees. He compromises. Most of the time he resists the temptation to conform, but some of the time he gives in to it.

After the experiment, John has a conference with Professor Asch that clears up the mystery. It was a put-up job: All the other members of the group had been confederates of the professor, agreeing in advance that on certain test trials they would lie with a straight face, giving the answer most different from what they actually saw. John was the only naïve subject in the experiment; it was designed entirely to discover whether, under strong group pressure, he would

[1] Asch, 1952, pp. 3–5.

deny the evidence of his own senses. John is chagrined to think that he compromised at all, but Professor Asch reassures him, telling him that such compromise is typical. Only a quarter of the previous subjects have completely resisted the temptation to conform; as many as a third have displaced their judgments toward those of the majority half or more than half the time. John at least did better than that. He goes away, still somewhat chagrined but not really resenting the deception practiced upon him, since he feels he has learned a wholesome lesson. He resolves that, the next time he finds himself disagreeing with others, he will be more self-reliant.

The strength of the pressure to conform in this experiment was clear. Even those who resisted often reported that they longed to agree with the majority. One of the most non-yielding said: "Despite everything, there was a lurking fear that in some way I did not understand I might be wrong; fear of exposing myself as inferior in some way. It is more pleasant if one is really in agreement." Other comments were: "I don't deny that at times I had the feeling: to heck with it, I'll go along with the rest." "I felt awfully funny; everything was going against me." "I felt disturbed, puzzled, separated, like an outcast from the rest. Every time I disagreed I was beginning to wonder if I wasn't beginning to look funny."

These findings and those of other investigators have a bearing on the problem of political misperception in several ways:

(1) The power of conformity helps to explain the momentum and staying power of the black-and-white picture in any group, *once it has become the view of a large majority* of the articulate members of that group. Once that point is reached, conformity with "what everybody is saying" provides a kind of momentum that keeps the black-and-white picture going. Those who disagree with it often tend to remain silent; the leaders know that they can retain their leadership only by appearing to be properly vigorous in the conflict or controversy to which the majority now feels committed; the followers continue to absorb each other's ideas and feelings by mutual reinforcement and also to follow the opinion leaders. What "all right-thinking people know" becomes for them self-evident truth.

The way in which this momentum can operate even on the highest level is suggested by the situation that has existed until recently in the United States Senate, as described by E. W. Kenworthy of the *New York Times*: "Some of the Senators hesitate even to criticize the bombing [of the North], which they regard as not only counter-productive but dangerous, because they fear the cry of 'appeasement of Communism' will be raised against them."[2]

It should be noticed however that this cannot explain how the whole thing got started. While conformity helps to explain the blind momentum of a black-and-white picture once it has become established—blind, that is, if the picture happens to be largely wrong—it cannot explain how that picture became established among the opinion-leaders in the first place. For that we must look at the individual motives and mechanisms of the opinion-leaders on all levels of society, during the period before the majority feeling became crystallized.

It should be noticed too that simple conformity, including the desire not to look inferior or "funny," is greatly intensified in political affairs by more practical considerations, including the desire to keep a job or to be elected or re-elected. During the 1964 campaign Barry Goldwater felt constrained to come out in favor of Social Security. In 1960, in his first debate with Richard Nixon, John Kennedy took a position on the Quemoy issue that he apparently decided was too non-militant for many of those who might vote for him; he quickly trimmed his sails and was less forthright from then on. In *Profiles in Courage* he argued persuasively for the political necessity and wisdom of compromises such as this.[3] Even Robert Kennedy and Senator Fulbright have rarely, if ever, raised forthrightly the basic issue of whether the assumption of Communist aggression, on which our policy in Vietnam is largely based, may be largely mistaken. To do so might sound "soft on Communism" and could be political suicide.

(2) Another of Asch's findings that is probably typical of the political world is that those who found themselves deviating from the perceived consensus did not conform completely. They compromised.

In political affairs the two most pervasive forms of conformity are, probably, compromise and silence. But silence, too, can be regarded as a form of compromise—not favoring a proposal but not conspicuously coming out against it either. In the Asch experiment John Jones must have longed for the opportunity to be silent and

2 Kenworthy, 1965.
3 Kennedy, 1957, pp. 1–18.

simply not advertise his divergent, "funny" perception. He could not; everyone expected him to say something, to commit himself. But in politics, silence is often possible, and many resort to it. The Senators referred to by Kenworthy did not necessarily come out in favor of the bombing they felt to be counterproductive and dangerous; they just kept still. Or if a Senator does feel constrained to say something about the Vietnam war, he can express an opinion somewhere between what he really feels and what he thinks would be fully acceptable to his colleagues and constituents. If, for instance, he believes that the wisest course would be a holding strategy, he may publicly come out only for an end to the bombing of the North. If he really wants to "clobber Red China now" he may publicly favor only a step-up in the bombing of North Vietnam.

One implication of this is that an apparent consensus can be deceptive. There is a constant pull toward the center in what is publicly said; both extremes tend to be underrepresented, since the people at both extremes are, some of the time, prudently compromising or keeping silent. It may be too that one extreme is more respectable than the other. Perhaps the hawks, who differ from the Administration in the direction of greater militancy, feel that theirs is the more virile and patriotic position, and usually they do not hesitate to proclaim it. Those in the center and also the general public thus have a picture of a consensus that is more concentrated and also closer to the seemingly virile and patriotic extreme than it actually is. There may be pluralistic ignorance among the non-militants regarding their own numerical strength.

This phenomenon of pluralistic ignorance should be better known than it is. It offers legitimate encouragement to anyone in any group who finds himself in basic disagreement with what seems to be a unanimous or nearly unanimous opinion. In small groups it occurs frequently. A proposal is made; at first, since none of those who oppose it feel quite ready to commit themselves publicly, there appears to be a consensus in its favor. Then perhaps some hardy soul, taking his courage in both hands, speaks out against it. To his amazement others chime in on his side, and not infrequently it turns out that the final consensus is with him, not against him.

In that connection another research finding is relevant. Crutchfield especially has shown that the hardy souls who dare to speak out are on the whole stronger human beings than those who timidly conform. On the average they are more intelligent, more self-confident, more able to cope with difficulties under stress, less authoritarian, and more effective as leaders. While the power of an emotionally involved majority is very great, it may be at least slightly mitigated by the higher average quality of those who resist it.[4]

(3) In the same connection another of Asch's findings is relevant: The courage to dissent publicly in a small group is often greatly increased if even one other person has already done so.[5]

What made John Jones's predicament so difficult was that not even one other person seemed to see the lines as he did. If one other had done so he could have thought "Well, at least I'm not the only one." His situation was like that of Winston in the first pages of Orwell's *1984*, before he met Julia. Utterly alone, with great doubts in his mind, but unsure that anyone else shared those doubts, he kept his doubts wholly to himself and even shared in the general overt glorification of the regime, contributing to the deceptive consensus that probably fooled a great many private heretics like himself. The "illusion of universality" reigned supreme. Then he met Julia. Calmly and confidently, she put his private thoughts into words. With immense relief, Winston realized that he was not alone, and not insane. Though they knew they were probably under constant surveillance, and knew the terrible consequences of detection, the two together actually dared to take some action against the regime.

Although this finding underlines the horror of a totalitarian system that is able to fragment all opposition and put every dissident into a situation of pluralistic ignorance, it has an encouraging implication when applied to our own relatively open society. In our society the tyranny of the majority, which De Tocqueville rightly deplored, is continually limited and resisted by the ability of dissenting individuals to find other like-minded dissenters and to form couples or small groups (or sometimes large groups) in which the courage to dissent is sustained by mutual reinforcement. As long as freedom of assembly is inviolate, dissent can be viable even if it exists only in tiny minorities. Each of these groups can be an important reference group for its members—more important to them than the majority feeling in the society as a whole.

(4) A final finding is more ominous: Crutchfield has shown that conformity on political questions is likely to be greater, more un-

---

[4] Krech, Crutchfield and Ballachey, 1962, pp. 522–29.

[5] Asch, 1952, pp. 7–9.

conscious and more permanent than conformity on visual perceptions such as the length of lines.

For example, in a large college-student group Crutchfield found that only nineteen percent expressed *private* agreement with the statement: "Free speech being a privilege rather than a right, it is proper for a society to suspend free speech whenever it feels itself threatened." In his experimental situation, when confronted with an apparently unanimous group consensus agreeing with the statement, fifty-eight percent expressed agreement. Moreover, when such political-opinion items are used, a considerable part of the change persists when the same people are questioned several weeks later. This suggests that there is often a real change of attitude. Apparently, after being told that everyone else agreed with a certain attitude item, many of the subjects really changed their minds.[6]

Loyalty

The power of conformity is greatly increased when a majority, feeling threatened by disunity, tries to get the misguided heretics to see the light. The experimental evidence provided by Festinger, Schachter, and Back has verified the everyday observation that majorities do often have this kind of anxiety and often make active efforts to bring dissenters back into line.[7] Dissent makes the majority feel uncomfortable.

If friendly persuasion of dissenters fails, and usually only after it fails, the majority tends to give up its effort, becoming less friendly to the dissenter, and ceasing to treat him as a full member of the group. Rokeach has shown that similarity of beliefs is a major element in the feeling of kinship and of liking.[8] In some degree, then, the dissenter is ostracized. Intentionally or unintentionally, this operates as a punishment, and fear of it tends both to bring him back into the fold and to deter others from leaving it.

That is one way in which group spirit or "loyalty" operates. The word is put in quotation marks here, since it is possible to doubt whether enforcing uniformity of opinion necessarily adds to the strength or the long-run welfare of a group. When healthy debate is

[6] Krech, Crutchfield and Ballachey, 1962, p. 509.
[7] Festinger, Schachter and Back, 1950.
[8] Rokeach, 1960, pp. 132–68.

needed, a premature uniformity can detract from the group's strength, or damage its well-being in the long run, or both.

Another form of "loyalty" that can lead to stifling dissent is especially familiar in time of war: the desire of those who are bent on accomplishing a task, such as winning a war, to get on with the job, and to have a united people behind them. Dissent then causes not merely a vague feeling of discomfort because one's own assumptions are challenged but also real anger at those whose dissent is believed—often with reason—to be hurting the war effort, hurting the impression of unity that the nation makes upon its enemies, postponing the confidently expected day of victory, and thereby postponing the peace that everyone wants. The result can be deliberate distortion of information toward the wartime black-and-white picture, or at least a judicious ignoring of facts that might conflict with that picture. It is not called distortion of course. It is called maintaining morale or uniting the country or not giving aid and comfort to the enemy. In this great morale-maintaining enterprise the government and the major elements in the mass media usually join hands. George Creel's office set up during World War I to propagandize the American people was accepted as legitimate or even necessary by the great majority of Americans.

Perhaps the Vietnam war, precisely because it has been much less than unanimously, enthusiastically supported by the more articulate elements in the American people, has seen also a less determined effort by the government and by the mass media to sustain and reinforce the typical wartime black-and-white picture. With a vigorous and articulate minority ready to pounce on flagrant distortions or omissions, and with the danger of nuclear war looming in the background as a possible consequence of too much oversimplification, there may have been fewer such distortions and omissions than has been typical of wartime in other countries, or in some other wars fought by this country.

Nevertheless there has been a good deal of distortion with the highest of motives: patriotism. The United States herself has embarked on an enterprise, and the prevailing feeling is that "it's a nasty enterprise but we've simply got to see it through." Loyal Americans, it is felt, will necessarily support our boys who are dying in Vietnam; "support" has been interpreted as saying nothing that might diminish their faith in the cause they are fighting for. Apparently most owners and managers of the mass media have shared this view, though the "working stiffs" of journalism and television who have seen the war at first hand or who have closely touched other grounds for skepticism regarding the official ideology do not always agree.

The need to put patriotism (as the military conceive it) ahead of candid reporting is likely to seem obvious. A poignant example is the privately expressed view of Admiral Cervera, commander of the Spanish fleet at the time of the Spanish-American war, who went into battle already recognizing the great odds against him: "We may and must expect a disaster. But as it is necessary to go to the bitter end, and as it would be a crime to say that publicly, I hold my tongue and go forth resignedly to face the trials which God may be pleased to send me."[9] He was right about the disaster.

The dignity and the absolute sense of duty that shine through this passage represent the military tradition at its best: "Duty, Honor, Country." But Cervera's conception of duty should be pondered. He was calmly, absolutely certain that it was his patriotic duty to suppress a fact. It would have been a crime to acknowledge publicly the weakness of Spain compared with the United States, since to do so would have impaired the fighting morale of his country and of his own men.

In addition to the high motive of loyalty to one's country, there is often the somewhat less high motive of loyalty to a team. Members of any team—the State Department, CIA, CBS, *Time,* or any of the smaller units that make up these large ones have a group reputation to maintain in a society that puts patriotism first and that tends to define patriotism more or less as Admiral Cervera did. The jobs and careers of the individuals within these units depend on keeping rapport with the others on the same team. The resulting group pressure on individuals who may be thinking heretically can be very strong.

The Military Mind

One institution has been so often regarded as a major cause of war that it calls for special discussion—the military establishment. The word militarism itself, defined as overweening importance of the

[9] Millis, 1931, p. 119.

military in the society as a whole (including undue influence in the conduct of foreign policy) is seen by many as a self-evident, war-producing evil.

The charge has at least enough evidence behind it to warrant careful review. In Japan the shift to a much more aggressive foreign policy after 1930 coincided with a new predominance of the military in the Japanese government. The Japanese militarists engineered the attack on Pearl Harbor, which in the long run proved a disaster for Japan. President Eisenhower spoke of the danger of the "military-industrial complex" in the United States. Roger Hilsman, who was near the center of policy-making on Vietnam in the Kennedy administration, holds that even President Kennedy felt he had to make concessions to the military—concessions that Hilsman thinks made a rational attack on the real causes of the trouble in Vietnam less possible. Hilsman also believes that Secretary Rusk's greatest limitation was and is his inability to stand up to the military.[10] Secretary McNamara is reported to have stood out stoutly against almost unanimous pressure from his military staff for more drastic escalation of the war in North Vietnam. But President Johnson listens to the military with respect; their constituency in Congress and the country is so strong that any President must do so.

In defense of the American military, it may be said that the higher echelons here, and probably also those in some other countries (Britain, Israel) represent a rather new breed. They are intelligent, incisive, broadly knowledgeable in world affairs, fully aware of the nature of nuclear war and of what it could do to the free societies it is their business to defend, hard-headed in recognizing elements of military weakness such as the danger of getting bogged down in a land war in Asia, and therefore sometimes actually more cautious than civilians who are less aware of military dangers. On the conscious level at least, they are very far from wanting war. These officers often say, and probably fully believe, that because they have seen war at first hand they know its horrors and hate it even more than civilians do.

It would also be a great mistake to regard the military establishment as monolithic. In addition to the service rivalries that often have the effect of opening the minds of men in one service to facts that are brushed aside by those in another, there is within the Penta-

[10] Hilsman, 1967; cf. Schlesinger, 1967, p. 40.

gon much the same diversity of opinion that can be found outside it. Six names—Eisenhower, Bradley, Ridgway, Gavin, Lansdale, and Taylor—should be enough to remind any well-informed American of the danger of generalizing, in negative terms, about "the military mind."

Nevertheless, there is a strong case for the proposition with which we started—that some characteristics found especially often in military men represent a danger to peace. More often than others, military men make mistaken predictions because of a gross inability to empathize realistically with their enemies or potential enemies. Whatever the causes may be, the record of history seems to be that the military have usually failed to meet the hard criterion of successful prediction, when that has demanded empathy.

A prime example is the decision of Japan's military men to attack Pearl Harbor. Militarily the attack was a brilliant success, but psychologically it was a disaster that after four years led to military disaster too. While it knocked out temporarily much of America's immediate capacity to wage war in the Western Pacific, it unified the American people and mobilized an American effort that would have been quite impossible without it. America had been deeply isolationist, and in December, 1941, was still torn between interventionists and isolationists. Even the interventionists were as a rule unready to sanction all-out war. Pearl Harbor ended that. Anger, hurt pride, and a feeling that the nation itself was in danger took over in the United States and catalyzed the tremendous latent power of the American people as no ideals or ideology could have done. Hitler had provoked a similar reaction in Britain two years earlier, but the Japanese military had apparently learned nothing vicariously. They had little or no insight into anything so intangible as the feelings of Americans, yet those feelings eventually translated themselves into a tremendous, highly tangible force that destroyed the military power of Japan.

Examples of military obtuseness in earlier times include Napoleon's persistence in war, though it arrayed most of Europe against him, and the unwillingness of the generals on either side in World War I to consider a compromise peace. MacArthur insisted that it was not dangerous to cross the 38th Parallel in Korea; according to his prediction, the Chinese would not or could not enter the Korean war with decisive force. Nasser, a military man, failed to understand the temper of Israel and therefore failed to predict its response in

June, 1967. The Pentagon and CIA apparently planned the Bay of Pigs without obtaining Lloyd Free's easily available data on Cuban public opinion.[11] The Pentagon (except Secretary McNamara) has seemingly miscalculated when it has advocated greatly increased bombing in North Vietnam, without giving due weight to psychological evidence such as the Strategic Bombing Survey and the evidence of James Cameron and others that anger at the bombing had actually stiffened the fighting spirit of the North Vietnamese. In the public statements of military men (Wheeler, Westmoreland) there has been little discussion of such psychological evidence. They have not said, for example, that "the Strategic Bombing Survey raises doubts about whether strategic bombing is a good way to break a proud enemy's will to fight, but we are inclined to discount the relevance of this evidence because . . ." Instead, they have simply ignored it. Nor have the military seemed aware that the North Vietnamese, leaders and followers alike, probably believe absolutely that whatever they do in the South is to defend their homeland against American aggression. This rather elementary proposition, which one would think ought to underlie any calculations about the probability of bringing the enemy to his knees by bombing, apparently has not been publicly discussed even as a proposition to be refuted.

My own conversations with several military men in Vietnam (mainly those ranked between sergeant and colonel) support this characterization of the public statements of officers of ranks higher than colonel. Their one most striking common characteristic seemed to be inhibition of curiosity, both about the viewpoint of the enemy and about the background of the war.

There are some exceptions to this rule. Hitler's generals, for instance, were more cautious than he was. It would seem, nevertheless, that mistaken predictions due to lack of empathy have been the rule, not the exception. No doubt the generals have always felt that they were friendly toward the common people or peasantry, hostile only to the Communists who were intimidating and oppressing them, willing to undertake "basic reforms" when the military task had been accomplished, and in the meantime doing what they could for the peasants. General Taylor's report to President Kennedy in 1961 was more realistic and thoroughgoing on this score

[11] Cantril, 1967, pp. 1–5.

than that of the civilian, Eugene Staley. At that point the incisiveness and the downrightness that characterize the military mind at its best showed to good advantage. Colonel Lansdale's approach is another outstanding exception. But, with a few exceptions such as these, the military record of understanding what the political war actually calls for has been meager, to say the least.

Another question on which the typical military view seems one-sided is the priority of military objectives versus psychological objectives in South Vietnam. To a military man who has never truly empathized with the peasants and who is blindly involved in winning the strategic and tactical war, the priority of military objectives is likely to seem self-evident whenever the two seriously conflict. By his own standards, the military man is already doing his utmost on the psychological side. He even sometimes sacrifices military objectives in order to spare civilian lives. He is doing more than any army ever has in history to be humane. But, except for concessions which civilian colleagues often regard as minor, he feels that winning the war comes first. To refrain from bombing a village or destroying a rice crop in order to avoid antagonizing civilians and driving them into the arms of the Viet Cong seems very desirable if it is practical, but it often seems impractical—if, for example, there are hiding in the village Viet Cong who need to be cleaned out and destroyed. A compromise peace which might deny us military victory appears similarly unthinkable. Such a peace is a no-win policy, and to a very large proportion of military men (as well as to a smaller proportion of non-military men) there is something less than virile—and therefore unthinkable—in a no-win policy.

The typical military belief is that when one's own tangible power is clearly greater than that of the enemy he will eventually be intimidated by it. If he is stubborn, the enemy must simply be made to hurt until he gives up. Weapons are the military's stock in trade, and it is natural for every profession (including psychology) to overestimate the importance and value of its own stock in trade. But such overestimation does interfere with empathy.

The habitual military use of the singular pronoun "he" to represent the enemy is revealing. Millions of people in an opposing nation are not "they," in military parlance; they are "he." Even the far from monolithic cluster of Communist nations is sometimes called "he." The word suggests a single coldly villainous intelligence sitting in

Hanoi or Peking, rationally comparing strengths, willing to retreat when the price he must pay for aggression rises too high.

Such simplicities are natural and perhaps inevitable in military men whose effectiveness in their own proper job of killing requires them to develop a dehumanized image of the people they kill. A soldier can keep his sanity and his self-respect most successfully if he develops the professional hardness of a surgeon, believing that in a broader perspective what he does is right and useful. To cut or to kill is his job, and he concentrates on doing it as intelligently, as efficiently, and as expeditiously as he can. This is a special form of the virile self-image. America is fortunate in having such men able and willing to fight its battles.

However, these are not the skills needed for making realistic judgments about whether a particular war is worth fighting, or escalating.

Omission and Distortion in the Channels of Communication

Many have played the parlor game Rumor, in which a message is whispered to a person at the end of a line of people, he whispers it to the next, and so on, the final product being spoken aloud. Usually the final version is very different from the original message.

The game illustrates a major source of group misunderstanding and group conflict. When an event is complex, far away, and full of the psychological factors that lead to perceptual distortion, the fact that change is likely to occur at several points in the chain of communication may result in a cumulative distortion that sometimes makes the final product radically different from the facts at the beginning of the chain. It is like a snowball rolling downhill. Unlike the random changes in the game of Rumor, those in the serious communication process are sometimes all or nearly all in the same direction—the direction of a particular country's black-and-white picture.

Psychological research, especially that of Allport and Postman,[12] has verified the everyday observation that real rumors are very far from random. The distortion that accumulates as rumors are passed along tends to express the conscious and unconscious emotional needs of the persons involved—hostility, fear, wishful thinking, con-

[12] Allport and Postman, 1945, pp. 160–71.

formity with prevailing stereotypes. The importance of hostility and of fear is especially striking. R. H. Knapp, analyzing 1000 rumors collected from all parts of the country in 1942,[13] classified them as follows:

Hostility (wedge-driving) rumors	66 percent
Fear (bogey) rumors	25 percent
Wish (pipe-dream) rumors	2 percent
Unclassifiable rumors	7 percent

The resemblance between this and the diabolical enemy-image is obvious. The tendency for rumors to conform to prevailing negative stereotypes is also conspicuous. Persons with strong prejudices against Negroes, Jews, the Administration, the brass hats, John Birchers, white supremacists, hippies, peaceniks, Nazis, or Communists are likely to modify a rumor at least slightly in the direction of their negative stereotypes. A striking case in point is reported by Allport and Postman.[14] The starting point of the rumor process they studied was a series of pictures: One showed a subway scene with a white man having an obviously heated argument with a Negro. The *white* man held a razor in his hand. In more than half of their experiments the razor moved (at some point in the transmission of the rumor) from the white man's hand to the Negro's. As these investigators put it, "This is a clear instance of assimilation to stereotyped expectancy. Black men are 'supposed' to carry razors; white men are not."

Another characteristic feature of rumors consists of what Allport and Postman call "leveling and sharpening." Leveling consists of a progressive shortening of the story as more and more details are omitted. After five reproductions, in their experimental situation, only about thirty percent of the details of the original story were retained. Obviously, there is abundant opportunity for distortion if this process of omission is a selective one, as it usually is. The story elements that are interesting, perhaps because they satisfy some unconscious need, are usually retained. Relatively speaking, they stand out more. This process of greater visibility of the emotionally significant material is what is called sharpening, and it can occur by ex-

[13] Quoted by Allport and Postman, 1945, p. 161.
[14] Allport and Postman, 1945, pp. 163-68.

aggeration of the significant material as well as by omission of the rest.[15]

Going a step beyond Allport and Postman, we can say that at each human link in the communication process three potential sources of distortion exist: distorted perception, distorted expression, and selective contact. The first two are familiar and obvious enough. Suppose there are four human links in a simple chain: A, B, C, and D. We can call A the source of the message, B and C the carriers of it, and D the receiver. B, the first carrier, may slightly misunderstand what A has told him; that is distorted perception. Then when he passes it on to C he may change it a little more, even as compared with his own initial perception of it. That is distorted expression. Both are forms of psychological distortion, since they occur within B's mind.

Selective contact is not itself psychological, though psychological factors can greatly influence it. It is familiar to social scientists chiefly through the writings of Hovland,[16] Klapper,[17] and others on the importance of "selective self-exposure" to various television programs, newspaper articles, etc. It is well known that any attempt to influence the public through the mass media is greatly influenced by the selective self-exposure of the audience. They will not turn on a particular television program, read a particular newspaper article, or expose themselves to a particular message in any other way unless it somehow satisfies their psychological needs. Since people's needs are usually satisfied by what they agree with and frustrated by what they disagree with, this gives a great advantage to messages agreeing with and supporting what people already believe.

What is less often realized is that a similar type of selective self-exposure can occur at any point in the chain of communication. Together with factors of physical accessibility, this can greatly influence the process of cumulative distortion. Usually it does so in the same direction as psychological distortion—that is, in the direction of closer and closer conformity to the nationalistic black-and-white picture.

[15] Allport and Postman, 1945, pp. 164–67.
[16] Hovland, 1959, pp. 8–17.
[17] Klapper, 1960.

SELECTIVE CONTACT AT THE SOURCE

One example is the self-selected character of escapees from Communist countries. It can be taken for granted that, by and large, it is the more disaffected, disgruntled, anti-Communist people who come out. The attitudes they express are thus (even apart from the problem of frankness) likely to be more anti-Communist than the attitudes of the general population in the countries from which they have come.[18]

Another example is the predominantly upper- and middle-class character of the contacts that Americans make in many countries overseas, including Vietnam. The point has been made that those whom Americans are most likely to meet in Vietnam—army officers, officials, educated people, city people, Catholics, foreign-oriented people who can speak French or English—are precisely the ones most likely to support the government or, at least, strongly oppose the Viet Cong.

Naturally, this source of distortion affects most the Americans who visit Vietnam for a short time and have contacts arranged for them by other Americans who are on the spot and who may have self-interested reasons to see that the visitor gets a "good" impression. A probably exaggerated but essentially valid picture of how the process works is contained in the chapter entitled "Senator, Sir . . ." in *The Ugly American,* by Lederer and Burdick.[19] Fall speaks of "the Catholic refugees, resettled in easily accessible areas, mostly around Saigon and along major roads, [who] become the political shock troops of the regime, providing the cheering crowds that for so long fooled American official visitors about the popularity of Diem."[20] The simple factor of language is often overlooked or underemphasized as a factor in distortion; Fall remarks on the higher quality of French reporting as against American reporting, simply because a much larger proportion of the people speak French than English. This gives the French-speaking reporter an important advantage in amount and representativeness of first-hand contact.[21]

The factor of class or economic position is also often underesti-

[18] USIA/IRS, 1963; Inkeles and Bauer, 1959.
[19] Lederer and Burdick, 1958.
[20] Fall, 1964a, p. 175.
[21] Fall, 1966b, p. 8.

mated. Malcolm Browne notes that "if you are a Saigonese, you probably are among the masses who earn even less than $20 a month, and who live in one of the vast slums that the visitors never see."[22] Those Americans who assume that the Vietnamese legislative body is at least roughly, reasonably representative of the South Vietnamese people may be suffering from a similar error. There is reason to think that the great majority of its members belong to the landlord class or share the viewpoint of that class, and therefore almost inevitably oppose many basic popular reforms.[23]

The self-selection factor exists in a subtler form in the tendency of the more pro-American and anti-Communist individuals, within any of these groups, to seek or cultivate contacts with Americans. Like seeks like; here again Rokeach's finding of the great importance of similar beliefs in establishing rapport is relevant. Those who have pleasant, friendly things they spontaneously want to say to an American are more likely to say them than those who do not. The same tendency is familiar in many contexts. Market researchers are familiar with the danger of relying on favorable findings from a mailed-in questionnaire when only a fraction of those who are asked to mail it in actually do so. They know that consumers who take the trouble to fill out and mail the questionnaire are likely to be much more favorable to the product, on the average, than those who do not. Politicians and the Voice of America know that fan mail is likely to be overwhelmingly favorable, even when real attitudes are mixed or mainly unfavorable. A speaker who does not want to fool himself realizes that those who enjoyed his speech are more likely to come up afterward and tell him their opinion of it than those who disliked it. Similarly, in Vietnam, those who do appreciate America's help against the Communists are more likely to make friends with Americans and express such feelings than those who sullenly resent our presence there. Any American who thinks he can generalize about Vietnamese attitudes simply because he has "been there," and who is not aware of intangible selective factors such as these, is probably fooling himself.

22 Browne, 1965, p. 202.
23 Buttinger, 1967b, pp. 6–110.

PSYCHOLOGICAL DISTORTION AT THE SOURCE

In interviewing escapees from Communist countries, another great problem is the extent to which they will speak truthfully and frankly. As strangers, newcomers to an anti-Communist world, they know how vulnerable they are, and how important it is to remove the stigma of coming from a Communist country by proving how anti-Communist they are. The normal desire of the respondent in any interview to say what the interviewer wants to hear is greatly magnified in escapees.[24]

Conversations with Soviet citizens on the streets of Moscow are subject to a similar bias in the opposite direction. There, the impulse and the ingrained habit are to say what a Communist society wants to hear. Someone might be listening, and report to the KGB. Understandably, therefore, there is a great gap between the predominantly anti-Communist sentiment expressed by escapees and the overwhelmingly pro-Communist sentiments expressed on the streets of Moscow. A Westerner seeking the truth about how Soviet citizens feel toward their system and their government can be fairly sure that it lies somewhere between the two extremes.

As we have seen, a peasant in a Viet Cong-controlled village must have a similar temptation to tell his Viet Cong controllers that he sides with them.

Similarly in a government-controlled city or village, Vietnamese with views disapproved by the government (such as neutralism, which is still a punishable offense) are not likely to speak up as freely as the orthodox supporters of the government do. They have good, tangible reasons to keep silent. On the day of Premier Quat's accession in February 1965, for instance, a meeting of Saigon intellectuals who favored a negotiated peace was broken up by the military police, and some of the leaders were arrested and deported.[25]

Another motive that may lead to conscious distortion at or near the source is group self-interest. For instance, many Vietnamese associated with Diem or with post-Diem governments have wanted to give Americans a good impression of what those governments were doing, in "revolutionary development," in keeping the loyalty

[24] USIA/IRS, 1963; Inkeles and Bauer, 1959.
[25] Nicolaus, 1965.

of the people, etc. Until 1963, at least, this led to much well-documented deception. According to Malcolm Browne, "Diem's touchiness about American spooks wandering around on their own . . . was always respected by the Americans, in the interest of preserving American-Vietnamese harmony, and somehow the intelligence reports always had it that the war was going well. Lodge was the first ranking American in Vietnam to ignore the niceties and send out his own crews. . . . The conclusion of these teams, in substance, was that the situation was worse than even the fears of the most confirmed pessimists (who included a number of resident American newsmen)."[26]

Unconscious motives may operate here too. When an anti-Communist Vietnamese collects his impressions of the prevailing feeling of his countrymen, he too wants to believe that the majority agree with him and are intensely anti-Communist. If he is an urban, middle- or upper-class person whose contacts are mainly with intensely anti-Communist people, his unconscious motives may lead him (like many Americans) to forget how atypical his social environment is and to focus on his middle-class world as if it were not very different from South Vietnam as a whole. Like many Americans, he may speak of "the morale of the Vietnamese" being bolstered by American bombing in the North, and really believe it, when what he really means is "my morale and that of the kind of people I associate with."

SELECTIVE CONTACT BY CARRIERS

This is partly a question of censorship, partly a question of physical access to first-hand and second-hand sources of news, and partly a question of the lines of communication that exist informally through friendship and rapport.

Censorship is an ugly word, but it has existed in Vietnam on a very large scale. John Mecklin, our Public Affairs Officer during the period that included the death of Diem, has written a book, *Mission in Torment*,[27] much of which is devoted to his long struggle against pervasive and often stupid censorship. The core of the difficulty at that time was State Department Directive No. 1006. "It was

[26] Browne, 1965, pp. 269–70.
[27] Mecklin, 1965a.

an incredible directive, and reflected an attitude of distrust in the American people which prevails today. . . . I went through a personal hell in trying to live with this directive and this attitude from Washington in my function as Public Affairs Officer."[28] Largely as a result of Mecklin's initiative that directive was changed, and the situation now seems to be considerably better,[29] but it is hard to tell how much is accomplished by unofficial censorship in the form of "gentlemen's agreements" between reporters and official sources of news.

Such "gentlemen's agreements," which can be wholly tacit and need not require anything more than a judicious omission of certain kinds of items from news dispatches, amount to a kind of informal censorship, the importance of which is very hard to estimate. In Washington as well as in Saigon, correspondents enter into a subtle relationship with government sources of news in which, more or less tacitly, correspondents who play ball with the government may discover that they are rewarded by somewhat greater access to the news that is their livelihood. In Vietnam, for instance, some correspondents say that when they have sent home material that is distasteful to the American authorities in Saigon they were denied transportation on military planes—a privilege freely enjoyed by other correspondents. In certain other capitals, Moscow, for instance, the process works the other way: Western correspondents who do not play ball with the Soviet government are the ones penalized by less access to important news. This is not the kind of thing that can be officially protested; access to government-controlled information is a privilege, not a right. But selective reports resulting from these practices add to cumulative distortion.[30]

Physical accessibility can be important, too. The access of newsmen to brutality on our side and not on the Viet Cong side is a case in point. On the other hand, much of the torture routinely practiced by our South Vietnamese allies has failed to be reflected in regular American news dispatches. It has been revealed mainly by

[28] Mecklin, 1965b, p. 25.

[29] Raymond, 1966.

[30] Tran Van Dinh (1967, p. 16) quotes a letter written on February 20, 1967, by seventy student leaders and professors in Saigon, addressed to U.S. students: "In South Vietnam cities, American power has become so great in support of the Ky government that no one can speak against the war without risking his life or his liberty. If it were not so, millions would speak out."

such men as Fall, Malcolm Browne, and Denis Warner—writers of books and articles for the *New Republic* and other magazines that do not have mass circulation. For a great many Americans, including some editors of newspapers and some Washington officials, this, too, is a matter of selective contact; they simply have not been physically fully exposed to this aspect of reality in Vietnam. (As we have seen, the rest of the world has probably been overexposed to the fact of torture as compared with other facts; brutality on our side has been "sharpened" for them while other things have been "leveled.") *Pro*-Viet Cong as well as anti-Viet Cong material has probably been denied to American newsmen because of their lack of actual contact with villages the Viet Cong controls.

There is finally the kind of selective contact that is based on friendship or rapport. During the Diem period, American Embassy officials were estranged not only from pro-Viet Cong elements but also from strongly anti-Communist intellectuals and even from American newsmen. They lived on a social island and were fed information by pro-Diem officials. People do not have contact unless they want to have contact, and they will not make the effort, even with a person who is an excellent source of information, if they are irritated with him and have formed an opinion that he is "irresponsible."

PSYCHOLOGICAL DISTORTION BY CARRIERS OF INFORMATION

If a typical communication sequence is thought of as A-B-C-D, with B and C playing the role of carriers of a message that starts with A and ends with D, then B and C represent a great variety of intermediate people: government officials of an allied nation, a nation's own government officials, soldiers, newspaper reporters, social scientists, editors, gatherers of government intelligence, carriers of intelligence to the top decision-making level, etc. There is ample room here for psychological distortion, partly conscious (chiefly for reasons of "patriotism" or "helping the war effort") and partly unconscious (because some messages are more consonant with the carrier's own black-and-white picture than others are). Conformity enters in, and desire to advance one's own career, and fear of fatally setting back one's career.

In all probability the distortion at this stage is greater in a closed society such as North Vietnam than in a much more open one such as the United States. There are indications for example that Hanoi itself has been quite fooled by reports of military successes coming from its men in South Vietnam, who exaggerated gains and minimized losses by fantastic ratios such as ten to one.

We know more about the distortion on our own side. Some of it has undoubtedly been antiwar distortion by deeply antiwar American reporters, and some has been an overplaying of what is violent and therefore dramatic. More of it, though, has probably been distortion in the other direction. The failures, the corruption, the unpopularity of Diem and his successors, and the torture widely used by the Vietnamese troops have occasionally reached the American public in full force, but only when there has been some break in the screen of official and unofficial resistance that normally diminishes the full impact of the facts. Fortunately this kind of distortion has been reduced to a minimum in the minds of seasoned first-hand observers. An anonymous writer in the *New Republic* says:

From the beginning, few reporters who spent any time at all in Vietnam (unlike columnists and special one-shot correspondents who are carted around by colonels like Americans in Russia by Intourist guides) could ignore the discrepancy between what they saw and what they read in handouts and heard in briefings. . . . When the Pentagon or the White House sends the chiefs to Saigon, they hear what they expect to hear. Although a military maverick may sometimes get to a visiting Secretary or Presidential adviser, most of the information filters through a fine screen of self-delusion.[31]

Editors and publishers too can think wishfully and "patriotically" (as they define patriotism) and can try to please a wishfully thinking and "patriotic" public. From the standpoint of militants who regard every departure from the black-and-white picture as a weakness that verges on disloyalty, the American press has been extremely, even dangerously free in its reporting on every sort of fact and opinion about the Vietnam war. But if one's starting-point is the perception of seasoned observers on the spot in Vietnam, rather than the American black-and-white picture, it seems rather that the typical attitude of the American press and periodicals has been a sort of compromise between the facts as reported to them and what would seem properly "patriotic" in the eyes of their readers and

[31] *New Republic*, 1966.

the American government. Also, editors have their own overall perceptions of the facts, and tend to regard as irresponsible those observers who see the facts differently. There have been exceptions, notably the *New York Times*. But other respected publications, such as *Time*, have not been insensitive to the pressures of "patriotism." At least, according to the anonymous *New Republic* article quoted above, "the *New York Times's* Charles Mohr resigned as a *Time* magazine correspondent in Saigon when his accurate on-the-spot reporting did not fit the fantasies of his editors in New York."

There is, of course, a question as to whether what is felt to be "patriotism" is actually that. It is questionable whether denying the American people full and undistorted access to the facts is an act of genuine patriotism. But even those editors and publishers who believe themselves to be fully committed to American principles of free expression are capable of the forms of misperception that afflict us all.

It should be noticed too that government intelligence is a medium, like the press or television, and it too can refract the light that shines through it. Presidents and Secretaries, briefed by heads of intelligence bureaus whom they regard as reliable, who in turn have been briefed by subordinates, may unknowingly encounter the same kind of cumulative distortion that afflicts the mass media. Even President Kennedy, one of the most intelligent and evidence-oriented Presidents we have had, was fooled. The full story of the evils of the Diem regime was not appreciated in Washington until perhaps six years after it could have been.[32] Some people on the spot realized it as early as 1957 but the reality did not strike Washington in full force until the summer of 1963, when it was dramatized by the self-immolation of Buddhist priests.

SELECTIVE CONTACT BY RECEIVERS

This takes chiefly the form of the selective self-exposure that has already been mentioned (p. 224).

PSYCHOLOGICAL DISTORTION BY RECEIVERS

Under this heading we can include both what happens in the mind of a citizen exposed to a newspaper or television program and what

[32] Buttinger, 1967a, II, pp. 925–39.

happens in his mind and that of his friends when he discusses the issue with them. As Katz and Lazarsfeld have pointed out,[33] there is typically a "two-step flow of communication," first to certain individuals who expose themselves to the mass media and then, through them, to many others whose primary source of fact and opinion is face-to-face contact. It follows that selection and distortion can occur as easily in this last link of the communication chain as in any earlier link. And the distortion here is likely to be even more definitely in the direction of an ethnocentric black-and-white picture than it is at earlier stages. Professional journalists have a certain professional pride and commitment to objectivity; the ordinary citizen has little realization of his own importance in the chain of communication and little awareness of the likelihood of conflict between an evidence-oriented and a "patriotic" approach to the facts. To be sure, he may take great pleasure in having what he thinks is inside information, especially if it casts discredit on an administration in his own country that he dislikes, and he may delight in passing along such information without checking as to whether it is true or not. The distortion in this final stage of communication may take many forms, not the least of which is an overplaying of what is startling and dramatic. Hostile misperception often dominates the picture, and it may be hostile misperception of one's own President, as well as of the diabolical enemy. But by and large the pseudo-patriotic black-and-white picture tends to prevail. Any individual who feels himself out of key with it is at least tempted to remain silent.

* * * *

Looking back over these six points where omission and distortion can occur, one cannot help being struck by the receiver's typical unawareness of how drastically distorted the picture he receives may be. Conformity, the tendency to avoid dissonance, and other forces within himself (see Chapter 10) predispose him to accept it. He is also handicapped by sheer lack of knowledge of the real facts at the other end of the chain, or of the kinds of distortion that may occur all along it. Perhaps he assumes that news reporters and others who provide information are, like himself, reasonably conscientious people who would not lie deliberately. In this he is largely

[33] Katz and Lazarsfeld, 1955.

correct. The increment of distortion added by a particular person along the way is usually small, usually unconscious and, when conscious, usually motivated by humanly understandable motives such as patriotism (perhaps misguided). Most of these individuals might be aghast if they saw the final cumulative magnitude of the distortion to which they modestly and more or less inadvertently contributed. Mercifully, they and the final receiver are spared that experience.

In this respect most citizens of a totalitarian state are perhaps more sophisticated than most citizens of the more open societies. A great many of the former *know* that the picture they get is distorted, because they have seen flagrant examples of distortion; they know their government distorts deliberately in order to reflect credit on itself and discredit on its enemies. Even so, the evidence from interviews with escapees suggests that the cynicism of the majority is rather spotty and indiscriminate. Any particular lie or distortion may be widely believed, partly because there is little access to competing sources of information and partly because, if the distortion is in line with that country's nationalistic black-and-white picture, the citizens really want to believe what is told them.

In a more open society there is much less widespread awareness that something might be seriously wrong with the general picture obtained through the mass media. In the United States, for instance, pride in our freedom of the press and the obvious diversity of fact and opinion to which we have access may create a quite spurious impression of how adequate and impartial our mass media are. Because distasteful facts and heretical opinions sometimes come through with full force, most Americans tend to feel that they come through adequately. That may be far from true. To be sure, there is generalized cynicism here, too: "You can't believe everything you read in the papers." But comparatively few clearly realize the full extent of the distortion, or even its characteristic direction. Few realize that it is precisely their own cherished, "patriotic" black-and-white picture that must be drastically discounted if they want a more realistic conception of the world.

Recently there has been much talk about a "credibility gap," with President Johnson pictured as the chief culprit. There is reason to think the talk is largely justified. Those with first-hand knowledge know of many instances, some unpublicized, of less than candid communication by the President and by his unfortunate aides. Naturally these omissions and distortions have served to defend his policies against one or another group of critics, and have generally fitted the pseudo-patriotic picture. They have added their increment to the cumulative total of distortion in that direction.

It would be an exaggeration, however, to think of these presidential distortions as deliberate deception that is qualitatively different from what other men do. It would also be unfortunate if criticism remains concentrated on the President rather than broadening out to include a critical awareness of what is inherent in the entire process of communication and, in fact, in human beings as communicators. The real "credibility gap" is much wider and more permanent than most of the President's critics realize. Distortions all along the line are so modest in size when considered separately, so unconscious often, and so natural for human beings who put their concept of "patriotism" before objectivity, that they probably can never be eliminated or even, in our lifetime, greatly reduced. We should have no illusions as to the probability of much success in the important enterprise of trying to reduce them. The amount of pseudo-patriotic distortion was great during the Eisenhower administration, it was great even during the Kennedy administration, and it will probably continue to be great during the administrations to come.

Ordinary citizens can try to shorten the chain of communication between themselves and the raw facts by listening directly to seasoned first-hand observers. They can read books as well as newspapers. They can cultivate the historian's critical analysis of sources, especially secondary sources, with continuing attentiveness to tangible evidence, various degrees of objectivity, and various directions of bias. They can cultivate the skeptical open-mindedness of the judge who is fully aware of the lawyers' "adversary procedure," taking for granted that people on opposite sides of a controversy will have opposing biases, and therefore listening attentively to what is said by their country's opponents as well as by its friends. They can even attempt the most difficult and painful discipline of all—to examine their own country's most basic assumptions with the same skepticism they automatically have when examining the assumptions of those whom they regard as their country's worst enemies.

Chapter 10

INDIVIDUAL FACTORS IN
BLACK-AND-WHITE THINKING

Unconscious Motives: Power, Prestige, Possession

One possible unconscious motive has already been discussed: the desire for prestige and certain other psychological factors that are closely related to it—the virile self-image (pp. 92–96) and the territorial self-image (pp. 160–65). To understand this whole egoistic side of our nature—the cluster of motives that Horney calls "power, prestige, and possession"—which often masquerades in moral guise (as self-defense, defense of others, defense of freedom, courage, fulfilment of commitments, etc.), is basic to any deeper understanding of the psychology of human conflict.

In this connection two familiar psychological mechanisms deserve special mention: rationalization (giving oneself morally good reasons for doing what one wants to do for less praiseworthy reasons), and projection (attributing to others, especially to an enemy, the non-praiseworthy motives that are unacknowledged or underacknowledged in oneself). In this case it could be argued that many American militants, though not necessarily all, are rationalizing when they do not see or do not emphasize their own reasons of power, prestige, and possession for insisting on complete victory in South Vietnam; and they are projecting when they exaggerate the intensity of Communist desires for world conquest, or perceive Communist aggression in South Vietnam (meaning a cold-blooded, power-motivated attack) as a self-evident fact. In keeping with our emphasis here on selective inattention, one could say that rationalization occurs when an American militant focuses more attention on his own moral motives and less on his egoistic motives than realism would require; projection occurs when he focuses more attention on the enemy's egoistic and aggressive motives (which are probably quite genuine), and less on the enemy's moral motives (such as defending his homeland and helping the economic underdog) than realism would require.

Since an emphasis on the power motive is very common among

both political scientists (for example, Morgenthau[1]) and political practitioners, one of them may object: "We do recognize the desire for power. In any power struggle such as the present struggle between East and West, it would be the height of unrealism not to recognize power as the main goal. But on our side, the Free World side, power is not an end in itself. It is only a means to the deterring of Communist aggression and the preserving of freedom in the Free World. The same is true of prestige and of defending territory such as South Vietnam that is still not under Communist control. America must have prestige in order that her warning to the Communist aggressors will be heeded in the future, and she cannot afford to give up territory such as South Vietnam, not because she values 'possession' as an end in itself, but because demonstrating her willingness to defend non-Communist territory is the only way she can decisively deter future Communist aggression."

Some interpretation is needed therefore. What is suggested here in calling the desire for power, prestige, and possession an unconscious motive is not that conflicting groups are unaware of their desire for these things. They are fully aware of it. But what they tend to gloss over is that they do want these things partly as ends in themselves. They get direct ego gratification from inflating their self-images. And then they rationalize by telling themselves that these things are merely means to an end, and that the end is wholly moral. The Communists, similarly, probably tell themselves that they must have South Vietnam not because they want land for its own sake but because the imperialists must be taught not to encroach flagrantly, as they have done in Vietnam, on the territory of weak, newly developing countries that are now beginning to shake off the imperialist yoke. On both sides, rationalization and projection operate partly by focusing on one's own good ends and on the enemy's evil means.

Rationalization operates largely by influencing perception of the concrete facts themselves. For instance, in order to feel virtuous about fighting in Vietnam it is almost essential for a militant American to believe that most of the Vietnamese people want his help; consequently, chiefly by focusing on some kinds of evidence and ignoring others, he manages to believe that they do want his help. In order to feel virtuous about killing Communists it is extremely

[1] Quote by Kelman, 1965, p. 602.

helpful to perceive Communists as aggressors; consequently (partly though not wholly for this reason) the militant American manages to perceive them as aggressors. In order to feel that no harm is being done to the Vietnamese people by our fighting on their soil, it is important not to believe, or not to think about, the fact that the military government and its local officials are on the whole anti-democratic, corrupt, and brutal; consequently the militant American often manages not to believe or not to think about it. Given the typical militant American way of perceiving the concrete facts, there would be no need to rationalize further, since that perception itself would be a fully adequate justification of what we are doing.

This is not a complete explanation of our behavior by any means, since it does not explain why, with great and genuine reluctance, we got involved there in the first place. We did not start by wanting to kill Communists and then decide that they were aggressors; we first saw them as aggressors and then got into the business of killing them, chiefly because we really believed that they were aggressors, and that it would be dangerous to let aggression be rewarded. The explanation of our behavior lies partly in the actual facts as any open-minded onlooker would have observed them (the Russian and Chinese Communists *have* committed aggression in a number of places since 1939, and the Vietnamese Communists *were* conducting a campaign of assassination in the villages). It lies also in reasons, other than rationalization, for our perceiving the Communists as more diabolical and aggressive than they actually are. But once our course of action had been determined upon, it would have been dissonant and painful to our egos to believe that the people were not on our side, or that from the Communists' own point of view they were not aggressors, or that the Vietnamese government was corrupt and brutal. It is at this later post-decision stage that the mechanism of rationalization, as defined by these examples, becomes a primary reason for the momentum of behavior.

Among the reasons other than rationalization for our perceiving the Communists to be more diabolical and aggressive than they actually are, projection is perhaps the most important. Psychiatrists regard projection as primary in the origin of paranoid delusions of persecution; in their view, intense but unacknowledged hostility must appear in consciousness somehow. It therefore appears as an attribute of others rather than of the self. This could have occurred before we became committed to a course of action. It could help to account for the fact that, although the behavior of many Communists has changed in a number of ways since the death of Stalin, many Americans still see Communism in Stalin's image, as if their world-picture had to include a figure as diabolical as Hitler or Stalin. This could be a case of simple perceptual lag (changes in perception failing to keep up with changes in reality), or it could reflect a need to deny and to project personal individual guilt. (This is not to deny that there is a sense in which "Communism" is a great evil and a great danger; it implies only a question as to whether many militant Americans are exaggerating that evil, whether they are failing to see the human side of the Communists, and whether they are picturing Communism in excessively monolithic terms.)

In any case it seems clear that projection is a major way of explaining to ourselves the morally questionable things we are now doing or are somehow associated with. Torture, for instance, is used by our allies, and we are using napalm. A typical defense when these things are challenged is to cite atrocities of the Viet Cong. Another is to speak of these things as "a regrettable necessity," or as inevitable in view of the nature of war itself, or of this particular war. In such expressions it is as if the guilt were shifted not to a concrete human enemy but to an impersonal Fate or Necessity.

In such expressions, too, projection comes close to what Bakan[2] has called "the externalization of necessity." The mythological figure of Satan and the primitive concept of being "possessed" by evil spirits are two illustrations of an extremely widespread human tendency to ignore evil in the spontaneous acts of the self and to see the causes of behavior rather as inherent in forces that are somehow alien to the self, "forcing" the self to do what it does.

Perhaps we can regard projection and the externalization of necessity as two alternative ways of transferring blame, though they also have much in common. In projection it is as if the individual says "I'm not to blame; *he* is." In the externalization of necessity it is as if he says "I did it, but only because I had to"—without necessarily blaming anyone. In Milgram's experiments on the readiness to inflict pain when commanded to do so by constituted authority[3] the authorities are not necessarily "blamed," because the feeling of compulsion keeps the individual from necessarily feeling guilt even at the outset; there is not necessarily any guilt to "project." In war-

[2] Bakan, 1965.
[3] Milgram, 1963.

time, typically, the two are combined in the formula: The enemy is diabolical, and his acts have forced us to do whatever we have done that might otherwise be blameworthy.

At the outbreak of war especially there is likely to be a great deal of externalization of necessity. The choice between war and peace is usually said to be wholly in the enemy's hands. "It was their decision to escalate." As for one's own actions: We cannot do otherwise; we had no choice; no proud nation could stand idly by and let such things happen; it is too late for compromise; we have made our decision and cannot back down. The little word "cannot" has all the ring of grim, realistic recognition of hard facts; yet it may serve psychologically as a shifting of blame to this imagined or misperceived necessity, and a weak evasion of responsibility that actually rests upon the self.

We have talked about the power-prestige-and-possession cluster of motives and about one sense in which it is unconscious: the tendency to think of power, prestige, and possession as only means to an end when they are also actually ends in themselves. There is also another sense in which this cluster of motives can exert an influence outside of consciousness: its effect on perception and misperception. The group self-image gravitates upward not only in terms of moral goodness but also in terms of strength. As the evidence on military overconfidence indicates, and also the expansive tendency of the territorial self-image, there is a strong wishful-thinking tendency to see one's own group as relatively stronger than it actually is. (On the American tendency to do so, see Almond.)[4] And although the desire to *be* strong is quite conscious and readily acknowledged, the tendency to distort perception in this direction is not. No normal person would admit "I want to kid myself and to think I am both better and stronger than I actually am." Yet, as we have seen, groups often have a marked tendency to do just that.

Unconscious Motives: Aggression, Simplicity, Significance

A familiar thesis of psychologists is that wars represent an indirect, rationalized expression of man's aggressive impulses; and an impressive array of evidence from animal behavior, child behavior,

[4] Almond, 1963.

and cultural anthropology as well as from psychiatry (see especially McNeil,[5] Dollard et al.,[6] Berkowitz[7]) supports the thesis that aggressive impulses are in fact very widespread and that they can be "displaced" onto a national enemy, real or imagined. The hypothesis is supported also by the gusto with which some Americans speak of "clobbering" Hanoi, by Joseph Alsop's "wonder and pride" inspired by the "deadly" efficiency of an American aircraft carrier, and by the tendency of the militant American mind to gravitate toward a definition of the situation that legitimizes, and even requires, violent action.

On the other hand, the word aggression may not be the most fortunately chosen word to describe the reality we are discussing. To the non-psychologist it has connotations not only of enjoying hurting, killing, and destroying for their own sake but also of initiating violence. What people actually feel, usually, is righteous indignation and a desire to hit back in a situation in which they believe, rightly or wrongly, that they have been attacked or that something they cherish has been attacked. Psychiatrists and psychologists are accustomed to a usage that extends the term aggression to this sort of thing—to any enjoyment of destroying, hurting or killing, even in a context of self-defense or righteous indignation such that the individual does not regard his behavior as aggression at all. It is in this latter, psychological sense that the term is used here.

Defined in this way, and in the context of the Vietnam war, the chief importance of the concept probably lies in its possible use in explaining the diabolical enemy-image (Christiansen,[8] Gladstone,[9] Rosenberg[10]). Since hurting or killing others is emotionally satisfying to a normally conscientious human being only when it is done in a mood of righteous indignation, there may be an unconscious need to work up such a mood, and in so doing to exaggerate all evidence of the enemy's criminality, while shutting off every impulse of empathy with the enemy as a human being like oneself. This exaggerated image of enemy criminality and aggression then takes on dynamic importance in creating, for instance, the conviction of

[5] McNeil, 1965, pp. 14–41.
[6] Dollard et al., 1939.
[7] Berkowitz, 1962.
[8] Christiansen, 1959.
[9] Gladstone, 1962.
[10] Rosenberg, 1965, pp. 322–29.

Communist aggression which, as we have seen, is basic in the reality-world of American militants.

Like the desire to think well of one's collective self, the desire for simplicity is in a sense completely conscious. Most of us would grant immediately that we enjoy it when simplicity emerges out of complexity, and also that uncertainty makes us anxious. What we are ordinarily unaware of is the effect of this on our assumptions about the world. We do not say, I will kid myself and imagine the world to be more simple than it is, or I will kid myself and imagine that this interpretation is certain when it is not. But we do it, just the same.

The familiar psychological terms for this process are "dissonance" (see below, p. 250) and "intolerance of ambiguity" (see below, p. 246). Whatever is dissonant with the simple black-and-white picture tends to be denied, reinterpreted, or selectively inattended (Cooper and Jahoda,[11] Holsti[12]). When evidence appears that is open to more than one interpretation there is a tendency to be intolerant of ambiguity—unwilling to suspend judgment—and a tendency to achieve a feeling of certainty illegitimately by settling prematurely for one interpretation (Heider,[13] Osgood and Tannenbaum,[14] Rosenberg[15]).

One particularly important result of this is an absence of empathy. Empathy normally has the disturbing effect of requiring us to see double—to hold in suspension two interpretations of the same facts, the other fellow's and one's own. Complexity and uncertainty are introduced. The human mind, seeking simplicity and certainty, rebels. And empathy is choked off.

Jerome Frank and others have emphasized a related but deeper reason for clinging to an ideology (a Communist ideology, a nationalist ideology, a democratic ideology, a world-peace ideology, or any other): It gives significance to the lives of individuals who otherwise might be overwhelmed by a sense of purposelessness and insignificance. Usually some kind of black-and-white picture is an inherent part of the ideology, and gives meaning to the struggle between good guys and bad guys, or between those who "see the truth"

[11] Cooper and Jahoda, 1947.
[12] Holsti, 1967.
[13] Heider, 1946, 1958.
[14] Osgood and Tannenbaum, 1955.
[15] Rosenberg, 1965, pp. 294–98.

and those who do not. When this occurs, the need to cling to that picture is reinforced by very deep psychological forces.

As Frank has pointed out, this suggests an additional answer to the question of why the Vietnamese Communists have shown such extraordinary stubbornness and tenacity even in the face of great punishment. Both their Communist ideology and the nationalist ideology that is fused with it have given significance to their lives, and when this occurs, the individual willingly gives up life itself rather than the cause that gives his life its meaning. Like the Christian martyrs, they go to their death praising God—their version of God. Such a mood is poles apart from the bargaining attitude of a merchant, or the attitude of a child who knows that what he wants to do is wrong, and desists when his parent's punishment becomes severe enough. It is much more like the mood of a child who feels that what he is doing is absolutely right and that his punisher is absolutely wrong. Such a child may stop what he was doing, but, whether he stops it or not, the punishment is likely to increase his tendency to look upon the punisher with grim, unforgiving hate. (Cf. Coser's proposition, based on Simmel, that conflict is intense if it is ideological; Coser,[16] summarized by Angell.[17])

Ethnocentrism, Dogmatism, and the Authoritarian Personality

The most important thing to teach children is absolute obedience to their parents.

Any good leader should be strict with people under him in order to gain their respect.

Prison is too good for sex criminals. They should be publicly whipped or worse.

There are two kinds of people in the world: the weak and the strong.

No decent man can respect a woman who has had sex relations before marriage.

These are sample items from the "F scale" (F for Fascism, see footnote 18), which is generally regarded as the best available meas-

[16] Coser, 1956.
[17] Angell, 1965, p. 107.

ure of "potential fascism" or the "authoritarian personality." A person who agrees with all or most of the items usually has more than his share of anti-semitism, anti-Negro feeling, anti-foreign feeling, conventionality, "authoritarian aggression," "authoritarian submission," narrow nationalism, religious dogmatism, superstition, lack of education, and lack of intelligence. Though not more likely to be neurotic than other people are, he is distinctly more likely to be a criminal.

It is an interesting exercise to examine any of the statements critically and to ask oneself what in it would correlate with any of the characteristics in this list. Despite certain criticisms, the correlations are now well established; the question is why they exist. For instance, take the first item: The most important thing to teach children is absolute obedience to their parents. A person who is properly skeptical of exaggerated statements and humane in his philosophy of child-rearing is likely to question it at several points. Obedience may be important, but is it the most important thing to teach children? What about other characteristics such as kindness, truthfulness, independent thinking? What about the word absolute? While it suggests a proper and wholesome firmness in the parents, doesn't it also suggest a completeness of submission and an abdication of critical thinking on the part of the child that might conflict with the development of a self-reliant, mature personality? Couldn't such a statement be a rationalization of a parent's need to dominate absolutely? And if a person hastily and thoughtlessly agrees with such a statement, not realizing its implications, isn't that a sign of a too-ready conformity—an overreadiness to agree with what others say, especially if what is said seems to represent the familiar, conventional wisdom and conventional morality? Similar questions can be raised with regard to the other four F-scale items listed above.

The scale itself and most of the findings mentioned above are the work of a group of psychologists at Berkeley[18] in which the late Else Frenkel-Brunswik and Nevitt Sanford were the senior investigators. It has inspired a large amount of research by others using the same scale (for a thoughtful summary of it, see Brown[19]), some of which has been critical of the research methods used by the

[18] Adorno, Frenkel-Brunswik, Levinson and Sanford, 1950.
[19] Brown, 1965, pp. 477–546.

Berkeley group (Christie and Jahoda,[20] Hyman and Sheatsley[21]), though not inclined to question seriously their essential conclusions. The existence of a large cluster of attitudes that correlate significantly with each other, and that therefore are presumably linked together by a basic psychological characteristic or cluster of characteristics, has been verified especially by a factor analysis conducted by Melvin.

Relationships between all of this and the kinds of misperception that lead to war are not hard to find. Consider the three anti's: anti-Semitism, anti-Negro feeling, and anti-foreign feeling. Together they make up what the Berkeley group calls "ethnocentrism," and that group developed an ethnocentrism scale that correlates highly with the F scale. With few exceptions the ethnocentrist is an authoritarian personality and vice versa, in spite of the fact that the F scale contains no items directly dealing with attitudes toward outgroups.

Ethnocentrism can be defined as a tendency to approve or to view as natural and right whatever is associated with one's own group (the ingroup), and to disapprove or view as unnatural and wrong whatever is associated with a contrasted group (an outgroup). There is an obvious, close relationship between this and the nationalistic black-and-white picture that has been encountered again and again in this book. It is encountered especially in the Communists (whose basis for dividing their world is not necessarily a nationalistic one, but is extremely black-and-white); it is encountered in militant nationalists such as the Nazis or the Arab nationalists; and it is encountered among some militant anti-Communists, especially those whose chief charge against Communism is that it is an alien or un-American philosophy. An ethnocentrist, as studied by Frenkel-Brunswik, Sanford, et al., tends to interpret ambiguous evidence as favorable to his own group or unfavorable to outgroups such as Jews, Negroes, or foreigners. This, it can be argued, is close to the psychological essence of all black-and-white thinking. With the substitution of the word "enemy" for "outgroup"—and an enemy is obviously an outgroup—the same tendency characterizes the nationalistic black-and-white thinker whose actions lead to war. Moreover, this relationship is not a matter of inference; it has been

[20] Christie and Jahoda, 1954.
[21] Hyman and Sheatsley, 1954, pp. 50–122.

confirmed empirically by Smith and Rosen,[22] who found a close relationship between the F scale and lack of "world-mindedness," and by Martin and Westie,[23] who found a clear correlation between anti-Negro prejudice and nationalism.

Another major connecting link between this kind of research and the psychological causes of war consists of the concept of dogmatism, clarified and investigated especially by Rokeach.[24] Dogmatism can be defined as a clinging to preconceptions in the face of contrary evidence, or as a tendency to interpret ambiguous evidence more or less automatically as supporting one's own preconceptions. This has a clear relation to black-and-white thinking, since the black-and-white picture is the most basic, most essential preconception in the mind of the black-and-white thinker. It also has a clear relation to Rapoport's concept of "the blindness of involvement," which means shutting one's eyes to evidence or ideas that conflict with an activity one is involved in. Its relationship to the authoritarian personality is also well established. Rokeach has shown this, and has brought out too the relationship of dogmatism to the kind of mental rigidity that consists of not recognizing, challenging, or changing an implicit assumption that happens to be false.

Intolerance of Ambiguity

One of the few ideas in modern psychology that really explains a number of different things is Else Frenkel-Brunswik's concept of "intolerance of ambiguity."[25] Introduced originally as an aspect of the "authoritarian personality," it has become more and more widely recognized and applied in more and more different areas.

It can be defined as *an inability to recognize that a situation is ambiguous,* that is, that the situation cannot yet be put clearly and confidently into a single familiar category, *and consequently an inability to suspend judgment while examining the available evidence more carefully.* A great many situations are ambiguous; that is, they give rise to more than one incipient interpretation in the mind of an observer. If the observer is at the moment intolerant of am-

[22] Smith and Rosen, 1958.
[23] Martin and Westie, 1959.
[24] Rokeach, 1960.
[25] Frenkel-Brunswik, 1949.

biguity he cannot or does not wait to examine these interpretations. He does not wait to let his thoughts play around them, to explore his own mind for relevant arguments and evidence, and perhaps to obtain new evidence to test their validity. Instead, he latches onto one interpretation, choosing it not primarily on the basis of evidence—he cannot do so because he has not taken the time to examine the evidence—but rather on the basis of what he wants to believe or what he already believes. Therefore, from the standpoint of realism, intolerance of ambiguity is unequivocally bad. It leads to misperception, to self-delusion, and sometimes to disaster.

Examples from the preceding pages are numerous: the military action that some interpret as aggression while others interpret it as self-defense; the disputed piece of land that some see as belonging to Nation A while others see it as belonging to Nation B; the state of opinion in a certain area which people on one side interpret as favoring them and people on the other side interpret as favoring them; the declaration of policy which some interpret as a commitment and others interpret as not a commitment; the course of action which some perceive as imperative and others perceive as misguided.

The word "tolerance" is used here in an unusual sense. It does not mean that the open-minded, evidence-oriented people—those who tolerate ambiguity—*like* ambiguity. They usually dislike it very much. In fact, they usually spend much more time and effort trying to resolve ambiguity (in legitimate, evidence-oriented ways) than the closed-minded people whom Frenkel-Brunswik would call intolerant of it. But the evidence-oriented person does tolerate ambiguity in the sense that he *looks at it steadily* and recognizes it for what it is. (Perhaps "recognition of ambiguity" would have been a more apt term than "tolerance of ambiguity.") The evidence-oriented person who recognizes (and in that sense tolerates) ambiguity does not compulsively seize the most attractive or the most familiar interpretation and then close his eyes to contrary evidence, with an unconscious need to save himself from the momentary anxiety of "seeing double" and from the blow to his ego that may be involved in admitting ignorance or uncertainty. That anxiety and that blow to his ego are what he tolerates. It is the closed-minded dogmatist who cannot stand the strain of seeing double or the humiliation of admitting uncertainty. His mind is in this respect soft and weak. He cannot or does not stand the strain of stretching his mind to hold two or more interpretations in suspension while looking for evidence on both. In self-defense he has to close it. And since he does not make his choice among the available interpretations on the basis of logic or evidence, he necessarily makes it primarily on the basis of "answers" he had already accepted.

Consonance, Dissonance, and Ambivalence

In the rapid development of social psychology during the past twenty years a major role has been played by the concepts of "balance," originated by Heider,[26] and of "dissonance," worked out especially by Festinger.[27] Both are at the root of misperception in international affairs. Balance, as studied by Heider, Newcomb, Osgood, and others is especially relevant to the formation of the black-and-white picture, and dissonance, as studied especially by Festinger and his co-workers, is especially relevant to what is called here the blindness of involvement.

The most inclusive term in this area is *dissonance*. It will be defined here as *the discomfort or psychological disequilibrium that results from bringing together psychological elements which, if separated, would not have this effect.*[*]

For instance, ambiguity—seeing double—is one form of dissonance. When two images or contradictory thoughts overlap and there is uncertainty as to which is valid, there is usually discomfort (as we have just seen), and the mind consciously or unconsciously resorts to various ways of eliminating the ambiguity. When there is tolerance of ambiguity, the methods are likely to be realistic, and when there is intolerance of ambiguity they are likely to be unrealistic. In both cases the ambiguity itself is unpleasant and the mind seeks ways to reduce or eliminate it.

Another kind of dissonance exists when a person or group or course of action is seen as simultaneously good and bad. The idea of a good deed is not ordinarily disquieting, but if one's worst enemy is said to have done something good, there is a kind of discomfort. The badness of the enemy and the goodness of his deed do not

[26] Heider, 1944; 1958, chap. 7.

[27] Festinger, 1957.

[*] Festinger's term is "cognitive dissonance" but the word "cognitive" is ambiguous in this context; we have therefore avoided it and spoken simply of "dissonance."

fit together. When bad people do bad things there is a feeling of fitness or consonance; when bad people do good things there is a feeling of dissonance. The person who hears a report that his enemy has done a good thing may restore consonance by deciding that the report must be wrong, or that his enemy did not do it because of goodness—it was forced upon him by circumstances, or he did it in order to curry favor with someone.

Similarly, there may be a need to believe that a course of action on which one has embarked is all good. For example, the idea of consulting with an ally is not ordinarily a negative idea, but if one's country is embarked on a firm policy from which it is felt that we cannot retreat, the idea of consulting with an ally known to be opposed to that policy is dissonant; it brings up the possibility of being led to reconsider the policy, which could be an acutely unpleasant thought. In all of these cases what causes discomfort is the bringing together of ideas or feelings that have a special relationship to each other, not the inherent nature of the ideas or the feelings considered separately. This is consistent with the meaning of the word "dissonance" in music; there, too, the bringing together of notes that have a special relationship to each other can be unpleasant, even though the notes sounded separately may be pleasant or neutral.

Broad as the term dissonance is, however, it should be noticed that it does not include the most common and familiar form of unpleasantness—frustration. Wanting food and not getting it, wanting sex and not getting it, wanting self-esteem or the approval of others and not getting it—these and many other forms of wanting and not getting are not dissonance. On the other hand, dissonance can perhaps be described as one form of frustration—frustration of a need that is not often recognized: a need for consonance in one's perceptions of the world.

Two main types of dissonance should be distinguished: dissonance between *ideas* (ambiguity) and dissonance between *feelings* (ambivalence). Ambiguity can be defined as *competition between two contradictory thoughts or two images of the same thing*. When there is uncertainty as to whether a particular military action is aggression or self-defense, that is ambiguity. When a person sees another person some distance away and does not know whether it is his friend John or his friend Jim, that is ambiguity. On the other hand, ambivalence can be defined as *liking and disliking the same thing at the same time.* If a person is forced to acknowledge that his worst enemy has done something good, he experiences ambivalence.

One final distinction will be useful: the distinction between liking and disliking a *person or group* (image-ambivalence) and liking and disliking a *course of action* (action-ambivalence). When an enemy has done something good, or when one's own group has done something bad, it is image-ambivalence; the black-and-white picture is disturbed. When a course of action on which one has embarked is seen as having a major disadvantage, it is action-ambivalence; whole-heartedness in action is disturbed.

The importance of this distinction is indicated by the fact that the two kinds of ambivalence roughly correspond to the two main-streams of psychological research and theory in this area: "balance theory," stemming largely from Heider, corresponds to image-ambivalence, and "dissonance theory," stemming largely from Festinger, corresponds to action-ambivalence.

Heider's "balance theory" is essentially a theory about what seems natural or harmonious in one person's perceptions of other people. It is ordinarily formulated in terms of three elements: the person who is doing the perceiving (P), some other person (O), and some action, attitude, person, or object (X) that is associated with O in P's mind. The combination of the three is called the P-O-X triangle, or the P-O-X triad. It is said to be "in balance" if, for instance, P likes O, P likes X, and O likes X. Let us say that P is a Republican voter, O is a Republican friend of his, and X is Senator Goldwater, who is running for president (the year being 1964). P and O are friends; they also both like Goldwater. In this cozy situation everything is in balance and there is no strain or feel-ing of incongruity in P's mind. His friend O "should" like Gold-water, and does. But now change one element in the situation: instead of being a Republican who likes Goldwater, P is a liberal Democrat who feels that Goldwater is a trigger-happy reactionary who will oppose the welfare of the economic underdog and greatly increase the danger of nuclear war. O is his favorite uncle—and O is planning to vote for Goldwater. To P this is distressing, and not merely because Goldwater is going to get another vote; it also seems distressingly incongruous. Uncle Jim is a good guy—but voting for Goldwater! The triad is out of balance. And it would be similarly out of balance if P's greatly disliked Uncle Horace were to feel as P does about Goldwater and vote against him.

What now needs to be brought out is an aspect of the problem that Heider himself has recognized from the outset, though he has not emphasized it: The feelings of balance or imbalance, harmony or disharmony, congruity or incongruity in P's mind can also be described in terms of ambivalence and the need to reduce or eliminate ambivalence. O's feeling about Goldwater, as perceived by P, is a part or aspect of O himself. If O is a favorite uncle, P's image of him is mainly positive. If now O declares for Goldwater, whom P regards as a trigger-happy reactionary, it is as if a part of O had suddenly become bad; bad is now mixed with good in the same "perceptual entity," negative with positive, and this is, by definition, ambivalence. Similarly, when a strongly disliked person comes up with a good, sound, socially constructive political attitude (from P's standpoint) there is a similar ambivalence; positive has become mixed with negative, and, though the change may be welcomed as an acquisition of an ally, it still seems puzzling, incongruous, and in that respect faintly unpleasant. In fact, all of the consequences Heider derives from ringing the changes on his P-O-X triangle can be derived also from the simple proposition that ambivalence (image-ambivalence, in this case) is unpleasant.

It should be noted that this is not a matter of logical inconsistency. It is not inconsistent for P to regard O as mostly good but partly bad. People *are* like that. Most of us would accept readily the general proposition that human beings are rarely all good or all bad, that almost any human being has bad aspects as well as good ones, that one's own judgment as to what is "good" or "bad" may be fallible. The juxtaposition of a plus with a minus is, in any case, not a logical contradiction. It is not a conflict between ideas at all but a conflict between feelings. It is not surprising, therefore, that the most rational, reasonable, evidence-oriented people are usually the ones who are most able to accept ambivalence as part of the natural order of things, and take it in stride. If P is evidence-oriented, he might say to himself, "Too bad Uncle Jim is for Goldwater. I thought he had more sense. Or maybe he has some argument for Goldwater that I haven't heard. Perhaps I'd better talk with him and find out." Mature love (it can be argued) requires an ability to see realistically and to accept at least some of the faults and limitations of the person who is loved. In any case, to do so is not irrational, illogical, or inconsistent. Neither rationality nor consistency, in the ordinary senses of those words, requires uniformity of feeling about all aspects of a person, a group, or a course of action. In fact the typical situation is a conflict between realism (defined as paying attention to evidence, respecting evidence, and trying to draw appropriate inferences from evidence) and the need for consonance. To be realistic and consistent with the evidence usually means to modify the black-and-white picture, while to be consonant means to retain it.*

Heider's balance theory, then, can be easily interpreted as a theory of image-ambivalence and consequently an explanation of black-and-white thinking. Similarly, Festinger's dissonance theory can be interpreted as largely, though not entirely, a theory of action-ambivalence, and consequently an explanation of the blindness of involvement.

Festinger is primarily concerned with cases in which some of a person's thinking is out of line with his actions. A case in point is the smoker who often feels a strong impulse to smoke but is told that smoking is bad for him. Festinger describes the rich variety of psychological devices a person may use to reduce or eliminate this kind of dissonance. He may simply ignore the evidence that smoking is injurious to health, he may deny the authenticity of the evidence, he may search for evidence that it is not injurious, he may interpret anti-smoking evidence as more inconclusive than it really is and pro-smoking or neutral evidence as more conclusive than it really is. He may even stop smoking. Or, if he is particularly able to tolerate dissonance, he may acknowledge all of the negative evidence and still make the conscious decision, "I'm going to smoke anyway. To me it's worth it."

In any case it seems clear that this is a matter of action-ambivalence, just as the situations Heider discusses are a matter of image-ambivalence. The smoker is ambivalent about his smoking. He wants to smoke because it gives him direct pleasure or relief

---

* A number of psychologists, including for example Zajonc (1960), Roger Brown (1965, pp. 549–609), Rosenberg (1960), and (in some of his writing) Osgood (1962, p. 26) have used the word consistency as an inclusive term to cover all the forms of what we are here calling consonance. The trouble with this is that in ordinary English usage the word "consistent" is honorific—it is good to be consistent—and that is not what these writers mean at all. To prevent confusion it seems desirable to use the more neutral term "consonance" and interpret it as good or bad depending on the circumstances.

from tension; at the same time he wants not to smoke because he wants to be healthy and he fully or partially believes that smoking will hurt his health. To him the act of smoking is good and bad at the same time.

The decision is not a question of logic versus feeling, although it is often conceived in those terms by the individual himself. Wanting health is as much a matter of feeling as wanting a cigarette. The decision is a question of two feelings in conflict, with one feeling (the desire to preserve health in the long run) being connected with the momentary decision by way of relatively elaborate cognitive processes, while the other (the desire for immediate satisfaction or relief from tension) is simple, direct, impulsive, and needs no elaborate cognitive structure to connect it with the act in question.

All of this is related to misperception and to war chiefly by way of another generalization that Festinger has brought out most clearly: Whatever the balance of positive and negative feelings may have been at the time of decision—51 to 49, let us say, or 60 to 40, or 80 to 20—the balance tends to shift further in the direction of the stronger force after decision occurs. It may become not 51 to 49, for example, but 55 to 45, or 60 to 40. There is usually a post-decision weakening of the forces that remain in opposition to the decision that has been made. Once a smoker in conflict has decided to smoke that one cigarette after all, and especially after he has made the same decision a hundred or a thousand times, his tendency to think about long-run effects on his health is reduced; he is more likely to ignore the evidence against smoking, to question its validity, etc.

Similarly, *if* a nation has fully decided on a course of action that involves a danger of war, the nation is happier, at least at the moment, if it does not look back and consider alternative courses of action it might have taken. There is much satisfaction in single-minded pursuit of a goal. The danger in this, however, is evident. Along with the psychological advantages of avoiding vain regrets about the past, and along with the practical advantages of effective, single-minded action, there is a danger that a basically blind and foolish course of action may be blindly persisted in. The goal itself may have been unwisely chosen.

We have then two rather basic propositions: The human mind unconsciously finds ways of reducing or avoiding image-ambivalence (this is Heider's balance theory); it also unconsciously finds ways of reducing or avoiding action-ambivalence (this is Festinger's dissonance theory).

Both of these are special cases of a broader and simpler proposition: Ambivalence is unpleasant. In support of this proposition the evidence is abundant and varied. It includes all the kinds of historical and contemporary political evidence covered in this book, and everyday observations such as the way liberals feel about favorite uncles voting for Goldwater, and the way smokers feel about the evidence against smoking. In addition there is psychiatric evidence; much of Freudian theory is an exploration of devices used by the mind to cope with intense ambivalence.[28] There is also a good deal of systematic research evidence: In support of Heider's balance theory (not necessarily as a major factor, but as one factor in the formation of attitudes) there is a large amount of research evidence.[29] More directly supporting the proposition that image-ambivalence is unpleasant is the experiment by Joseph Cooper[30] that shows an increase in the galvanic skin reflex (an indicator of emotional disturbance) when unfavorable things were said about a liked group or favorable things about a disliked group. The experiment of E. S. Gollin[31] has shown that a woman depicted in a film as having both good and bad characteristics—a "kindly immoralist" —was very often remembered as either good or bad but not both. There is the evidence on national stereotypes[32] and their tendency to an all-good or all-bad character. There is the evidence of a general tendency, accentuated in ethnocentric and authoritarian personalities, to favorable perception of any ingroup and unfavorable perception of any outgroup. There is finally the large amount of research, experimental and non-experimental, on Festinger's dissonance theory. Although the inferences drawn in some of this research are controversial,[33] the weight of research conclusions supports the basic theory as stated here.

[28] Brown, 1965, pp. 604–8.
[29] Jordan, 1953; Tannenbaum, 1956; Osgood and Tannenbaum, 1955; Morrissette, 1958.
[30] Cooper, 1959.
[31] Gollin, 1954.
[32] Buchanan and Cantril, 1954.
[33] Chapanis and Chapanis, 1964.

Ways of Reducing Ambivalence

How does the mind manage to maintain the blackness of the black and the whiteness of the white in the face of contradictory evidence? When involved in an enterprise such as a war, how do human beings manage to remain blind to the elements of unwisdom and of immorality that it contains? The previous section focused on the psychological need to reduce the discomfort or pain of ambivalence. This one focuses on how that is done. It is primarily a review of historical evidence already considered, but in this chapter the same evidence is put in a psychological matrix and the main effort is to understand its psychological nature.

IMAGE-AMBIVALENCE—REALISTIC WAYS OF REDUCING IT

It often happens that a good self-image and an evil enemy-image are simultaneously threatened. For instance this probably occurred in many Austrian minds on July 25, 1914, when Austria broke relations with Serbia and set in motion the escalation that led to World War I. Austria's own initiation of violence was a basic threat to her peaceful self-image. As seen by most of the rest of the world it was aggression, and even the German Kaiser, who had loyally supported Austria but who thought the conciliatory Serbian reply to the Austrian ultimatum had "done away with every reason for war," must have had great qualms about it. To see it as aggression, however, would have threatened the Austrians' image of themselves as an essentially good, peaceful nation. That was unthinkable, and they managed not to think it, using various psychological devices, the chief of which, perhaps, was to perceive their action as firmness or a renewal of virility rather than as aggression. At the same time, the conciliatory Serbian reply itself was a threat to their diabolical enemy-image. They had been picturing the Serbian government in Belgrade as the center of the plot that had led to the assassination of the Archduke and that was now threatening the very existence of the Austro-Hungarian Empire. Incongruously, these assassins were now having the effrontery to put up a façade of reasonableness and conciliation. It was unthinkable that they could be sincere, and here too the Austrians managed not to think the unthinkable. The present question is: How?

As a preliminary to consideration of these unrealistic thought processes, a simpler question should be asked: What could we regard as a realistic way of avoiding ambivalence? In the case of Austria we have the advantage of hindsight and the answer seems relatively clear. It now seems that the aggression in Austria's action was almost unmistakable and that the conciliatory nature of Serbia's reply to Austria's ultimatum was also relatively clear. Austria had her diplomatic triumph and war had become unnecessary even on the basis of Austria's own assumptions. In such a case the realistic response would have been a modest, discriminating, and flexible response, focused on the evidence rather than on inflexible pride.

This would not have destroyed an Austrian's basic loyalty to his country, or even his faith in its goodness, nor would it have destroyed his belief that basically the Serbians were in the wrong. However, both his national self-image and his national enemy-image would have had to become more *differentiated,* with good and bad aspects clearly distinguished. He would have had to perceive Austria as basically good, but in some senses bad, and to perceive Serbia as basically bad, but in some ways good. Four days later, when Austria had stubbornly gone forward while Germany was urgently trying to restrain her, to have accepted the German viewpoint would have involved actually admitting guilt or unwisdom. Either admission would have involved a painful self-depreciation and the additional discomfort of ambivalence. But this would have been more realistic than the arrogant definition of the situation that the Austrians continued to hold.

IMAGE-AMBIVALENCE—UNREALISTIC WAYS OF REDUCING IT

Six less realistic ways of reducing the discomfort of ambivalence are:[34]

1. Selective inattention
2. Angry denial

[34] This list is to a large extent a composite of the ideas of Heider (1958, pp. 174–217), Allport (1958, pp. 19–24, 161–73, 360–68), Smith, Bruner, and White (1956, pp. 241–79, esp. p. 251), Roger Brown (1965, pp. 549–609), and Holsti (1967, pp. 16–39).

3. Avoiding the communicator
4. Bolstering
5. Selective interpretation
6. Separation

1. *Selective inattention:* Examples of selective inattention in conflict situations are scattered throughout the pages of this book more thickly than examples of any other psychological process. When a dissonant idea is selectively inattended it is soft-pedaled, pushed out of the mind at least temporarily.

It is not necessary for it to be completely repressed or suppressed. Berchtold, for instance, probably could not completely rid himself of the nagging thought that perhaps he had done a wrong and foolish thing. At certain moments this thought may even have become fully conscious, only to be pushed out of his mind again with varying degrees of success.

How is it possible to push something out of your mind? The difficulty of doing so by a mere act of will is illustrated by the children's game of "pink elephant." In that game the players sit in a circle; whenever one of them thinks of a pink elephant he is in honor bound to get up and leave the circle; the last one to remain seated wins. Those who have played the game know that it can be won only by the very young or by those who cheat. The moment anyone tries not to think about a pink elephant he is already thinking about it, and has lost the game. *Is* it possible, then, to push something out of your mind?

Everyday observation suggests a partial answer: The effort is successful only when the person succeeds in focusing attention on something else. While an idea cannot fade out spontaneously it can be *crowded* out by another idea or group of ideas. The span of attention (or more correctly, the span of apprehension) is limited; much research has shown that even an intelligent individual is not able to think of more than seven or eight things at the same moment even when they are simple things, and if any of them are at all complex, or if emotion enters the picture, the number that can be clearly thought about simultaneously is a good deal less than seven.[35]

This much is, perhaps, simple common sense. But what is seldom clearly recognized even by psychologists is the further proposition

[35] Woodworth, 1938, pp. 684–95.

that *the focus can shift successfully only when the reason for shifting it is not fully conscious.* The mind unconsciously, or only partly consciously, learns ways of turning its attention to something other than what is embarrassing or painful to contemplate. The process of self-distraction can be no more than partly conscious, because if it were fully conscious—if the person were saying to himself "I am paying attention to Idea B in order not to think about Idea A"—the pink-elephant process would occur and he would find himself paying attention to Idea A after all. He can do it successfully only if he does not fully realize what he is doing.

To a large extent the unrealistic ways of reducing ambivalence that remain to be discussed are of this nature; they serve the unconscious or only partly conscious purpose of filling the mind with ideas other than dissonant ones. Selective inattention is not a mechanism separate from the others; it is, rather, a goal or end result that several of the others tend to bring about.[36]

2. *Angry denial,* often linked with an effort to discredit the communicator of dissonant ideas. When a Southern gentleman of the old school hears a slighting remark about a certain woman, he proverbially says "Suh, you are talking about the woman I love!" and reaches for his pistol. He is not less likely to do so if he thinks or suspects that the slighting remark may be true. Nor is he, in that case, less likely to shout "Liar!" as well as "Scoundrel!"

In addition to conforming to the dictates of his subculture, this gentleman is illustrating the ambivalence-reducing mechanism that is here called "angry denial." At the moment when someone else has presented or may be about to present dissonant evidence challenging an emotionally cherished image, he has a not fully conscious impulse to turn his attention instantly away from the substance of the challenge, and at such times the most immediately available thought object on which to focus attention, other than the substance of the challenge, is the person who has communicated it. Our Southern friend is fortunate if at such a moment he can immediately remember some occasion on which the person who has insulted his lady has actually told a lie. In that case his shouting "Liar!" is not merely a way of crowding out the idea of his lady's possible misdemeanors and substituting the mind-filling emotion of anger. (For that purpose "Scoundrel!" would have done equally well.) In addition, the

[36] Bartlett, 1932; Levine and Murphy, 1943, pp. 402–9, in Swanson, Newcomb, and Hartley, 1952.

idea of the communicator's previous lying really casts doubt on the substance of what he has just said.

Angry denial as a factor in the background of war has already been illustrated at a number of points. It is related to the mechanism of autistic hostility; whatever the enemy says that might justify his actions or promote empathy with his reality-world is often disregarded as lying or propaganda (which, of course, it often is). Some non-militant Americans dismiss what General Westmoreland says about Vietnam as a typical product of the military mind, and some militant Americans, instead of listening to what Senator Fulbright says, denounce him as disloyal.

One of the more curious examples of trying to discredit the communicator of a disturbing idea, and doing so in ways that are actually irrelevant to the point at issue, appears in the typical criticisms of the late Bernard Fall by those who found his non-militant ideas disturbing. Probably the most frequent criticisms of him were that he was arrogant, that he was glib, and that he was French. To be sure, there may well have been varying degrees of truth in these three charges. His voluminous knowledge and great self-confidence were accompanied by an impatience and a readiness to attack others which sometimes could be fairly called arrogant; his extreme articulateness and fast talking could be called glib by those who did not realize how much knowledge and thinking lay back of what he said; he was French, and his French background may indeed have led to a pro-French bias in what he said about events in Vietnam during the years 1946–54. But no one of these charges was actually in any degree a refutation of what he said about the situation in Vietnam or American policy in Vietnam during the years 1954–67. To those who made the criticisms they may have seemed to "discredit the communicator," and the aura of disfavor they spread may have seemed to include also the things he said, but there was little or no logic in this assumption.

3. *Avoiding the communicator of a dissonant idea:* If Mr. X has quarreled with Mr. Y and, without having decided to settle their differences, sees Mr. Y at some distance down the street, he may do one or the other of two rather curious things: He may pretend not to have noticed Mr. Y (perhaps acting absorbed in conversation with his own companion) with the result that their eyes do not meet, even though they pass each other on the sidewalk, or he may actually cross the street in order to avoid meeting Mr. Y. One interpre-

tation of this behavior would be that it is simple hostility; Mr. X does not want to give Mr. Y the satisfaction of being greeted by him. At the same time there is another explanation that may contain more of the truth: Mr. X may be embarrassed by the part he himself has played in the quarrel, and he may have been repressing (selectively inattending) this embarrassment along with the quarrel itself and the person with whom he has quarreled. The sight of Mr. Y may therefore cause anxiety and an avoidance reaction motivated, partly unconsciously, by fear of having to talk with Mr. Y and to think clearly about the source of embarrassment. Because he is a potential communicator of dissonant, ego-threatening ideas, Mr. Y is dangerous.

The same kind of thing may happen when the communicator is a columnist, a commentator, a newspaper, a magazine, or a political figure. Let us say that an arch-segregationist in Montgomery, Alabama, sees an article in the *New York Times* magazine section written by Martin Luther King. Despite some feeling of irritation at King as a trouble maker, curiosity may lead him to start reading. The first paragraph confirms his worst fears; King is citing evidence that real-estate values do not necessarily go down when Negroes enter a previously all-white neighborhood. This information he not only angrily denies and selectively inattends; in addition he turns the page and becomes absorbed in an article on the Baltimore Orioles, or tosses the whole paper aside, with anger at the *Times* for printing such a thing, and goes to the refrigerator to get a beer. The following Sunday he may watch television instead of looking at the *Times* at all.

As we have seen (pp. 198–204), this kind of inattention can contribute much to the pseudo-patriotic distortion that produces war.

4. *Bolstering* a consonant idea by seeking or focusing on evidence and ideas that support it. The reader probably knows the old, old story (told by Freud, among others) of the peasant woman whose neighbor took her milkpail without permission and returned it full of holes. Confronted by the angry peasant woman, the neighbor roundly declared: "I returned it in perfectly good condition. Besides, it was full of holes when I got it. And anyway, I never took it in the first place."

This reaching out, regardless of logic or evidence, for anything and everything that will justify what one has done, illustrates what is here called "bolstering." Everyone seeks ideas and evidence that may be relevant to a problem he has, but some try to give weight to whatever seems most solidly established in the light of all the available evidence, and most genuinely relevant to the problem, while others give priority, often more or less unconsciously, to whatever will bolster what they already believe or want to believe.

Examples relating to war are legion. When Serbia accepted all but one of the points in the Austrian ultimatum, Berchtold brushed aside all concessions as merely examples of Serbian duplicity, focusing instead on Serbia's refusal of the final Austrian demand as evidence that the Serbs were still defiant and unwilling to end their "criminal agitation." When Hitler undertook one of his most flagrant acts of aggression, the march into Prague, he focused on one of the few pieces of evidence that might have been plausible justification, the fact that Czechoslovakia possessed air bases from which Germany could be attacked.

When the Chinese Communists feel a need to justify their demand for Taiwan they do not focus on any desire of the Taiwanese to be part of Communist China, though this would seem to be required by their own philosophy of championing national independence against "imperialism." To do so would be difficult, because there is little evidence that either the mainland Chinese on the island or the Taiwanese themselves want to be part of Communist China. Instead, the Communists fall back on the idea that "Taiwan has always been part of China"—an appeal to history and tradition that ill befits a movement committed to the upsetting of tradition in the name of true democracy and national independence. When militant Americans want to justify prolonging the war until all of South Vietnam is reclaimed for an anti-Communist government, they usually do not invoke any evidence that the majority of the South Vietnamese want to be defended from the North even at the cost of prolonging the war. Such evidence would be hard to find. Instead they usually seize upon every idea or piece of evidence indicating that "we aren't sure what the people want," and focus mainly on the indubitable fact that North Vietnamese soldiers are still on South Vietnamese soil.

5. *Selective interpretation* of ambiguous evidence: A certain employee is slow and inaccurate, but very conscientious. He often works overtime, keeping a careful record of it whenever he does so. After some years he begins to feel aggrieved that he is not promoted while others who never work overtime are promoted over his head. He talks with his boss, and in doing so displays all the processes we

have discussed. He selectively inattends his slowness and inaccuracy. He angrily denies them when his boss brings them up. He avoids discussing the office tasks in which his slowness and inaccuracy are especially handicapping, and expatiates at length on his own accumulated evidence of overtime work. What now needs to be noticed is that all of these are parts of, and subordinate to, a complex overall process of selective interpretation of ambiguous evidence.[37] To be sure, from his supervisor's point of view it may not seem ambiguous; it may seem very clear to him that the employee does not deserve promotion. But it is nevertheless ambiguous in the sense that different people can interpret it in very different ways. It is complex enough, and the processes of selective attention and slanted interpretation are potent enough, at least in the employee's mind, to enable him to perceive it as something radically different from what his supervisor believes it to be, though they have been working in the same office for years.

The story of how wars come can nearly always be described in a similar way, both in the over-all interpretation of the total situation on both sides and in the interpretation given to specific questions of fact. In both world wars (with the possible exception of Hitler in World War II) both sides regarded their enemies as in some sense aggressors, and themselves as victims of aggression. The same is true today of the East-West conflict and of the Vietnam war.

The same selective interpretation appears in the answers given to a great many specific questions of fact embedded in these over-all pictures of a conflict. Berchtold could have perceived the Serbian reply as evasive or as conciliatory; he saw it as evasive. Hitler could have seen the airfields in Czechoslovakia as aggressive or defensive; he saw them (or claimed to see them) as aggressive. The Communists could have seen the Marshall Plan as generosity or as an attempt to extend capitalist domination; they saw it (or claimed to see it) as an attempt to extend capitalist domination. Non-militant Americans could see Vietnam's neighbors as very vulnerable to a domino process if the Communists win in Vietnam or as not particularly vulnerable; many see them as not particularly vulnerable. Militant Americans could see America's past behavior as innocent or

---

[37] Experimental evidence on the process of selective interpretation or reinterpretation is provided by Bartlett, 1932; Murray, 1933; Edwards, 1941; Abelson and Rosenberg, 1958, and many others. On its role in Soviet thinking, see White, 1965, pp. 238–76.

aggressive; typically they see it as innocent. Egyptians could see the Strait of Tiran as international or as part of Egypt; most of them see it as part of Egypt. In any conflict situation a number of specifics, which to an overwhelming degree conform to the black-and-white picture, add up to one big black-and-white picture; and the big picture in turn influences all the specifics, predisposing the individual to see each specific fact or incident in the way that justifies his side or incriminates its enemies. There is enormous momentum here, since each new fact or incident, if it has any inherent ambiguity at all, is interpreted in such a way that it only seems to confirm what is already believed.

6. *Separation* of a dissonant idea from the image that is challenged by it. "Dissonance," it should be remembered, does not consist of the mere presence of an unpleasant or negative idea in the mind. When we are talking about images it consists rather of having to admit that the self has done something bad or that the enemy has done something good. It exists only when a negative idea comes uncomfortably close to the self-image or when a positive one comes uncomfortably close to the enemy-image.

A final device for avoiding ambivalence exists: An idea of something bad can be handled readily if it is *kept separate* from the self-image, and an idea of something good can be handled readily if it is kept separate from the diabolical enemy-image. In this kind of psychological physics opposite signs do not attract; they repel each other, and tension can be kept at a minimum by keeping them far enough apart.

How can such separation be accomplished? As we have seen, the best way not to think about a particular thing is to think about something else. A similar psychological principle is that if a particular thing is not to be seen as part of Image A it should be seen as part of Image B. Experiments on "embeddedness" as an important element in visual perception have made it clear that if a visual item is embedded in one figure it is often difficult to segregate it and see it as a separate thing at all, let alone seeing it as part of some other figure.[38] In political psychology the application of this principle would be: If a particular bad action is not to be attributed to the self, it should be attributed to somebody or something other than

[38] Gottschaldt, 1926.

the self; and if a good action is not to be attributed to the enemy, it should be attributed to somebody or something else.

On July 29, 1914, when Berchtold threw away the last hope of peace, he could tell himself not only "we have always sought to avoid this war"—a direct denial of guilt—but, more effectively, he could focus on Serbian or Russian guilt. "They did it. They left us no choice." Communists and Americans today feel compelled to explain somehow the horror of war in Vietnam; both are more vocally insistent on the total guilt of the enemy than they are on their own innocence.

In these cases the term "projection" would be equally applicable; a country that has any doubt as to whether it may share the guilt of starting a war is likely to feel a great need to "project" the blame onto its enemy, partly because doing so provides a full justification for whatever acts of intervention or of violence the country itself has engaged in. All of these acts can then be defined as defense against aggression. In such cases, projection is reinforced by rationalization. But there are other cases in which projection seems to serve more purely the cause of separating guilt from oneself by attaching it to someone or something else. The "someone else" need not be the enemy. Francis Joseph, at a late stage in the crisis of 1914, said, "We cannot go back now," as if responsibility now rested on an impersonal Fate or Necessity. Also, as a variation on this theme, blame may rest on past mistakes of persons in one's own or another country. Americans can blame France, or Diem, or John Foster Dulles, or commitments made by Presidents Eisenhower and Kennedy that "we can't go back on now."

The same mechanism may serve to defend the enemy-image against contamination by something good. The Communists, let us say, are looking back on the period when the United States had a monopoly of the atom bomb, and they are asking themselves the question—a very serious question from the standpoint of their ideology—"Why didn't America simply wipe us out when it had such a good chance to do so?" What is challenged here is actually not their image of all of America, since in the typical Communist black-top image of their number-one enemy the American "people" are good and friendly toward the Soviet Union, while the "ruling circles" of America, in Wall Street and the Pentagon, are bad and implacably hostile. More precisely stated, then, the problem is: "Why didn't America's ruling circles simply wipe us out when they had such a good chance?"

A simple if not wholly valid answer is available: They probably wanted to wipe us out but were forced to refrain from doing so by their fear of the American people. They knew that if they had attacked their wartime comrades in cold blood there would have been a tremendous, irresistible wave of protest by the people. To be sure, this hypothesis would be inconsistent with a literal acceptance of the term "ruling circles." If the rule of the "ruling circles" were absolute, America's ruling circles could have erased the Soviet Union and defied the resulting wave of popular protest. But Communist propaganda does not actually picture capitalist rule in the West as absolute; it frequently implies that, although "the people" do not ordinarily rule, when sufficiently united and aroused on a particular issue they can set limits to the evil perpetrated by their rulers. The problem is then solved. The action in question (refraining from attack) is still seen as good, but it is separated from the all-bad image of America's hidden capitalist leadership, and attributed to, or embedded in, the already good image of "the American people."

Any attribution of a good act to evil motives has the same effect of separating it from the evil enemy-image and leaving that image intact. For instance, when America offered Marshall Plan aid even to the Communist countries of Eastern Europe, the Communists could dismiss this as a subtle, insidious technique for acquiring dominance over them. When America (at least in its own eyes) is defending the small and helpless country of South Vietnam, the Communists can perceive this as a desire to establish imperialist rule, or as establishing a base for an attack on Communist China. When the USSR's behavior became more conciliatory after the death of Stalin, some Americans, including John Foster Dulles, could attribute this primarily to weakness rather than to any diminishing of the intensity of the Communists' drive to rule the world. "They had to," not "they wanted to."

ACTION-AMBIVALENCE

Since the need to reduce action-ambivalence goes far to explain the blindness of involvement (which ranks with the black-and-white picture as a major cause of war), the devices used by the mind to do so are perhaps fully as important as those used to reduce image-ambivalence and to sustain the black-and-white picture. However, since they appear to be essentially the same as the six mechanisms described above, they can be described, in the context of action rather than images, very briefly. It will be enough to give a single illustration of each:

1. *Selective inattention:* The Strategic Bombing Survey, with its implication that bombing can be psychologically counterproductive, is typically ignored by those who have set their hearts on bombing as a way of bringing the North Vietnamese to the conference table.

2. *Angry denial:* People who bring up evidence that a particular war is unwise are often called disloyal.

3. *Avoiding the communicator:* When the Kaiser rejected negotiation, saying that "in vital matters and those of honor one does not consult others," he was avoiding a situation in which the ideas of others might cast doubt on the wisdom of his support of Austria.

4. *Bolstering:* Opponents of our involvement in Vietnam may eagerly latch onto the thought that Ho Chi Minh might be another Tito.

5. *Selective interpretation:* North Vietnamese Communists, having decided to fight in the South, tend to interpret all evidence on South Vietnamese attitudes as supporting the wisdom of this decision.

6. *Separation:* Arguments against a course of action that one has decided upon are often dismissed as irrelevant when they are not. Hitler, for instance, treated the reactions of the British, French, and Americans as irrelevant to his decision to attack Poland: "When statesmen in the West declare that this affects their interests, I can only regret such a declaration. It cannot for a moment make me hesitate to fulfil my duty."

Usually action-ambivalence and image-ambivalence are intimately interrelated. Any course of action that I have voluntarily chosen becomes, in a sense, a part of me, and it is defended in the same ways and for much the same reasons. A great deal of the blindness of involvement as described by Rapoport and of the momentum of escalation as described by Frank and by Osgood can therefore be accounted for by the six mechanisms that have just been described.

Diabolism

Among the images discussed in this book the diabolical enemy-image is probably the most dangerous as a cause of unnecessary war. It includes the crucial proposition: *They* have committed aggression. It is also the most complex and puzzling. It is puzzling chiefly because it is not obviously pleasant. To think well of oneself or of one's own group, in terms of virility or morality or both, is in line with an obvious and well-nigh universal need for self-esteem. When it leads to exaggeration or selective inattention those processes are obviously forms of wishful thinking. But even if we grant a certain obviously pleasurable dramatic quality in the belief in devils, one might suppose that it would be more than outweighed by the unpleasurable quality of physical fear, since fear is based upon the biologically basic motive of self-preservation. Is there really a *net* pleasure in believing that a diabolical enemy has placed one's own country or an ally in mortal danger? On the face of it, it looks like the opposite of wishful thinking. On the conscious level it typically appears as a grim reality that we must face up to, not as anything pleasurable.

For the sake of compactness we will use the word "diabolism," from this point on, to mean the tendency to see another person or group as more diabolical than the facts warrant, and an enemy will be said to be "diabolized" when he is seen as more diabolical than the facts warrant. The psychological question can then be stated: Why is the tendency to diabolize an enemy often so extremely strong?

Even leaving the Vietnam war completely aside (which seems desirable at this point, since it brings in the distracting question of whether either side has actually committed aggression in that war) the problem of diabolism as a cause of war is ubiquitous. It includes, but is not by any means confined to, the problem of abnormal persons with paranoid tendencies, including delusions of persecution. One is tempted to invoke abnormality as an explanation of the Kaiser's despairing outcry against what he thought was an English plot to destroy his country, Hitler's apparent belief in a world conspiracy of the Jews, the belief of a possibly senile Mao Tse-tung that his domestic opponents (good Communists all) are "monsters and demons" in cahoots with a treacherous Moscow and an imperialist Wall Street, and perhaps the behavior of a "megalomaniac" Nasser with delusions of grandeur as a leader of the Arabs (including a gross form of military overconfidence) and delusions of persecution about the "aggression" of Israel against the Arab world. But not one of these four persons was or is demonstrably psychotic, since each of them functioned or is functioning with at least some effectiveness as the head of a state. Each of them successfully persuaded many others in his own country that his delusions of persecution were reality, not fiction, which testifies not only to the non-psychotic character of the persuader but also to some special receptiveness to paranoid ideas in the many millions who were persuaded. Also, there are many instances of large groups diabolizing their enemies without being headed by any especially paranoid individual. We ourselves in World War I assumed that Wilhelm II was the arch-criminal of that war and a would-be world conqueror (and Woodrow Wilson, who represented the views of a great many Americans in 1917, was not psychotic); the Communists assume a world in which Wall Street is the center of worldwide forces supporting an evil, moribund system called capitalism (and neither Marx nor Lenin was demonstrably psychotic); many Americans other than Joseph McCarthy have perceived American liberals and internationalists as undercover Communists. Primitive men seem to accept almost universally the idea of evil spirits; medieval men apparently accepted almost universally the idea of witches and devils. Some degree of spontaneous diabolism on a mass basis seems to be the rule, not the exception. It can be accentuated in individuals to the point of paranoid psychosis, and those who have more than their share of it can be national leaders. Such leaders could get nowhere, however, if there were no ready mass response to which they could appeal.

Before trying to explain diabolism it will be useful to describe five of its characteristic forms:

1. The Black-Top Enemy-Image
2. The Puppet Enemy-Image
3. The Alien-Agitator Image
4. The Phony-Ally Image
5. The Traitors-in-Our-Midst Image

1. *The Black-Top Enemy-Image:* The black-top image is the only one of the five that has been rather fully illustrated and dis-

cussed in previous pages. Examples of it include, for instance, the American belief that the Kaiser was the villain of World War I and the Communist belief that America is sharply divided between good "people" and evil "ruling circles."

What can now be added is that the black-top image is a remarkably effective way of handling ambivalence. Ambivalence often exists, even in feelings about an enemy nation. There is much evidence that the Russians, for example, have a basic image of America that is at least as favorable as it is unfavorable. What has apparently happened is that, with much help from Communist propaganda, the ordinary Soviet citizen has concentrated his friendly feelings upon the American people and his hostility upon their capitalist rulers. He can think, "I have only friendly feelings toward the *people* of America," and this not only gives the positive element in his basic ambivalence a legitimate form of expression; it also enables him to feel that *he* is an essentially friendly, tolerant person, with good will toward the vast majority of the human race, including all of the poor and downtrodden, and with hostility only to those who oppress the people. "Differentiation" has been described as a realistic way of resolving ambivalence when, for instance, the self or a loved person is seen as good in some ways and bad in others. The black-top image represents another kind of differentiation, probably equally effective as a way of handling ambivalence, though its realism is often questionable.

2. *The Puppet Enemy-Image:* When there is an arch-enemy who has allies, there is a recurrent tendency to see those allies as mere puppets of the arch-enemy.

In 1914–18 most of Germany's enemies assumed mistakenly that she was the prime instigator of the war; we and our allies had no notion of the extent to which the initiative was actually Austria's during July, 1914, and of how obstreperously independent Austria had been when Germany tried to hold her back on July 29. Similarly the Arabs have tended to see Israel as an outpost of American imperialism, and the Communists have tended to see Chiang Kai-shek, Diem, Thailand, Iran, Israel, and most of the governments of Latin America as puppets or lackeys of the United States. When some of our puppets have acted obstreperous, unconscionably dragging their feet on land reform and other things that we really wanted them to do, we have listened a little wryly to these Communist accusations. As McGeorge Bundy put it, "Anyone who thinks that the lines of influence from Washington are like so many strings to so many puppets has never sat at the pulling end."[39]

There are puppet-imaginers on our side too. Before Tito's defection there were many in the West who assumed that he was as subordinate to Moscow as the other Communist leaders in Eastern Europe, and until 1960 there were many who attributed a similar subordination to Peking. With the wisdom of hindsight we can see how mistaken Dean Rusk was in 1951 when, as Assistant Secretary of State for Far Eastern Affairs, he said "The Peiping regime may be a colonial Russian government—a Slavic Manchukuo on a larger scale. It is not the government of China. It does not pass the first test. It is not Chinese." At the time, though, there were many other well-informed Americans who saw it as he did. Now there are many militant Americans who see the Viet Cong as more completely puppetlike in relation to Hanoi, and Hanoi as more puppetlike in relation to Peking, than is warranted by the evidence as seen by some well-informed persons (Fall, Devillers, Chaffard, Gottlieb, Schlesinger, Buttinger).[40]

Why? Why is this distortion such a persistent one?

One reason may be the tendency to limit and concentrate hostility, focusing it on a single enemy and preferably on a single individual. Like the black-top image, the puppet image limits feelings of guilt. One does not need to feel hostile to the puppets since they are only puppets and cannot do otherwise. At the same time there is no need to try to empathize with them. The puppet image is in a sense a rationalization for the absence of empathy. Why bother to understand *their* point of view when they are only puppets anyway?

More importantly, perhaps, the puppet image satisfies a need to see oneself as more shrewd and unfoolable than others are. It is pleasant to think: "They can't pull the wool over *my* eyes. They pretend to be independent allies, but I know better!" There is a luxury in cynicism and in looking down on others as naïve. It is a luxury that can be enjoyed easily and cheaply by those who think they see plots and inner meanings and dominance-submission relationships that others cannot see. This is perhaps a major element in the appeal of Marxism, especially to intellectuals and pseudo-intellectuals. It enables them to think: "*We* know the dark inner meaning of history.

[39] Bundy, 1967.
[40] See especially Schlesinger, 1967, pp. 76–88.

We know who pulls the strings in the capitalist world. *We* know who owns the newspapers and bribes the legislators. They can't fool us!"

Very often the puppet image contains a kernel of truth. Some countries do dominate other countries or exert undue influence over them. The USSR has been dominant in Eastern Europe to a degree that we in the West sometimes wishfully forget; Hitler dominated most of Europe in his day; France dominated its puppet, Bao Dai. The United States government has at times categorically denied an effort to influence the internal politics of South Vietnam, though some independent and well-informed observers have believed that that influence was large. In the case of Vietnam, the truth probably lies in an ambiguous middle zone, with people on one side usually exaggerating the extent of a particular case of puppetry and people on the other side usually underestimating it. What is typical is a puppet *enemy*-image. Militant Americans probably tend to over-estimate the extent to which our direct enemy, the Viet Cong, is a puppet, and the Communists probably overestimate the extent to which their enemy, Saigon, is a puppet.

3. *The Alien-Agitator Image:* Whenever possible an enemy is pictured as alien in the territory in which he is operating, and when it is obvious that natives of that area are on the enemy side they are often pictured as stirred up and instigated to action by alien influences.

The white Southerner sees contented Negroes inflamed by carpet-bagging agitators who know nothing about the South's problems. Opponents of the New Deal often saw it as a form of socialism—an alien ideology imported from Europe. Communists in the developing countries see native anti-Communists as influenced by alien American "imperialists," and militantly anti-Communist Vietnam-ese and Americans often see the Viet Cong as a group of outsiders who are inflaming and capitalizing upon the discontent of the vil-lagers, as well as intimidating them. In fact, anti-Communist mili-tants often see the fighting in Vietnam as caused by three successive kinds or layers of outsiders: the North Vietnamese aggressors, the Chinese who are backing them up, and the worldwide Communist movement, professing a Marxist ideology that is as un-Chinese and un-Vietnamese as it is un-American.

In each of these beliefs there is probably a sizable kernel of truth. Ideas do spread, and outsiders can often articulate these ideas better than insiders can. Struggling groups inside a country often want and get help from outside it. But what the diabolizer usually underestimates is the actual extent of the discontent that has made a local population receptive to ideas coming from outside, the extent to which its leadership is local as well as foreign, and the extent to which the discontent might have been remedied by the diabolizer himself or by his group.

Like the black-top image and the puppet image, this one serves to limit hostility and relieve guilt by exonerating most of those who constitute the actual enemy. The diabolizer can feel that he is a man of good will, tolerant of the local group as a whole, and hostile only to the outsiders who have misled it. His hostility is displaced onto the outsiders. The image serves also as a substitute for empathy and for sympathy; as long as a person believes it he does not have to understand what made the group receptive to outside influence, or do anything drastic to relieve their sources of discontent. There is also direct or vicarious satisfaction of his own ethnocentric prejudice. To whatever extent he himself is ethnocentric and tends to regard what is foreign as automatically bad, and to whatever extent he is able to project himself and his own ethnocentric prejudice into the group in question, he can smear what he dislikes as "alien" just as he would if the group were his own.

4. *The Phony-Ally Image:*[41] Many examples support the proposition that the greatest political weakness of the dogmatic diabolizers and the greatest boon to their opponents is their distrust of actual or potential allies and their consequent tendency to alienate those allies.

Stalin thoroughly alienated the democratic socialists of the world by trying to dominate them and by attacking them. Hitler alienated millions of Russians who at first welcomed him as an ally against Stalin's oppression. Stalin alienated Tito and thereby began the long break-up of monolithic Communism. Joseph McCarthy finally alienated even conservative Americans by attacking the Army and President Eisenhower. Khrushchev alienated Mao and Mao alienated

[41] The term "phony ally" comes from Davis Bobrow (1966, private communication) who has done a particularly systematic analysis of Chinese Communist imagery in terms of the various roles in which they cast the various actors in the world drama as they see it. Bobrow discusses at length the "phony-ally role" which was once played by the Nationalist Chinese, in the war against Japan, and is now, as the Chinese Communists see it, being played by the Russians.

Khrushchev. By pressing the Indian border dispute (in which he had a legitimate case) Mao needlessly alienated India. Mao has disrupted and weakened China by his paranoid suspicions and violent attacks on Communist comrades. Diem systematically alienated almost all of his own natural allies in South Vietnam, finally including the army. The Arabs alienate each other. Right-wing conservatives in America cast beady eyes upon moderate, middle-of-the-road liberals, suspecting them of being undercover Communists or dupes of Communists, and thereby alienate the middle-of-the-road vote. John Foster Dulles alienated neutrals by calling neutralism immoral.

Why? In addition to some factors already discussed, there is probably here the additional factor of intolerance of ambiguity. An uncertain or merely potential ally is ambiguous, and the dogmatic diabolizer is, as a rule, a person who is made anxious and hostile by shadings and overlappings and in-betweens. Tito was frustrating and exasperating to Stalin because Stalin, demanding complete and uncritical loyalty, could not really tell whether he was getting loyalty from Tito or not. Consequently, he denounced him and drove him away.

5. *The Traitors-in-Our-Midst Image:* The paranoid element in politics rises to its most irrational, most freedom-destroying pitch when it turns inward and seeks the destruction of "traitors in our midst." It happened in Germany in the years after World War I when Hitler, indiscriminately attacking liberals, democratic socialists, Jews, and Communists, and accusing them all of joining in the "stab in the back" that had allegedly led to Germany's downfall, engineered the establishment of a regime dedicated to the purging of such poisonous elements. It happened in Stalin's great purges of the 1930s. It happened to some extent in the United States in the McCarthy era, and it is happening to a nightmarish extent in Communist China as the main theme of the great "cultural revolution." It happens on a far smaller scale in the United States whenever an opponent of the Vietnam war, or an advocate of a compromise peace, is denounced as disloyal or as soft on Communism; and it happens whenever a right-wing conservative asserts that the danger of Communism "right here at home" is greater than the danger of Communism abroad.

If we ask how such irrationality is psychologically possible, these last examples suggest at least part of the answer. The ideas of the dissenters may touch the diabolizers on a vulnerable spot, leading to angry denial and to "avoidance of the communicator" by trying to shut him up. Here also is a kind of ambiguity. The dissenters at home are Americans, yet "they don't talk like Americans." It is incongruous. A Communist is expected to talk like a Communist, but not these people! As in the case of the phony-ally image, the frustration caused by ambiguity itself may be a major source of aggression.

The Roots of Diabolism:
It should be clear by now that diabolism is a many-sided and many-rooted process, embodying several themes which have appeared repeatedly in these pages. One is partial truth; not all devil-seeing is misperception by any means. Some devils are really there, and many devils are partly there. There are also a number of roots of unrealistic, exaggerated diabolism: projection, rationalization, displacement of hostility, intolerance of ambiguity, and disturbance of an unrealistically expanded territorial self-image.

There is another root of diabolism that has not been discussed:
The mystery of weapons directed against an "innocent" self. Each side arms, believing that its weapons are essential for self-defense. The other side, feeling wholly peaceful and innocent because of rationalization and all the other psychological processes we have considered, cannot understand what these arms portend unless it is aggression. Similarly, any actual military action by either side, no matter how great the provocation, and no matter how defensive the motive, is perceived by the other side almost inevitably as aggression. The Arab-Israeli dispute is an outstanding instance of this process. The vicious-spiral possibilities here are obvious.

Finally, *all the mechanisms that sustain an enemy-image once it is established come into play,* including social mechanisms such as conformity, loyalty, and distortion in the channels of communication, as well as psychological mechanisms stemming from the need to reduce ambivalence.

The Mirror Image and the Nature of Nationalism

Looking back over these sources of misperception in the minds of American militants, American non-militants, Communists and others, one is struck by two relationships.

The first is the similarity of the psychological processes described, even between cultures that in other respects are very different. The ethnocentric black-and-white picture is a transcultural, almost universal phenomenon, the details of which vary greatly from nation to nation, but the essence of which remains much the same. Similarly, the desire for prestige is very widespread. Americans have a stereotype of Orientals that pictures them as peculiarly sensitive to the fear of losing face, and circumstances that are regarded as humiliating do vary a good deal from culture to culture. However, the desire for prestige and the fear of humiliation were so strong in Europe in 1914 and are so strong in America today that one wonders whether they could be any stronger in the Far East. In view of this it is not surprising that there is a "mirror image" quality in the reality-worlds of combatants on both sides of the present struggle, even though the cultures of Vietnam and of Communist China are in some ways very different from that of the United States.

The other generalization that emerges is the basic character of identification with a nation. The black-and-white picture is typically a dichotomy between one's own nation (plus its allies) and the enemy of one's own nation (plus its allies). The desire for power and prestige is the desire for national power and prestige. The "self" that is virile and moral is a national self. This lends strong support to the proposition that when we fully understand nationalism we will have gone far toward understanding the causes of war. It seems to support also Emery Reves's contention, in his chapter on "A Copernican World," that:

There is not the slightest hope that we can possibly solve any of the vital problems of our generation until we rise above dogmatic nation-centric conceptions and realize that, in order to understand the political, economic, and social problems of this highly integrated and industrialized world, we have to shift our standpoint and see all the nations and national matters in motion, in their interrelated functions, rotating according to the same laws without any fixed points created by our own imagination for our own convenience.[42]

[42] Reves, 1963, p. 29.

BIBLIOGRAPHY

Abelson, Robert P., and Rosenberg, Milton J., "Symbolic Psycho-logic: A Model of Attitudinal Cognition." *Behavioral Sciences,* 1958, *3,* pp. 1–13.

Adorno, T. W., Frenkel-Brunswik, Else, Levinson, Daniel J., and Sanford, R. Nevitt. *The Authoritarian Personality.* New York: Harper & Brothers, 1950.

Allport, Gordon W., *The Nature of Prejudice.* New York: Doubleday Anchor Books (abridged edition), 1958.

——, and Postman, Leo J., "The Basic Psychology of Rumor," in Proshansky and Seidenberg, eds., *Basic Studies in Social Psychology.* New York: Holt, Rinehart and Winston, Inc., 1965, pp. 47–58.

Almond, Gabriel A., "Public Opinion and the Development of Space Technology: 1957–60," in J. Goldsen, ed., *Outer Space in World Politics.* New York: Frederick A. Praeger, Inc., 1963, pp. 71–96.

Alsop, Joseph, Article in *The New Yorker,* 1955. Quoted by Scheer, *How the U.S. Got Involved in Vietnam,* 1965, pp. 46–47.

——, "Uncle Sam's Money's Worth." Syndicated Column, October 8, 1965.

American Friends Service Committee, *Peace in Vietnam.* New York: Hill & Wang, 1966.

——, *The United States in Vietnam.* San Francisco: AFSC Northern California Regional Office, 1966.

Anonymous, "According to Informed Sources . . ." *New Republic,* February 20, 1966.

Ardrey, Robert, *African Genesis.* New York: Atheneum Publishers, 1963, pp. 33–58.

Asch, Solomon E., "Effects of Group Pressure upon the Modification and Distortion of Judgments," in Swanson, Newcomb & Hartley, eds., *Readings in Social Psychology.* New York: Henry Holt & Co., 1952, pp. 2–11.

Bakan, David, Contribution to Symposium on "The Legitimation of Evil," American Psychological Association. Chicago, September, 1965.

Baldwin, Hanson, "The Case for Escalation." *New York Times Magazine,* February 27, 1966, pp. 22–82.

——, "There Are Clear Signs of Progress." *New York Times,* December 3, 1967, p. E3.

Barnett, A. Doak, *Communist China and Asia*. New York: Vintage Books, 1961.

Barrymaine, Norman, "Bombing in the North Takes Its Toll." Article in *Look* reprinted by the *Washington Post,* November 27, 1966, p. E4.

Bartlett, F. C., *Remembering*. Cambridge, England: Cambridge University Press, 1932.

Berkowitz, Leonard, *Aggression: A Social Psychological Analysis*. New York: McGraw-Hill, Inc., 1962.

Brezhnev, Leonid, Speech to Central Committee, Moscow, September 29, 1965. *Washington Post,* September 20, p. A16.

Brightman, Carol, "The Weed-Killers." *Vietnam Report,* June–July, 1966, pp. 10–14, 33–45.

Bronfenbrenner, Urie, "The Mirror-image in Soviet-American Relations: A Social Psychologist's Report." *Journal of Social Issues,* 1961, pp. 45–56.

Brown, Roger, *Social Psychology*. The Free Press, 1965.

Browne, Malcolm, *The New Face of War*. New York: Bobbs-Merrill, 1965.

Browne, Robert S., "Vietnam Revisited." *Viet Report,* August–September, 1965, pp. 12–14.

——, "Vietnam—From Disorder to What?" *New Republic,* April 23, 1966, pp. 11–12.

Buchanan, W., and Cantril, Hadley, *How Nations See Each Other*. Urbana: University of Illinois Press, 1954.

Bundy, McGeorge, "The End of Either/Or." *Foreign Affairs,* 1967, *45*, pp. 189–201.

Bundy, William P., "Bundy Comments on Galbraith's Plan." *New York Times Magazine,* November 12, 1967, pp. 31–135.

Burchett, Wilfrid G., *Vietnam: Inside Story of the Guerrilla War*. New York: International Publishers, Inc., 1965.

Buttinger, Joseph, *The Smaller Dragon*. New York: Frederick A. Praeger, Inc., 1958.

——, *Vietnam: A Dragon Embattled*. New York: Frederick A. Praeger, Inc., 1967a. 2 vol.

——, "Vietnam: Fraud of the 'Other' War." *Dissent,* May–June 1967b, pp. 3–11.

Cameron, James, *Here is Your Enemy*. New York: Holt, Rinehart and Winston, Inc., 1966.

Campbell, Alex, " 'Our' War, 'Their' Peace: Who Wants What in South Vietnam?" *New Republic,* March 19, 1966a, pp. 19–23.

——, "Who's Afraid of China?" *New Republic,* April 9, 1966b, pp. 12–16.

Cantril, Hadley, *The Human Dimension: Experiences in Policy Research*. New Brunswick: Rutgers University Press, 1967.

Carpenter, C. Ray, "Behavior and Social Relations of the Howling Monkey," *Comparative Psychology Monthly*, Johns Hopkins University, 1934.

Carthew, Anthony, "Vietnam is Like an Oriental Western." *New York Times Magazine*, January 23, 1966, pp. 8–20.

Carver, George A., Jr., "The Real Revolution in South Vietnam." *Foreign Affairs*, 1965, *43*, pp. 387–408.

——, "The Faceless Viet Cong." *Foreign Affairs*, April, 1966, *44*, pp. 347–72.

CBS, *The People of South Vietnam: How They Feel about the War*. (privately printed, March 13, 1967.)

Chaffard, Georges, "Talks with the Viet Cong." Paris, *L'Express*, April 19, April 25, 1965. Translated in *Viet Report*, July, 1965.

Chapanis, Natalia, and Chapanis, A., "Cognitive Dissonance: Five Years Later." *Psychology Bulletin*, 1964, *61*, pp. 1–22.

Cherne, Leo, Article in *Look*, January 25, 1955.

Childs, Marquis, "War Psychology: Costly Consensus." *Washington Post*, November 19, 1965, p. A24.

——, "A Swedish View of War in Asia." *Washington Post*, November, 1965.

Chou En-lai, Speech in Peking, April 30, 1966. *New York Times*, April 31, 1966, p. 4.

Christiansen, Bjørn, *Attitudes Toward Foreign Affairs as a Function of Personality*. Oslo: Oslo University Press, 1959.

Christie, Richard, and Jahoda, Marie, *Studies in the Scope and Method of "The Authoritarian Personality."* The Free Press, 1954.

Clubb, Oliver E., Jr., *The United States and the Sino-Soviet Bloc in Southeast Asia*. Washington, D.C.: The Brookings Institution, 1962.

Collias, N., "Aggressive Behavior among Vertebrate Animals." *Physiol. Zoology*, 1944, *17*, pp. 83–123.

Cooper, Eunice, and Jahoda, Marie, "The Evasion of Propaganda." *Journal of Psychology*, 1947, *23*, pp. 15–25.

Cooper, Joseph B., "Emotion in Prejudice." *Science*, 1959, *130*, pp. 314–18.

Coser, L. A., *The Function of Social Conflict*. The Free Press, 1956.

Crow, Wayman J., "A Study of Strategic Doctrines Using the International Simulation." *Journal of Conflict Resolution*, 1963, *7*, pp. 580–89.

Defferre, Gaston, "De Gaulle and After." *Foreign Affairs*, 1966, *44*, pp. 434–45.

Deutsch, Karl, *Nationalism and Social Communication*. New York: Wiley, 1953.

Deutsch, Morton, "Trust and Suspicion." *J. Conflict Resolution*, 1958, *2*, pp. 265–79.

——, and Krauss, R. M., "Studies of Interpersonal Bargaining." *J. Conflict Resolution*, 1962, *6*, pp. 52–76.

——, "Vietnam and the Start of World War III: Some Psychological Parallels." Presidential Address to the New York State Psychological Association, May 7, 1966. (Privately mimeographed, 1966.)

Devillers, Philippe, "The Struggle for Unification of Vietnam." *China Quarterly*, January–March, 1962, pp. 2–23.

Dinh, Tran Van, "Ky vs. Buddhists—Round 2." *New Republic*, May 13, 1967, pp. 15–19.

Dollard, John, Doob, Leonard, Miller, Neal, Mowrer, O. Hobart, and Sears, Robert, *Frustration and Aggression*. New Haven: Yale University Press, 1939.

Donnell, John, "The War, the Gap, and the Cadre." *Asia*, 1966, No. 4, pp. 49–71.

Doob, Leonard W., *Patriotism and Nationalism: their Psychological Foundations*. New Haven: Yale University Press, 1964.

Dudman, R., "The Rules They Use in Vietnam." *New Republic*, June 12, 1965, pp. 20–21.

Duncan, Donald, *The New Legions*. New York: Random House, 1967.

Eden, Anthony, "The Burden of Leadership." *Foreign Affairs*, 1965, *44*, pp. 229–38.

Edwards, Allen L., "Political Frames of Reference as a Factor Influencing Recognition." *Journal of Abnormal and Social Psychology*, 1941, *36*, pp. 35–40.

Eisenhower, Dwight D., *Mandate for Change*. Garden City, New York: Doubleday & Company, Inc., 1963.

Fairbank, John K., *The United States and China*. New York: Viking, 1958.

——, "Why Peking Casts Us as the Villain." *New York Times Magazine*, May 22, 1966, pp. 30–109.

Fall, Bernard B., "Sociological and Psychological Aspects of Vietnam's Partition." *Journal of International Affairs*. 1964a, *18*, pp. 173–87.

——, *The Two Vietnams*. New York: Frederick A. Praeger, Inc., rev. ed., 1964b.

——, "Vietnam: European Viewpoints." *New Republic*, August 21, 1965a, pp. 13–14.

——, "Vietnam Blitz: a Report on the Impersonal War," *New Republic*, October 9, 1965b, pp. 17–21.

——, "The Year of the Hawks," *New York Times Magazine*, December 12, 1965c, pp. 46–116.

——, "And Still the Little Men of the Vietcong Keep Coming." *New York Times Magazine*, March 6, 1966a, pp. 20–70.

——, "Vietnam: The Undiscovered Country." *New York Review*, March 17, 1966b, pp. 8–9.

Fay, Sidney B., *The Origins of the World War*. New York: Macmillan, 1928.

Festinger, Leon, *A Theory of Cognitive Dissonance*. Evanston: Row, Peterson, 1957.

——, Schachter, Stanley, and Back, Kurt, *Social Pressures in Informal Groups: A Study of Human Factors in Housing*. New York: Harper & Brothers, 1950.

Fishel, Wesley R., ed., *Problems of Freedom: South Vietnam Since Independence*. The Free Press, 1961.

——, in *Vietnam, Is Victory Possible?* Foreign Policy Association, Headline Series No. 163, February 1964.

——, "Vietnam: the Broadening War," *Asian Survey*, May, 1966, pp. 249–63.

Foisie, Jack, *Washington Post*, September 29, 1965.

Foley, John P., *Archives of Psychol.*, 1935, *184*.

Frank, Jerome D., Statement on South Vietnam, inserted in *Congressional Record* by Senator Gruening, March 9, 1965.

Frenkel-Brunswik, Else, "Intolerance of Ambiguity as an Emotional and Perceptual Personality Variable." *J. Personality*, 1949, *18*, pp. 108–43.

Freud, Sigmund, *The Basic Writings of Sigmund Freud*. New York: Random House (Modern Library), 1938.

Fulbright, Senator J. W., "The Fatal Arrogance of Power." *New York Times Magazine*, May 15, 1966a, p. 103.

——, ed., *The Vietnam Hearings*. New York: Vintage, 1966.

Gavin, General James M., Statement to Committee on Foreign Relations. In Fulbright, ed., *The Vietnam Hearings*, 1966, pp. 59–106.

Gayn, Mark, "To Mao We Are the Prime Enemy." *New York Times Magazine*, October 24, 1965, pp. 46–182.

Gerassi, John, "Report from North Vietnam." *New Republic*, March 4, 1967, p. 16.

Gettleman, Marvin E., ed., *Vietnam*. New York: Fawcett, 1965 (Paperback).

Giap, V. N., *People's War, People's Army*. New York: Frederick A. Praeger, Inc., 1962. (More correctly listed as Vo Nguyen Giap, Vo being the family name, though he is better known in the U.S. as Giap.)

Gilpatric, Roswell L., "Vietnam and World War III." *New York Times*, May 30, 1965.

Gittinger, J. P., Article in *Far Eastern Survey*, January–February, 1960.

Gladstone, Arthur I., "Relationship Orientation and Processes Leading toward War." *Background*, 1962, *6*, pp. 13–25.

Gollin, E. S., "Forming Impressions of Personality." *J. Personality*, 1954, *23*, pp. 65–76.

Gooch, George P., *Before the War: Studies in Diplomacy*. London: Longmans, Green, and Co., Ltd., Vol. I, 1936, Vol. II, 1938.

Gottlieb, Sanford, Report on talks with NLF, Hanoi. *Sane World*, September, 1965, pp. 1–6.

——, Report on talks with NLF and North Vietnamese in France and Algeria. *New York Times*, March 17, 1967.

Gottschaldt, K., *Psychologische Forschung*. 1926, *8*, pp. 261–317.

Graff, Henry F., "How Johnson Makes Foreign Policy." *New York Times Magazine*, July 4, 1965, pp. 4–20.

Greenspoon, Joel, "The Reinforcing Effect of Two Spoken Sounds on the Frequency of Two Responses." *Amer. J. Psychol.* 1955, *68*, pp. 409–16.

Guetzkow, Harold, Alger, Chadwick F., Brody, Richard A., Noel, Robert C., and Snyder, Richard C., *Simulation in International Relations*. Englewood Cliffs, New Jersey: Prentice-Hall, 1963.

Hammer, Ellen E., *The Struggle for Indochina*. Stanford: Stanford University Press, 1954.

Harwood, Richard, "The War Just Doesn't Add Up." *Washington Post*, September 3, 1967, p. B5.

Heiden, Konrad, *Der Fuehrer*. Boston: Houghton Mifflin, 1944.

Heider, Fritz, "Attitudes and Cognitive Organization." *J. Psychology*, 1946, *21*, pp. 107–12.

——, *The Psychology of Interpersonal Relations*. New York: Wiley, 1958.

Hickey, Gerald, *Village in Vietnam*. New Haven: Yale University Press, 1964.

Hilsman, Roger, Quoted by Fall, *New York Times Magazine*, December 12, 1965.

Hitler, Adolf, *My New Order*. Speeches, ed. by De Sales. New York: Reynal & Hitchcock, 1941.

Ho Chi Minh, Interview with Felix Greene. *Washington Post*, December 14, 1965, pp. A1–10.

——, Letter to Communist Heads of State. *Washington Post*, January 29, 1966, p. A12.

——, *On Revolution*. New York: Frederick A. Praeger, Inc., 1967.

Hoang Van Chi, *From Colonialism to Communism*. New York: Frederick A. Praeger, Inc., 1964.

Holsti, Ole, "Cognitive Dynamics and Images of the Enemy." *J. Internat. Affairs*, 1967, No. 1, pp. 16–39.

——, and Robert C. North. "The History of Human Conflict," in McNeil, ed., *The Nature of Human Conflict*, pp. 155–71.

Honey, P. J., ed., *North Vietnam Today: Profile of a Communist Satellite*. New York: Frederick A. Praeger, Inc., 1962.

——, "Vietnam: To the Bitter End?" *The Spectator,* December 17, 1965. Also in *Survival,* February, 1966.

Hovland, Carl I., "Reconciling Conflicting Results Derived from Experimental and Survey Studies of Attitude Change." *Amer. Psychologist,* 1959, *14,* pp. 8–17.

Hyman, Herbert, and Sheatsley, Paul B., "The Authoritarian Personality: A Methodological Critique." In Christie and Jahoda, *Studies in the Scope and Method of "The Authoritarian Personality,"* 1954.

Inkeles, Alex, and Bauer, Raymond, *The Soviet Citizen.* Cambridge: Harvard University Press, 1959.

Janis, Irving L., and Feshbach, Seymour, "Effects of Fear-arousing Communications." *J. Abnor. & Soc. Psychol.,* 1953, *48,* pp. 78–92.

——, and King, Bert L., "The Influence of Role-Playing on Opinion Change." *J. Abnor. & Soc. Psychol.,* 1954, *49,* pp. 211–18.

Johnson, General Harold K., "End of Vietnam War in Sight?" *U.S. News & World Report,* September 11, 1967.

Johnson, Lyndon B., "Vietnam: The Third Face of the War." Speech to Assoc. of Am. Editorial Cartoonists, May 13, 1965, *Dept. of State Pub.* 7897.

Jordan, N., "Behavioral Forces that are a Function of Attitudes and of Cognitive Organization." *Human Relations,* 1953, *6,* pp. 273–87.

Just, Ward, "This War May Be Unwinnable." *Washington Post,* June 4, 1967, p. B5.

——, "The Heart-Mind Gap in the Vietnam War." *Washington Post,* November 19, 1967, pp. B1–2.

Kahn, M. W., "The Effect of Severe Defeat at Various Age Levels on the Aggressive Behavior of Mice." *Journal of Genetic Psychology,* 1951, *79,* pp. 117–30.

Kamenetzky, Joseph, "Anxiety and Attitude as Variables Affecting Perception of Persons." Unpub. dissertation, University of Illinois, 1955.

Karnow, Stanley, *Washington Post,* October 24, 1965, pp. E1–4.

Katz, Elihu, and Lazarsfeld, Paul F., *Personal Influence.* The Free Press, 1955.

Kelman, Herbert C., "Attitude Change as a Function of Response Restriction." *Human Relations,* 1953, *6,* pp. 185–214.

——, ed., *International Behavior: A Social-Psychological Analysis.* New York: Holt, Rinehart and Winston, Inc., 1965, pp. xiv–626.

Kennan, George F., *Russia and the West under Lenin and Stalin.* Boston: Little, Brown, 1960.

——, Testimony to Foreign Relations Committee, February 10, 1966. *New Republic,* February 26, 1966, pp. 19–30.

Kennedy, John F., *Profiles in Courage.* New York: Harper & Brothers, 1956.

Kenworthy, E. W., "Johnson's Policy in Vietnam—Four Positions in Congress." *New York Times,* July 25, 1965.

Klapper, Joseph, *The Effects of Mass Communications.* The Free Press, 1960.

Krech, David, Crutchfield, Richard S., and Ballachey, Egerton L., *Individual in Society.* New York: McGraw-Hill, 1962.

Labin, Suzanne, *Vietnam: an Eye-Witness Account.* Springfield, Virginia: Crestwood, 1964.

Lacouture, Jean, *Vietnam Between Two Truces.* New York: Random House, 1966.

——, "The Military Situation in Vietnam," *New Republic,* May 22, 1966, p. 20.

Ladejinsky, Wolf, "Agrarian Reform in Vietnam," in Fishel, ed., *Problems in Freedom,* 1961.

Langguth, Jack, "Saigon Tries to Live in a Hurry." *New York Times Magazine,* August 8, 1965.

Lansdale, Major General Edward G., "Vietnam: Do We Understand Revolution?" *Foreign Affairs,* 1964, *43,* pp. 75–86.

Lederer, William J., and Burdick, Eugene, *The Ugly American.* New York: W. W. Norton, 1958; Crest Paperback, 1961.

Leites, Nathan, *A Study of Bolshevism.* The Free Press, 1953.

Lerner, Daniel, *The Passing of Traditional Society.* The Free Press, 1958.

Levine, J. M., and Murphy, Gardner, "The Learning and Forgetting of Controversial Material," in Swanson, Guy E., Newcomb, Theodore M., and Hartley, Eugene L., eds., *Readings in Social Psychology.* New York: Henry Holt & Co., 1952.

Levine, S., "Emotionality and Aggressive Behavior in the Mouse as a Function of Infantile Experience." *J. Genet. Psychol.,* 1959, *94,* pp. 77–83.

Lifton, Robert J., *Thought Reform and the Psychology of Totalism: A Study of "Brain-Washing" in China.* New York: Norton, 1961.

Lin Piao, "Long Live the Victory of the People's War." Peking, September 2, 1965. Condensed in *Survival* (London Inst. for Strategic Studies), November, 1965.

Lippmann, Walter, Syndicated column, September 21, 1965.

——, "Defining Our War Aims." Syndicated column, December 28, 1965.

——, "The White Man's Burden." Syndicated column, April 28, 1966.

——, Syndicated column, June 2, 1966.

Lipset, Seymour Martin, "The President, The Polls, and Vietnam." *Transaction,* September–October, 1966, pp. 19–24.

Lockwood, Lee, "Recollections of Four Weeks with the Enemy." *Life,* April 7, 1967, pp. 44B-D.

Loomis, J. L., "Communication, the Development of Trust and Cooperative Behavior." *Human Relations,* 1959, *12,* pp. 305–15.

Lorenz, Konrad, *On Aggression*. New York: Harcourt, Brace & World, 1966.

Lowenthal, Richard, "Can We Make Common Cause with Russia?" *New York Times Magazine*, November 21, 1965, pp. 34–74.

Luchins, Abraham S., "Primacy-Recency in Impression Formation," in C. I. Hovland, ed., *The Order of Presentation in Persuasion*, Vol. I. New Haven: Yale University Press, 1957.

McCarthy, Eugene J., *The Limits of Power: America's Role in the War*. New York: Holt, Rinehart and Winston, Inc., 1967.

McNeil, Elton B., ed., *The Nature of Human Conflict*. Englewood Cliffs: Prentice-Hall, 1965.

Mannes, Marya, "A Visit with U Thant." *New Republic*, January 8, 1966, pp. 10–12.

Markel, Lester, "Public Opinion and the War in Vietnam." *New York Times Magazine*, August 8, 1965, pp. 9–72.

Marr, David, "Political Attitudes and Activities of Young Urban Intellectuals in South Vietnam." *Asian Survey*, May, 1966, pp. 249–63.

Martin, J. G., and Westie, F. R., "The Tolerant Personality." *American Sociological Review*, 1959, *24*, pp. 521–28.

Mecklin, John, *Mission in Torment*. New York: Doubleday & Company, Inc., 1965.

——, Reed College Conference on U.S. Policy in Vietnam. Reed College *Sallyport*, April, 1965.

Milgram, Stanley, "Behavioral Study of Obedience." *J. Abnor. & Soc. Psychol.*, 1963, *67*, pp. 371–78.

Millis, Walter, *The Martial Spirit: a Study of our War With Spain*. Boston and New York: Houghton Mifflin, 1931.

Mohr, Charles, *New York Times*, November 28, 1965, pp. 1–2.

Mok, Michael, "In They Go—to the Reality of This War." *Life*, November 26, 1965.

Montgelas, Max, *The Case for the Central Powers*. New York: Knopf, 1925.

——, and Walter Schucking, eds., *Outbreak of the World War: German Documents Collected by Karl Kautsky*. New York: Oxford University Press, 1924.

Montgomery, John D., *The Politics of Foreign Aid: American Experience in Southeast Asia*. New York: Frederick A. Praeger, Inc., 1962.

Moore, Robin, *The Green Berets*. New York: Avon Books, 1965.

Morgenthau, Hans J., "War with China?" *New Republic*, April 3, 1965, pp. 11–14.

——, "Russia, the U.S., and Vietnam." *New Republic*, May 1, 1965, pp. 12–13.

——, "Globalism: Johnson's Moral Crusade." *New Republic*, July 3, 1965, pp. 19–22.

Morrissette, Julian O., "An Experimental Study of the Theory of Structural Balance." *Human Relations,* 1958, *11,* pp. 239–54.

Moser, Don, "Eight Dedicated Men Marked for Death." *Life,* September 3, 1965, pp. 30–33.

Murray, Henry A., "Effect of Fear upon Estimates of Maliciousness of Other Personalities." *J. Soc. Psychol.,* 1933, *4,* pp. 310–29.

Mus, Paul, Quoted by Scheer, *How the U. S. Got Involved in Vietnam,* 1965, p. 28.

Myrdal, Gunnar, "With What Little Wisdom the World is Ruled!" *New York Times Magazine,* July 18, 1965, pp. 20–26.

Nevin, David, "The Dissent." *Life,* February 25, 1966, pp. B56–62.

Nicolaus, Martin, "Saigon: The Wheel Comes Full Circle." *Viet Report,* July, 1965, pp. 13–16.

Nixon, Richard M., "Why Not Negotiate in Vietnam?" *Reader's Digest,* December, 1965, pp. 49–54.

North, Robert C., "Perception and Action in the 1914 Crisis." *J. Internat. Affairs,* 1967, No. 1, pp. 103–22.

Orwell, George, *1984.* New York: New American Library, Signet Books, 1950.

——, *Animal Farm.* New York: New American Library, Signet Book Edition, 1956.

Osgood, Charles E., *An Alternative to War or Surrender.* Urbana: University of Illinois Press, 1962.

——, *Perspective in Foreign Policy,* Second Edition. Palo Alto: Pacific Books, 1966.

——, and Tannenbaum, P. H., "The Principle of Congruity in the Prediction of Attitude Change." *Psychol. Review,* 1955, pp. 42–55.

Pike, Douglas, "How Strong is the NLF?" *Reporter,* February 24, 1966a, pp. 20–24.

——, *Viet Cong.* Cambridge: M.I.T. Press, 1966b.

Pool, Ithiel de Sola, "Political Alternatives to the Viet Cong." *Asian Survey, 7,* 1967, pp. 555–66.

Pustay, Major J. A. (USAF), *Counterinsurgency Warfare.* The Free Press, 1965.

Pye, Lucien, *Guerrilla Communism in Malaya.* Princeton: Princeton University Press, 1956.

Rapoport, Anatol, *Fights, Games and Debates.* Ann Arbor: University of Michigan Press, 1960.

Raskin, Marcus G., and Fall, Bernard B., eds., *The Vietnam Reader.* New York: Random House, 1965.

Raymond, Jack, "When G.I. Joe Meets Ol' Charlie." *New York Times Magazine,* July 25, 1965, pp. 4–21.

BIBLIOGRAPHY 287

——, "It's a Dirty War for Correspondents, Too." *New York Times Magazine*, February 13, 1966, pp. 32–95.

Reston, James, "We May Win the War but Lose the People." *New York Times Magazine*, September 12, 1965a, pp. 43–117.

——, "Washington: Where Did We Go Wrong?" *New York Times*, November 21, 1965b, p. E10.

Reves, Emery, *The Anatomy of Peace*. New York: Viking, 1945; Compass Books Edition, 1963.

Richardson, Lewis F., *Arms and Insecurity*. Chicago: Quadrangle Books, 1960.

Ridgway, Matthew B., Quoted by Schlesinger, *The Bitter Heritage*, 1967, p. 26.

Roberts, Chalmers M., "Ho Steals U.S. Thunder." *Washington Post*, January 9, 1966, p. E1.

Rock, Vincent P., *A Strategy of Interdependence*. New York: Scribner's, 1964.

Rokeach, Milton, *The Open and Closed Mind*. New York: Basic Books, 1960.

Ronning, Chester A., Quoted by Schlesinger, *The Bitter Heritage*, 1967, pp. 108–9.

Rose, Jerry, *New Republic*, October 12, 1963. Quoted in Scheer, *How the U. S. Got Involved in Vietnam*, 1965, p. 76.

Rovere, Richard, "Letter from Washington." *The New Yorker*, December 18, 1965.

Rusk, Dean, Testimony to Foreign Relations Committee, February 18, 1966. *Washington Post*, February 19, p. A10.

Sacks, Milton, "Marxism in Vietnam." In Trager, Frank N., ed., *Marxism in Southeast Asia*. Stanford: Stanford University Press, 1959, pp. 102–70.

Salisbury, Harrison E., *New York Times*, January 15, 1967, p. E2.

Sansom, Robert L., "Working Paper on Viet Cong Economics." (USAID Economic Division). Unpublished. April, 1967.

Scheer, Robert, *How the United States Got Involved in Vietnam*. Report to Center for the Study of Democratic Institutions, Santa Barbara, 1965.

Schell, Jonathan, "A Reporter at Large: The Village of Ben Suc." *New Yorker*, July 15, 1967, pp. 28–93.

Schelling, Thomas C., *The Strategy of Conflict*. Cambridge: Harvard University Press, 1960.

Schlesinger, Arthur M., *The Bitter Heritage*. New York: Fawcett Crest Books, 1967.

Scigliano, Robert, *South Vietnam: Nation Under Stress*. Boston: Houghton Mifflin, 1963.

Scott, J. P., "Dominance and the Frustration-Aggression Hypothesis." *Physiol. Zoology,* 1948, *21,* pp. 31–39.

——, *Aggression.* Chicago: University of Chicago Press, 1958.

Scott, William A., "Attitude Change through Reward of Verbal Behavior." *J. Abnor. & Soc. Psychol.,* 1957, *55,* pp. 72–75.

——, "Attitude Change by Response Reinforcement: Replication and Extension." *Sociometry,* 1959, pp. 328–35.

Sen, Chanakya, *The Future of Vietnam: an Asian Assessment.* September, 1965. (Privately mimeographed.)

Shaplen, Robert, *The Lost Revolution.* New York: Harper and Row, 1965.

——, "Letter from South Vietnam." *The New Yorker,* June 7, 1967, pp. 37–91.

Sheehan, Neil, "How Saigon Sees All Those G.I.s," *New York Times,* May 8, 1966, p. E3.

Sheehan, Susan, *Ten Vietnamese.* New York: Knopf, 1967.

Sherif, Muzafer, Harvey, O. J., White, B. J., Hood, W. R., and Sherif, Carolyn W., *Intergroup Conflict and Cooperation: The Robbers Cave Experiment.* Norman, Oklahoma: University Book Exchange, 1961.

Smith, Howard P., and Rosen, Ellen W., "Some Psychological Correlates of World-mindedness and Authoritarianism." *J. Personality,* 1958, *26,* pp. 170–83.

Smith, M. Brewster, Bruner, Jerome S., and White, Robert W., *Opinions and Personality.* New York: Wiley, 1956.

Snow, Edgar, "Is Peace Still Possible?" *New Republic.* May 22, 1965, pp. 15–20.

Spock, Benjamin, "Why Do We Betray Peace and Justice?" *Sane World,* July, 1965, pp. 5–6.

State Department, "White Paper, 1961." *Dept. Pub. 7308,* Released December, 1961. In Raskin and Fall, eds., *Vietnam Reader,* pp. 123–25.

Steiner, Ivan D., and Fishbein, Martin, eds., *Current Studies in Social Psychology.* New York: Holt, Rinehart and Winston, Inc., 1965.

Sulzberger, C. L., "Foreign Affairs: Vietnam through French Eyes." *New York Times,* February 20, 1966, p. E12.

Tanham, George K., *Communist Revolutionary Warfare: The Viet-Minh in Indochina.* New York: Frederick A. Praeger, Inc., 1961.

Tannenbaum, Percy H., "Initial Attitude toward Source and Concept as Factors in Attitude Change through Communication." *Pub. Opin. Quart.,* 1956, *20,* pp. 413–25.

Taylor, Edmund, *The Fall of the Dynasties.* Garden City: Doubleday & Company, Inc., 1963.

Taylor, General Maxwell D., (Testimony to Foreign Relations Committee of February 17, 1966). *Washington Post,* February 18, 1966, p. A18.

Topping, Seymour, "Vietnam Issue Divides Communists as Well as West." *New York Times,* June 20, 1965, p. E3.

Toynbee, Arnold, "Reunified Vietnam under Communism Preferable to Continued Division." *Yomiuri Shimbun* (Japan), July 9, 1965.

Trager, Frank N., "The Impact of Marxism," in Trager, Frank N., ed., *Marxism in Southeast Asia.* Stanford: Stanford University Press, 1959.

——, "Pax Asiatica?" *Orbis,* 1966, *10,* pp. 673–89.

Tucker, Robert C., *Philosophy and Myth in Karl Marx.* Cambridge, England: Cambridge University Press, 1961.

USIA/IRS, *The Rationale of Drawing Inferences from Interviews with Escapees.* Washington, 1963.

U. S. Strategic Bombing Survey, *Over-all report (European War).* Washington, D.C. Government Printing Office, September 30, 1945.

Verplanck, William S., "The Control of the Content of Conversation: Reinforcement of Statements of Opinion." *J. Abnor. & Soc. Psychol.,* 1955, *51,* pp. 668–76.

Vo Nguyen Giap, *People's War, People's Army.* New York: Frederick A. Praeger, Inc., 1962. (also listed under Giap).

Warner, Denis, Article in *The Reporter,* October 10, 1963. Quoted by Scheer, *How the U. S. Got Involved in Vietnam,* p. 73.

——, Article in *The Reporter,* September 13, 1962. Quoted by Scheer, *How the U. S. Got Involved in Vietnam,* p. 72.

White, Ralph K., "The Case for the Tolman-Lewin Interpretation of Learning." *Psychol. Review,* 1943, *50,* pp. 157–86.

——, "Hitler, Roosevelt, and the Nature of War Propaganda." *J. Abnor. & Soc. Psychol.,* 1949, pp. 157–74.

——, *Value Analysis: the nature and use of the method.* Society for the Psychological Study of Social Issues, 1951.

——, "Socialism and Capitalism: an International Misunderstanding." *Foreign Affairs,* 1966, *44,* pp. 216–28.

——, and Lippitt, Ronald, *Autocracy and Democracy: an Experimental Inquiry.* New York: Harper & Brothers, 1960.

Woodworth, Robert S., *Experimental Psychology.* New York: Henry Holt & Co., 1938.

Zagoria, Donald S., "How Hardnosed is Hanoi?" *Washington Post,* December 19, 1965, p. E3.

Zietlow, Carl P., *Washington Post,* April 27, 1967, p. A31.

Zinnes, Dina A., North, Robert C., and Koch, Howard E., "Capability, Threat, and the Outbreak of War," in James N. Rosenau, ed., *International Politics and Foreign Policy.* The Free Press, 1961.

A LARGE-AREA HOLDING POLICY IN VIETNAM

Note: In this Appendix the writer abandons the effort to be analytical and descriptive, and says what he thinks should be done, and why. Earlier parts of the book have been diagnosis; this part is "prescription." It is obviously not "objective" in the sense of being neutral. It argues for one course of action and answers certain arguments that are commonly raised against it. On the other hand, there is a continuing attempt to be objective in another sense—to avoid wishful thinking and selective inattention. Both Appendixes try to gather all the elements in the rest of the book that have a bearing on what we should do now, to look at them steadily, and to consider their relationship to the fateful choices that confront us.

Probably most Americans see Vietnam as a bloody quagmire from which we would gladly escape if we only knew how to do so honorably and safely. But the two paths of escape most often advocated seem to many of us wholly unacceptable. One, drastic escalation in the North, immediately risks a much larger war. The other, withdrawal, most of us regard as a form of appeasement—humiliating, dishonorable, and an invitation to Communist aggression elsewhere.

In this predicament a possible alternative is some form of compromise peace, but here too there are great difficulties. The kind of compromise that has been most often discussed—a coalition government with the Viet Cong participating—is open to serious question on the ground that it would be only a way station on the road to Communism. Even though the Viet Cong now appear to represent only a minority, they are organized, dedicated, and power-hungry, and their disorganized opponents would probably be no match for them in the power struggle that would ensue.

This particular difficulty, at least, is avoided by the other major form of compromise peace that is open to us: the "holding policy" advocated in various forms by Lippmann, Kennan, Gavin, Reston, Sevareid, Galbraith, Morton, McCarthy, and others. It deserves a good deal more thought and discussion than it has usually been given.

It not only has various possible forms; it also goes by various names. The name is important because a person's emotional reaction to the policy is partly determined by the words in which he first hears it described. Perhaps the term most often used has been "the enclave policy." General Gavin used the term "enclave," and the word has stuck. That has been enough to condemn it in the eyes of a great many Americans, since "enclave" ordinarily means a small patch of land completely surrounded by foreign territory. Not many Americans would want to settle for a few small patches of land. But smallness is not a necessary characteristic of the areas that would be held, if a holding policy were adopted. The word "holding" is a broader, less limiting term, better for our present purpose since it leaves open the possibility that the territory held by non-Communists might be large rather than small.

Sometimes the term used is "retreat to enclaves." That is even more damning, since any retreat is a humiliation and implies a net gain in territory for the Communists. Another automatically damning phrase is "hunkering down." President Johnson has spoken scornfully of hunkering down in enclaves. Most of us would probably agree with him that hunkering down in anything as small as an enclave would be an undignified posture for a proud nation like the United States. But neither retreat nor hunkering down is necessary. Holding does not by definition imply either retreat or hunkering down. In fact, one form it could take is first to *advance* to positions stronger than those we and our allies now occupy, and then to hold those positions, pursuing a more active, dynamic policy within them than any we have yet attempted.

I

A basic fact that a great many Americans have never clearly grasped is that we and our Vietnamese allies now hold firmly a great deal less than half of the land and the population of South Vietnam. Many have been misled by the fact that elections have been held in localities representing more than half of the population. But an election held in a locality in the daytime does not mean that our side holds that locality firmly by night as well as by day. Although less than half of the hamlets are now firmly held by the Viet Cong, a good many more than half are either held by the Viet Cong or in dispute, with the inhabitants subjected to the demoralizing process of acknowledging one set of masters by day and another by night.

What we have now is in fact an enclave situation, the enclaves being the larger cities and towns, plus one sizable rural area controlled by the Hoa Hao sect in the northwest, upriver part of the Mekong Delta. The few major connecting roads are usually fairly secure—in the daytime—as is the territory extending perhaps two kilometers on both sides of the major roads. That is about all. Like the French during their long and ultimately disastrous war in Indochina, and like the Japanese in China, we hold the strong points and (precariously) most of the lines of communication, but not much that lies between. If we could change this to a situation in which nearly all the city people and as many as half of the peasants enjoyed real security in solidly non-Communist territory it would be a great advance in terms of real power and also in terms of human welfare. Americans who do not realize what a great advance it would be are deceiving themselves about the reality of our present situation. It is only in comparison with a hope of total victory in South Vietnam—a hope which many now regard as illusory—that a holding policy could possibly be regarded as a retreat.

It is rather surprising that there have been few concrete suggestions as to how this policy could be implemented. In the hope of promoting concrete discussion of various possibilities, one such suggestion is offered here. It is that we and our allies should hold, and establish real security in, two large areas: (1) The lion's share of the Delta—roughly the northern three-fifths of it, including Can Tho and My Tho—plus Saigon and the surrounding area (see Figure 1). Close to half of all of South Vietnam's population lives within this fertile, relatively rich, densely populated area. It would contain both of the two heavily populated areas that are now fairly free from Viet Cong harassment—the Saigon area and the Hoa Hao area—and all of the territory between them. It would be economically viable and (with strong defense and patrolling of the Cambodian border from the ocean to Hau Nghia) militarily defensible. (2) The geographically large but poor and thinly populated montagnard area (at least the provinces of Kontum, Pleiku, Darlac, and Phu Bon) plus the coast from Binh Dinh down to our strong base at Cam Ranh.

To consolidate non-Communist strength more easily in these two large areas (and for other reasons below), we would simultaneously withdraw, in a gradual and orderly way, from our precarious, hard-to-hold positions in other parts of the country. For example, it might be regarded as wise to withdraw from all of "I Corps," from most

Figure 1. Areas in South Vietnam proposed for the "Large-Area Holding Policy"

of the area between Cam Ranh and Saigon, and from the southern two-fifths of the Delta. During our gradual withdrawal from our outposts in these precarious areas, anti-Communists living in them might be helped to withdraw with our troops and to establish themselves in one of the two large non-Communist areas. A reverse movement of pro-Viet Cong Vietnamese could also be permitted.

Meanwhile, inside the large non-Communist areas, we and our Vietnamese allies could pursue a dynamic policy of social, economic and political advance. With even half the money we are now spending on military operations (which could probably be cut by more than half during the year or two after shifting to a holding strategy) we could make many long-term investments, especially in education, that would promote stable, healthy economic growth rather than the present unstable, unhealthy kind. Such investments would also build confidence and morale in the South Vietnamese people in the holding areas, since they would demonstrate tangibly that we intended to stay as long as we were needed. We could press for a drastic program of land reform, starting with complete elimination of rent paid to absentee landlords. (If the landlords and their political allies were recalcitrant it might be necessary for the United States to use its military and economic leverage more firmly than in the past.) We could push elimination of the restraints on democracy that still exist on the national level (for example, the exclusion of neutralists as political candidates) and especially on the village level, with a rebuilding of the kind of village democracy that existed before 1956 (see Chapter 2, p. 29).

A vigorous anti-Viet Cong police program would, unfortunately, still be necessary, along with adequate military defense, but our emphasis could shift strongly away from the inhuman business of "counterinsurgency" (which in Vietnamese hands has torture as a frequent accompaniment) to providing positive incentives for enlisting in the common constructive effort. Such measures could make the non-Communist parts of South Vietnam a showcase—not of "democracy" exactly (since with all our efforts we could hardly make the country very democratic very soon), but of practices at least as democratic as the present activities of the Viet Cong in the villages it controls. We could see to it that these areas were much better off economically than the others, and progressing economically at a faster rate. It seems likely that, if these things were done, our areas would become a magnet, as West Germany has been for East Germans, and West Berlin for East Berliners. In the long run a peaceful unification of South Vietnam around these large nuclei might well be possible, and even, in the longer run, a unification of all of Vietnam.

This kind of holding strategy would be difficult. It would probably require, for at least one or two years, at least as many troops and at least as much money and effort as we are investing now. But, unlike the present strategy, it might show clear progress within a short time—perhaps months. And, unlike the other main form of compromise peace that has been proposed (a coalition government) it would be feasible immediately. It would not require any negotiation or agreement with the Viet Cong or with North Vietnam. It would not require trusting them in any way. It could be done by us and our allies on our own initiative, without continuing the present agonizing process of waiting for the Communists to come to the conference table.

II

The great virtue of this strategy is that it faces up to the grim fact of the present stalemate and offers a path to an honorable peace that takes the nature of that stalemate fully into account. The nature of the stalemate, therefore, calls for close examination.

Essentially it consists of the fact that the Viet Cong cannot be defeated on their own terrain and that the Americans cannot be defeated on theirs. The United States has now dug in and, with its tremendous superiority in modern weapons, cannot be pushed out. But the Viet Cong cannot be pushed out either. If they maintain the extraordinary courage and tenacity that they have shown up to now—and there is much reason to expect that they will—they cannot be defeated on their own preferred terrain of mountain, jungle, swamp, and the acid-soil, soggy desert of the Plain of Reeds—from all of which they make forays at will into the densely populated areas nearby. In the Delta the Viet Cong use for this purpose the network of innumerable tiny canals, and the coconut groves, which provide admirable cover. In the Delta, also, food is plentiful. Rice, fish, bananas, coconuts, and vegetables are abundant. The Viet Cong have ready access to this food, since a large part of the population of this area is willing (due to intimidation and also to other reasons) to feed them, to help them conceal themselves, to give them intelligence about the movements of government troops, and to deny such intelligence to their enemies. Joseph Alsop and others have pictured the misery of the Viet Cong, now suffering from malnutrition and the skin diseases of the tropical jungle, with their places of rest largely destroyed, and exhausted from being constantly on the move. But Alsop was talking of conditions in the mountainous jungle north of Saigon, not about the Delta. In the Delta the Viet Cong are in no such predicament.

Moreover, a distinction should be made between their capacity to wage conventional warfare, which may be seriously reduced by present and future American operations (including the bombing of the North and the barrier we now plan to build across Viet Cong supply lines from the North), and their capacity to wage guerrilla warfare with very simple weapons, which may not be seriously reduced at all. The kind of stalemate described here would not be disproved by evidence that the Viet Cong was losing in the field of conventional warfare, or that their supplies of heavy weapons were being gradually choked off, or that the economy of North Vietnam was suffering. The essential point is their capacity, at least in the Delta, to return to a primitive but effective form of guerrilla warfare, and to continue it indefinitely. That is their fall-back position, and we have not yet forced them back to it. In that fall-back position they probably could hold out and remain a formidable enemy even if we invaded or destroyed North Vietnam.

This is the hard, basic fact that most of our military men, who pride themselves on their hard thinking, have not yet fully grasped. The American military cling to the belief that their own stock-in-trade, the superweapons modern technology has produced, could win the war if only the peaceniks and the politicians would allow them to use these weapons rationally, without needless restraints. If the enemy in Hanoi is only made to hurt enough, they hold, he will issue orders to his subordinates in the South and the aggression will stop. Implicit in this argument is the assumption that our forces could handle, perhaps with difficulty but quite adequately, the Viet Cong resistance that might continue in the South even if supplies and direction from the North were cut off. Probably most of the American public still assume the same. It seems to most of us unbelievable that the strongest country in the world, with the most awesome weapons, cannot put its foot down and simply win the war. Most civilian Americans, like most American military men, probably assume that the Viet Cong in the South could not hold out without large-scale help from the North.

It is just this assumption, however, that my own recent experience in South Vietnam, especially in the Delta, has led me to question most fundamentally. It has all the earmarks of the fatuous optimism (fatuous, at least, in retrospect) that characterized the military thinking of the French throughout their disastrous nine-year war in the same country. The typical American view disregards, or under-emphasizes, the burning conviction of the Viet Cong that Americans are aggressors like the French, and that if necessary the Vietnamese must sacrifice all they have to defend their homeland. Mistaken as this conviction may be, it is not less real on that account. The typical view also leaves out of account, or underemphasizes, the extraor-dinary success of the Viet Cong, especially in the Delta, during the period between 1957 and 1961. During those years very little ma-terial help was forthcoming from the North, and their opponent, Diem, was already drawing heavily on the enormous material re-sources of the United States. The typical American view ignores or underemphasizes the fact that our very heavy (if not maximal) use of superweapons in South Vietnam since early 1965 has been singu-larly ineffective in breaking the stalemate. It ignores or underempha-sizes the fact that guerrilla warfare needs only small, light weapons and ammunition, which the Viet Cong now seem to have in large quantity and which they could continue to construct, capture, buy through third parties, or obtain by sea—even if the Ho Chi Minh trail and the Cambodian border were completely blocked, which seems unlikely. It ignores or underemphasizes the fact that we are still far from achieving the ten-to-one ratio of counterguerrilla to guerrilla forces which has often been regarded as necessary for counterguerrilla success, and that we are unlikely to achieve that ratio as long as the Viet Cong are able to recruit locally, by intimida-tion or other means, at the rate they have been recruiting since 1965. It ignores or underemphasizes the considerable possibility that the tough Viet Cong cadres in the South might refuse to disband even if officially ordered to do so by Hanoi.

Finally, the prevailing American view ignores or underemphasizes the dubiousness of the assumption that Hanoi would ever really order the Viet Cong to disband, no matter what punishment it may take from us. To be sure, if the Communist leaders in the North were made to hurt very badly, they might come to the conference table, as their counterparts in Korea did, and they might verbally agree to some kind of truce. The truce might even be partially and temporarily observed, in order to induce Americans to believe that the war is over. The mortaring of airfields and mining of roads might cease—for a while. But that would hardly be the end of the war. The Viet Cong could continue to hold their present dug-in political position at least throughout most of the Delta, as they did between 1954 and 1957, waiting for a chance to regain the initiative under favorable circumstances. Knowing this, the tough, grimly determined, power-minded men in Hanoi would hardly abandon their almost impregnable position of power in the South, even if they themselves were in hiding in the hills of the North.

The Strategic Bombing Survey conducted immediately after World War II in Germany and Japan (it is remarkable how seldom this survey is publicly cited by our military men) made clear that non-total strategic bombing is likely to stiffen the fighting spirit of the country bombed. Total bombing, such as the atom bombing of Japan, can break a nation's fighting spirit, but it is doubtful that we would ever bomb North Vietnam totally; short of that, the Communist leaders are not likely to give up their entrenched strength in the South. Even an American invasion of the North seems likely to transform the war into a guerrilla war throughout the whole country —doubling our present problem, rather than solving it.

In another context Walter Lippmann has talked about the battle between the elephant and the whale. The elephant cannot defeat the whale in the whale's element and the whale cannot defeat the elephant in his element. In Vietnam, we are the elephant and the Viet Cong is the whale.

III

What can the United States do to break the stalemate?

What we cannot do is to change stalemate into victory. For all the reasons indicated above, a stalemate of some kind seems the most probable situation in the foreseeable future—one year from now, two years from now, five years from now. Even if we invade the North. Even if we use nuclear weapons. This is the most probable shape of the future, whether we like it or not.

What we can do is to work toward changing an intolerable form of stalemate into a tolerable form. Ruling out either withdrawal or a futile and quite possibly suicidal escalation, there are two choices available to us: to back into the future with our eyes closed (as they have been closed during the past eighteen years), passively accepting the stalemate in its bloodiest, most needlessly destructive form, or to face it with our eyes open, consciously seeking the best solutions possible for the Vietnamese and for ourselves, given the fact of stalemate.

In making this choice we would be wise to take candidly into account all the costs and risks of the present form of stalemate, including some which have grown so familiar that we are sometimes not vividly aware of them. Such a stalemate means not only blood and needless destruction. It means also continual disintegration of the economic and moral fabric of South Vietnamese society. It means several kinds of loss inside the United States. It means a continual poisoning of our relations, in the United Nations and elsewhere, with many of our friends and with most of the neutral nations as well as with our potential enemies. It means a continual and probably increasing danger of a greatly enlarged war, chiefly because of the increasing danger that we ourselves may escalate in North Vietnam beyond the point that the USSR or Communist China (or some militant faction in Communist China) is willing to accept. While the present kind of stalemate continues, the American military and most of the American public, impatient and exasperated, are increasingly likely to say, "If we're going to fight, let's fight to win."

An opposite danger, that hardly any of those who reject a compromise peace appear to have considered, is that, as Ho Chi Minh has been hoping, the American public will tire of unending, fruitless bloodshed and simply pull out. The pendulum may swing in that direction. It is more likely to do so if the public has been encouraged to cherish unrealistic hopes of victory; it is more likely to do so if the bloodshed does not produce visible, tangible progress toward security, prosperity, real democracy, and an honorable compromise peace.

Seen in this context, a large-area holding policy in Vietnam presents at least three clear advantages:

(1) It would permit concentration of the competent, strongly motivated manpower of South Vietnam.

A critical fact that is generally recognized by informed persons, though seldom mentioned in this context, is the severe shortage of capable Vietnamese to do the innumerable jobs of war-making and of reconstruction. And we Americans cannot replace them, much as some of us would like to. The language barrier alone is sufficient reason. The supply of capable interpreters is already wearing thin. This applies to pacification or "revolutionary development," which involves direct dealing with the peasants, even more than it applies to military operations.

A rationally planned holding operation would permit concentration of the capable people within a limited area rather than spreading them out over the entire South as the Saigon government is doing now. Shaplen has estimated that at its current pace the "revolutionary development" program would take ten years to reach all of the peasants. It might be done more than twice as fast if limited to half of the peasants, and if those peasants were mainly in the areas where it is easier for the government and harder for the Viet Cong to operate.

(2) Our own military strength would be more effective if concentrated in relatively favorable areas, not dissipated over the whole of South Vietnam.

It is true that our great strength and pride now lie in the super-weapons which, if the holding strategy were adopted, would no longer be as useful as they have seemed in the past. While helicopters would still be greatly needed, the brunt of the fighting would presumably be borne, much more than it is now, by foot-slogging infantrymen who would have to learn the dangerous and frustrating business of staying in a disputed hamlet at night as well as in the daytime. To some extent they would have to learn to swim like a whale. They would also have to operate in the Delta, where up to now our troops have done little. But we would then know that our strength was not being misapplied. We would know that it was being applied on the ground and in the hamlets, where it really counts in establishing security for the villagers, rather than in air and artillery actions. Such operations are spectacular and soul-satisfying to the military but usually rather ineffective for any purpose except physical destruction, which alienates the people without winning the war.

What parts of South Vietnam would be most defensible if the United States adopted a holding strategy, and how should they be defended? This is obviously a question for the military professional, who has access to classified information. It would be presumptuous for a civilian without such access to do more than raise pertinent questions.

One highly pertinent question is: What areas are now most free from Viet Cong control? In what areas are the people most on our side already, or least against us? This is an important question if we are to reduce to a minimum the slow, brutal process of trying to root out the Viet Cong in places where they are deeply entrenched and have most of the people on their side, which appears to be true in most of the hamlets in the southern two-fifths of the Delta, including the Camau peninsula and the provinces of Vinh Binh and Kien Hoa. That area would be a very hard nut to crack—which is one good reason not to try to crack it, when our resources and those of the South Vietnamese government are limited.

Unfortunately the Viet Cong are entrenched also, though to a lesser extent, in much of the connecting area between the Saigon population center and the non-Communist Hoa Hao stronghold in the northwest part of the Delta. The intervening provinces of Phong Dinh, Vinh Long, Dinh Tuong, Long An, Go Cong, and Hau Nghia are by no means solidly "pacified," and a long, intelligently directed effort of reconstruction, persuasion, and coercion would be necessary in order to pacify them. Like nearly all of rural South Vietnam, they are an intricate patchwork of Viet Cong-controlled, Government-controlled and disputed hamlets, with scarcely any discernible pattern except the tendency for hamlets near main lines of communication to be more often Government-controlled. But in these provinces the need to link the two solidly non-Communist areas that now exist is a very strong reason to make the effort, difficult as it will be, and to concentrate here the resources that are now scattered over a much wider area. If it is successful, a broad, solid belt of secure and prosperous country would be established.

Another question the military professionals would have to answer is whether we would have to prevent or minimize the infiltration of men and materiél from Cambodia and from the ocean into the two-fifths of the Delta that remained under Viet Cong control. It might be necessary to continue patrolling the coast and the Mekong itself, and to exercise a good deal of control over the Cambodian border. This would at least isolate the Viet Cong in the Plain of Reeds, which is within the proposed holding area but has been a Communist stronghold for many years. Eliminating the Viet Cong from their expertly concealed hideouts in this wilderness would be very difficult and costly, but perhaps it would suffice to establish control only in the northern part of the provinces of Kien Phong and Kien Tuong, along the Cambodian border, cutting off the Viet Cong in the Plain of Reeds from their chief source of military supply. Here, as in Hau Nghia, a good deal of land reclamation seems feasible, bringing in non-Viet Cong settlers to occupy the reclaimed land.

The montagnard area plus Binh Dinh and Phu Yen, comprising the second large non-Communist area suggested here, raises quite different problems. With its mountain-and-jungle terrain, in which the Viet Cong can operate easily, and with Viet Cong territory both north and south of it, the montagnard area would be very hard to defend against a determined assault. From a purely military point of view its borders are indefensible; they are very long and in very rugged country. However, if we gave the montagnards something valuable to defend they might defend it successfully themselves, with only a moderate amount of help from us. This is one place where our emphasis might shift strongly from military priorities to political and economic ones. Continuing to defend present centers such as Pleiku and Ban Me Thuot, we might add a vigorous effort to give the montagnards all the autonomy they can handle, and to develop with them (especially with Fulro, the present intertribal montagnard organization) plans and activities that would give them a real stake in their own country and in continued cooperation with us. The montagnards' hostility to the Vietnamese of both North and South is such that they might then want to defend themselves against all comers.

To be sure, the South Vietnamese government might stand in the way. With its typical Vietnamese scorn for the montagnard "savages" and its compulsive clinging to the fiction of national unity, the Government neglected previous opportunities to win the active, voluntary support of the mountain peoples, and has on the whole continued to alienate them. If it continues to do so, we Americans might be wise to do in this limited area what some have urged us to do in Vietnam as a whole—to bypass the Vietnamese government, setting up what would be in effect an American protectorate dedicated to the rapid development of autonomy for the people in it.

How much of the I Corps area should be kept is another complex question the professionals would have to decide. Danang might be kept, and perhaps Hue and Chulai. But recent fighting there has underlined what a physical map makes plain. The whole area is vulnerable not only because of its long Laotian border but also because most of it is mountainous jungle, coming right down to the narrow, fertile coastal areas where the Vietnamese live. To maintain these precarious outposts strung along the coast, harassed by rocket and mortar fire and by the Viet Cong's continual forays into them from hideouts in the mountains, would be a continual fight against odds and a major diversion of human resources badly needed in the Delta.

(3) With a holding strategy we could give the Viet Cong strong positive as well as negative incentives to stop fighting.

Most of our military men in active service and our military-minded civilian strategists have shown up to now an almost total absence of genuine, realistic empathy with their Communist enemy. Most of them do not seem to have considered any way, other than more and more "punishment," to make the leaders of the Viet Cong and of North Vietnam, in their own interests, want to stop fighting.

A principle applies here that is supported by research as well as everyday observation, and that applies to children as well as adults —the principle of "positive reinforcement." Sensible parents know how futile it is to use nothing but continual punishment in dealing with a "bad" child. They know that continual hostility to a misbehaving child and continual punishment regardless of whether his recent behavior has been better or worse than usual is not the way to make him "good." It is necessary rather for parents to demonstrate their own good will and fairness by showing him, through repeated experience, that there will be rewards when he is good and punishments only when he is bad.

All of this everyday wisdom has been disregarded in our treatment of the Viet Cong. (Both sides disregard it in almost any war.) The one major exception is the Chieu Hoi program to encourage defection, which is well worthwhile, but half-heartedly carried out by militant anti-Communists in South Vietnam, and scarcely likely to affect the decisions of hard-core Viet Cong or North Vietnamese. We have in effect demanded unconditional surrender or total retreat of the Communist cadres in the South, since this is how we appear to define "an end to aggression," and we have indicated no clear willingness to settle for anything less than "an end to aggression"—"letting their neighbors alone." Given the intense conviction of the Viet Cong that they are defending their homeland against American aggression, and in the absence of any real life-saving and face-saving alternative, it is not surprising that up to now they have found this total retreat completely unacceptable.

The holding strategy would offer the Viet Cong a lifesaving and face-saving alternative: to settle down and live a normal life in certain parts of South Vietnam which are, by and large, the parts they are strong in now. They would be alive, they could work, and those with families in the South (still the large majority) could go back to their families, which in the family-centered Vietnamese culture would mean a great deal. Though they would be frustrated in their final avowed purpose of "pushing the imperialist aggressors into the sea," their pride could be legitimately sustained by the thought that they had taken on the United States, the strongest military power in the world, and had fought it to a standstill. We and our Vietnamese allies would in effect say to them: "From now on we will live and let live if you do the same. If your home is in South Vietnam you can go back to your family and your farming, without fear that we will blast you or your crops or your children—as long as you and your comrades do not molest us in the area we have staked out for ourselves. If your home is in North Vietnam you can either go back home or stay here and help your comrades to work out, in peace, the way of life that you think best. We insist only that you grant the same safety to those who want a different way of life, including those in your area who want to move into ours—and, of course, we would reciprocate."

A movement of Viet Cong sympathizers out of "our" area into "theirs," to the extent that it occurred, would be a particularly wholesome thing from the standpoint of long-run stability. It would drain away from the non-Communist area many of those whose pro-Viet Cong convictions would make them an active threat as long as they stayed. Our effort to root out the Viet Cong from hamlets in our area would be much more effective if, in addition to the negative inducements provided by the police, there could be positive inducements in the form of an opportunity to live their own lives in peace not too far away. This would also be more humane. Making a helpless man suffer for his genuine political convictions is not a role congenial to most Americans. We could with better conscience support the Vietnamese police in tough treatment of cap-

tured Viet Cong cadres if we knew that they had been given a fair
opportunity to live elsewhere and had refused it.

*   *   *   *

It will be noticed that each of the three points discussed above
is an advantage even in strictly military terms.

Counterbalancing them, to an extent that only a military professional could validly estimate, is a military disadvantage that should
be given due weight. Our artillery and air strikes and our harassment of lines of supply are now keeping the Viet Cong somewhat
off balance, as far as offensive operations are concerned, and denying them safe areas for supply, regrouping, rest and recuperation.
In the mountainous areas at least, our war of attrition has been
getting some results. It follows that any abrupt and complete abandonment of our search-and-destroy operations, in areas that we might
relinquish to the Viet Cong, would mean at least a short-term loss
of military advantage. Until the Viet Cong learned from our consistent policy of retaliation that they would be ill-advised to attack
our areas, they would probably take full advantage of any slackening of our offensive operations by mounting more effective offensive operations of their own.

It seems likely, however, that this disadvantage could be mitigated by not halting our offensive operations completely and abruptly.
We could reserve the right to attack and to spoil any Viet Cong
operation that, on the basis of continuing air reconnaissance, we regarded as offensive in nature. Our control of the air could continue to be a major military advantage. It seems likely, too, that
any disadvantage would be only temporary. As the Viet Cong
learned the penalties attached to any offensive operations against our
areas, through their experience of our consistent and severe retaliation, their bases of supply and recuperation would probably become
less and less a threat to us and our allies.

IV

What are the non-military arguments against a large-area holding
policy?

Probably the central argument, which has seemed decisive to a
great many Americans, is that a holding strategy in any form would

not give us victory. It would be a "no-win" policy. Since it would not completely drive the Communist aggressors out of South Vietnam, it would not decisively teach them (and other Communists) that a policy of subversion and guerrilla warfare—the Chinese Communist policy of assassination and intimidation in the villages—does not pay. There is much more at stake here, it is argued, than the welfare of the South Vietnamese or their right to self-determination. All countries in the less-developed two-thirds of the world are vulnerable to the Chinese Communist technique of "wars of liberation," and we must protect them from it by punishing the Communists decisively whenever they resort to that technique.

It can be readily granted that this is a strong argument against pulling out of Vietnam, and also a strong argument against "hunkering down" in small enclaves or "retreating" to them. Any policy that would give the Communists in Vietnam and elsewhere the impression that *they* had won a victory in Vietnam might encourage them to attempt new seizures of power in any of scores of vulnerable developing countries. But is it a valid argument against the kind of dynamic, large-area holding policy we have been considering? Would the Communists feel "rewarded for their aggression" if the war ended with more than half of the people of South Vietnam, and more than half of the good land, in firm non-Communist hands?

We in America too often forget the twenty-odd years of heartbreaking struggle and suffering that the Viet Cong have already gone through, in order (from their point of view) to "liberate" their country and defend it against foreign aggression. However misguided they may be, their courage and tenacity in the face of these decades of suffering have been extraordinary. If after paying such a price they are forced to settle for less than half a loaf, leaving the imperialist aggressors and their lackeys in firm control of the better half of the country, it is hard to see how they could possibly regard it as a reward, or how Communists elsewhere could regard it as a rational basis for deliberately resorting to similar tactics.

Also, we Americans tend to forget how close to victory the Viet Cong were in early 1965, and how strong their position in the countryside still is. If we and our South Vietnamese allies were able with great effort to establish ourselves firmly in the economically betterendowed half of South Vietnam, it would be a real gain in power as compared with the present situation, and a very great gain in power compared with the situation in 1963–65. We Americans could legitimately feel that we had stopped and reversed the Communist tide, which would be no mean accomplishment. And we should not underestimate the blow to Communist pride that it would represent.

This means too that whatever the element of truth may be in the domino theory, increased danger elsewhere would be largely prevented by a vigorous and successful holding operation. The military strength of the United States in Thailand is now considerable. Communist China is distracted and weakened by internal troubles. If, then, we can establish large firm bastions of non-Communist strength in South Vietnam—which do not exist now—it seems likely that the power situation in Southeast Asia could remain in equilibrium for a long time to come.

V

To some Americans, a moral argument against a holding policy carries more weight than any practical one: It is wrong to compromise with evil. The Communists are aggressors; they are endangering the right of South Vietnam to determine its own destiny; we are committed to driving them out of South Vietnam completely; and we therefore must do so, whatever the cost. Anything less would be dishonorable.

This definition of the situation cannot be adequately discussed here, but a brief review of what has been discussed at length in the body of this book may be appropriate.

One basis of disagreement is historical. It is sometimes argued that by supporting the French army against a clear majority of the Vietnamese people we ourselves committed aggression against them during the period 1950–54. By supporting Diem in his unwillingness to hold internationally supervised elections even in South Vietnam in 1956 we committed aggression again. Against this historical background, it is argued, the Vietnamese Communists are not cold-blooded, Hitler-like aggressors. The evidence covered in Chapter 3 suggests that, misguided or not, they see themselves as patriots defending their homeland against what they really believe to be aggression by us. Therefore punishing them is not for us a moral imperative.

A more important basis of disagreement is contemporary: It is argued that the South Vietnamese people are probably at least as much against us as they are for us, and that a live-and-let-live compromise is therefore the only democratic solution.

On this question there is some disagreement even among those who are relatively well-informed. (There are no "experts.") Some think that more than half of the South Vietnamese people are leaning at least slightly toward our side in the war.

The evidence described in Chapter 2 suggests an estimate that is both more complex and more pessimistic. It is that, even as a first approximation, we should recognize three groups in South Vietnam: (1) The Viet Cong themselves and those peasants who—partly from intimidation and partly from genuine conviction—are actually on their side. Largely because of extraordinarily effective propaganda, a pro-Viet Cong conviction probably exists in 15 to 25 percent of the population. (2) A smaller group—perhaps 5 to 15 percent of the population—have similarly strong convictions on the anti-Communist side. (3) A very large group—perhaps 60 to 80 percent of the population—are outwardly passive, serving in a perfunctory way whatever master it is in their personal self-interest to serve at the moment, and saying, usually, what they think that master wants to hear.

If this is accepted as a more or less valid first approximation to the complex and elusive truth, the question of what would now be an honorable policy takes on a rather different character from that envisaged by those who assume that the Vietnamese are on our side, counting on us to defend them against Communist aggression. It suggests that, although we are not literally waging war on behalf of a minority against the majority of the South Vietnamese people, we are doing something that is questionable on similar moral and practical grounds: fighting on behalf of a small minority against a larger minority. By any definition of democracy this is not democratic.

This points to a redefinition of the moral issue. Can we realistically claim to be defending democracy, or the right of the Vietnamese people to determine their own destiny? We have intervened much more heavily on behalf of a small minority than the North Vietnamese have on behalf of a larger one.

This definition of the situation also raises a practical question much broader than Vietnam: In any developing country can we afford—considering our global responsibilities and also our domestic needs—to take on the difficult and expensive task of helping a small minority to defeat a larger one? Our massive intervention on behalf of a small minority, although much greater than the North Vietnamese intervention on the other side, has still been only just about enough to counterbalance the advantage of the Viet Cong in number of dedicated human beings. We have clung to the hope that we could persuade large numbers of the indifferent sixty to eighty percent to join our side. Now the hope that we can do so in any near future is fading. Is it either moral or practical, then, to continue the unequal battle in expectation of final victory? Or should we cut our losses, settle for a fair compromise, and resolve not to tilt with this kind of windmill again, in Vietnam or anywhere else?

Actually, as a rationale for a live-and-let-live holding policy, it is not necessary to accept even the proposition that the dedicated pro-Viet Cong minority is larger than the dedicated anti-Viet Cong minority. For purposes of evaluating this policy, the ratio could be one-to-one instead of two-to-one. Since the holding policy is not a proposal for a majority vote in a unified South Vietnam, but rather for the continued existence of both sides, with an opportunity for the members of the passive majority to gravitate toward whichever side they prefer (voting with their feet), there is no need to decide in advance which side is more numerous. It is enough to remember that both sides are composed of human beings, with human needs. In the absence of any clear aggressor on either side, and in the absence of any clear moral obligation to punish the aggressor, we are free to consider the needs and desires of the dedicated human beings on both sides, as well as those of the great passive majority whose one passionate desire is for peace. (By one interpretation of democracy, it is our democratic obligation to respect what this clear majority wants. It clearly wants a compromise peace if that is the quickest way to get peace.)

We may indeed feel a special obligation to preserve life and livelihood for the dedicated minority (ten percent, or whatever the figure may be) who are on our side. Some of them have risked much by enrolling on the anti-Communist side, relying on our implicit and explicit commitments to continue the struggle. In a strong, large-area holding operation we would be fulfilling that obligation on a very large scale. But their claim on us is not unlimited. We have never promised to enable this minority to dominate the remainder of the people (which they are still doing, behind a façade of democracy) or to enable them to destroy the equally dedicated and equally human twenty percent (or whatever the figure may be) on the other side. Both of these might occur if we won a complete victory in the South. The bitterness created by the long civil war, with innumerable atrocities on both sides, is such that our intervention may be needed to make sure that neither side destroys the other. A holding operation in which the dedicated minority on our side takes the political lead in half the country while the dedicated minority on the other side leads the other half would at least assure that neither minority is destroyed, or decimated. It would fully discharge our special obligation to the dedicated anti-Communists, as well as our wider, human, democratic obligation to let both sides, and the passive majority in the middle, determine their own destiny as far as humanly possible.

This is the live-and-let-live policy, and as such it is consistent with all that is best in the American character and tradition. It is only in moments of aberration that we Americans have ever attempted to rule, to conquer, or to force our way of life on others. A policy that permits both sides to live, to go back to the constructive activities of peace, and to work out their own political expedients in their own ways, is not simply the most honorable and the most practical policy, it is also the only policy that will enable us, as Americans, to be ourselves.

Appendix B

A BALANCE SHEET

THE NEED FOR BALANCE SHEETS

The one result of our analysis that stands out above the others is the omnipresence and the danger of selective inattention. Most of the misperception in every point of view involves it, directly or indirectly. Most of the disagreement and the rancor in America today on the issue of Vietnam is traceable to the fact that some Americans focus strongly on a few parts of the extremely complex reality, while others focus on other parts, and each tends to regard the parts he focuses on as *the* reality. As McGeorge Bundy put it, "In a situation in which easy solutions do not exist and in which commitments of purpose and hope are high, it is only natural that there be a tendency in each observer to emphasize the part of the truth to which he is nearest. . . . Where danger comes is not in these equally right perceptions of important phenomena but in the human tendency . . . to suppose that one's own reality is the only reality, so that the observation of the other man is somehow misleading."[1]

One time-tested device that any individual can use to force himself to stretch his own perspective and to take into account "the other man's observation" is to make a written list of pros and cons on a given issue, including every point that seems to him to have any validity in viewpoints other than his own. He can then assign weights on the basis of his own considered judgment and arrive finally at a more balanced view of the whole. This device has at least the advantage of giving some assurance that no very important consideration has been left out of account by sheer inadvertence. Benjamin Franklin long ago discovered the value of such a balance sheet, and many others have discovered it independently. It has the great virtue of transcending the span of attention, which limits the number of ideas that can exist simultaneously in anyone's mind at a given moment. A much broader and more differentiated picture can

[1] Bundy, 1963, in Raskin and Fall, pp. 163–64.

be built up piecemeal, with separate judgments as to whether any given item should be included at all and then as to how much weight it should be given; and full use is made of the help that writing can give to our slipshod, systematically biased memories in retaining those unwelcome ideas that we know should influence our final judgment but that all too easily slip out of the mind and get lost.[2] The mere act of writing down an unwelcome, dissonant idea may fix it more firmly in the mind, and the act of reviewing all of the arguments, with a conscious effort to give each its proper emphasis, further safeguards against inadvertent inattention.

In the hope that some readers who have not yet undertaken such an enterprise may be moved to do so, the writer presents in this appendix his own personal balance sheets, with each step in the process spelled out as clearly and explicitly as possible:

A. Five courses of action (escalation, reclaiming, holding, coalition, and withdrawing) are defined.

B. Ten values or objectives (avoiding World War III in the long run, keeping our commitment to self-determination for the South Vietnamese, avoiding the domino tendency, etc.) are defined.

C. Each of the five policies is evaluated in terms of its estimated relationship to each of the ten values.

D. The values are assigned weights representing the writer's own sense of their relative importance, and an over-all evaluation of each policy is obtained.

This strenuous pursuit of explicitness has been useful in forcing me to clarify and to challenge a number of implicit assumptions that I had not realized I was making, and to think more clearly about a number of aspects of the problem that I had not clearly thought about before. The results of the exercise are presented here, not to urge my own conclusions on the reader, but to illustrate a method that anyone can use to check and expand the thought processes that have led him to his own conclusions. If the reader wants to try out the method he can do so by examining critically each step in the process, substituting his own definitions, his own evaluations, and his own weights wherever he disagrees with those presented here, and adding up his own totals to see how his over-all conclusions compare with these.

[2] Edwards, 1941.

The method is not easy. It demands closer attention and more careful step-by-step thinking than any other part of the book. But there is no evident short-cut. The complexities and uncertainties are in the world situation rather than in the method of analysis.

A. Definitions of Five Policies

1. *Limited escalation:* Not extreme measures such as occupation of all of North Vietnam, a large-scale bombing of the dikes or use of nuclear weapons, but more moderate measures such as occupation of limited areas or greatly increased ordinary bombing directed at the economy rather than at the civilian population. It is assumed that the more extreme forms of escalation are ruled out for a number of reasons, especially the danger of involving Communist China.*

2. *Reclaiming:* Doing all we reasonably can to reclaim all of South Vietnam for an anti-Communist government, but without escalation in the North as defined above. A further large increase in the use of American troops is not excluded if our military men so advise. Judicious bombing of the North is also not excluded, if it is justified wholly or almost wholly by the need to support our troops in the South.

3. *Holding:* Not a retreat to enclaves, but a consolidation of strength in certain large areas (see map, p. 294), and an orderly withdrawal from hard-to-hold positions elsewhere; no bombing of the North; an active policy of reform in government-held areas; military action in Viet Cong areas limited to retaliation (see Appendix A).

4. *Coalition:* Not "leaving it all to the Vietnamese" (which might enable the well-organized Viet Cong to dominate its disorganized opponents) but an internationally supervised interim coalition government in which the Viet Cong would be given substantial minority representation. After the interim, internationally supervised elections to obtain a more representative government.

5. *Withdrawal:* Not a precipitate, disorderly pull-out, but a planned operation that includes doing whatever is feasible to pro-

* Like the other four definitions, this one is an arbitrary choice among several possible courses of action; in this exercise the other possibilities are left undefined and unevaluated. The reader is free to define any one of the five differently, providing that his definitions are as clear and specific as these.

tect Vietnam's neighbors and the militant anti-Communists in the South. The latter could be given time to emigrate if they wanted to, and helped to do so without serious personal loss.

B. Definitions of Ten Values or Objectives
(in estimated order of importance)

It will be noticed that there is a certain amount of overlap among the values listed below. Though I have tried to minimize it, overlap is unavoidable because of the fluid quality of values, which cannot actually be separated into neat intellectual compartments.

1. *Avoiding World War III in the long run:* Not rewarding (and thereby encouraging) aggression. Not undermining the UN and thereby preventing or reversing progress toward enforceable world law. Not reinforcing the vicious circles of the East-West conflict by increasing hostility to the United States in Communist countries or by increasing "the blindness of involvement" in the United States.

Except for the general desire not to allow clear Communist aggression to be rewarded, these long-range considerations are seldom put first in American thinking about Vietnam. However, in view of the immeasurably larger scale of destruction in a major nuclear war, compared with the present non-nuclear one, the case for putting them first is very strong.

2. *Our commitment to self-determination for the Vietnamese:* Enabling South Vietnam as a whole to determine its own destiny if that is feasible. Enabling pro-Viet Cong and anti-Viet Cong segments of the population to determine their own destiny separately if they are more or less equal and effective unification of the area is not feasible. Taking into account the inevitable differences between Western-style democracy and the kind of democracy that is possible in Vietnam. (Many Americans have not included in their definition of self-determination a respect for the intense anti-war feeling of the large middle group in Vietnam, but this perhaps should be included.)

The right of the South Vietnamese to determine their own destiny is our chief avowed reason for being in Vietnam. It represents both the value of fulfilling commitments and the values of democracy and national self-determination as such. It also represents our opposition to aggression as such. If aggression is defined as the use of force on another country's territory, against the wishes of a majority of the politically conscious people in that country, then those who believe we are defending South Vietnam against North Vietnamese aggression are invoking the value of self-determination. But those who believe the United States itself has been inadvertently committing aggression by opposing what more than half of the politically conscious people in South Vietnam want are invoking the same value.

3. *Avoiding the domino tendency:* Not a mechanical one-after-another conception of the domino process (though in Southeast Asia this may actually occur), but General Taylor's more sophisticated conception of the worldwide effects of an American defeat or pull-out: encouraging Communists, discouraging anti-Communists (who would see the non-fulfillment of American pledges to protect anti-Communists in Vietnam), and appearing to confirm the feasibility of the Chinese Communist policy of "wars of liberation" in developing countries. Avoiding any appeasement of Communist aggression in Vietnam that would encourage Communist aggression elsewhere.

This bears on the long-run survival of freedom and democracy in the countries where effective democracy now exists. It bears also on the long-run chances for peace. If "new Vietnams" appear elsewhere, the United States and other non-Communist countries may feel obliged to intervene.

4. *Ending the war quickly:* "Ending" here means either literal ending, perhaps through negotiated agreement, or a dwindling of the war to a fraction of its present intensity without negotiation or agreement. "Quickly" here is a relative term; it means for example that ending in six months would be better than in a year, and two years would be far better than five.

This means ending the suffering and the atrocities on both sides, ending the progressive disintegration of the fabric of Vietnamese society, and ending the loss of American lives. In order to minimize confusion, this definition does not include certain values that are represented or implied elsewhere in our list of ten: danger of escalation leading directly to nuclear war, long-run effects of the war on the likelihood of World War III, erosion of America's position of leadership in the world, ammunition given to Communist propaganda, splitting of the Western alliance, economic cost to the United States. If these had been included it would have seemed necessary to rank "ending the war quickly" higher than fourth place in the list.

5. *Avoiding World War III in the short run:* Avoiding the danger

that escalation by us might draw in Russia and/or China, and avoiding a long-continued indecisive war that would continually confront the United States with the temptation to escalate—"let's win and get it over with."

This is ranked as high as fifth because of the enormous scale of destruction that world war, in our nuclear age, would probably entail. The value of avoiding it in the *short run* is ranked only fifth, however, because escalation does not seem likely to lead directly to a major war as long as it is "limited escalation." The danger that Russia or China will enter on a large scale seems not very great. The logistic difficulties of Chinese intervention, the reluctance of the North Vietnamese to permit it, the distracting effect of civil disorder in China and other factors operate to make it less likely. On the other hand, the inherent momentum of escalation implies that limited escalation might become unlimited, in which case the danger of World War III would be immediate and very great.

6. *Combating Communism in other ways:* That is, other than avoiding the domino tendency covered by the third point above. This includes not giving propaganda ammunition to the Communists, not pushing the USSR and Communist China closer together, not pushing together the contending factions in Communist China, not eroding America's position of leadership in the world, not splitting the Western alliance, not turning developing countries toward Communism by associating the United States with war and imperialism. Positively, it means rebuilding their conception of the United States as a country identified with peace and with respect for the independence of small nations—including non-white nations. (Since it contains so many intangibles, this value is peculiarly difficult to rank in comparison with the others. Perhaps it should be on a par with number three, "avoiding the domino tendency.")

7. *Minimizing the war's economic cost to the U.S.:* some thirty billion dollars a year. This is not just money. It means neglected cities, a neglected war on poverty, and slackening concern about unequal opportunity for Negroes. It may mean riots, fear, and bitterness in the United States.

8. *Security for anti-Communists in Vietnam:* In view of the hatred that the war has generated on both sides, this is a very real problem. It includes whatever special commitment we have made to the anti-Communist group, by actions as well as by words. It also includes the international effects of ignoring their security—the in-

tensifying of the domino tendency that might occur if anti-Communists elsewhere felt that they could not believe future assurances of American support and protection. The likelihood that no more than five percent to fifteen percent of the South Vietnamese people can be described as dedicated anti-Communists does not diminish our commitment to them, and it does not greatly reduce the prospects of international repercussions if we appear to abandon them.

9. *Rebuilding Vietnam:* A re-knitting of the economic, political, social, and moral fabric of Vietnamese society, raveled as it has been by twenty-odd years of intermittent civil war. To whatever extent we may feel responsible for the war, we must also feel obligated to help repair the damage it has caused. Even those who do not hold America at all responsible for the war may feel that the Vietnamese have had more than their share of suffering.

10. *Unifying Vietnam,* or laying a basis for its unification in the future: To Americans, accustomed to thinking of Vietnam as naturally divided at the 17th Parallel, this often does not seem an important value at all. Many Vietnamese patriots feel differently. To many of them it is paramount, or at least as important as anti-Communism (or Communism).

C. Evaluations of the Five Policies in Terms of the Ten Values

1. Avoiding World War III in the Long Run

++	**Holding**	Holding would probably keep the Communists from feeling rewarded for what we regard as their aggression. At the same time it would not undermine the UN or intensify the vicious circles of the East-West conflict. It would reassure our friends as well as our enemies. Neither side would be "learning aggression."
0	**Withdrawal**	Withdrawing would cleanly end this war and all the dangers directly associated with it, but it might encourage "wars of liberation," with heightened danger of future wars.
0	**Coalition**	Coalition might end this war, but not cleanly. If the Communists soon came to dominate, they might feel rewarded, with a heightened danger of later wars.
—	**Reclaiming**	Reclaiming would probably aggravate all the present evils, including undermining the UN and intensifying the basic East-West conflict.
— —	**Escalation**	In addition to its immediate danger of precipitating World War III, escalation would humiliate the Soviet and Chinese Communists and deeply embitter them, even if they swallowed their pride and took no effective steps against what they would regard as aggression by us.

2. *Our Commitment to Self-Determination for the Vietnamese*

++ **Holding** — Holding would permit self-determination for the estimated 20% who are strongly pro-Viet Cong as well as for the estimated 10% who are strongly anti-Viet Cong. Also, if it were the quickest way to peace, it would represent the desire of the great middle group whose only strong desire is for peace.

+ **Coalition** — If a coalition government did not become Communist-dominated it would give self-determination, in the sense of majority rule, to South Vietnam as a unit. Probably, though, it would become Communist-dominated, with intense coercion of the 10% who are strongly anti-Communist and not much freedom, in the long run, for the 70% or so who are now indifferent.

— **Withdrawal** — Our complete withdrawal would almost certainly lead to domination by the organized, intensely motivated Communists, with the results described above.

— **Reclaiming** — Reclaiming would give self-determination only to the estimated 10% who are anti-Communist, denying it to the 20% who are pro-Viet Cong, and—if it prolonged the war—overriding the intense desire of the 70% for peace.

—— **Escalation** — Escalation, like reclaiming, would mean self-determination for the 10% but not the 20% or the 70%. In addition, it would be coercion of North Vietnam.

3. Avoiding the Domino Tendency

++	**Escalation**	Escalation would presumably be the most effective way of showing Communists everywhere that "wars of liberation" do not pay off, and may bring severe penalties.
+	**Reclaiming**	Reclaiming would be only less effective than escalation as a way of "punishing" Communists for tangling with the United States.
0	**Holding**	Holding, like reclaiming, would probably keep the Communists from feeling "rewarded" for what they have done, but it presumably would not be seen as "punishment" either and would not have much deterrent effect on others.
—	**Coalition**	Coalition might be seen by Communists as a reward, making their whole effort worthwhile, if—as seems probable—they came to dominate the political scene.
— —	**Withdrawal**	Withdrawal by us would probably be seen by the Communists as a real triumph for them; it probably would encourage Communists elsewhere, discourage anti-Communists, and appear to confirm the Chinese Communist policy of "wars of liberation."

4. Ending the War Quickly

++	**Withdrawal**	Withdrawal by us would probably lead fairly soon to ending the war through a complete Communist victory.
+	**Holding**	A strong, large-area holding policy probably offers the best hope of a fairly early peace, not through negotiation but through a dwindling of fighting on both sides. It could also make real give-and-take more possible if negotiation did occur.
0	**Coalition**	A negotiated agreement to set up a coalition would presumably end the war completely, at least temporarily. But agreement might be very hard to get, and even after agreement the war could flare up again. Mortal enemies find it hard to cooperate.
—	**Escalation**	Though many Americans assume that an even tougher policy would force the enemy to come to terms, and quickly end the war, this hope is probably illusory.
——	**Reclaiming**	The present reclaiming policy does not offer even an illusory hope of quickly bringing the war to an end.

5. *Avoiding World War III in the Short Run*

++	**Withdrawal**	Withdrawing would completely end the immediate danger that American action might bring in the USSR or China.
++	**Holding**	Holding—since it would be clearly less belligerent than escalation or fighting to get all of the South (which has not yet brought in the USSR or China)—would seem almost as good in this respect.
+	**Coalition**	Coalition might be somewhat less stable; war could flare up again and the present dangers could re-emerge.
0	**Reclaiming**	Reclaiming—a large-scale effort, probably with little sign of victory—would always tempt the American people and government to drastic escalation as a way of "winning and getting out," and this could lead directly to World War III.
——	**Escalation**	Given the inherent momentum of escalation, even limited escalation in the North carries with it the danger of unlimited escalation and nuclear war. Even limited escalation might overstrain the patience of the intensely humiliated Russians and/or Chinese.

6. Combating Communism in Other Ways
(that is, other than by avoiding the domino tendency)

++	**Holding**	Holding would probably give an impression of strength and firmness combined with reasonableness and desire for peace. It would give little if any ammunition to Communist propaganda accusing the U.S. of war and imperialism or picturing it as a paper tiger; it would not tend to unify China or the Sino-Soviet alliance; it should end the present splitting of the Western alliance.
+	**Coalition**	Coalition would appear reasonable and peaceful, but if the government proved ineffective, and especially if it became Communist-dominated, we would appear weak.
0	**Withdrawal**	Withdrawing now would probably be interpreted by Communists everywhere as simply a defeat—a sign of our weakness rather than our good will.
−	**Reclaiming**	The present reclaiming policy provides a steady flow of propaganda ammunition for the Communists. It does not yet seem to have pushed Russia and China closer together, or unified factions in China, but it has tended to split the Western alliance.
−−	**Escalation**	Escalation would give much more ammunition to Communist propaganda and split the Western alliance more deeply. Though the present policy does not seem to have done so, further escalation might effectively push Russia and China together, and unify factions in China.

7. *Minimizing the Economic Cost to the United States*

++	**Withdrawal**	Immediate, drastic reduction of cost, even if we subsidized emigration of anti-Communist Vietnamese. (Probably most of them would not want to leave.)
0	**Coalition**	An internationally supervised coalition, probably with strong U.S. participation on the financial side, could be expensive; and war could flare up again—expensively for us.
0	**Holding**	Holding too would be expensive at least for one or two years, if we did enough to make a showcase of the non-Communist areas. After that, the expense might greatly diminish; we could return to our problems at home.
——	**Reclaiming**	Reclaiming offers only a continuation of present expense—some 25–30 billion per year—with all that that means in neglect of our own cities, etc.
——	**Escalation**	Escalation offers a hope (probably illusory) of cutting down the expense by winning. If it led to a bigger war the expense would increase enormously.

8. Security for Anti-Communists in Vietnam

++	**Reclaiming**	Escalation, reclaiming and holding seem about the same in amount of security for anti-Communists, since none of them would give the Communists power in more than about half of the country, and the 5–15% who are strongly anti-Communist could easily survive in the non-Communist part of it.
++	**Holding**	
++	**Escalation**	
—	**Coalition**	A coalition might be much less healthy for anti-Communists, since the Viet Cong probably would use its former methods of assassination and intimidation to get total power.
——	**Withdrawal**	Even if we tried to minimize the danger by gradual, orderly withdrawal and by financing the emigration of some Vietnamese, this would still be the worst policy from the standpoint of strong anti-Communists. Few would *want* to leave, and those who remained would face liquidation.

9. Rebuilding Vietnam

++	**Withdrawal**	With the war completely ended, with the country united and with strong Communist leadership, the rebuilding process might well be more rapid than would be possible with any other policy.
+	**Holding**	Holding would permit, to the extent that it was successful, rapid rebuilding in the non-Communist "showcase" parts of the country. Much of our effort could shift, even at the outset, from destruction to construction.
0	**Coalition**	Coalition might permit much construction, with American help, but the government would probably be divided and highly inefficient, and the whole process would be unstable.
—	**Reclaiming**	The present reclaiming process in South Vietnam is judged by many to be destroying faster than it is building.
——	**Escalation**	With escalation the emphasis would be even more on destruction.

10. Unifying Vietnam

++	**Withdrawal**	Withdrawal would probably lead quickly to Communist control of the whole country, and unification on that basis.
+	**Coalition**	If coalition led to a Communist take-over, that too would at least unify the country. Conceivably, with a revival of the Geneva principle of nationwide elections, the whole nation might be unified on a semi-Communist, semi-neutralist basis.
— — — — — —	**Escalation** **Holding** **Reclaiming**	Since the United States is not defining victory as including unification of the country (although many of the South Vietnamese would like to do so), not one of these three policies offers a real prospect of unification.

The ten analyses described above are brought together in the following chart:

Table 1

ONE SET OF ESTIMATES OF HOW FIVE POLICIES RELATE TO TEN VALUES

	Policies				
Values:	Limited Escalation	Re-claiming	Holding	Coalition	With-drawal
Avoiding World War III in Long Run	—	–	++	0	0
Commitment to Self-Determination for Vietnamese	—	–	++	+	–
Avoiding Domino Tendency	++	+	0	–	—
Ending the War Quickly	–	—	+	0	++
Avoiding World War III in Short Run	—	0	++	+	++
Combating Communism in Other Ways	—	–	++	+	0
Minimizing Economic Cost to U.S.	—	—	0	0	++
Security of Anti-Communists in Vietnam	++	++	++	–	—
Rebuilding Vietnam	—	–	+	0	++
Unifying Vietnam	—	—	—	+	++

D. Overall Evaluation

There are many ways in which these assigned values could be added together to get an overall judgment of the desirability or undesirability of the five policies. All would be somewhat subjective and arbitrary, since there is no "objective" way of deciding which of the values is most important.

For example, the writer's own feeling is that the first value, "avoiding World War III in the long run," is by far the most important of the ten. It could easily involve death for hundreds of millions or billions of human beings, and perhaps loss of freedom for hundreds of millions of others who might be unfortunate enough to survive. The fact that the human mind boggles at such thoughts should not lead us to push them out of our minds, or give them too little weight, just at the moment when we are making decisions that could significantly increase or decrease the risk of realizing them, not only in the present but also in the long future. Perhaps this value should be given greater weight than all the others put together. Arbitrarily, I have given it here a weight of only 6. The second in the list, "self-determination for the Vietnamese," is equally arbitrarily given a weight of 4; the third, fourth and fifth each have a weight of 3; the sixth, seventh, and eighth a weight of 2 each, and the ninth and tenth a weight of 1 each.

A double-plus was counted as 2, a single-plus as 1, a zero as 0, a single minus as −1, and a double-minus as −2. These figures were then multiplied by the weights of the corresponding value. For instance, limited escalation was evaluated as double-minus in the value of "avoiding World War III in the long run." The figure −2 was multiplied by 6, the result being −12. Ten such calculations for limited escalation, with the products simply added up, led to a score of −31. Holding had the highest score (36); withdrawal and coalition were almost tied for second place (6 and 5 respectively); reclaiming was next (−18), and escalation last (−31).

Reader, if you disagree, please look again at Table I and find out just how and why your judgments differ from these.

INDEX

Absence of empathy, 22, 208, 242; Vietnam, 99–101, 196–98; World War I, 6, 9, 10–11, 14; World War II, 20–21, 22, 23

Action-ambivalence, 250, 252, 265–66

Adorno, T. W., 128, 244

Aggression, 208–9, 240ff.; appeasement and learning of, 177–85; meanings of, 165–68, 173–74, 241; Vietnam, 49–50, 88–90, 141–54, 155–85, 186–204, 236–40ff.; World War I, 8; World War II, 16–21, 24

Ahmad, on guerrilla activity, 193, 195

Albania, 151

Alger, Chadwick F., 204

Algeria, 22, 23, 107, 148, 161; success of counterguerrilla campaign in, 193; world opinion and French pull-out, 195

Alien-agitator image, 268, 271–72

Alliances, competitive, 12, 13, 25

Allport, Gordon W., 222, 223–24, 256

Alsace-Lorraine, 161

Alsop, Joseph, 54–55, 241, 296; and virile self-image, 189

Ambiguity, 168–70, 182–84; dissonance and, 246–61ff.

Ambivalence, 36–37, 74, 81; balance, dissonance and, 249–56ff.; ways of reducing, 255–66ff.

American Friends Service Committee, 114, 203

Angell, on ideology conflict, 243

Angry denial technique, 258–59, 266, 273

Animal Farm (Orwell), 207

Anti-foreign feelings. *See* Xenophobia

Anti-Semitism, 244, 245. *See also* Jews: Hitler and

Anti-war protests, 152, 188

Appeasement, 119, 155, 156, 157, 169, 170; and bombing, 212; and learning of aggression, 177–85

Apple, R. W., Jr., 68, 77

Arabs, 22, 123, 151, 161, 268, 274

Arbenz, Communist aid to, 151

Ardrey, Robert, 160

Arms race, 12, 25. *See also* Weapons (weaponry)

ARVN (South Vietnamese Army), 31, 33, 52

Asch, Solomon E., 202, 210–14

Assassination(s): Kennedy, 138–39; Vietnam, 59, 68, 74, 88, 98, 119, 166, 188; World War I, 5, 7, 24, 187–88

Atrocities. *See* Torture

Attitudes (*See also* specific aspects, studies, techniques): selective contact and, 224–26; study of, 65–70, 78–84; and unconscious motives, 236–43ff.

Australia, 129, 169

Austria (Austria-Hungary): World War I, 4–15, 22, 24–26, 118, 128, 131, 161, 188, 255–56; World War II, 20

Authoritarian personality, 92, 128, 243–48, 254

Authority, attitude among Vietnamese toward, 33–34

Autistic hostility, 196–98, 259

Autocracy and Democracy: An Experimental Inquiry, 131

Avoiding communicators of dissonance technique, 259–60, 266, 274

Power, 137, 207–9, 275 (See also Virile self-image); as unconscious motive, 236–40
P-O-X triangle, 250–51
Prague. See Czechoslovakia
Press (news; newspapers; journalists), 202, 216–17, 228–35. See also specific newspapers, periodicals, writers
Prestige ("face"), 95–96, 137, 138, 189; as unconscious motive, 239–40, 275
Profiles in Courage (Kennedy), 212
Projection mechanisms, 92, 236, 239–40, 264. See also specific mechanisms
Propaganda: Communist, 85–92ff., 318; NLF, 85–92, 107; Viet Cong, 30, 31, 35n, 41, 50, 57; World War I, 15–18, 216
Pruitt, on hostility, 197
"Psycho-logic" (or Neanderthal) mentality, 167
Publishers, 231–32
Pull-out. See Withdrawal
Punishment, and learning, 185
Puppet enemy-image, 268, 269–72
Pustay, J. A., 51
Pye, Lucien, 71

Quakers, 114, 203
Quang Lien, 68
Quat. See Phan Huy Quat
Quemoy, 151, 183, 212

Rajagopalachari, C., 130
RAND Corporation, 43n
Rapoport, Anatol, 8, 202, 246, 266
Raskin, Marcus G., 89
Rationalizations, 236–40ff. See also specific aspects, rationalizations, techniques
Raymond, Jack, 192
Reclaimers (reclaiming), 141ff., 155ff., 181–82, 314, 315; evaluation of, 321–30
Recruitment: South Vietnam govern-

ment, 68, 76; Viet Cong, 52, 55, 59, 193, 298
Reforms, 42–44, 78, 226, 295; land (See under Land)
Refracting-lens hypothesis, 109–12
Refugees, 55, 62–65, 70, 153; and selective contact, 225, 227, 234
"Regroupees," 49
Reporters. See Press
Repression. See Selective inattention
Reston, James, 48, 59, 291
Reves, Emery, 275
Revolutionary development program, 77, 194, 227, 300–1
Rewards, and learning of aggression, 177–85
Ribbentrop, Joachim von, 19
Richardson, Lewis F., 197
Ridgway, Matthew B., 113, 191
Rock, on mutual trust, 197
Rokeach, Milton, 215, 226, 246
Ronning, Chester A., 113
Rose, Jerry, 51
Rosen, Ellen W., 246
Rosenberg, on unconscious motivation, 241, 242, 252
Rovere, Richard, 122, 123
Rumania, 19, 151
Rumors, 222–23
Rumpf, on bombing effectiveness, of Germany, 113
Rusk, Dean, 155, 202, 270; and the military, 218; and war enthusiasm, 188–89
Russell, Senator, 130, 188
Russia. See U.S.S.R. and the Russians

Saigon (See also South Vietnam [government]): and U.S. holding (enclave) policy, 293–94, 302
Salisbury, Harrison E., 114
Sanford, R. Nevitt, 128, 244, 245
Santo Domingo, 121, 138. See also Dominican Republic
Saturday Evening Post, 51
Scalopino, Robert, 38, 67, 125
Schachter, Stanley, 215